D1765946

THE ISLANDS OF SCOTLAND:
A LIVING MARINE HERITAGE

© Crown copyright 1994

Applications for reproduction should be made to HMSO

First published 1994

British Library Cataloguing in Publication Data

A catalogue record for this book is available from the British Library

ISBN 0 11 494243 9

PREFACE

Scottish Natural Heritage (SNH) was born on 1 April 1992. It has a distinguished lineage, being formed by the merger of the Countryside Commission for Scotland and the Nature Conservancy Council for Scotland, which itself had existed for just one year after the split up of the Nature Conservancy Council. This new agency not only inherited the powers and responsibilities of its predecessors but was also charged with being concerned with, and promoting, the concept of sustainability. The Natural Heritage (Scotland) Act 1991 says

> **1.**-*(1) There shall be established a body to be known as "Scottish Natural Heritage" (in this Part of this Act referred to as "SNH") whose general aims and purposes shall be (a) to secure the conservation and enhancement of; and (b) to foster understanding and facilitate the enjoyment of, the natural heritage of Scotland; and SNH shall have regard to the desirability of securing that anything done, whether by SNH or any other person, in relation to the natural heritage of Scotland is undertaken in a manner which is sustainable.*

Conservation of the Scottish environment, its enjoyment, and its management on a sustainable basis are therefore fundamental aspects of the work of SNH.

One of the SNH Directorates, based in Edinburgh, is the Research and Advisory Services Directorate. As part of the planning of this directorate the staff felt enthusiastic about starting a series of annual conferences. Each conference would explore a facet of the natural heritage, endeavouring to maintain the breadth of interests that characterizes SNH. The proposal for such a series of conferences was warmly supported by the newly formed research board, established to advise the staff and main board of SNH on all aspects of research. It is simple enough to establish a series of annual conferences, but a much more difficult task to choose a topic for the first.

A particular feature of Scotland is the wealth of islands that surround its coastline, especially to the west and north. A conference featuring on the islands of Scotland was a first step, but was that a sufficiently focused theme? The Countryside Commission for Scotland had been active in the area, with a number of National Scenic Areas (NSAs) taking in whole islands, or parts of larger islands, from Arran in the south, with islands such as Jura, Mull, Rum, Skye, North and South Uist, Harris and Lewis in the west, to parts of Orkney and Shetland in the north. The Nature Conservancy Council had also been active, with many island Sites of Special Scientific Interest (SSSIs) and National

Nature Reserves (NNRs), such as Loch Druidibeg, Gleann Diomhan, the Keen of Hamar and Hermaness, and whole islands such as Noss, Rum and St. Kilda. A conference with such a theme could, therefore, have emphasised the scenic and wildlife importance of the islands, but in a very real sense this had been achieved by CCS and NCC. Was there a new perspective that the conference could take?

We found this by concentrating on the marine environment. The conference's title was therefore 'The Islands of Scotland: our Marine Heritage'. No longer was it sufficient to reiterate the importance of the Scottish islands for landscape or wildlife; we needed to ask what research was being undertaken on the marine heritage and to explore the land/sea interface. As Professor George Dunnet highlights in his introduction, so much has been written about the land of the islands whilst so little has been written about the sea surrounding those islands. We hope that this first RASD conference will, at least partially, redress this imbalance.

The book, like the conference, is divided into three sections.

First, we felt it important to review the features which have shaped the island heritage as we know it today. Besides the ever-changing climate, it is the processes of the rocks and the waters and the transport of marine sediments that have shaped the lands and provided the landscapes and seascapes that we value so highly.

Second, the wildlife of the islands contributes to their enormous importance for Scotland's natural heritage. Inevitably it is the birds and marine mammals that are best known, but the profusion of wild flowers on the machair, the innumerable invertebrate and fish species in the intertidal and subtidal zones, and the range of coastal habitats from salt marsh and sand dune to cliffs provide niches for many other plants and animals. However, it is some of this wildlife that has traditionally supported the people who live on the islands – the fish for food, the seaweed for compost and fertilizer, some birds (e.g. guga) for food, for example. The list is long.

Third, the dimension of sustainability needed to be introduced. Can we use the marine gravels and sands in a sustainable way? Can the species of the coast and sea – be they fish, shellfish or seaweeds – be harvested sustainably? Can people use this island resource in their recreational activities so that its quality is never impaired? These are important questions if the inhabitants of Scotland, and the visitors to Scotland, are to continue enjoying the island marine heritage for as far as we can see into the future.

The conference therefore brought together these three strands. Many of the speakers at the conference were associated with SNH, either as staff or as members of the boards and committees associated with SNH. Other speakers were not directly associated with SNH but, in a spirit of partnership, were prepared to share with us the results of their studies on the Scottish island marine heritage. We should like to thank all of these speakers for their contributions to the conference. We are grateful to them for preparing the written versions of their papers, but we should particularly like to thank the band of anonymous referees (each paper has been refereed by two independent people) who so willingly agreed to read and comment critically on the manuscripts. As editors we are extremely grateful for all of the advice that we received from these referees, all of which has been passed on to the authors for them to revise their manuscripts.

Very early in the planning of the conference we decided that a venue away from Edinburgh would be appropriate. Perhaps it would have been attractive to have each theme of the conference in a different island archipelago, but such logistics would have been formidable. So we chose Inverness as a venue for the whole conference, a city more or less equidistant from all of the main archipelagos! We are particularly grateful to the Inverness District Council for hosting a reception on the evening of the first day of the conference. This gave us an opportunity to meet the local councillors and their staff in the magnificent surroundings of the Town House.

During the second day of the conference we 'launched' the Geological Conservation Review publication *British Tertiary Volcanic Province*; part of a series which involves the appraisal of key earth science sites throughout Britain. Some 48 sites are described in this volume which is a public record of key sites being considered for notification as Sites of Special Scientific Interest (SSSIs). The occasion of this conference was considered especially appropriate as many of the sites are to be found on the Inner Hebrides. By any standards, these sites represent some of the most outstanding features of British geology as they contributed in large measure to the development of the science and are still at the forefront of current research.

It is difficult to imagine, but around 55 million years ago a series of volcanoes, stretching from Skye in the north to Arran in the south, were pouring lava and ash from their vents and fissures, smothering the contemporary land surface. Fifty million years of erosion has seen some of that evidence disappear as the volcanic stumps were eroded by rivers and by ice. However, much has survived and what remains has acted as a magnet for geologists for the last 150 years or more. The craggy peaks of the Black Cuillins, Askival on Rum, the Sgurr of Eigg, to name but a few, all owe their origin to this tempestuous time in geological history.

Finally, we should like to thank the many people whose efforts contributed to the smooth planning and running of the conference. In particular we thank the organizing committee (Mike Matthew, Dr Pat Monaghan, Dr Jim Munford and Dr Jeff Watson), Jackie Graham for much of the administrative work, Mhari Smith and staff of the Caledonian Hotel, and Caroline Munro of the Inverness District Council.

Michael B Usher and John M Baxter
Edinburgh, June 1993

CONTENTS

LIST OF CONTRIBUTORS

S. Angus, Scottish Natural Heritage, 17 Francis Street, Stornoway, Isle of Lewis PA87 2NB, UK

R. S. Bailey, Scottish Office Agriculture and Fisheries Department, Marine Laboratory, P.O. Box 101, Victoria Road, Aberdeen, AB9 8DB, UK (Present address: International Council for the Exploration of the Sea, Palægade 2–4, DK–1261, Copenhagen K, Denmark)

J. M. Baxter, Scottish Natural Heritage, 2 Anderson Place, Edinburgh EH6 5NP, UK

D. W. Connor, Joint Nature Conservation Committee, Monkstone House, City Road, Peterborough, PE1 1JY, UK

D. W. Donnan, Scottish Natural Heritage, 2 Anderson Place, Edinburgh EH6 5NP, UK

G. M. Dunnet, Whinhill, Inverebrie, Ellon, Aberdeenshire AB41 8PT, UK

D. J. Ellett, Dunstaffnage Marine Laboratory, PO Box 3, Oban, Argyll PA34 5AD, UK

I. Fuller, Scottish Natural Heritage, 2 Anderson Place, Edinburgh EH6 5NP, UK

M. R. Hall, Shetland Islands Council, Environmental Services Department, Greenhead, Lerwick, Shetland, ZE1 0PY, UK

J. Hunter, 22 Borve, Portree, Isle of Skye IV51 9PE, UK

W. J. Lambert, Gatty Marine Laboratory, School of Biological and Medical Sciences, University of St. Andrews, St. Andrews, Fife KY16 8LB, UK

A. P. McKirdy, Scottish Natural Heritage, 2 Anderson Place, Edinburgh EH6 5NP, UK

P. Monaghan, Applied Ornithology Unit, Zoology Department, Glasgow University, Glasgow G12 8QQ, UK

J. G. Munford, Scottish Natural Heritage, 2 Anderson Place, Edinburgh EH6 5NP, UK

W. Ritchie, Department of Geography, University of Aberdeen, Old Aberdeen AB9 2UF, UK

P. M. Thompson, University of Aberdeen, Department of Zoology, Lighthouse Field Station, Cromarty, Ross-shire IV11 8YJ, UK

J. P. Thorpe, Department of Environmental and Evolutionary Biology, The University of Liverpool, Port Erin Marine Laboratory, Port Erin, Isle of Man, UK

C. D. Todd, Gatty Marine Laboratory, School of Biological and Medical Sciences, University of St. Andrews, Fife KY16 8LB, UK

J. R. Turner, Scottish Natural Heritage, Fraser Darling House, 9 Culduthel Road, Inverness IV2 4AG, UK

M. B. Usher, Scottish Natural Heritage, 2 Anderson Place, Edinburgh EH6 5NP, UK

B. Wilson, WILDLAND – Natural Heritage Services, Achlunachan, Inverbroom, Ullapool, Ross-shire, IV23 2SA, UK

Introduction: The Marine Heritage of the Islands of Scotland

G. M. Dunnet

The conference title, 'The Islands of Scotland – our Marine Heritage', is an appealing one, calling to mind the political and cultural history of such contrasting groups as Shetland, Orkney and The Hebrides, the romance of living on and visiting islands, the spectacular land and seascapes of our coasts and archipelagos, the rich wild life, especially perhaps the seals and the seabirds, and also the flora and vegetation of such communities as the machair. Though there were many earlier naturalists visiting the Scottish islands it was perhaps Fraser Darling who first described their great attractiveness, bringing together his appreciation, as a scientist, of the natural history, the archaeology, the culture and the romance of our island heritage. His book *A Naturalist on Rona* (1939), subtitled *Essays of a Biologist in Isolation*, was for me, at least, a compelling introduction to island life. His later books *Island Years* (1940) and *Island Farm* (1943) described his continuing commitment to islands, and in 1947 he published *Natural History in the Highlands and Islands* the sixth volume in the impressive New Naturalist series.

Around that time and later many distinguished naturalists wrote on aspects of the natural history of Scottish islands; for example Robert Atkinson, Kenneth Williamson, James Fisher and Pat and Ursula Venables. More recently Sam Berry and Laughton Johnston have published a New Naturalist volume on the natural history of Shetland (1980) and Sam Berry on the natural history of Orkney (1985). Morton and Ian Boyd recently published their book *The Hebrides* (1990) and the Royal Society of Edinburgh has produced two symposium volumes on the natural environment of the Outer Hebrides (Boyd, 1979) and of the Inner Hebrides (Boyd and Bowes, 1983). In addition, much has been written about the natural history of Foula, Fair Isle, the Bass Rock and the Isle of May. We have therefore a very considerable literature on many aspects of the natural heritage of our islands.

What about the marine heritage of our islands? First impressions are that this would be a major component of the nature conservation interest, but somewhat surprisingly this has not been the case. Much has been written on seabirds and seals for which islands are relatively safe and convenient breeding platforms, close to the inshore and open seas on which they depend. Seabirds and grey seal *Halichoerus grypus* breeding colonies have not only appealed to the general naturalist as exciting, fascinating and often spectacular, but have also permitted scientists to undertake extensive studies of the biology of every one of these species. However, other aspects of marine biology such as the plants and animals of the littoral and sub-littoral environment, their ecology and the dynamics of their populations and communities, have only recently been the subject of preliminary studies by specialist biologists. In particular, the sub-littoral environment has posed difficult problems for the scientific observer, though recent advances in technology and SCUBA diving have enabled us to reach areas we could not reach before. In the extensive literature on islands referred to earlier, these aspects of island biology have been treated only very briefly. For example, in the Royal Society of Edinburgh Symposia on the Inner and Outer Hebrides only 4 out of 35 and 4 out of 32 chapters, respectively, refer to these matters; and in the accounts of the Natural History of Orkney, Shetland and the Hebrides, only 1 in 12, 1 in 14 and 2 in 20 chapters, respectively, deal with shore communities in general.

At first I was surprised to find this, but on reflection it becomes clear that much of the interest in island faunas and floras concentrates upon terrestrial biology, for which islands provide separate and more or less isolated areas where the terrestrial communities are much influenced by area, degree of isolation and heterogeneity of island topography, together with the powers of dispersal, establishment and persistence of species in what are usually somewhat impoverished communities. These factors and processes have much less significance in relation to the marine life in coastal communities around islands. The dispersive phases in the life history of many species of marine plants and animals, and the tides and currents which transport them, suggest that these communities should not be nearly as isolated and distinct between islands as the terrestrial ones. The theories of island biogeography which have been developed for terrestrial communities (MacArthur and Wilson 1967) are less relevant to the marine environment, and hence the distinctiveness of the communities in similar habitats on different islands is not marked. However, now that new information is being gathered on the composition, structure and dynamics of these communities, it may well be that some species will show patterns of distribution which are clearly associated with islands. If we are properly to conserve the marine wildlife associated with our islands it will be essential to have information on and understanding of these ecological patterns and processes. It is, however, also important to understand the human activities that impinge on the natural heritage (Table 0.1).

Much work has been done over the years on the marine fauna and flora of our shores. The Scottish Association for Marine Science and its precursors (notably the Scottish Marine Biological Association up until 1991) have carried out such research. This started in 1884 on a ship moored in the Forth, and has continued through the work of the marine biological station at Millport, Isle of Cumbrae, and more recently at the Dunstaffnage Marine Laboratory near Oban. Several Scottish universities have also contributed substantially to our knowledge of marine fauna and flora. The Scottish Office Agriculture and Fisheries Department have monitored commercial stocks of fish and shellfish

Table 0.1   Examples of human activities which impinge upon the marine natural heritage

Activity	*Description of impacts, and opportunities for SNH*
Fisheries	Exploitation of commercial stocks (note the Sea Fisheries Conservation Act 1992, with responsibility for the conservation of marine fauna and flora; also the review of rare marine fish in British waters
	Mechanical harvesting of seaweed and shellfish
	Industrial fisheries – sandeels and sprats are the basic food for a wide range of predators implying a need for collaborative approaches and holistic interpretations of marine ecosystems
Fish farming	Salmon and shellfish (site selection and consultations by the Crown Estate Commissioners)
	Environmental change (cf. the joint programme on recovery of benthos during fallowing supported by SNH, Scottish Salmon Growers' Association, Highlands and Islands Enterprise, BP Nutrition)
	Use and effects of pesticides
	Effects of predation – seals, piscivorous birds, eiders
Oil exploration, production and transport	SNH is consulted re offshore exploration and production licences and planning for on-shore development
	Oil spill contingency planning and clean up (SNH input to the training facility at BP's oil spill unit at Dundee)
	MPCU's activities following oil spill incidents
	Collaboration in monitoring e.g. SNH's formal membership of SOTEAG
Land claim and coastal protection	Impacts on designated and other sites of natural heritage value.
Pollution	A wide range of pollutants, from many sources, affect marine biological systems and species
Recreation	Increasing development of marinas, windsurfing, water-skiing, etc., can cause undesirable disturbance in sensitive areas

MPCU   –   Marine Pollution Control Unit
SOTEAG –   Shetland Oil Terminal Environmental Advisory Group

and their environment for many years, and in recent years the oil industry has commissioned survey and monitoring of coastal marine communities in the Moray Firth, Orkney and Shetland in particular.

Perhaps the first critical assessment of the needs for marine conservation in Britain was carried out by a joint working party of the Nature Conservancy Council (NCC) and the Natural Environment Research Council (NERC), whose remit was to study the needs of marine wildlife conservation (Anon., 1979). After careful review of the public interest in marine wildlife conservation, the report identified the needs to describe and classify the wildlife of the coastal zone and to look at the impacts of man on marine ecosystems. It identified considerable difficulties with the implications of a wide variety of relevant legislation, listed scientific needs for marine conservation, and produced a strategy for marine conservation. Many of its 15 recommendations remain valid today.

Provision was made in Section 36 of the Wildlife and Countryside Act 1981 for the Nature Conservancy Council to recommend to the Secretary of State that suitable areas of the sea extending to the seaward limit of territorial waters could be designated as Marine Nature Reserves (MNRs). To date only two such MNRs have been declared, the island of Lundy in Devon, and the island of Skomer in Dyfed. To provide the basic structure within which decisions about the quality of marine sites can be taken, the Marine Nature Conservation Review (MNCR) was established by the Nature Conservancy Council in 1987. This has progressed well but suffers from the fact that it was designed as a 20-year programme of survey and classification. The objectives of the MNCR are to extend our knowledge of British marine ecosystems in the littoral and shallow sub-littoral, to identify sites of nature conservation importance (requiring description and classification of biological communities and criteria for nature conservation values) and to provide information to support measures required to minimise adverse effects of development and pollution on the marine ecosystems. It should be possible to speed up the production of selection criteria and site assessments and this would be welcomed. The EC Habitats and Species Directive will impose time scales and provide an opportunity which must not be missed for developing this work, especially in relation to the brackish environments around the islands' coasts.

At present SNH has five National Nature Reserves (NNRs) which are islands or island groups – but they extend only down to the mean low water level of Ordinary Spring Tides. These NNRs are Rum, St. Kilda, Isle of May, North Rona and Sula Sgeir, and the Monach Islands.

In 1978 the Countryside Commission for Scotland published a report (Anon. 1978) in which 40 National Scenic Areas were defined. Many of these are coastal and some are islands, e.g. parts of Shetland, Hoy in Orkney, Fair Isle and Foula, the Small Isles, Dornoch Firth, St. Kilda and some of the Western Isles.

Although Scotland has no MNRs other approaches to site-specific conservation include Marine Consultation Areas (a non statutory label devised by NCC in Scotland as a strategic response to the increase in fish farming; these often overlap with the Very Sensitive Areas, identified by the Crown Estate Commissioners, using their own criteria, as areas where there is a presumption against siting fish farms), and Marine Protected Areas (promoted by the Marine Conservation Society; the precise meaning of this designation is under discussion by Scottish Natural Heritage, English Nature, Countryside Council for Wales, Joint Nature Conservation Committee, Department of Energy and Non-Governmental Organizations).

During its first year the Nature Conservancy Council for Scotland, recognizing the importance of conservation of our marine environment, organized a wide-ranging symposium entitled *Marine Conservation in Scotland* in the Spring of 1991 at Stirling. This two-day symposium was designed to consider all aspects of the marine environment and thus provided a comprehensive review from which an appropriate and relevant programme could be designed to meet conservation needs. The conference included thematic workshop discussions and the results of the meeting have been brought together in a paper by John Baxter and Jim Munford entitled *Towards a Marine Conservation Strategy* (1992). The results of this important meeting were published by the Royal Society of Edinburgh.

The Inverness symposium, on which this book is based, is a logical development for Scottish Natural Heritage. After describing various features of our islands and their associated biological resources, the symposium concentrated on sustainable use, an aspect of the marine environment for which SNH has been given specific responsibility. The Inverness conference was closely followed by a full-day meeting of the Scottish Marine Group at Battleby, a meeting targeted at conservation of the marine environment. In February 1993 the Marine Conservation Society held a two-day symposium at Crieff to consider Marine Protected Areas. Scottish Natural Heritage was well represented at both of these meetings as well as many other organizations charged with protection of Scotland's marine heritage. It is good to see this ongoing discussion of marine issues, and to know that there are many people and organizations who will be working with Scottish Natural Heritage to promote the conservation of our islands and marine heritage.

References

Anon. 1978. *Scotland's Scenic Heritage*, Countryside Commission for Scotland, Perth.

Anon. 1979. *Nature Conservation in the Marine Environment*. Report of the NCC/NERC Joint Working Party on Marine Wildlife Conservation, Nature Conservancy Council and the Natural Environment Research Council, Duplicated, 65pp.

Baxter, J. M. and McIntyre, A. D. (Eds) 1992. Marine conservation in Scotland, *Proceedings of the Royal Society of Edinburgh (B)*, **100**, 1–204.

Baxter, J. M. and Munford, J. G. 1992. Towards a marine nature conservation strategy, *Proceedings of the Royal Society of Edinburgh (B)*, **100**, 185–96.

Berry, R. J. 1985. *The Natural History of Orkney*. Collins, London.

Berry, R. J. and Johnston, J. L. 1980. *The Natural History of Shetland*. Collins, London.

Boyd, J. M. (ed) 1979. Natural environment of the Outer Hebrides, *Proceedings of the Royal Society of Edinburgh (B)*, **87**, 1–568.

Boyd, J. M. and Bowes, D. R. 1983. Natural Environment of the Inner Hebrides, *Proceedings of the Royal Society of Edinburgh (B)*, **91**, 1–648.

Boyd, J. M. and Boyd, I. L. 1990. *The Hebrides*. Collins, London.

Darling, F. F. 1939. *A Naturalist on Rona*. Clarendon Press, Oxford.

Darling, F. F. 1943. *Island Farm*. Bell, London.

Darling, F. F. 1946. *Island Years*. Bell, London.

Darling, F. F. 1947. *Natural History in the Highlands and Islands*. Collins, London.

MacArthur, R. H. and Wilson, E. O. 1967. *The Theory of Island Biogeography*. Princeton University Press, Princeton, N.J.

PART ONE
SHAPING OUR ISLAND MARINE HERITAGE

PART ONE

SHAPING THE ISLAND MARINE HERITAGE

In his Introduction, George Dunnet has mentioned many of the books dealing with the Scottish islands, but equally he has stressed how uncommon it is to consider the sea around these islands. If one is writing a book about an island, where does one begin? The most common approach is to concentrate on the factors that have shaped the island that we see today. The main factors are the rock which the island is made of and the climate that has prevailed since at least the last glaciation. Two sciences are thus involved – geology and climatology. However, these two factors give rise to three others: the formation of soils, the development of a vegetative cover and the use of the area since prehistorical times by human populations. Taken as a group of five – geology, climatology, pedology, botany and land use history – they have shaped the Scottish islands we see today. The landscape is a product of these factors and of their interactions.

What factors have shaped the marine heritage? To a limited extent, the same set of factors have been at work. However, for the marine heritage it is the geomorphological processes that are more important than the actual geology of the area. The sea buffers climatic extremes, and hence it is the currents and waves that are more important than temperature maxima and minima. It is these two branches of science – geomorphology and oceanography – that are highlighted as being of prime importance in the shaping of the marine heritage of Scotland's islands. Here, as on land, the operation of these two factors has been modified by the biological communities as well as by the patterns of human use of the sea and the coastline.

The interactions between geology and geomorphology are clearly shown by Bill Ritchie where he relates these closely to climate and the history of sea-level change. The picture that he paints in his chapter is one of dynamism where the biological communities have developed in a situation of long-term changes in the environment. To help our understanding of the dynamism, David Ellett demonstrates clearly how the waters around Scotland's islands are continually moving. The Atlantic and Slope Currents are remorselessly moving in a north easterly direction, with the associated coastal current that impinges on all of the western islands moving in a similarly northerly direction. The patterns become much more complex around Orkney and Shetland, with the currents tending to be northerly off their west coasts and southerly off their east coasts. It is both these overall patterns of water movement, and the local variations of eddies and reversals, that determine, for example, the fate of marine pollutants. This was demonstrated by the south easterly Fair Isle Current and the southerly East Shetland Atlantic Inflow, both of which had a major influence on the location of the deposition of the oil that was released into the sea by the *MV Braer* in January 1993 near the southern tip of the Shetland Islands.

The term 'landscape' is often used to describe the shape of the land together with an indication of the aesthetic sense that that landform engenders in people. There is no similar term for the sea, largely because the opacity of the sea itself makes it impossible for the majority of people to appreciate – to like or dislike – the underwater panorama. This is essentially a landscape, with rocks, plants and animals, that is bathed in water rather than in air. However, the term 'seascape' is gaining greater popularity, as demonstrated in Russell Turner's chapter. Seascape is very much associated with the land/sea interface; few seascapes as presently discussed have no land in them. Essentially it is a landscape concept where the landscape is *dominated* by a marine vista. Russell Turner's analysis of the seascape concept must rank as an important step in the recognition that Scotland's seascapes are every bit as important as Scotland's landscapes. Just as on land, the seascape brings together all of those factors that have been integrated to produce the forms and shapes of Scotland's coastal zone. We now need to assess what we value most in seascapes.

An introduction to Scotland's marine heritage would not be complete without an analysis of the communities of plants and animals that live around Scotland's islands. This is essentially the content of Part Two of the book. However, ever since MacArthur and Wilson's (1967) book there has been a heightened interest in island biogeography. Can one predict how many species will occur on an island, and which species these might be? How dynamic are island populations, and do new species colonize or extant species become extinct? What are the genetic effects on populations that are isolated from other populations? These are some of the questions that have been of concern to biogeographers, ecologists and conservationists alike. Soulé's (1987) book has particularly stimulated an interest in the genetical aspects of small populations, with inbreeding due to the small size of isolated populations generally being detrimental to the long-term survival of that population or species. The chapter by Chris Todd and his co-workers is therefore important. In the marine environment, with flows of currents that have already been mentioned, it might seem that isolation of populations is unimportant. Chris Todd's results with the mollusc, *Adalaria proxima*, are striking; there is very significant genetic differentiation of populations even over distances of a few hundred metres along West Coast islands. How general is this result? Do we have to take island biogeography and genetic isolation of marine species as seriously as we do for terrestrial species? The research field here is enormous.

This collection of four introductory papers aims to demonstrate just how the marine heritage of the Scottish islands has arisen. It is clear that we understand many of the factors that have produced this dynamic heritage, especially the physical factors that move the water and shape the seabed and coastal surfaces. It is equally clear that there are biological surprises as demonstrated with the considerable genetic differentiation in one of the species that Chris Todd and his co-workers studied. But there is still the question of the appreciation of that natural heritage, how the islands and their surrounding seas contribute not only economically but also in an aesthetic sense to the quality of life enjoyed by the people who live in Scotland and by visitors to Scotland.

References

MacArthur, R. H. and Wilson, E. O. 1967. *The Theory of Island Biogeography*. Princeton University Press, Princeton.

Soulé, M. E. (Ed) 1987. *Viable Populations for Conservation*. Cambridge University Press, Cambridge.

1 PHYSICAL ENVIRONMENTS OF THE COASTLINES OF THE OUTER HEBRIDES AND THE NORTHERN ISLANDS OF SCOTLAND AND THEIR POTENTIAL FOR ECONOMIC DEVELOPMENT

W. Ritchie

Summary

1. The outer islands of Scotland, Shetland, Orkney and the Outer Hebrides, have diverse coastlines which reflect the prime formative factors of geology, inherited landforms, sea level changes, marine and terrestrial processes (which are driven by climate) and sediment supply. Orkney and Shetland have distinctive high energy outer coastlines and very sheltered inner coastlines. Wave energy on the Atlantic coast of the Outer Hebrides is reduced by a wide, shallow continental shelf.

2. There is a relative lack of development, with most use being extensive and low value, especially agriculture where, except for Orkney, grazing is dominant. In contrast, there are some high intensity, high value developments, e.g., oil terminals.

3. The richness of the marine environment should provide a diverse and sustainable fishing industry but history, political decisions and extrinsic factors have led to a decline and an uncertain future. Current developments in fish and shellfish farming are of great importance and epitomise many of the problems of development.

4. Tourism and conservation are prime assets which could be developed further.

5. Developments should take place in an integrated planning context, taking into account local interests while recognizing the natural and heritage value of the special coastal landscapes of the islands.

1.1 Introduction

The physical characteristics of the island groups of Scotland have little in common. At a superficial level, Orkney, Shetland and the Outer Hebrides (Figure 1.1) share similar attributes of distance, cool maritime climate, a high percentage of poor agricultural land (although many of the Orkney islands have large areas of good land), a traditional dependence on the sea and, as a summary of the level of economic activity, low populations. At a smaller scale of analysis, all these similarities disappear and many landscape generalizations become increasingly untenable. The topographic diversity of the islands as a whole is mirrored in their coastal and nearshore areas. Nevertheless, the coastal zones of all the islands do share the common attribute of a comparative lack of intensive economic development. This absence of commercial interest, other than in localized points of growth such as harbours or unique concentrations of oil-based activity, might be explained by posing the hypothesis that the options for the economic development of the coastlines of these diverse islands are limited; limited by the economic friction of distance and insularity, and limited by the absence of those coastal environments that favour development on the mainland, ie, estuaries and fertile coastal plains. Equally, it could be argued that any coastline development reflects high levels of activity and wealth-generation in hinterland areas, and again this is conspicuously absent in most of the islands.

1.2 Coastal Environments

In the context of this paper, it is impossible to describe and explain in detail the wide spectrum of coastlines of the islands of Scotland which range from fragile salt-marshes to some of the highest, storm-swept rock cliffs in Europe. Instead, a systematic approach is followed by examining, in turn, the main factors that singly or in combination determine the main physical and, to a lesser extent, ecological characteristics of any coastline. These are: (1) geological setting, rock type and structure; (2) history of sea-level change; (3) land processes; (4) marine processes; and (5) inherited land-forms. The two process environments – land and marine – are essentially driven by climatic factors. The all-important additional variable of sediment supply derives from a combination of all five factors but is rendered more complex by the inclusion of biologically derived sediment, for example, shell sand, which is common in all the islands. Although being dependent on a range of other variables is not a prime factor, it is convenient to give prominence to the biological factor which, like sediment supply and to some extent geology, is both a factor and an element in all coastal environments.

It is important to emphasize the interrelationship of factors and elements and the multiplicity of system loops and feedbacks. Faced with such complexity (which provides the self-regulating resilience of all natural systems), the role of the coastal geomorphologist is to attempt to select the dominant factors that provide most explanation and to leave the consequential cascade of lesser

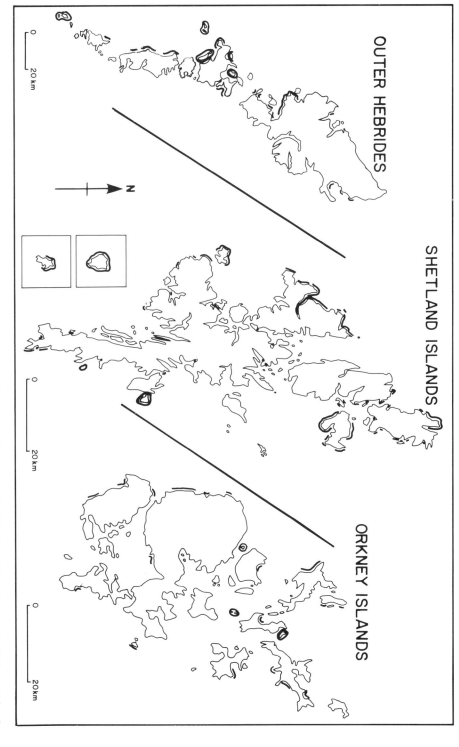

Figure 1.1. Maps of the three island archipelagoes discussed in the text – the Outer Hebrides, the Shetland Islands and the Orkney Islands. Conservation designations of coastal zones are indicated by thick lines.

interactions for the stage of more detailed, finer-scaled study. Thus, it is necessary to describe at a general regional scale each island group, in turn, using the main systematic headings of geology, inherited landforms, sea-level changes, sediments and land and marine processes. The main factor that is omitted at this stage, is the impact of existing land use and various types of engineering works; factors which often override all other natural processes of change.

1.2.1 The coastline of Shetland

The geological structure of Shetland is complex. Most of the coastline, especially on the eastern side of the islands, consists of ancient metamorphic and igneous rocks (Mykura, 1976). On both sides there are areas of later sedimentary formations including sandstones of Old Red Sandstone age e.g., Bressay, and Sumburgh Head and Foula on the west side. Rocks of volcanic origin are unusual, although dyke swarms e.g., in Muckle Roe and Northmaven, provide classic examples of local variations in the resistance of cliff and rock platform sections. The geological map shows strong structural orientations, mainly in a series of north to south junctions and dislocations, three of which, Melby, Walls and Nesting are major features. The well-known cliffs of Esha Ness and Papa Stour are also of volcanic origin. At a general level there is some correspondence between inlets and voes and these geological trends. Many of the rocks have steeply inclined bedding and foliation planes which give rise to dramatic coastal features. In general, a greater diversity of rock types occurs along the western coasts, producing rugged and varied cliffs and rock platforms. Coastal lowlands and bays are rare. Sand beaches are infrequent. Rock type and structure have determined that Shetland has an outer coastline that is dominated by cliffs, skerries and other rock features (Flinn, 1974). In contrast, the long, complex and often narrow, inner coastlines of voes and fjards have gentle slopes, pseudo cliffs and low energy lag beaches of mixed sediments, including gravel.

A history of postglacial submergence is the prime factor explaining the general nature of the Shetland coast. The coastline is most easily understood by envisaging a complex mountainous topography of steep ridges, plateau remnants and intervening valleys; a varied topography which reflects the underlying complexity of rock types and frequent faults, folds and fractures: a glaciated landscape; all these landforms have all been drowned by a substantial relative rise in sea level.

A coastline of submergence consists of inherited landforms which have been intersected by the sea and which have been exposed to different levels of incident wave energy. This concept is best explained by a single example. Picture two steep-sided mountainous ridges with an intervening valley which after submergence has high energy Atlantic waves on one side, a very sheltered flooded valley (a voe) in the centre and a lower energy (North Sea) coast on the other side. There may also be tilting, contrasting rock types and differences in glacial history, but at a basic level, marine energy will erode the Atlantic side to produce spectacular high cliffs above which lies the original mountain slope. The voe will be a very low energy environment with the original valley sides sloping downward without change of gradient into the sea, and there will be deltaic stream infill at the head of the inlet (Figure 1.2). The North Sea coast will have low cliffs, and more of the 'old' inherited landforms will remain visible.

Figure 1.2. Dales Voe, Shetland. The inner, sheltered coastline of Shetland provides close-spaced interdigitation of land and sea. A distinctive landform of the northern islands is the ayre. The origin of these shingle bars is not fully understood. In places they retain small lochs which provide distinctive wetland habitats.

Thus, in summary, the fundamental character of the Shetland coastline lies in the contrast between some of the highest marine energy zones in Britain on the outer, west coastline and great lengths of some of the most sheltered deep waters to be found in Europe. Rock type, structure and submergence have combined to minimize the number of bays and sediment sinks which might give rise to beaches and sand dunes. The inland topography tends to rise steeply; the glacial sediment legacy lacks any fluvio-glacial deposits; nearshore depths tend to be greater than effective wave base. There are exceptions, eg, extensive low areas of dunes and beaches at Sumburgh, the

St. Ninians' tombolo and scattered beaches in the northern islands – but it is a meagre legacy – and like Orkney and the Hebrides much of the precious sand is of a biogenic origin. The tidal range is not great (about 3 to 4 m), and does not give rise to significant coastal processes. Storms, onshore wind vectors and North Sea surges are important in raising water levels above predicted tides and thereby initiating flooding of low coastal barriers e.g. ayres and beaches, but, again, this is only of local significance.

1.2.2 The coastline of Orkney

Unlike Shetland, the islands of Orkney are almost all composed of some type of sandstone formation of Old Red Sandstone age (Mykura, 1976). Igneous and schistose rocks are rare (e.g. near Stromness) and there are many small-scale volcanic features including numerous dyke swarms. Some of the cliffs of Hoy are characterized by the presence of basaltic rocks at the waterline. Bedding and hardness differences are more important controls of coastal landforms than geological age and account for spectacular cliff formations (Figure 1.3),

Figure 1.3. The West Coast of Orkney Mainland. These dipping flagstone cliffs provide one of the most dramatic coastal views in Europe. Both bedding planes and joints have been exploited by the power of Atlantic waves to create the distinctive cliff profile of this plateau-dominated coast.

especially when hard beds overlie softer strata. Vertical faults and cracks produce deep geos and stacks e.g. Old Man of Hoy. Indeed, the Atlantic coastline of Orkney is probably the finest example in Europe of landforms that are controlled by rock type and structure, and one of the great coastal vistas is the view north from Yesnaby to the sequence of dipping flagstone cliffs of this exposed Atlantic coast.

Like Shetland, there has been a history of recent submergence but the pre-existing land mass was more rounded and dissected by an ancient pre-glacial river system draining southeastwards towards the remarkable submarine cliff between 40 and 60 m deep. The latter is described by Steers (1973) as an extension of the fault line of the east Caithness coastline, and continues as the Walls Boundary Fault in Shetland.

As a consequence of the drowning of this ancient series of low hills, broad plateaux and valleys, the islands experience a similar wave energy climate to Shetland in having high energy outer coastlines, especially the west mainland, and sheltered inner coastlines between the islands, for example Stronsay Firth, Wide Firth and Scapa Flow. There are no equivalents to the narrow Shetland voes (fjards), but there is a similar scatter of islands. The Orkney landscape (with the exception of Hoy) is significantly lower and flatter. Most of the islands are covered in thick glacial deposits which were conveyed by ice from the Scottish mainland and which were derived from the floor of the North Sea. Again fluvio-glacial deposits are rare. The lower landforms, softer rocks and similar abundance of shell and glacial sands on shallow sea beds has enabled extensive beaches and dune systems to develop on most of the islands, notably on Westray, Sanday, Stronsay and North Ronaldsay (Mather *et al.*, 1975). Thus, Orkney has more than double the number of dune systems of Shetland; there are over 80 examples in Orkney, some of which are extensive, especially in the northern islands (Mather and Ritchie, 1977).

In general, marine and land processes are similar in both the Orkney and Shetland archipelagos. With deep water to the west and a prevalence of storm and swell waves from the same sector, some of the most spectacular cliffs in Britain occur in west facing coastlines but as a consequence of the relative absence of geological variety, their forms have less diversity than the Shetland equivalents. Frost action is rare and most cliff-top erosion is by spray and running water but periglacial activity in the Late-glacial period was probably very effective in these latitudes and prepared the rock surfaces for relatively rapid disintegration. In contrast, the inner coastlines are low-wave energy environments, but in the wider firths of Orkney some fetch-limited wave action can develop and beach processes occur on many inner coastlines. Nevertheless, the sinuosities of the coastlines and the shallow water depths produce complex wave refraction patterns which give rise to subtle changes in small-scale coastal formations. These differences are also related to local sources of sediment, e.g., cliffs of glacial materials.

A common factor in all the islands is a climate that is characterized by very powerful wind vectors which drive high-energy wave processes and, where the terrain is suitable, build dunes and sand plains, often to great distances inland. The average dune heights are lower than in the Hebrides and have a more subdued, streamlined shape (Mather and Ritchie, 1977). Nevertheless, from a topographic point of view, the dune landscapes of the Northern Islands often resemble machair formations (Ritchie, 1976), but there is some discussion if the Gaelic term 'machair' should be used beyond the Hebrides.

Although a hazard to sailing and small ships, the tidal races between the islands and in the Pentland Firth have little effect on adjacent coastlines. The effect of tidal currents is mostly at the surface and as few currents come close to the coastline, there is little consequent nearshore sediment transport. Similarly, normal tides are in the medium range (2 to 3 m) but storms and surges have the same effects as in Shetland in producing elevated water levels.

The inherited landforms of rolling hills and gentle basins that dominate the landscape of Orkney are the prime controls of coastal types, with the west coasts of Rousay, Westray, Mainland and Hoy having bold, often overhanging cliffs, where the sea has eroded back into higher hill and plateau surfaces; elsewhere it is a subdued, low altitude coastline of beaches and low-angle coastal slopes and rock platforms, most of which vary in topographic detail as a consequence of differential hardness and variations in the bedding angles of the ubiquitous sedimentary rock formations. Many of the lower cliffs are also formed in glacial deposits which provide sediment for adjacent beaches.

1.2.3   The coastline of the Outer Hebrides

On a regional scale, the bedrock of the Outer Hebrides is entirely composed of ancient Lewisian gneiss with local areas of younger rocks, including sedimentary formations near Stornoway, and ancient igneous intrusions in central Harris and southwest Lewis. A massive fault provides the arcuate boundary of the Minch coastlines, with subsidiary faults forming the important 'sounds' for example, between North Uist and Harris, and Barra and South Uist. Similar structural weaknesses have been exploited by the main west-flowing ice movements which overdeepened the sea lochs which penetrate from the east into this island chain. Most of the lowland areas are covered by hummocky, relatively thin, boulder-rich moraine interspersed by numerous small lochs, especially in the islands south of Harris. Lewis has more extensive thick and continuous glacial deposits in the north but, like Harris, the mountainous central and south areas are characterized by severe glacial erosion and scouring (Peacock, 1984). Although the islands are typically covered in a blanket of peat, this is not true of most coastal areas which have been 'skinned' for agricultural purposes.

More important than the archaean basement rocks is the very extensive shallow continental shelf, the widest in Europe, extending into the Atlantic towards St. Kilda. Thus, unlike the northern islands, deep water lies on the relatively sheltered Minch coasts whereas the high-energy Atlantic swell and storm waves are attenuated by the shoaling effect of shallow water.

The coastal landforms of the Uists mirror the east-west contrast with small islands, sea lochs, cliffs and pseudo cliffs on the Minch coast and extensive low machair covered plains on the Atlantic littoral. Harris and Lewis are different. Harris and South Lewis have a central mountain massif with sea lochs and two extensive, sand-filled complex bay environments, – south of Luskentyre and at Uig. There are also a number of bay-head beaches between high cliffs, e.g. Mangersta. Lewis has an extensive peat-covered low plateau in the north with occasional areas of higher hills. The broad central and north parts of Lewis have a few areas of high and low cliffs, some which have been cut in glacial deposits, and, on the northwest coast, wide sand beaches and machair systems are common.

Throughout the Hebrides, the sequence of sea-level changes has been one of submergence but the mountains of Harris and Lewis were sufficiently high and extensive to sustain a local ice cap and subsequent isostatic changes appear to have produced higher sea levels, the fragmentary evidence of which can be found especially in Lewis (Von Weymarn, 1979). Fluvioglacial deposits are not common, but, exceptionally are found in abundance in the Uig area of South Lewis (Peacock, 1984). Nevertheless it is certain that vast quantities of sands and gravels were also laid down during the Ice Age on the wide, shallow continental shelf. The rising sea level carried these sands landwards. The huge volumes of sand in the Outer Hebrides coasts, especially in the Uists, are believed to contain over 25% of the entire sand supply in the Highlands and Islands (Mather and Ritchie, 1977). This sand is derived partly from this glacial sediment source but more than 50% comes from organic (shell) sources; the origin of this biogenic source is largely unknown but must be related to the extensive rock platform and constructive Atlantic wave energy from the west side (Mate, 1992). Unlike the glacial sand, the shell sand might be in continuous supply. As in Orkney and Shetland these calcareous sands give rise to sandy alkaline soils which contrast with the ubiquitous acid soils and peats of the rest of the islands. These sandy areas are therefore regions of relative fertility and have long been attractive to settlement. The machair coastal lowlands are especially important in the Uists and occupy 10% of the land area (Ritchie, 1979; 1985).

1.3 A Review of the Existing Use of the Coastal Zone

All parts of the coastal zone of the outer islands of Scotland are used but could they be used for greater economic return? Increasingly, the answer to both questions cannot be determined without reference to unpredictable national, European and local political attitudes which are based at the regional level on social, and tenurial factors and at the national level on extrinsic strategic and economic policies. As a crude example, it is clear that a powerful factor in the future of salmon farming in Scotland is the outcome of marketing policies in Norway and there are dozens of similar examples of key factors that lie outwith the control of the island economies. Although the use of the coastal zone may, in the end, be determined as much by policies made elsewhere, two powerful factors must always be considered – current use (which both offshore and onshore is controlled by powerful historical factors) and the fundamental physical and ecological characteristics of the area.

At a more general level, a survey of the onshore component of the existing use of the coastal zone of the outer islands resembles most of the Highlands and Islands in Scotland showing predictable areal patterns of extensive, low value, low intensity usage and punctiform, sometimes short-lived, high intensity developments. Like mainland areas in the West Highlands and other islands, for example the Inner Hebrides, most of the coastal land is upland, poor quality and, in the cool climate, most suitable for extensive grazing (some areas are also managed for shooting and fishing interests). From a management point of view, a positive factor, however, is the fact that with the exception of crofting common land and rotational arable strips, the land retains the advantage of remaining in large ownership blocks. The inevitable consequence of these extensive forms of use is a sense of wilderness and open space – both of which are seen as assets by two sectors of society which can be described as being related to tourism and to conservation. Thus the overwhelming use of the coastlines of all the outer islands is essentially the same as the inland areas of the islands, – extensive, open, low value per hectare and, of necessity, lightly managed, with the coastal zone being croftland and the inland areas common grazings.

The low coastlines – beaches, machair and coastal plains – permit more valuable developments with consequent higher population densities. Agriculture is relatively more intensive with some arable use, especially in the richer coastlands of Orkney, being added to the ubiquitous dependence on grazing. Routeways and other infrastructure developments are, of necessity, concentrated on lowland areas, and, in the islands, this is normally within the coastal zone. Other land uses, again locally important, that occupy low coastal areas are airfields, including the strand of Traigh Mhor (Barra), military facilities and some housing developments. Sand beaches and adjacent dunes, which are accessible, provide the focus for many recreational and tourist-related opportunities, including a few caravan sites, golf courses and a variety of beach-based water sports. A few dune systems are sources of quarried sand. The two categories of use, collectively described as conservation and passive tourist/leisure, are equally dependent on these low areas – and, arguably, the ecological and scientific interest and the scenic impact of beaches, dunes and machair are often much greater than the superficially more dramatic exposures of cliffs and rocky offshore islands. In this respect a useful survey would be the total and seasonal use of different types of coastlines by visitors. The surveys of beaches which are reported in the various 'beach reports' for the Countryside Commission for Scotland (Ritchie, Mather and Smith, 1970–74) indicated that tourist use of beaches was concentrated for a few weeks in summer and associated with one of the following factors: good road access with parking (although this is often on the machair), caravan sites, proximity of a large town and juxtaposition with an interest feature, e.g. Skara Brae. These factors remain paramount but in a few areas local and national bodies have improved access and parking facilities and the level of use has probably increased since the surveys of the 1970s, for example St. Ninian's Isle in Shetland.

Point developments, including ports and harbours, are scattered and diverse. With the exception of fish farming, the activities are sufficiently rare to permit almost complete listing – the oil-based activities in Shetland and Orkney, including Sullom Voe and Flotta, fish processing units, airfields, seaweed collecting points, (for the alginate industry), small-scale sailing and boating activities, (usually associated with existing harbours) and notable tourist attractions most of which are essentially historical and archaeological. A special category of importance relates to viewing positions for spectacular coastal scenery or wildlife (usually seabirds).

In general, it is difficult to see any expansion of these existing forms of coastal land use especially in relation to the agricultural base. Specific tourist and leisure uses will develop in response to local initiatives which include the increasing provision of good information sources. All forms of tourist or leisure activities, including conservation use, are ultimately controlled by the overriding importance of access and throughout all the islands this factor has improved substantially. It would be foolish to deny the possibility of significant major oil-based expansion or some military/strategic imperative, but the evidence of the previous 30 years indicates that, with the exceptions of the salmon and shellfish industries, most developments both areal and point-based have been extensions of existing patterns of activity. Some forms of use have also declined, such as the intensity of arable use on some machair land, or disappeared, such as whaling stations.

It is clear that the fundamental physical and biological characteristics of the coastlines of these islands are not exceptional; examples of the main types of high and low coastlines in the islands can be found elsewhere on the Scottish mainland. There are no coastal types in the islands that are uniquely advantageous for specific developments. Location is more important than intrinsic environmental attributes. For example, the vastly important Sullom Voe terminal exploits deep sheltered water but its development was a consequence of the position and distance of the producing offshore oilfields. The army base and firing range of Benbecula and South Uist require the relatively empty waters of the Atlantic out to St. Kilda for their existence.

In contrast, where the physical and biological characteristics are truly exceptional and valuable are in their unspoilt, relatively empty, 'wilderness' landscapes and in the scientific interest which has often been preserved by lack of development. Most of the conservation areas including Sites of Special Scientific Interest are coastal and, collectively, are so extensive that most of the coastlines of all the islands have some form of conservation status (Figure 1.1).

These designations give rise to the possibility of management conflict which might be more apparent than real since much of the present use already embodies coexisting land uses which are sympathetic to conservation values. Although this is, of necessity, a value judgement, the number of coastal areas that could be described as having outstanding scenic beauty is very high and compares only with the mainland of the West Highlands and the Inner Hebrides.

1.4 The Importance of Fishing Including Fish Farming

The single most important use of the coastal zone is some form of fishing activity. Exploitation extends across the adjacent shelves, reaches into every inlet and sea loch and is the *raison d'etre* of most harbours and coastal villages. It sustains an elaborate infrastructure and an array of dependent economic activities, especially in Shetland. Traditional fishing activities have been greatly expanded by massive investment in fish farming, especially for salmon.

Any attempt to approach this complex industry from the point of view of a simple assessment of the physical and biological environments of the nearshore zone and the contiguous coastline is almost an unreal exercise. The level and nature of current activity requires an intense scrutiny of the historical development of an industry which is controlled by market forces, technological change, national and European legislation and powerful political and social factors. If it were possible to turn the clock back for 100 years before sophisticated fishing technology, before transport development, before the incursion of vessels from distant ports, refrigeration, the expansion of marine science and several other important changes and developments, then the physical and biological base, as many entrepreneurs such as Lord Leverhume, recognized, was the greatest single source of potential economic development for the outer islands. The variety of marine habitats, the flux of rich Atlantic water masses, the intricate coastline of bays, sheltered firths and fjords – (both as habitats and sites for ports and harbours) – unpolluted water, sufficient water mixing processes, a rich variety of seabed sediments and habitats combined to provide an abundance of populations of highly marketable fish and crustacea. In summary, there is a convergence of factors that would and did provide one of the richest fisheries areas in the world. Curiously, with the exception of the severe damage to complex food chains and to delicate balances within trophic levels of biomass production, which are a product of selective overfishing, all the environmental factors remain unchanged a century later in the 1990s. Thus the future of the fishing industry, whether it expands or declines, lies in the hands of human decision and judgement, not in the fundamental assets of the natural environments of the coastline and adjacent waters, which are comparatively secure and renewable. Factors that damage fisheries industries elsewhere such as pollution, competing forms of sea-use and the environmental problems associated with enclosed marine areas, bordered by different nation states, are also almost absent from the islands.

Salmon and shellfish farming is a special recent development and numerous reports have been produced on its growth and future prospects. Again, from the environmental point of view, the basic attributes of sheltered sea water, unpolluted water columns, sufficient water exchange, good sites for mooring and shore-based facilities, appropriate water temperatures and salinity are readily available around the coastlines of the islands. Unlike traditional fishing these are new commercial undertakings and, by definition, must be located close to the shore where there is road access and the nets and cages are sometimes highly visible. Developments of salmon and shellfish farming have occurred at a time when considerations of possible conflicts of interests which include scenic effects, cumulative environmental impacts, relationships with conservation designations and a heightened awareness of problems of waste disposal and litter have become matters of substantial public interest. All of these factors pose problems for further development but, in reality, these environmental difficulties, although not inconsequential, are less important than current commercial considerations.

Fish farming epitomizes some of the central issues of the potential of the coastal zones for economic developments. From an economic point of view it is estimated that the value to the islands is worth £20 million annually, and the industry employs about 450 people directly. It exploits the fundamental attributes of the physical and biological environments of the coastal zone but in so doing *might* be detrimental to other forms of use; such as scenic and conservation values which are almost impossible to assess quantitatively. Nevertheless, most recent reports on the future of the industry are concerned with marketing, quality assurance, pricing and, especially competition from as far afield as Alaska (Lloyd and Livingstone, 1991; Scottish Office, 1991; Hopper and Gillespie, 1992).

1.5 The Use of the Coastal Zone: Conflict and Coexistence

There are few conflicts in the use of the coastal zone of the outer islands, especially on the higher coastal landforms such as cliffs and steep moorland slopes. Scenic value for tourism, conservation and grazing are rarely in conflict. For the lower coastlines, especially of beaches, dunes and machair there is a greater risk of a conflict of interests. The most destructive use is sand quarrying, especially in those areas where fluvio-glacial sources are absent. Traditionally crofters have also removed sand for roads and agricultural use, including improvements to acid soils using shell sand. Camping and caravanning (which is affected by the cost of sea crossings) are not common. Many areas of conservation value require the maintenance of traditional methods of grazing and husbandry. Airfields and military use have become important direct and indirect inputs into island economies and, in some areas, grazing can still be allowed within the airfield or military area. Large-scale industrial and commercial developments are rare compared with the vast lengths of coastline in the islands. Similarly, on the regional scale, although the environmental impact would extend beyond the zone of activity, superquarries would utilize only a small fraction of the total coastal resource.

When the scale of reference shifts to particular sites, to lengths of coastline measured in a few kilometres, problems of competition can arise. Specific agricultural improvement schemes, such as drainage, run against conservation management and could be seen as damaging operations against the preservation of the preferred habitat. A superquarry will remove a specific coastal feature and will introduce infrastructure changes, including associated roads, buildings and other exporting facilities.

In the voes and sea lochs there are both ecological and visual objections to salmon farms. There may be local sea-bed contamination. If there are serious problems, the only remedy is regional planning and island-wide coastal zone management. Coastlines, sector by sector, should be identified as being optimum for specific uses, and it is important to stress the plurality of usage, ideally within an integrated planning framework. In theory this situation might not be codified at present but it probably exists; long sections of coastlines have been identified and zoned in Structure Plans for specific types of use, usually the existing use. It could be argued that the all-purpose nature of planning and local government powers in the islands are a great strength since they facilitate an increasingly holistic approach to the exploitation of coastlines, but the legal definition of the coastal edge, low-tide level, poses special problems for effective management (Ritchie, 1991).

1.6 Conclusion

This broad overview of the nature and potential for development of the long and varied coastlines of the outer islands tends to confirm the view that the existing and potential use is closely adjusted to both environmental determinants and economic reality (Table 1.1) [(pg 27–28)]. The corollary is to recognize that the chances of recognizing unexploited opportunities other than on a very local scale are extremely low. Arguments have been made elsewhere that the damaging effects of history, for example, deforestation, excessive sheep and deer grazing, depopulation, overfishing, could be reversed by a programme of rehabilitation and replenishment. It is difficult, however, to envisage how this worthy concept can be translated into tangible work programmes. In relation to many criteria, the use of the coastline is not a special area which is different from inter-montane valleys, upland moorland or rolling hills and plateau surfaces, but the *range* of actual and potential uses is much higher than in inland areas: there are more options available. The greatest asset of these island coastlines lies in their marine environments, broadly defined to include scenic and biological richness. The coastline is different in several other respects: it is immensely long; it is remarkably varied both geologically and scenically: the range of ecological niches both offshore and onshore is great; historical and archaeological interest is relatively greater than inland. The future therefore lies in maintaining and expanding forms of use that are sympathetic to the natural development of the coastal zone; in preventing visual and environmental pollution; in focusing developments at the most suitable site, preferably within a wide coastal zone management framework. Decision makers must find ways to exploit diversity without destroying the asset for the future, and without

Agriculture:	Limited by climate, poor soils and distance to markets. Requires subsidy. Sandy machair soils might have some potential for special crops but previous schemes, eg, bulbs in the Uists, have a history of failure. There are no special advantages in any of the islands, other than in the current trend to organic farming which could favour traditional husbandry.	**Forestry:**	Inhibited by climate, especially strong winds and salt-effects, and a lack of markets, but selective non-commercial afforestation could enhance habitat diversity and scenic value. Crofting-type land holding and grazing operations introduce a special difficulty.
Fishing:	In theory, this should have greatest economic potential. All the natural factors are conducive to a strong industry. In reality, over-fishing, political and extrinsic economic decisions and some marketing problems, including transport costs, place severe constraints on growth. The main advantages lie in the proximity of a wide variety of habitats and marine conditions, ranging from open oceanic to sheltered voes, lochs, inlets and firths.	**Aquaculture:**	In theory, all the physical and biological marine factors are propitious. Future developments are likely to be determined by marketing factors and possibly some local conflicts. The islands have no special advantage over the West Highland sea lochs but environmental conditions are significantly better than most other parts of Britain.
Military:	Difficult to assess but growth and change will be determined wholly by external and strategic considerations. Islands have some advantage in low unit costs of land but, in some areas fragmented crofting tenure might pose problems. Strategic and security conditions are also favourable factors.	**Industry:**	Many forms of industrial and commercial developments do not require coastal sites. Existing processing factories related to the fishing industry are reflections of the strength of traditional fishing and now aquaculture. There is also a substantial multiplier effect in support industries, including transport. Oil dependent industries are presently very

Table 1.1. Potential coastal developments that could affect the marine heritage of Scotland's islands.

Table 1.1 Continued.

Special Developments:	These include proposals for renewable energy. Wind energy devices to drive generators are better sited on hillsides. Electricity generated by the powerful Atlantic waves is technically possible but seems to have doubtful economic viability other than at a very local scale. There are also possible underestimated damaging environmental side-effects.	**Industry cont:**	important but are not in an expansion phase. Future developments are dependent on the possibility of offshore finds, especially west of Shetland. There are also promising offshore blocks elsewhere. Exploitation will be determined by world oil-prices. Two superquarries are under consideration. Their development will be strongly influenced by current Environmental Impact Analyses.
Conservation:	This must be considered to be a viable land use and not a form of management for sterile preservation. In general, conservation is compatible and does not compete with most forms of existing use. In the outer islands this is a prime asset for the special types of tourism that are not found elsewhere in Britain. Very large sections of the coastlines of most of the islands are already under some kind of conservation management but, in reality, the management regime is essentially to maintain the status quo and allow nature to shape change.	**Tourism:**	This is dependent on scenic value, relative quietness, special interests, eg, wildlife, archaeology, history, but, in the end, is controlled by vigour of economic conditions elsewhere in Britain, and travel and transport costs. Attractiveness to visitors could be enhanced by selective small scale developments such as well-designed viewing positions at the coast. The scenic and scientific interest values of most of the coastlines of all the islands are prime assets. They could be exploited further and with careful planning, design and management, such expansion would not damage the resource base which, in nature, is very resilient if the fundamental properties of the coastal environment and its controlling processes are not altered, eg, by inappropriate coastal structures or large changes in nearshore bathymetry such as might be produced by sand and gravel extraction. Pollution from a landward source is a special problem but is minimal in the islands.
Ports, Harbours and Marinas:	The varied coastlines offer some of the finest natural anchorages and harbours in Western Europe, but developments are likely to be improvement of existing facilities rather than "greenfield" constructions. Certainly, the recent ferries between smaller islands, eg, in the Uists, have been at new locations but the impact on the coast has been very localised. There might be some scope for additional water-based leisure and tourist-based activities but, arguably, such expansion is also likely to occur in well-established, existing ports and harbours since the high capital cost of development may deter the exploitation of new sites.		

introducing imbalance. Further, any view that there are special advantageous factors and that the coastlines of the islands are lying ripe for development, but only require capital and the import of entrepreneurial skill, should be discouraged. Perhaps more than elsewhere in the UK, coastal development has maintained a mature and sensitive balance between the environment and economics, especially where local knowledge and experience have been taken into account.

Widespread proposals for coastal development are therefore unlikely and, probably, unwise. History shows that productive investment is more likely to occur in small, selective areas where this is controlled by good planning, sound environmental advice and management. If there is also an input of local knowledge and enthusiasm, the success rate is likely to be high and durable.

References

Flinn, D. 1974. The coastline of Shetland. In R. Goodier (Ed.), *The Natural Environment of Shetland*, Nature Conservancy Council, Edinburgh. pp. 13–23.

Hopper, A. G. and Gillespie, M. J. S. 1992. Marine fish farming in the United Kingdom – A challenge for the 1990s. In H. D. Smith (Ed.), *Advances in the Science and Technology of Ocean Management*, Routledge, London.

Lloyd, M. G. and Livingstone, L. 1991. Marine fish farming, planning policy and the environment. *Scottish Geographical Magazine*, 107, 52–7.

Mate, I. 1992. The theoretical development of machair in the Hebrides. *Scottish Geographical Magazine*, 108, 35–8.

Mather, A. S., Ritchie, W. and Smith, J. S. 1975. An introduction to the morphology of the Orkney coastline. In R. Goodier (Ed.), *The Natural Environment of Orkney*, Nature Conservancy Council, Edinburgh. pp. 10–18.

Mather, A. S. and Ritchie, W. 1977. *The Beaches of the Highlands and Islands of Scotland*. Countryside Commission for Scotland, Perth.

Mykura, W. 1976. *British Regional Geology: Orkney and Shetland*. NERC Institute of Geological Sciences, Keyworth.

Peacock, J. D. 1984. Quaternary geology of the Outer Hebrides. *Report of the British Geological Survey*, 16, 2, 1–26.

Ritchie, W., Mather, A. S. and Smith, J. S. 1970–74. Series of beach reports for the Countryside Commission for Scotland, Perth: Lewis and Harris (1970), Uists and Barra (1971), Shetland Islands (1974) and Orkney Islands (1974).

Ritchie, W. 1976. The meaning and definition of machair. *Transactions of the Botanical Society of Edinburgh*, 42, 431–40.

Ritchie, W. 1979. Machair development and chronology in the Uists and adjacent islands. *Proceedings of the Royal Society of Edinburgh*, 77, 107–22.

Ritchie, W. 1985. Inter-tidal and sub-tidal organic deposits and sea level changes in the Uists, Outer Hebrides. *Scottish Journal of Geology*, 21, 161–76.

Ritchie, W. 1991. The law and coastlines. In H. Smith and J. Vallega (Eds), *Development of Sea Use Management*, Routledge, London.

Scottish Office 1991. *Survey of Fish Farms for 1991*. Report of the Scottish Office Agriculture and Fisheries Department, Edinburgh.

Steers, J. A. 1973. *The Coastline of Scotland*. Cambridge University Press, Cambridge.

von Weymarn, J. A. 1974. A new concept of glaciation in Lewis and Harris, Outer Hebrides. *Proceedings of the Royal Society of Edinburgh*, 77, 97–106.

2 THE OCEANOGRAPHIC SETTING OF THE SCOTTISH ISLANDS

D. J. Ellett

Summary

1. The origins of the waters around the Scottish islands are traced from their oceanic, continental shelf and coastal sources.

2. Estimates of the quantities of water in motion around the Scottish west and north coasts are reviewed, and estimates of transit times within the coastal system noted.

3. The variation of hydrographic conditions on annual and interannual timescales is examined.

4. Local factors important in determining the character of the marine environment of individual islands are discussed.

2.1 Introduction

It is not possible to describe the oceanographic environment of the Scottish Islands by reference to a 'typical' island. On the grounds of exposure alone, examples range from the extreme case of Rockall, sitting upon its own micro-continental shelf and swept to its crest by winter waves, to Bute and the Cumbraes, where the greatest fetch for waves is a few tens of miles. For these reasons, the paper will describe the origins and variations of the waters which reach the islands and attempt to indicate the general oceanographic factors which affect individual islands to greater or lesser degrees. Cruises from the Dunstaffnage Marine Laboratory (DML) over the past 20 years have largely been in the waters to the west of Scotland, but although this may lead to examples being drawn from the environment of the west coast islands, I shall note the extensive work by our colleagues of the Marine Laboratory, Aberdeen, around the Shetlands and Orkneys. Much basic data concerning the environment of the Scottish coasts can be obtained from the atlas of Lee and Ramster (1981), now expanded into the form of the UK Digital Marine Atlas (BODC, 1991).

Four major questions about the marine environment may be suggested:

1. What are the origins and the paths of Scottish continental shelf waters?

2. What quantities of water pass through the shelf system, and at what rates?

3. How do conditions vary with time?

4. What local oceanographic processes influence islands?

2.2   The Origin and Paths of Scottish Shelf Waters

The chief types of water upon the Scottish shelf enter the area from the south-west or south and circulate in a clockwise direction around the coast. They are not only warm by contrast with seas in similar northern latitudes elsewhere, but bring species of marine life from southern European coasts and the western Atlantic. Although the outermost waters originate from the Atlantic Current flowing north-eastwards from the vicinity of Newfoundland, they have been modified by mixing with the more saline waters of the eastern Atlantic. The outer edge of the continental shelf west of Scotland is marked by an unusually steady northward current over the slope zone bringing Atlantic water from the south. The coastal current entering the region from the North Channel, the passage between Kintyre and Antrim, also contains a major proportion of Atlantic water which has entered the system from the Celtic Sea, the broad shelf area between southwest Ireland and Ushant, and which has been modified in its northward passage by fresh water inputs from sources such as the Bristol Channel, Liverpool Bay and the Solway estuary. Along the Scottish west coast further fresh water outflows from the firths, rivers and lochs influence the inshore waters.

2.2.1   *The Atlantic Current*

The Gulf Stream terminates to the southeast of the Grand Banks of New-foundland, where a large proportion of its volume recirculates southwards to the west of the Mid-Atlantic Ridge and another part drifts south-eastwards in the Sub-tropical Gyre. The remainder combines with colder, less saline water from over the Canadian continental slope to flow north-eastward as the Atlantic Current, the southern sector of the Sub-polar Gyre. The surface layers, bearing some western Atlantic organisms, are swept towards Britain by the prevailing winds, but the shoaling bottom topography of the North-eastern Atlantic further subdivides the current at intermediate depths so that part flows west of the Rockall Plateau and part towards the deep water channel immediately to the west of Britain, the Rockall Trough. Within the trough, the flow is often in the form of large eddies (Ellett *et al.*, 1986) which drift northwards from the deep water to the west of Porcupine Bank to between Rockall Bank and Anton Dohrn Seamount, an isolated feature some 220 km west of the Uists which rises in the centre of the trough from depths of 2200 m to within 550 m of the sea surface. From this vicinity the Atlantic water takes a north-easterly course towards the Faroe-Shetland Channel (Figure 2.1). However, compared

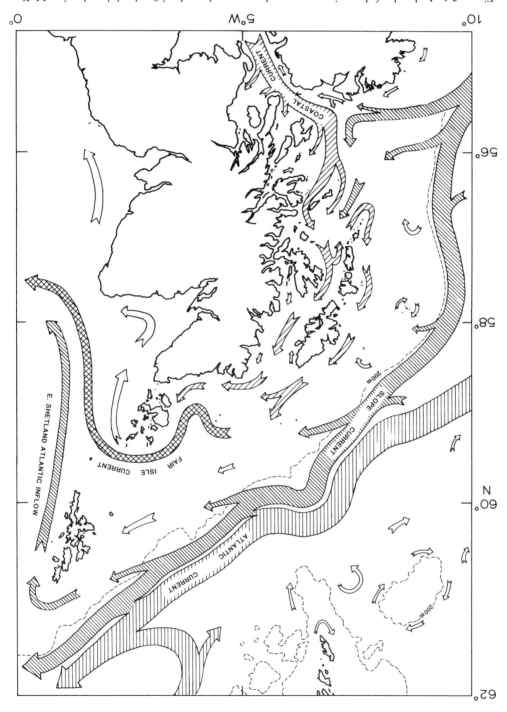

Figure 2.1. A sketch of the main current paths west and north of Scotland, largely after McKay et al. (1986) and Turrell et al. (1992).

with the branch flowing west of Rockall, this portion of the Atlantic Current has become modified by additional influences in the region at the southern entrance to the Rockall Trough.

2.2.2 *North-eastern Atlantic influences and the Slope Current*

The salinity of the upper North-eastern Atlantic is some 0.1 practical salinity units (psu) greater than water of equivalent temperature in the Western Atlantic. The chief source of this additional salt content is the subsurface outflow from the Mediterranean at the Straits of Gibraltar (Cooper, 1952). Although this outflow plunges down from the sill at the straits to spread northwards and westwards with its core at about 1000 m depth, mixing processes against the European continental slope raise salinity at lesser depths (Ellett and Martin, 1973).

This process is aided by a northward flowing current along much of the European continental boundary. The existence of such a current was partly deduced from biological evidence (Ellett *et al.*, 1979): Lusitanian plankton reaches the shelf edge north of Scotland and blue whiting migrations follow the shelf edge southward in late winter to spawn west of Porcupine Bank, so a slope current would provide a reliable mechanism for the return of the eggs, larvae and young fish to the Norwegian Sea. Although complete continuity between Iberia and Spitsbergen has yet to be fully demonstrated, segments of such a current have been observed over the larger part of this track, in particular from Porcupine Bank to the west of Islay and from west of Uist to the Norwegian continental shelf (Huthnance, 1986). This slope current appears to be relatively broad and slow to the west of Ushant, but narrows and becomes more rapid as it approaches the northwest Scottish slope (Figure 2.1). A good degree of continuity from southern sources is supported by a slightly higher salinity core over the slope zone west of Scotland (Booth and Ellett, 1983), but the current does not appear to constitute a complete barrier against the penetration of Atlantic current water onto the shelf; it seems probable that there is a cross-current flow by which Atlantic water is taken in on the western flank to balance water spreading on to the shelf on the shoreward side of the slope current, such as occurs between Barra Head and Malin Head (Ellett, 1979). Here the Atlantic water which has flooded over the shelf meets the Coastal Current water in a marked frontal zone west of Islay and penetrates northwards towards the Little Minch. Between Mull, Barra Head and the shelf edge, the relationships between these water masses and phytoplankton production have been studied by Savidge and Lennon (1987).

The next major incursion of slope water on to the shelf occurs just north of Rona, where mixing with Coastal Current water takes place (Turrell *et al.*, 1992). The main slope current continues north-eastwards parallel to, and mixing with, the Atlantic Current (Figure 2.1). From north of Shetland a branch of Slope/Atlantic Current water has been shown to flow southward off the east coast of Shetland (Turrell, 1992). This branch, the East Shetland Atlantic Inflow, seems to have been weaker or absent during the later 1970s, at a time of lower Atlantic salinity levels and decreased westerly winds over the UK.

2.2.3 The Coastal Current

Between Galloway and the Irish coast there is a net northward flow out of the Irish Sea (Figure 2.1). The relatively high salinity of this water shows it to be of Atlantic origin from the Celtic Sea shelf edge south of Ireland, although modified by fresh water additions in its passage through St. George's Channel and the Irish Sea (McKinley *et al.*, 1981). Some of this water enters the Outer Firth of Clyde, and after circulating and mixing with fresh water from the rivers and lochs which drain into the firth, returns to the North Channel (Edwards *et al.*, 1986). Inflow is often along the Ayrshire coast, and outflow close to the Mull of Kintyre, but water movements within the Clyde Sea are very wind dependent (Dooley, 1979). The strong tides and irregular bottom topography of the North Channel ensure that the Coastal Current flowing northwards from the area is well mixed. This current keeps close to the west coast, the greatest proportion of its flow passing between Coll and Mull, with less drifting to the west of these islands (McKinley *et al.*, 1981). The current passes the Small Isles, but between Skye and South Uist divides into two branches, one to turn south to round Barra Head and flow northward up the west coast of the Long Island, the other to continue northward through the Minches (McKay *et al.*, 1986).

Off Cape Wrath the Minch branch continues along the north coast towards the Pentland Firth, but despite the strong tidal currents between Orkney and the mainland, net transport of water through the firth is small (Turrell and Henderson, 1990), and the coastal current becomes diverted clockwise around the islands (Figure 2.1). The branch which travels up the west coast of the Outer Hebrides mixes little with the oceanic water upon its offshore flank until it has passed north of the Butt of Lewis. In the vicinity of Rona increased mixing with water from the slope current takes place (Turrell *et al.*, 1992) and the resultant water passes eastwards, roughly along the 100 m isobath, to become the Fair Isle Current, passing into the North Sea between that island and the northern Orkneys, turning south, then south-east to the east of the Moray Firth. During the late 1980s the East Shetland Atlantic Inflow, noted above, has run in a greater parallel stream on the left flank of the Fair Isle Current as it entered the North Sea, but in the previous decade the Fair Isle Current may have been the major inflow (Turrell, 1992).

2.3 The Magnitudes and Rates of the Shelf Flows

To appreciate the impact of the source waters on conditions upon the Scottish shelf it is important to compare their relative volumes and to examine the rates at which water passes through sections of the shelf. Rapid tidal streams do not necessarily lead to large residual (net) flow through the areas in which they are found, for example. Observations of mass transport from a variety of sources are discussed below, and some estimated transit times are shown in Figures 2.2 and 2.3. Determinations of seasonal transport variations are few but are mentioned where available.

2.3.1 The volumes of the flows

Oceanic transport over deep water is typically of the order of millions of cubic metres per second. In the Rockall Trough large quantities of water are in motion within eddies which propagate up the trough, and the mean net transport above 500 m on twelve crossings during 1963–68 was estimated at $2.7 \times 10^6 m^3/sec$ (Ellett and Martin, 1973). Slope Current estimates are tabulated by Huthnance (1986) and average about $1.5 \times 10^6 m^3/sec$ between the Celtic Sea slope and the Wyville–Thomson Ridge. North of the ridge and northwest of Shetland the Atlantic flow is increased by water which has crossed the Faroe–Iceland Ridge, and observations by Gould *et al.* (1985) measured a seasonal change

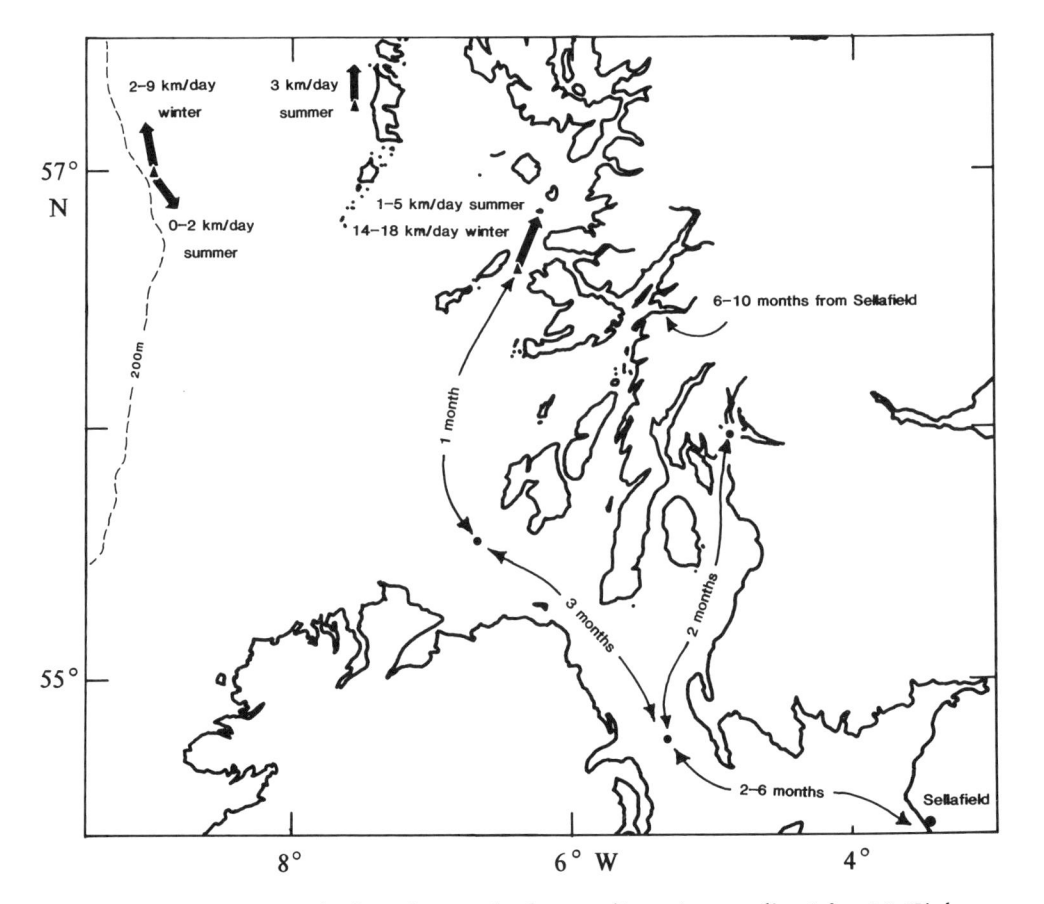

Figure 2.2. West coast transit times in months from radiocaesium studies (after McKinley *et al.*, 1981 and McKay *et al.*, 1986), and typical winter and summer residual current speeds (km/day) at three DML long-term current meter sites.

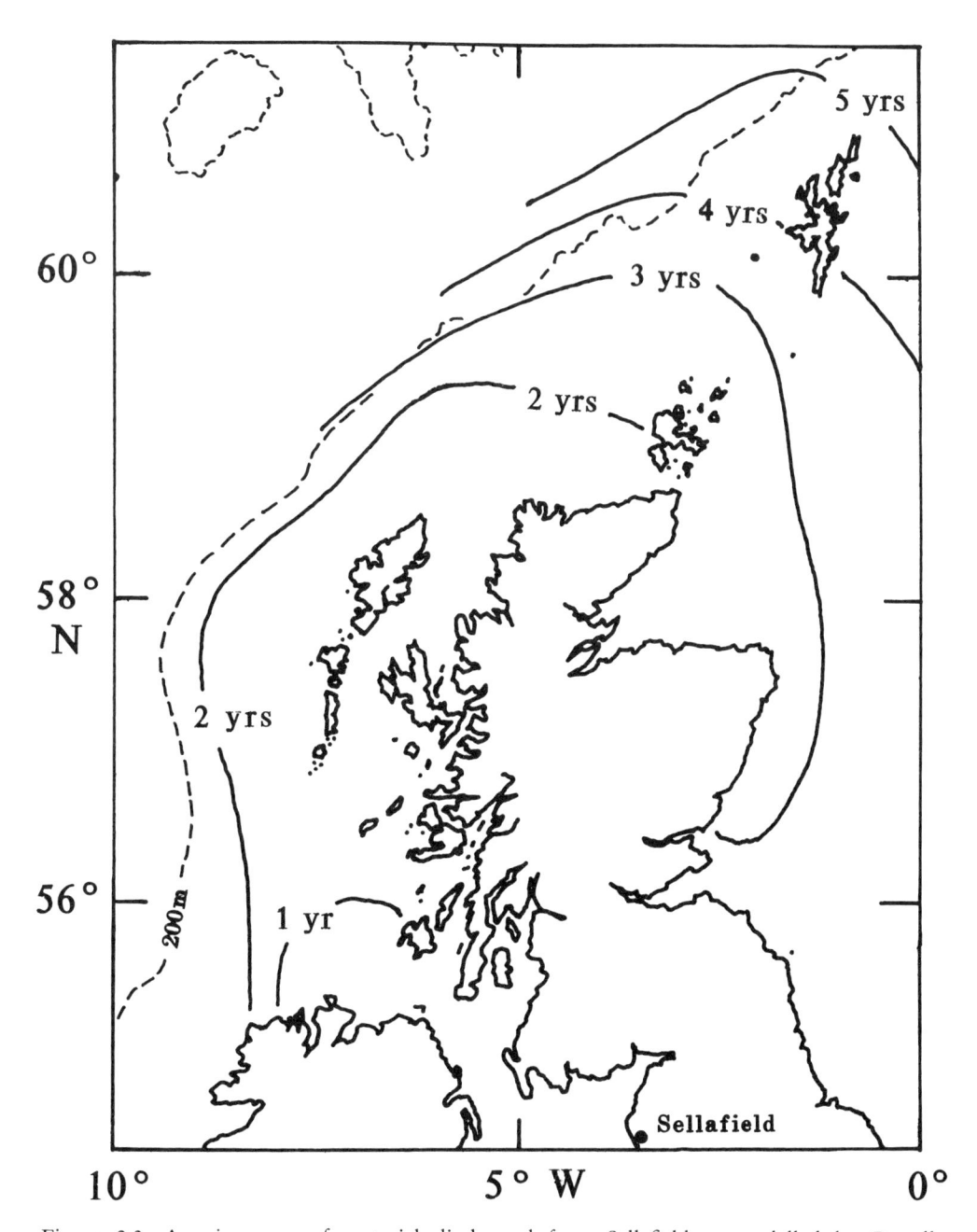

Figure 2.3. Age in years of material discharged from Sellafield as modelled by Prandle (1984).

from a monthly mean of $4 \times 10^6 \text{m}^3/\text{sec}$ in August 1983 to $13 \times 10^6 \text{m}^3/\text{sec}$ in February 1984. These latter values include both the Atlantic water and the Slope Current transport.

Over the shelf, the order of water movements is largely in the range of 10,000 to 200,000 m³/sec. On the west coast, a survey in July 1981 (McKay *et al.*, 1986) found about 5×10^4m³ of mixed Irish Sea and Clyde water leaving the North Channel between the Mull of Kintyre and the Antrim coast. Small quantities of this water were lost to the sea-lochs and the Irish coastal current, but the two branches of the Scottish Coastal Current, east and west of the Outer Hebrides, had gained about 7×10^4m³/sec of Atlantic water to total 11×10^4m³/sec in the latitude of Cape Wrath. Calculations made by inverse compartmental analysis (ICA) using data of the dispersion of Sellafield radiocaesium (Bradley *et al.*, 1991) indicate that long-term mean values are about three times greater than this summer value, which would agree with the observed seasonal variations in transport through the Tiree Passage, between Mull and Coll. Current meters maintained here from February to November 1983 gave transport estimates of about 3×10^4m³ in August and of about 13×10^4m³ in February (Economides *et al.*, 1985).

The long-term ICA box modelling, the July 1981 survey and the surveys during October 1987 of Turrell *et al.* (1992) agreed in finding a greater transport of Coastal Current water through the Minches than to the west of the Outer Hebrides, but data from December 1987 to January 1988 showed equal amounts passing by both routes (Turrell *et al.*, 1992). This may reflect another aspect of seasonal variation, with south-westerly winds being able to increase the outer flow more effectively than that through the restricted passages of the Minches.

Along the north coast, surveys by the Aberdeen Laboratory in October 1987 and December 1987 to January 1988 found the coastal flow from the North Minch to be of the order of 5 to 11×10^4m³/sec, but the mixed Atlantic and Coastal Current water from the vicinity of Rona was carrying 16 to 21×10^4m³/sec. Because of mixing between these streams during their passage around the Shetlands, the inshore water flowing south down the east coast of Orkney was somewhat diminished, and the major flow, now the Fair Isle Current, had increased in volume. Turrell and Henderson (1990) and Turrell *et al.* (1990) show that variations in wind stress clearly affect the transport of this current, which increases with south-westerly winds.

By comparison with the offshore flows, the freshwater input is surprisingly small, reflecting to some degree the west–east asymmetry in the drainage of Scotland. Values for runoff can be calculated from the mean rainfall estimates for west and north coast catchments of Barnes and Goodley (1958) using the value for evaporation (350 mm) given by them. Their estimate by this method of 350 m³/sec for the flow into the Clyde Sea area is remarkably close to the largely gauged average value (340 m³/sec) given by Poodle (1986). Annual mean run-off from Barnes and Goodley's four other catchments using the same evaporation value would be West Kintyre, 20 m³/sec; Firth of Lorne, 230 m³/sec; Ardnamurchan–Cape Wrath, 280 m³/sec; North coast, 73 m³/sec.

2.3.2 *Drift rates through the shelf system*

Residual currents (i.e. the net water movement when tidal excursions are removed) are notably lower than the peak tidal velocities. During the past 20 years the use of recording current meters has expanded our knowledge of both tidal and residual currents, but instrumental observations, seeking small differences between large quantities, need special care to obtain accurate results. The presence of natural or anthropogenic tracers in the water provides an additional method. Irish Sea water has been traced by the presence of radiocaesium isotopes from the reprocessing of fuel rods at BNFL Sellafield. During the mid-1970s, when emissions were at a peak, both the short-lived [134]Cs (half-life 2.05 years) and the longer lived [137]Cs (half-life 30.23 years) were accurately determinable throughout the coastal zone. Hence, from the ratio between the two isotopes at points within the Coastal Current, the time elapsed since input to the Irish Sea could be calculated. Figure 2.2 shows a selection of values determined in this way by McKinley *et al.* (1981) and McKay *et al.* (1986), and typical near surface winter and summer residual currents obtained at three long-term current meter sites. Figure 2.3 shows the 'age' since discharge of material from Sellafield as modelled by Prandle (1984); for example, the waters west of Islay should contain the largest remaining part of radiocaesium released one year before, according to the model.

2.4 Temporal Variations of Temperature and Salinity

Seasonal changes provide the largest variations in conditions, but the effects of longer term changes are becoming apparent as records grow longer, and also need to be considered. Because of the differing origins of the Scottish shelf waters, both local and distant variations are relevant.

2.4.1 *Seasonal changes in temperature*

The most obvious seasonal variation is in temperature, and here the role of the ocean in moderating climatic extremes is clear. Figure 2.4 shows annual cycles of air and sea surface temperature towards the southern and northern limits of Scottish island waters. On both parts of the figure the temperature of the oceanic waters west of the shelf edge is shown for comparison. At Millport, on Great Cumbrae in the Firth of Clyde, the sea temperature has a range of 6.7° K (7.0 to 13.7° C), whereas the air temperature at Rothesay on the nearby island of Bute has a range of 10.3° K (4.1 to 14.4° C) (Barnes, 1955). From May to August the air temperature is the greater, but during the other eight months the sea is warmer than, or as warm as, the air. Over the deep waters to the west of Scotland surface winter minima are almost 3° K warmer than in the Clyde estuary waters, though the maxima are closely similar, giving an annual range of only 4.2° K (9.7 to 13.9° C). This reflects the deep overturning which takes place in the Northeast Atlantic in winter, when the surface layers give up their heat to the atmosphere and sink, to be replaced by the warmer waters beneath, a process

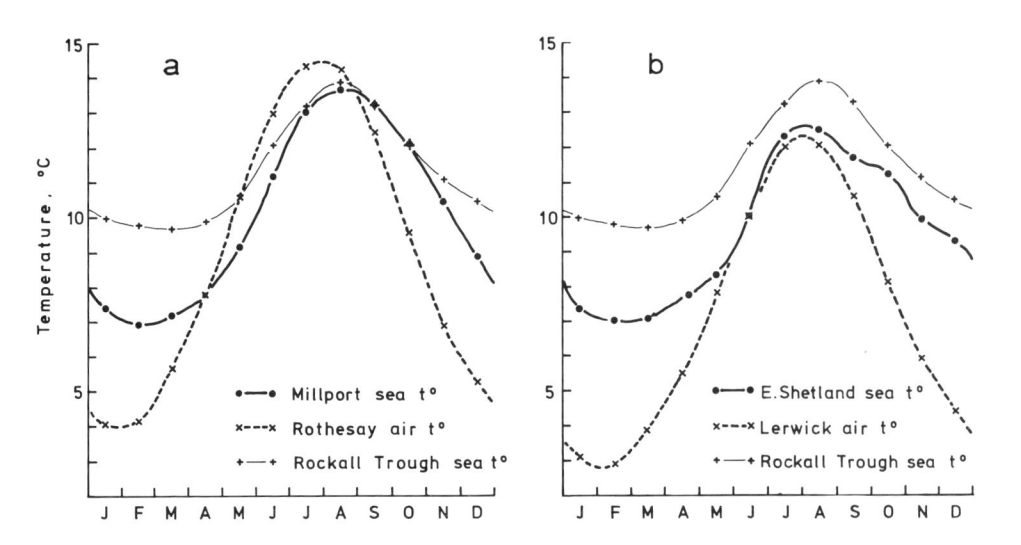

Figure 2.4. (a) Mean monthly sea temperature at Millport, 1949–53; mean monthly air temperature at Rothesay, 1931–58, mean monthly sea temperature, central Rockall Trough, 1951–90. (b) Mean monthly sea temperature, E. Shetland Inshore, 1960–90, mean monthly air temperature at Lerwick, 1931–60, mean monthly sea temperature, central Rockall Trough, 1951–90. (See text for references.)

which continues until the end of the winter, by which time the overturning can reach to depths of 600 m or more (Ellett and Martin, 1973).

Surface sea temperatures from the inshore region off the east coast of Shetland (Turrell and Slesser, 1992) (Figure 2.4b) have a range of 5.5° K (7.0 to 12.5° C). In Lerwick the annual air temperature range is 9.2° K (Meteorological Office, 1963), about 1° K less than at Rothesay, but monthly mean temperatures are notably lower (2.9 to 12.1° C), and do not exceed the sea temperature, although equal to it in June and close to it in July and August. Thus for 11 months of the year the sea is warmer than the air, even though the maximum sea temperature is 1.2° K below that at Millport. The sea temperature remains well below that over the deep water to the southwest, reflecting the general loss of heat to the atmosphere in the well mixed sections of the coastal current and the influence of the mostly cool run-off waters entering the sea along the west coast.

Away from the coasts, in soundings of 100 m or more, subsurface water may become isolated in the spring as the upper layers warm rapidly and become less dense, preventing the surface heating from spreading to the lower layers (Ellett, 1979). In such circumstances midwater and bottom temperatures warm only slowly during the summer, and reach their maximum annual temperature in the autumn or early winter when gales can once again overturn the water column. Figure 2.5 is for a position on the shelf west of Barra, and shows how the dates of the maxima are progressively later as the depth increases. The same pattern is observed in the isolated deeps which are found on the shelf in many locations between the Sound of Jura and the North Minch, and where tides are

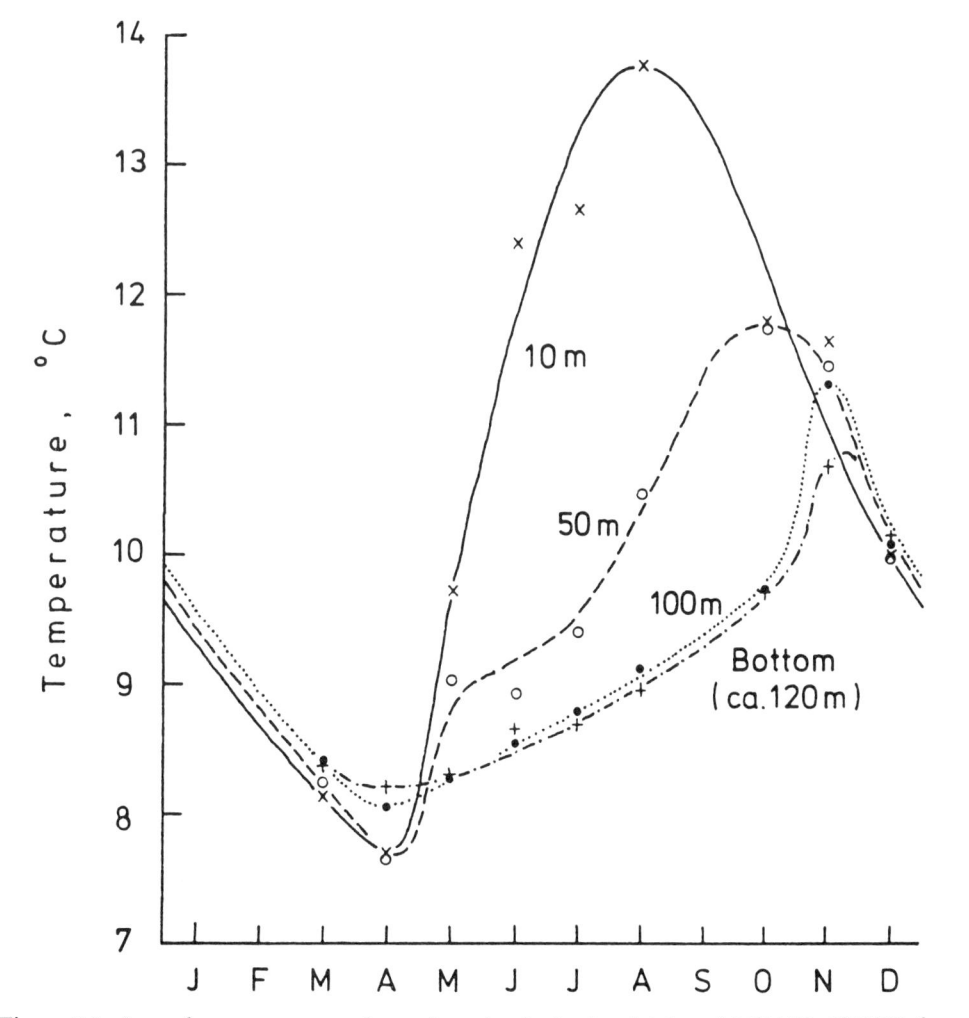

Figure 2.5. Annual temperature cycles at four depths in the vicinity of 56°52′N, 8°22′W, from observations taken during 1973–77 (Ellett, 1979).

relatively weak: an example is the trench with soundings exceeding 250 m to the east of Barra Head, where dense water from the previous winter has been observed until well into the autumn (Ellett and Edwards, 1983). A somewhat similar sequence of events happens in the Arran Deep and Kilbrannan Sound, which surround three sides of Arran (Edwards *et al.*, 1986). Here from late autumn to spring dense subsurface water from the North Channel spills over the sill across the entrance to the outer Firth of Clyde, descending into the deep and spreading anticlockwise around the island into the sound. As the inflows become colder and denser they displace the previous inflows upwards, until in spring lighter water over the sill again isolates the deep until autumn.

2.4.2 Seasonal salinity changes

Over the deep water the annual cycle of surface salinity change is governed principally by the balance between evaporation, highest when winds are strongest, and precipitation, highest in late summer to early winter. Other factors are summer stratification and deep winter mixing. In the Rockall Trough this gives a cycle with a small range of monthly mean values (0.066 psu) which has a spring maximum and summer minimum (Figure 2.6). Inshore conditions are very different however, with a winter minimum and summer maximum resulting in large part from fluctuations of run-off water from the land. At Millport the monthly mean salinity in 1949–53 (Barnes, 1955) ranged over 1.72 psu, between 31.26 psu in January to 32.98 psu in June, reflecting the changes in a major river estuary. Probably more representative of salinity changes around the larger islands is DML station C1 from the western end of the Sound of Mull (Figure 2.6) which shows the same general pattern

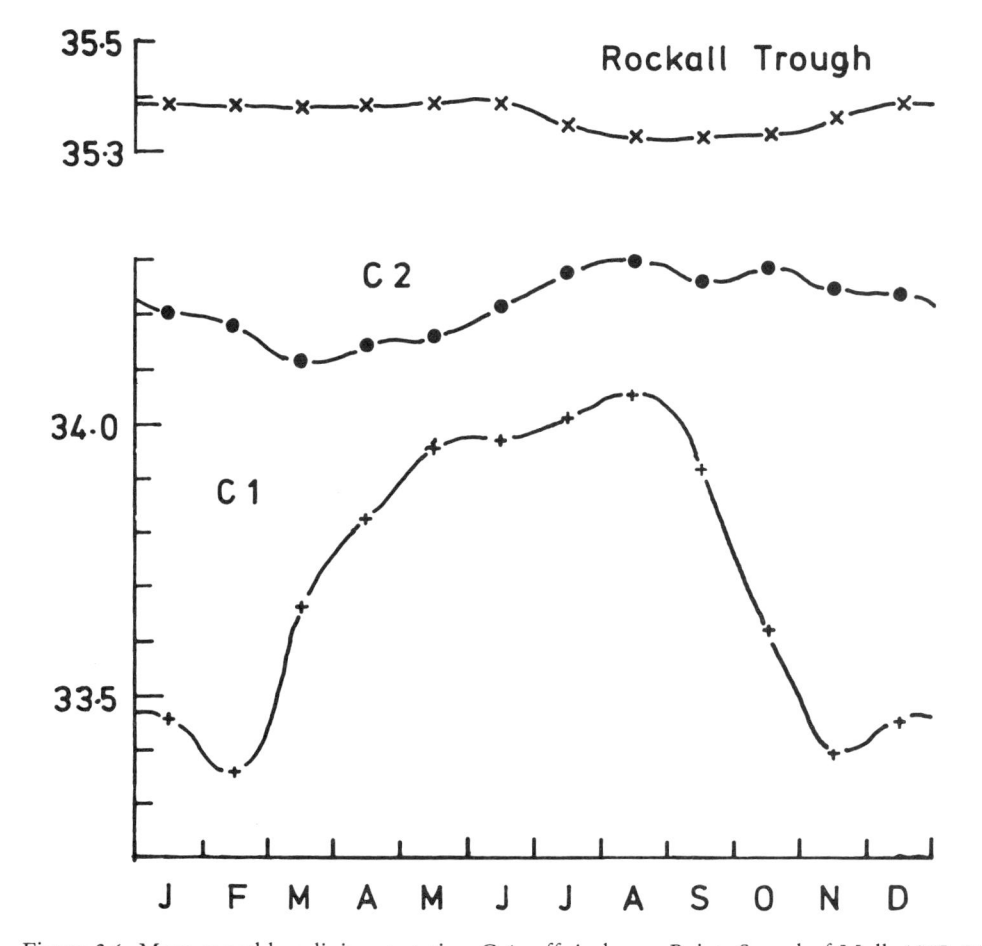

Figure 2.6. Mean monthly salinity at station C 1, off Ardmore Point, Sound of Mull, 1975–86, at station C 2, in the Tiree Passage, 1975–86, and in the central Rockall Trough, 1951–90.

of variation, from a minimum of 33.36 psu in February to a maximum of 34.06 psu in August, but is more oceanic and has a smaller range of values (0.70 psu). Orkney and Shetland, where the sealochs have minimal fresh water catchment areas and generally lack the entrance sills of mainland sealochs, are probably even closer to oceanic conditions; sections along the axis of Sullom Voe by Dooley (1981) during 1976–78 show that surface salinity was in the range 34.7 to 35.2 psu.

Surface salinity and its seasonal variation can vary notably over short distances. Station C2 in Figure 2.6 is less than 10 km to the west of C1, but is in the northern exit for the coastal current from the Tiree Passage. Here the annual range of the monthly means is reduced to 0.19 psu, from 34.11 psu in March to 34.30 psu in August. This reflects the history of strong tidal mixing in the current as it has passed through the North Channel and the uneven topography between Mull and Tiree and Coll. To the west, at positions between Coll and Barra Head, variability increases due to incursions of oceanic water from the outer shelf.

The subsurface salinity cycle in deeper areas where tidal mixing is weak is similar to the temperature changes described earlier. Dense oceanic water can persist beneath the pycnocline as fresher water spreads out from the coasts in spring and summer, until autumn gales overturn, or new incursions of oceanic water displace, the older water (Ellett, 1979).

2.4.3   Long-term changes

Long-term variations in the atmosphere are not evenly distributed across the globe. Whilst it is agreed that there has been a general warming over the past century, the recent history of the North Atlantic area shows that the relatively steady rise in temperature until the 1940–50 period was followed by a decline. Parker and Folland (1988) demonstrate a fall of 0.5 to 1.0° K in the surface temperature of the Atlantic Subpolar Gyre for the period 1971–87, relative to the values for 1951–60, centered upon the waters south of Greenland, and a decline in the annual mean air temperatures for northern Scotland approaching 0.5° K over the period 1951–87. Winter sea surface temperatures in the Rockall Trough reached a peak in 1960 (Figure 2.7), and have since fluctuated at a lower level by approximately 0.2° K about the mean value for 1961–70. Such changes will not be very evident in the coastal waters of the islands, where inter-annual variability is markedly greater.

The bottom part of Figure 2.7 shows that there have also been long-term changes in surface salinity. Despite the fall in temperature in the early 1960s, salinity continued to rise until 1968, but fell markedly to a minimum in the mid-1970s. This minimum has been connected (Dickson *et al.*, 1988) to an unusual influx of fresh water noted off the east coast of Greenland in 1968, which circulated around the Subpolar Gyre, passing west of Scotland in late 1975. Although this 'Great Salinity Anomaly' as it has become known, with a peak to trough difference west of Scotland of about 0.2 psu over 8 years,

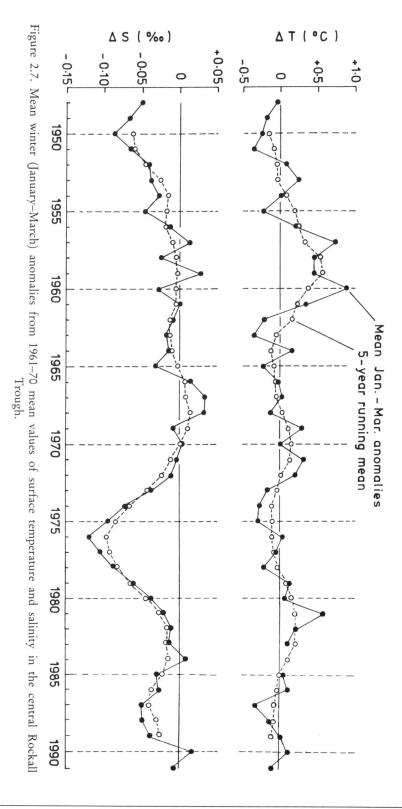

Figure 2.7. Mean winter (January–March) anomalies from 1961–70 mean values of surface temperature and salinity in the central Rockall Trough.

was significant in oceanic waters, its effects upon the shelf were masked by the greater annual and inter-annual changes. The most notable salinity event in Coastal Current waters was an unusual outflow of fresher water from the Irish Sea at the end of 1976 (McKinley *et al.*, 1981). This passed through the Tiree Passage in early March 1977 and had reached Barra Head by mid April, spreading to the shelf edge west of Barra by July. It is tempting to connect this flushing event either with increased stability of the upper layers of the Irish Sea during the preceding hot summer of 1976 or with the effects of the Great Salinity Anomaly, delayed due to 12 to 18 months' residence time between the Celtic Sea and the North Channel, but neither hypothesis can at present be substantiated.

2.5 Local Influences upon the Oceanography of the Islands

So far we have mostly been concerned with the effect of large scale processes upon the marine environment of the islands. However, local factors are particularly important in modifying these processes in the greatly differing situations around Scotland's coasts and as will be apparent, often interact with one another.

2.5.1 *Bottom topography*

The form of the bottom topography in the vicinity of the islands is one of the most important factors in determining the marine 'climate' of individual islands. A useful overview of the character and nature of the seabed around the Scottish coasts has been given by McManus (1992). The deeper sounds and channels provide paths which tend to steer currents over them, but conversely tides are generally weaker over deeper water. Thus tides off the east coast of the Outer Hebrides, where the bottom descends within a kilometer of the shore to depths of over 50 m, are weaker than off the west coast, where southwards from Lewis the 50 m isobath is over 10 km from the coast. Currents are strong where they are constrained by narrow passages such as the Sounds of Islay, Mull and Sleat and the several Kyles, from Bute to Lochalsh. Another aspect of topographic influence, previously noted, is the persistence during the summer of cold dense water in the deepest troughs.

A combination of shallow water and strong tides ensures that the water column is well mixed, an important factor in both the physics and the biology of the area. Figure 2.8 shows the very variable depth of mixing during a summer survey along the west coast (McKay *et al.*, 1986). In the North Channel and to the west of Islay and across the sill between the Little and North Minches the water was homogeneous to the bottom, as at many of the inshore stations. Elsewhere, where the depth was greater, the tides and currents weaker, or lighter coastal current water was present, stratification had occurred. Jones *et al.* (1984) found in a summer survey of the Sound of Jura that diatoms, the plant plankton, predominated in well mixed regions, whereas zooplankton populations were found in the stratified water. At the boundaries between stratified and well

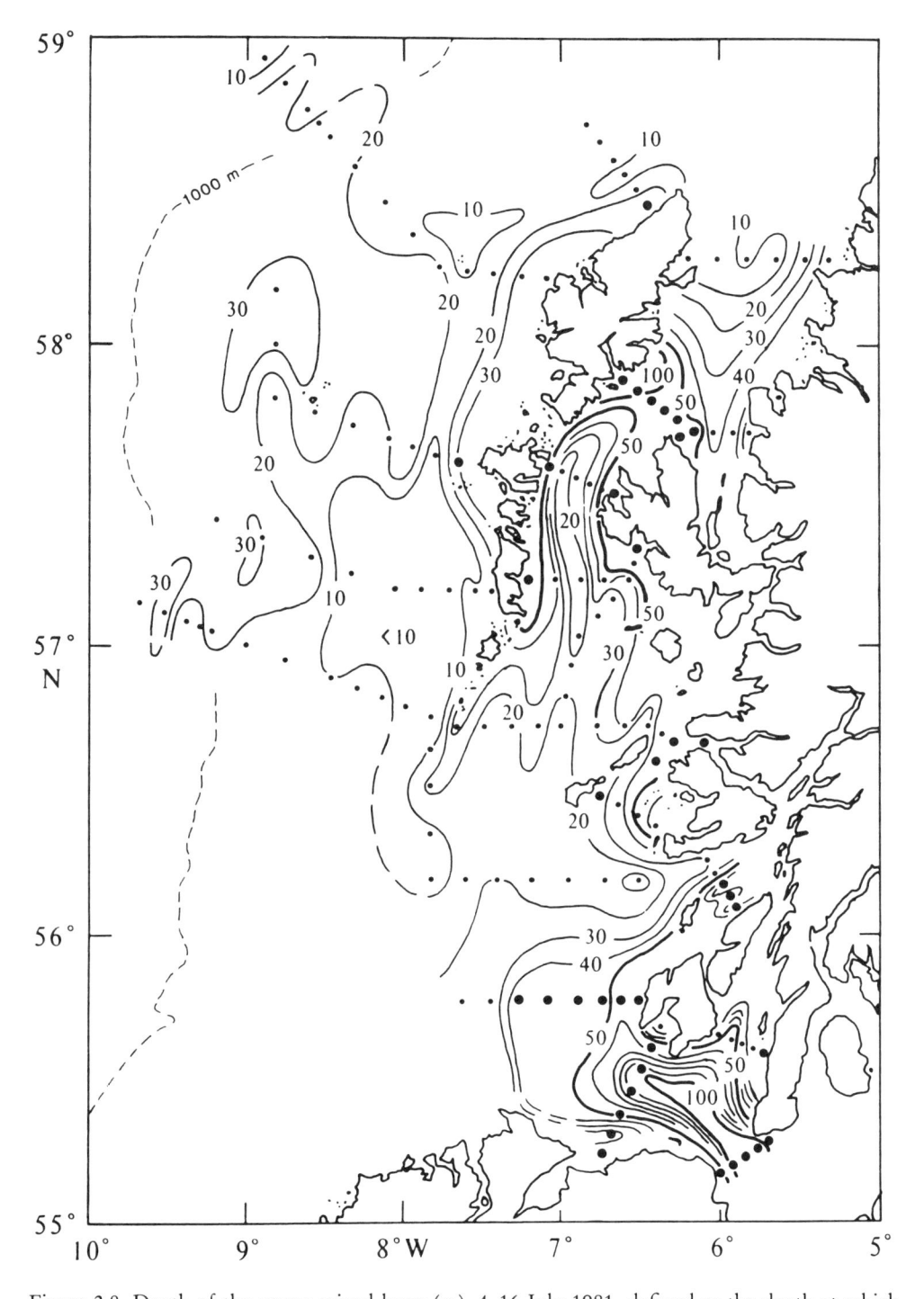

Figure 2.8. Depth of the upper mixed layer (m), 4–16 July 1981, defined as the depth at which temperature had declined by 0.25 °K from surface temperature. Large dots show stations homothermal throughout the water column (McKay *et al.*, 1986).

mixed water plankton production is high, due to the availability and recycling of nutrients.

2.5.2 Fronts

Boundaries of the type just discussed are predictable as forming at a critical value of hu^{-3}, where h is the depth and u is the maximum spring tidal velocity (Simpson and Hunter, 1974). For much of the year, during spring to autumn, they are detectable at the surface by sharp horizontal gradients of temperature and salinity, somewhat analogous to weather fronts in the atmosphere, and are often clearly visible on infrared satellite images. Examples occur in the Minches, to the west of the Hebrides and around St. Kilda, but more transient examples may be found in many situations around islands and headlands, some perhaps only during spring tides.

One of the most marked fronts is that running south to north due west of Islay in longitudes 7° to 8° W (Ellett, 1978; Simpson *et al.*, 1979). This appears to be maintained by two mechanisms; whereas fronts of the mixed/stratified type necessarily disappear in winter, when strong winds overturn the formerly stratified water, the Islay Front remains traceable as a salinity boundary between oceanic water on the outer shelf and the Coastal Current water shorewards (Economides *et al.*, 1985). Other fronts due to salinity differences occur on a smaller scale in estuaries, where river water meets the sea.

2.5.3 Fresh water input

Besides forming visible fronts at sea-loch and river mouths, the addition of fresh water to the coastal system modifies the buoyancy of the nearshore waters. The resulting mixture, being less dense than the waters offshore, is affected by the Coriolis force and tends to flow out keeping the coast on its right-hand. This mechanism operates on a wide range of scales, from stream outflows to the major additions to the Coastal Current from the Firths of Clyde and Lorne. Simpson and Hill (1986) suggest that the seasonal contribution of rainfall run-off from these sources is an important factor in the pattern of annual variability in the strength of the current through the Tiree Passage, supplementing the annual variation due to the wind regime (Economides *et al.*, 1985).

2.5.4 Wind

Local conditions are strongly wind influenced. In some areas such as the Outer Firth of Clyde the currents are largely wind driven (Dooley, 1979), and throughout the coastal system wind speed and direction act to modify the flows. We have earlier noted the work of Turrell *et al.* (1990) dealing with the effect of wind upon the north coast currents. In sounds and channels gales can sometimes stop the normal semi-diurnal reversal of tides and dramatically increase the rate of the down-wind tidal current. Current meters moored between Mull and Coll not infrequently in winter show a mean north-east going current of 50 cm/sec

(1 kt) over 24 hours with south-westerly gales, and on one occasion in March 1985 recorded a similar south-west going average with a northerly gale. The wind direction can itself be modified by local land-forms, so that westerly winds for instance can be channelled to blow from the north-west down the Sound of Mull, and the sight of spray being lifted some 30 m into the air by south-westerly gales descending from the cliffs of Hirta, St. Kilda, is a memorable one, particularly to those in ships seeking shelter.

Large scale weather systems can affect the whole coastal system (Prandle, 1987), the more intense depressions causing storm surges which produce abnormally high and low waters, but these are not normally as disastrous on the west and north coasts as they can be when they run into the shoaling waters of the southern North Sea. Townson and Collar (1986) have examined the effect of the west coast storm surges of December 1972 and March 1979 in the Clyde and show surges of the order of 1 m at Millport. Depressions crossing the shelf edge north of Scotland have been observed to generate continental shelf internal waves on the outer shelf north-west of Orkney (Huthnance et al., 1988). Two types were distinguished, 'oscillatory responses' which generated currents rotating over the inertial period of about 23 hours, and 'quasi-steady responses' which flowed along the isobaths during the duration of the storms. Gordon and Huthnance (1987) found that these processes typically generated currents of 20–40 cm/sec. The oscillatory responses were mostly forced by storms which passed within a day, but could continue for three 23-hour cycles before abruptly disappearing, whereas the quasi-steady responses gave increased current velocities for as long as the strong winds persisted.

2.5.5 Tides

The effect of tides upon the structure of the water column has been discussed above, but here we will note the general patterns of tidal range and velocities and two unusual tidal features of Scottish waters. The areas of shoreline habitats available to intertidal communities are of course greatly dependent upon tidal range, and greater ranges can encourage greater variability of species. The significant points of Figure 2.9 are the small range (<1 m) in spring tides east of Islay where an amphidromic point is centered, the northward increase to a maximum (>4 m) around Skye, and a decrease thereafter northwards and eastwards. Tidal velocity, usually greater than residual currents, also helps to determine the settlement of organisms and the dispersal of their offspring, but is subject to more local variations than the range. Figure 2.10 shows maximal velocities in the North Channel, the Pentland Firth and among the sounds of north Orkney. The figure cannot show the detailed rates in the narrower channels; the appropriate tidal stream atlases (Hydrographic Department, 1980, 1983) show mean maximal spring tide rates of up to 5.1 m/sec (10.0 kt) in the Pentland Firth and 4.1 m/sec (8.0 kt) in Kyle Rhea. Viewing the progression of the time of high water as a tidal wave moving in a clockwise direction around the Scottish coast northwards from Tiree, and anticlockwise around

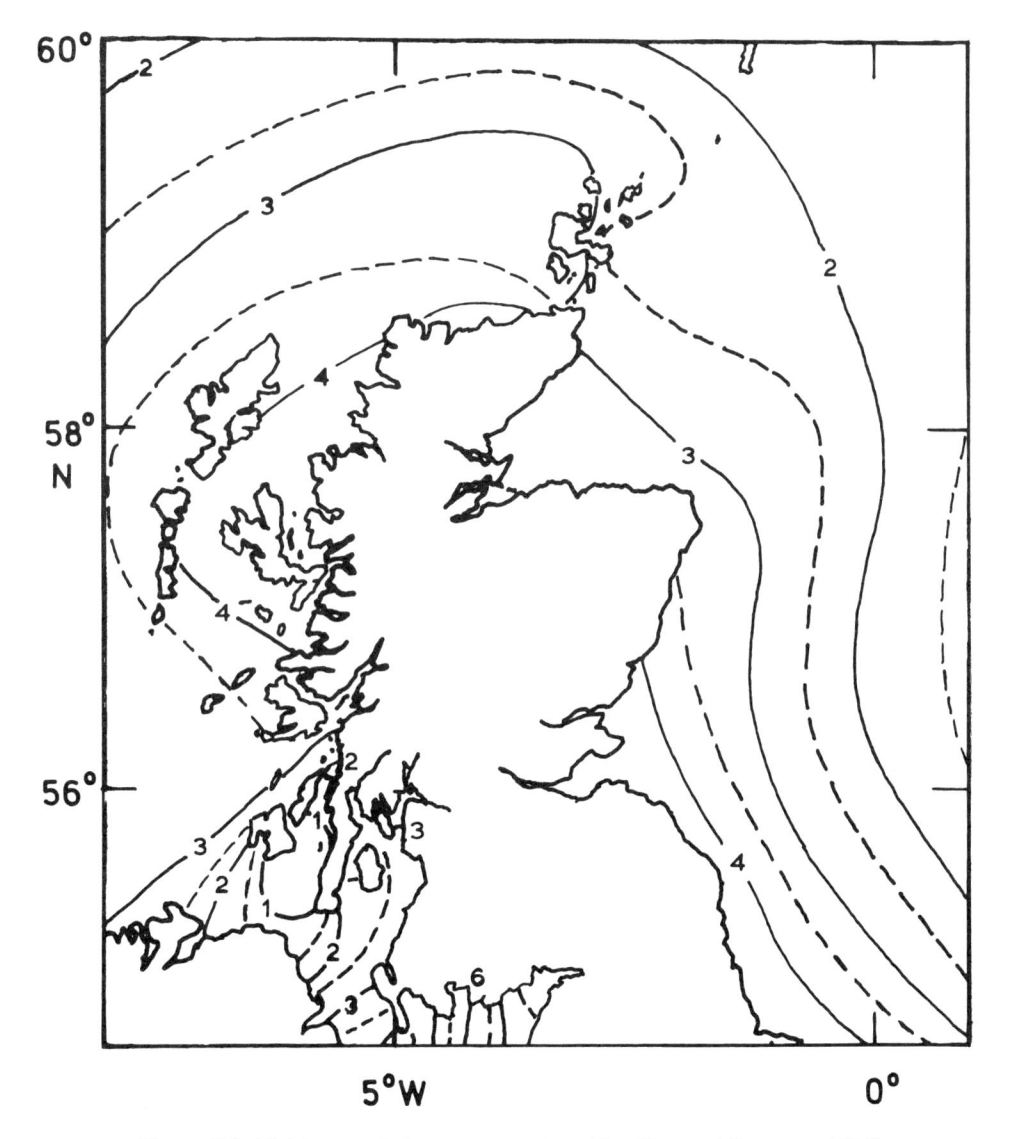

Figure 2.9. Tidal range (m) at mean spring tides (Lee and Ramster, 1981).

Islay in the south (Lee and Ramster, 1981), it can be readily appreciated that differences of level may arise between opposite entrances to channels between islands due to differing routes taken by the wave. Thus McManus (1992) has found that the greatest differences in level over the 20 km distance between the western and eastern entrances to the Pentland Firth occur at high and low waters, giving peak tidal velocities at these times, with slack water occurring at mid-tide. Such effects give rise to fast streams between the islands of Shetland, but there is sparse information about their velocities: Blackman *et al.* (1981) measured speeds of up to 1.4 m/sec (2.7 kt) in Yell Sound, but suspected that

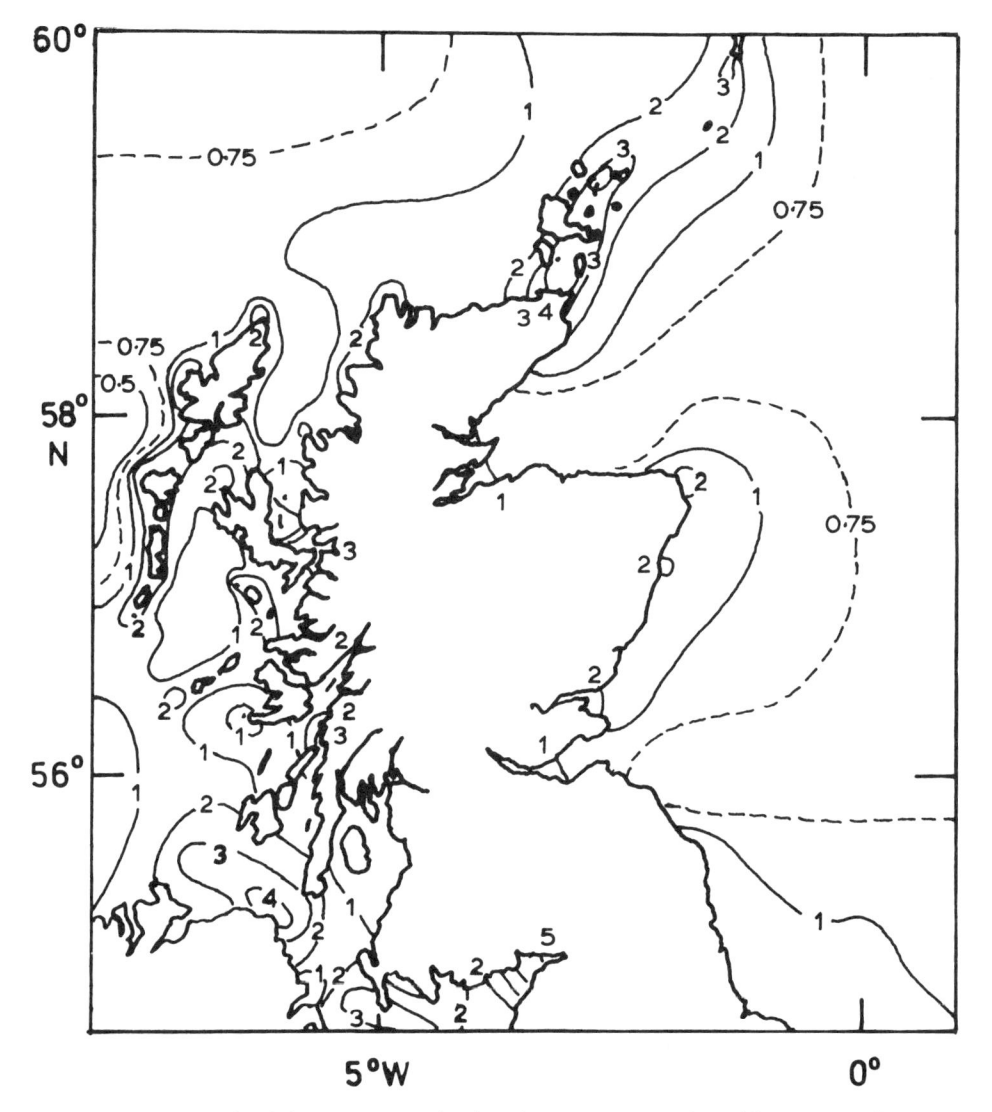

Figure 2.10. Maximal tidal current speeds (kt) during mean spring tides (Lee and Ramster, 1981).

this was significantly less than the true speed because of the difficulties of measurement.

No measured velocities are available for the Gulf of Corryvreckan, the passage between Jura and Scarba notorious for the eddies with dangerous turbulence and overfalls which form on both sides of the main stream, but especially to the north of the west going stream (Warburg, 1946). The sea level difference at springs over the distance of about 2 km between the eastern (Sound of Jura) end of the gulf and its western (Firth of Lorne) end is estimated at about 1 m, giving a velocity of about 4.4 m/sec (8.5 kt). Warburg says, 'The gulf was certainly navigated in the middle ages by Norse and Hebridean pirates . . . more in a spirit of bravado than as a useful channel', and it is still treated with as much respect.

A final tidal phenomenon which deserves notice is one which was brought to the notice of the Royal Society in 1665, by a founder member, Sir Robert Moray. In the Sound of Harris at neaps in summer the tide flows westward all night and eastward all day. During winter neaps the opposite is the case, with westward flow all day and eastward flow all night. This results from the marked diurnal tide found to the west of the Outer Hebrides and has been studied by Cartwright (1969) who has characterized it as a non-divergent continental shelf wave which propagates across this broad shelf area. Cartwright *et al.*, (1980) find that diurnal effects are normally much reduced at coasts, but the general tendency for consecutive semi-diurnal tides to be of unequal range in Scottish waters has been noted by McManus (1992).

2.5.6 Waves

Waves are probably the oceanographic processes with the greatest local variability, due to differing 'fetch', the clear distance downwind available for wave generation. Apart from Rockall and the outer skerries, there can hardly be an island without at least one bay sheltered from the worst winter storms. McManus (1992) notes the significance of wave action upon sediment transport and the disturbance of benthic life, and although such bays are likely to accumulate sediments, continuity of life may at rare intervals be disrupted by storms from directions offering the greatest fetch to that shore. The south-western to north-western coasts are exposed to both the greatest fetch and the prevailing wind direction, so that sand and sediments are disturbed every winter.

Here we may indicate the waves to be expected upon the most exposed shores of the islands. The comprehensive atlas of Draper (1991) shows that within the comparative shelter of the Clyde Sea, the most exposed coast, that of south Arran, can expect to experience waves exceeding 0.5 m for 50% of the winter and exceeding 2 m for 10% of the winter. For Rockall the figures are >4 m for 50% and >7 m for 10% of the winter. The western coasts of the islands from Islay to Shetland can expect >2 m waves for 50% and >3–4 m waves for 10% of the winter, but in the Inner Hebrides, Small Isles and Skye the values are >1.0–1.5 m for 50% and >2.0–2.5 m for 10% of the winter. Draper's estimates of the 50-year extreme wave heights (given by Lee and Ramster, 1981) are for 32–35 m waves along the western shores of the Long Island, 30–32 m waves to the west of Orkney and Shetland and 15–20 m waves around the Inner Hebrides.

2.6 Conclusion

I have briefly reviewed the contribution made by the ocean to shaping our marine heritage of islands, sketching, the main features of the waters, their origins, paths and variability, and some of the local factors which make for the great variety in the physical marine environment of individual islands. It is to be hoped that I have demonstrated that the sea which surrounds the islands has fascinations which can compete with the attractions of the islands themselves.

References

Barnes, H. 1955. Climatological and salinity data for Millport, Scotland. *Glasgow Naturalist,* **17,** 193–204.

Barnes, H. and Goodley, E. F. W. 1958. A note on the rainfall in the west of Scotland. *Glasgow Naturalist,* **18,** 45–54.

Blackman, D. L., Graff, J. and Vassie, J. M. 1981. Tidal currents in Yell Sound and the outer regions of Sullom Voe. *Proceedings of the Royal Society of Edinburgh,* **80B,** 73–90.

BODC 1991. *United Kingdom Digital Marine Atlas.* British Oceanographic Data Centre, Bidston Observatory, Merseyside, (3 diskettes).

Booth, D. A. and Ellett, D. J. 1983. The Scottish continental slope current. *Continental Shelf Research,* **2,** 127–46.

Bradley, P. E., Scott, E. M., Baxter, M. S. and Ellett, D. J. 1991. Radiocaesium in local and regional coastal water modelling exercises. In Kershaw, P. J. and Woodhead, D. S. (Eds), *Radionuclides in the study of marine processes,* Elsevier, London and New York, 61–73.

Cartwright, D. E. 1969. Extraordinary tidal currents near St. Kilda. *Nature,* **223,** 929–32.

Cartwright, D. E., Huthnance, J. M., Spencer, R. and Vassie, J. M. 1980. On the St. Kilda shelf tidal regime. *Deep-Sea Research,* **27,** 61–70.

Cooper, L. H. N. 1952. The physical and chemical oceanography of the waters bathing the continental slope of the Celtic Sea. *Journal of the Marine Biological Association of the United Kingdom,* **30,** 465–510.

Dickson, R. R., Meincke, J., Malmberg, S.-A. and Lee, A. J. 1988. The 'Great Salinity Anomaly' in the northern North Atlantic. *Progress in Oceanography,* **20,** 103–51.

Dooley, H. D. 1979. Factors influencing water movements in the Firth of Clyde. *Estuarine and Coastal Marine Science,* **9,** 631–41.

Dooley, H. D. 1981. Oceanographic observations in Sullom Voe, Shetland in the period 1974–78. *Proceedings of the Royal Society of Edinburgh,* **80B,** 55–71.

Draper, L. 1991. Wave climate atlas of the British Isles. *Department of Energy Offshore Technology Report,* **OTH 89 303,** 11pp, 22 charts.

Economides, B., Baxter, M. S. and Ellett, D. J. 1985. Observations of radiocaesium and the coastal current west of Scotland during 1983–85. *International Council for the Exploration of the Sea,* **CM 1985**/C:24, 10pp.

Edwards, A., Baxter, M. S., Ellett, D. J., Martin, J. H. A., Meldrum, D. T. and Griffiths, C. R. 1986. Clyde Sea hydrography. *Proceedings of the Royal Society of Edinburgh,* **90B,** 67–83.

Ellett, D. J. 1978. Temperature and salinity conditions in the Sea of the Hebrides, 25–29 May 1976. *Annales Biologiques, Copenhagen,* **33,** 28–30.

Ellett, D. J. 1979. Some oceanographic features of Hebridean waters. *Proceedings of the Royal Society of Edinburgh,* **77B,** 61–74.

Ellett, D. J., Dooley, H. D. and Hill, H. W. 1979. Is there a North-east Atlantic Slope Current? *International Council for the Exploration of the Sea,* **CM1979**/C:35, 11pp.

Ellett, D. J., Edwards, A. and Bowers, R. 1986. The hydrography of the Rockall Channel – an overview. *Proceedings of the Royal Society of Edinburgh,* **88B,** 61–81.

Ellett, D. J. and Edwards, A. 1983. Oceanography and inshore hydrography of the Inner Hebrides. *Proceedings of the Royal Society of Edinburgh,* **83B,** 143–60.

Ellett, D. J. and Martin, J. H. A. 1973. The physical and chemical oceanography of the Rockall Channel. *Deep-Sea Research,* **20,** 585–625.

Gordon, R. L. and Huthnance, J. M. 1987. Storm-driven continental shelf waves over the Scottish continental shelf. *Continental Shelf Research*, **7**, 1015–48.

Gould, W. J., Loynes, J. and Backhaus, J. 1985. Seasonality in slope current transports NW of Shetland. *International Council for the Exploration of the Sea*, **CM 1985**/C:7, 13pp.

Huthnance, J. M. 1986. The Rockall slope current and shelf-edge processes. *Proceedings of the Royal Society of Edinburgh*, **88B**, 83–101.

Huthnance, J. M., Loynes, J. and Edden, A. C. 1988. An investigation of meteorological effects on currents. *Proudman Oceanographic Laboratory Reports*, **2**, 211pp.

Hydrographic Department, 1980. *Tidal Stream Atlas, Orkney and Shetland Islands*. Hydrographic Department, Taunton, Somerset, 28pp.

Hydrographic Department, 1983. *Tidal Stream Atlas, West Coast of Scotland and North Coast of Ireland*. Hydrographic Department, Taunton, Somerset, 28pp.

Jones, K. J., Gowen, R. J. and Tett, P. 1984. Water column structure and summer phytoplankton distribution in the Sound of Jura, Scotland. *Journal of Experimental Marine Biology and Ecology*, **78**, 269–89.

Lee, A. J. and Ramster, J. W. 1981. *Atlas of the Seas around the British Isles*. Ministry of Agriculture, Fisheries and Food, Fisheries Laboratory, Lowestoft, 75 charts.

McKay, W. A., Baxter, M. S., Ellett, D. J. and Meldrum, D. T. 1986. Radiocaesium and circulation patterns west of Scotland. *Journal of Environmental Radioactivity*, **4**, 205–32.

McKinley, I. G., Baxter, M. S., Ellett, D. J. and Jack, W. 1981. Tracer applications of radiocaesium in the Sea of the Hebrides. *Estuarine, Coastal and Shelf Science*, **13**, 69–82.

McManus, J. 1992. A hydrographic framework for marine conservation in Scotland. *Proceedings of the Royal Society of Edinburgh*, **100B**, 3–26.

Meteorological Office, 1963. Averages of temperature for Great Britain and Northern Ireland. *Meteorological Office*, **Met.O. 735**, 42pp.

Parker, D. E. and Folland, C. K. 1988. The nature of climatic variability. *Meteorological Magazine*, **117**, 201–10.

Poodle, T. 1986. Freshwater inflows to the Firth of Clyde. *Proceedings of the Royal Society of Edinburgh*, **90B**, 55–66.

Prandle, D. 1984. A modelling, study of the mixing of ^{137}Cs in the seas of the European continental shelf. *Philosophical Transactions of the Royal Society*, **A310**, 407–36.

Prandle, D. 1987. Response of the NW European Shelf Sea at subtidal frequencies. *Continental Shelf Research*, **7**, 267–84.

Savidge, G. and Lennon, H. J. 1987. Hydrography and phytoplankton distributions in north-west Scottish waters. *Continental Shelf Research*, **7**, 45–66.

Simpson, J. H., Edelsten, D. J., Edwards, A., Morris, N. G. C. and Tett, P. B. 1979. The Islay front: Physical structure and phytoplankton distribution. *Estuarine and Coastal Marine Science*, **9**, 713–26.

Simpson, J. H. and Hill, A. E. 1986. The Scottish coastal current. In Skreslet, S. (Ed.), *The role of freshwater outflow in coastal marine ecosystems*, Springer-Verlag, Berlin, 295–308.

Simpson, J. H. and Hunter, J. R. 1974. Fronts in the Irish Sea. *Nature*, **250**, 404–6.

Townson, J. M. and Collar, R. H. F. 1986. Water movement and the simulation of storm surges in the Firth of Clyde. *Proceedings of the Royal Society of Edinburgh*, **90B**, 85–96.

Turrell, W. R. 1992. New hypotheses concerning the circulation of the Northern North Sea. *ICES Journal of Marine Science*, **49**, 107–23.

Turrell, W. R. and Henderson, E. W. 1990. Transport events within the Fair Isle Current during the Autumn Circulation Experiment. *Estuarine, Coastal and Shelf Science*, **31**, 25–44.

Turrell, W. R., Henderson, E. W. and Slesser, G. 1990. Residual transport within the Fair Isle Current observed during the Autumn Circulation Experiment. *Continental Shelf Research*, **10**, 521–43.

Turrell, W. R., Henderson, E. W., Slesser, G., Payne, R. and Adams, R. D. 1992. Hydrographic observations at the continental shelf edge northwest of Scotland. *International Council for the Exploration of the Sea*, **CM 1992**/C:19, 30pp.

Turrell, W. R. and Slesser, G. 1992. Annual cycles of physical, chemical and biological parameters in Scottish waters. *Scottish Fisheries Working Paper*, **5/95**, 7pp text + tables.

Warburg, H. D. 1946. *Tidal streams of the waters surrounding the British Islands and off the west and north coasts of Europe*. Hydrographic Department, Taunton, 599pp.

3 DEVELOPMENT PRESSURES ON COASTAL AND INTER-ISLAND SEASCAPES AND THE PRESENT DESIGNATION SYSTEM

J. R. Turner

Summary

1. Seascape is not a well-developed concept. Except in popular art, it is not clearly distinguished from landscape.

2. Nevertheless there is a rich and diverse variety of coastal landscape and inter-island seascape in Scotland, but with varying degrees of statutory protection.

3. Changes to seascape may originate in a wide variety of human uses, governed by a complexity of agencies and legislation.

4. It is concluded that management of the coast and protection of seascapes, needs to be based on integrated environmental principles. The adoption of Coastal Zone Management is advocated, and the need for the development of an assessment of the visual values of inshore waters emphasized.

3.1. Introduction

Despite millennia of venturing upon the sea, it remains an alien environment for man. We have of course an extensive vocabulary of words to do with the sea, especially among those whose cultures have developed in island or coastal circumstances. Nevertheless, our lay vocabulary to describe seascape is relatively limited and the concept of 'seascape' is an unfamiliar one to most people. Even the *Shorter Oxford English Dictionary* offers only two definitions:

- A view of the sea, or

- a picture representing a scene at sea.

If we compare popular use of the word 'seascape' with that of 'landscape', 'seascape' features hardly at all. We are used to talking of landscape photography, landscape painting, landscape architects, landscape designers, landscape gardeners, but scascape? One has yet to hear of any coast dweller talking of having the view in front of his house 'seascaped'. Perhaps because the possibility of major developments at sea is a relatively recent phenomenon, our terminology for the impacts of such development is very limited. Techniques for landscape assessment are still at the formative stage, and although the interplay of land and water is approached in methodologies, assessment of the impacts of changes at sea have hardly been addressed.

Yet love of the sea is very strong in maritime peoples. The seaside has been a classic recreation environment since the Hanoverians turned Brighthelmstone into Brighton, or perhaps ever since the Norsemen went 'a-viking'. Today the amount of world tourism aimed at helping people escape to remote islands must be considerable.

Although total seascapes or sea and skyscapes feature in popular art, the sea appears only to have featured as a backdrop or a scenic incident in classical art. Even when man resorts to the submarine world for recreation and enjoyment, it seems that he is really concerned with the submarine or seabed landscape, the

Figure 3.1. Duncansby Stacks. Seascapes of this kind are characteristic of northern and eastern coasts and islands. While little at risk from landward development, major offshore structures inevitably alter perception of scale and impair the 'presence' of features like the Duncansby Stacks.

Figure 3.2. Sandwood Bay. Surge power converters harnessing the fetch of the ocean could entirely alter the dynamics of western or northern facing bays like this one. The remote location would not, of course, be changed but the elemental atmosphere that underpins the feeling of remoteness would be.

Figure 3.3. Kyle of Lochalsh. Some Inner Hebridean waters seem almost landlocked. Nevertheless, the sea crossing to Skye has been one of the romantic elements in enjoyment of a scene such as this view of Skye from Lochalsh. Will the construction of a bridge impair this quality? It will certainly change it.

Figure 3.4. Inner Sound of Raasay. The apparent scale of this seascape can change with light and weather. A strong factor in its present character is the absence of the major artefacts which give a point of reference for scale, and change the subtle relationships between the landward components and the sea.

Figure 3.5. Dunbeath. Simple coastal relationships between the land and the sea like this can more easily withstand change. A major installation offshore could add variety and dimension to this scene, in which it is otherwise somewhat lacking.

Figure 3.6. Valtos. The offshore skerries in this scene, heavily influenced by local cultural activities, provide an opportunity to integrate a new activity like fin fish farming without necessarily impairing the beauty of the bays.

flora, fauna and land forms that occur at the interface between the terrestrial and the marine environment. Seascape for most of us is therefore really to do with the interplay of land and sea, and is most likely to mean landscape in which the sea is a considerable component (Figures 3.1–3.6).

Scotland is blessed with a high degree of 'interlock' between the land and the sea from the firths of the east coast to the fjords of the north and west coasts, and the archipelagoes of the Inner and Outer Hebrides, Orkney and Shetland.

Seascape most frequently comprises the sea as perceived from this myriad coast, or in the land as perceived from the intervening and surrounding sea. Islands are land masses with a high proportion of coast, and inter-island seascapes necessarily enjoy a high degree of coastal landscape. The transition from coastal landscape to seascape is one of degree and development is likely to have a more adverse impact in waters where there is some landform against which the eye can judge its scale. However the configuration and relative visual scales of island and coastal scenes can vary enormously, as can the scale of modern developments. The interactions of land and sea and the visual characteristics arising from coastal dynamics are very particular and assessing the impacts of proposals, therefore, becomes relatively more complex than assessing land-based proposals. The effects of distances become more difficult to assess over open water, and open waters often form political boundaries, making an integrated view of effects more difficult to achieve and complicating conservation initiatives.

3.2   Heritage Protection

Recognition of the heritage value of this rich diversity of seascapes is still only vestigial. The St. Kilda Archipelago has been accorded World Heritage Listing by the United Nations Educational, Scientific and Cultural Organisation, (UNESCO) because of its dramatic landform in an oceanic setting, salt tolerant flora, idiosyncratic fauna, outstanding sea bird populations and peculiar human history. One of the best monitored ecological sites of its kind, it was also accepted by UNESCO as having adequate protection, in being wholly owned by the National Trust for Scotland and designated as a National Nature Reserve (NNR) and National Scenic Area (NSA), with the islands remoteness underpinning this degree of protection.

In considering further sites for nomination for World Heritage Listing, the two predecessor agencies of Scottish Natural Heritage (SNH) agreed to advise the Scottish Office that, apart from the Cairngorms, the most likely candidate area in Scotland was the North Western Seaboard including all the offshore islands, because of its striking landforms and rich cultural history. No detailed submission was ever worked up in support of this, and proposals ranged from most of the North Western Tertiary Volcanic Province to a more limited area based on the National Scenic Areas of the north west mainland. Particular emphasis was given in either approach to the significance of the interplay of the marine and terrestrial environments.

Of the 40 National Scenic Areas designated by the Secretary of State for Scotland, 26 have a marine dimension and most of these have an island component or inter-visibility with islands offshore (CCS, 1978). National Scenic Areas were selected on the basis, as their name implies, of their scenic values, and although there is a large measure of coincidence with nature conservation designations they represent only a partial view of heritage values, so that for example the ecological, cultural and seascape values of the islands in say, the Firth of Forth are ignored by them. The concept of Heritage Coasts, developed in England and Wales, has not been translated to Scottish circumstances, perhaps in part because of the high number of already established NSAs with a coastal character.

To date we have no Marine Nature Reserves (MNR) designated in Scotland, but 17 National Nature Reserves have coastline and provide protection for intertidal and coastal fringe habitats many of them including islands. Over 350 Sites of Special Scientific Interest (SSSI) have a coastal component and afford some protection to fauna, flora, geological or physiographic features which make up the sites down to low water mark of ordinary spring tides. There are 29 Marine Consultation Areas (MCA) in Scotland (Nature Conservancy Council, 1990), with a similar concentration to National Scenic Areas on the northern and western island and fjord coasts, although together with Marine Nature Reserves these have been recognized by the House of Commons Environment Committee as largely unworkable (Anon., 1992a).

A range of other designations (Dasman, 1973) to give protection to various species, wild birds and wetlands is available and not irrelevant to landscape and seascape conservation, since the experience of these 'living' components of the seascape is as germane to appreciation of its scenic value as both the inert and the dynamic physical components. Measures such as Special Protection Areas (SPAs), the Ramsar Convention, the Convention on International Trade in Endangered Species (CITES), the Bonn Convention and the International Whaling Convention all have their contribution to make to the conservation of our heritage of seascape by conserving biodiversity, but are not directly concerned with seascape qualities.

3.3   Development Pressures upon Seascape

It is not possible in the short space of this paper to deal comprehensively with all of the possible threats to the quality of seascape. To give but an indication of their range an attempt to group them in a roughly ascending scale of impact under four generic headings has been made: hunter-gathering, extracting, depositing and harnessing. The scale of impact varies depending on whether one is thinking ecologically or simply visually; the real purpose is more to indicate the complexity of possible changes than to achieve a ranking of effects.

3.3.1   Hunter-gathering

The gathering and collecting of resources from the sea has helped to sustain man from the beginning of recorded time. Most traditional forms of these activities have little adverse impact and contribute positively to landscape and seascape through association of visual pleasure with things that we value as part of our cultural heritage. Thus fishing harbours, fishing settlements, shell-fish gathering, and seaweed collection add to our enjoyment of seascapes. This small-scale exploitation still occurs in a variety of forms, especially in the remoter parts of the Highlands and Islands. In addition, other traditional uses such as machair grazing, use of seaweed for agricultural fertilizer, and guga culling still occur. However, commercial fin and shell fish farming have escalated in recent years (Anon., 1988a,b) and although there is a small percentage of locally based fishing in North West coastal waters the efficiency of the Scottish sea-fishing fleet has vastly increased, to the extent that there are few examples of sustainable fishing. This change has its effect in the seascape through impoverishment and decline of locally based fishing and its associated usually visually pleasant artefacts.

On a different scale, collecting, be it of bait, curios such as sea urchins, birds' eggs, or higher seaside plants can lead to subtle changes and impoverishment of seaside landscapes, such as the knock-on effects of mechanical dredging for lugworm.

3.3.2 Extracting

Into this category come sand extraction, dredging whether for biota or minerals and quarrying for aggregates either from the landward coast or the seabed. Even small-scale removal of beach sand, shingle or gravels for local use can have an uncertain and irreversible effect on sediment dynamics, leading to possible changes in the stability of beaches or water channels, often with a deterioration of their visual quality.

Hydraulic dredging is carried out as a means of collecting molluscan shellfish such as oysters, clams, cockles, mussels and scallops. It can destroy habitat and non-target species which are damaged or destroyed by the passage of the dredge. Frequently these areas are close inshore and of high habitat and species diversity and amenity value. It can release toxic materials and heavy metals locked up in deeper anoxic sediments. Both water quality and the food chain for birds can be affected and consequently enjoyment of the inshore seascape.

Dredging also occurs at sea for aggregates – for sand and gravel, for maerl, metalliferous sediments and to aid shipping and navigation, although it has to be said that the bulk of these uses occur in lowland offshore waters and do not much affect Scottish seascapes. However Barra has been the subject of interest in maerl, a kind of red calcareous algae, and Rum has been of interest because of chromium-rich deposits containing rare metals such as osmium and platinum. A lease for such dredging must be obtained from the Crown Estate Commissioners. Inshore dredging may contribute to beach draw down with consequent loss of both intertidal and coastal habitats and may cause re-suspension of sediment with loss of visual quality. Dredging has been known to accelerate foreshore erosion by changing the wave régime, making it more likely that coastal defence works may be required.

Large coastal quarries, popularly termed 'superquarries', have been of concern recently. Although quarries are of course a land-based industry, their visual impact can affect a wide area of open water because of their scale. The visual impact of the quarry at Glensanda has been greater than anticipated by most of those concerned in advising the Planning Authority about its impact although measures to ameliorate many of the impacts have still to be effected. New proposals at Lingerabay in Harris, at Haggrister in Shetland and possibly Loch Eriboll give rise to anxiety about the impact on valued coastal landscapes. The quarry at Lingerabay is likely to prove visible from Skye across the Minch in clear conditions. Impact arises from the construction of jetties and shipping facilities, sediment washed down from the site, changes in coastal configuration, pollution from ballast water discharge and adverse effects from blasting and dust. While the effects above low water mark are subject to control under the Town and Country Planning Acts those below are not.

3.3.3 Depositing

Inshore and offshore waters have a relatively high density of merchant ships, passenger and fishing related traffic; dredging, recreational and military traffic.

While shipping is usually regarded as an attractive feature of seascapes, navigational improvements have not meant that there are no longer accidents at sea. There are many adverse consequences for seascape from shipping, ranging from cargoes being spilled, of which the most dramatic and visually unpleasant is usually oil although other chemicals may be far more inimical to marine life and health, to all sorts of other discharge. Ships are a major source of pollution at sea, discharging oily waste from bilges and refuse of all kinds despite regulations. While flotsam is sometimes attractive to beachcombers, jetsam seldom is, and the presence of plastics and hazardous items on beaches reduces the visual and other sensory qualities of the shore, and reduces the visual amenity of the area. Ships also need docks, wharves and navigation channels and these tend to lead to problems of where to dump excavated spoil.

The marine environment has long been used for dumping waste. Not only is sewage discharged raw into the sea with a consequent effect on all the senses in the intertidal zones, but sewage sludge is also disposed of offshore although this is to be phased out. There are many other kinds of dumping including industrial wastes and spoil from excavations and these last are sometimes used for landfill on the coast. Coastal land claim is of course subject to planning control, but it nevertheless results in losses of intertidal and surrounding terrestrial habitats, and consequent change in the visual characteristics of a wider area than just the landfill project, removing from the ecosystem a diversity, the loss of which also impoverishes landscape and seascape. Much landfill facilitates the construction of major artefacts on the coastal scene such as power stations, port and harbour construction and tourist and recreational developments, the scale of which can diminish the seemingly indeterminate open nature of seascapes and coastal landscapes, and may be of greater impact in the often slighter scale of island or inter-island topography.

3.3.4 Harnessing

In this group are placed factors of the sea which make special use of its physical characteristics. They include military use, recreational use, fish farming, alternative energy and oil and gas.

Military use of the sea is somewhat equivocal in terms of the conservation of seascape. The use by British Underwater Test and Experimental Centre (BUTEC) of the Inner Sound of Raasay was a factor in reducing its attraction for platform construction for the North Sea Oil and Gas Industry and today its very emptiness as a stretch of inshore water contributes to its sense of scale and remoteness. But there are disadvantages. Incongruent coastal tracking installations are alien features in an apparently untrammelled seascape, where the views are among the most dramatic from our shores. They do not dominate such a seascape but neither do they enhance it. It has been estimated that a quarter of all hazardous items washed up on the beaches around the UK have a military origin.

Recreation has a considerable number of factors which impact on the marine environment but, without attempting to categorize them all, they generally fall into two broad groups: those of the physical developments to enable recreational activity to be pursued, and the actual pursuit of the activity at the coast in the intertidal zone or in open water. In an island context the most commonly encountered forms of recreation other than relatively benign activities like ornithology, botanical identification and whale watching are likely to be yachting and sailing. The greatest adverse impact on seascape, for boats and yachts, with the possible exception of motorboats and jet skis is likely to come from infrastructure developments which can cause long-term and irreversible changes to the marine environment. Problems of erosion, destabilization of coastal systems, land claim, habitat loss, disturbance to species and dredging and contamination of marine berths and channels can all have adverse visual consequences for the quality of seascapes and coastal landscapes.

Fin and shellfish farming has expanded greatly in the last decade (Anon., 1988a,b). Although fin-fish farming with its rafts of cages has the greater visual impact on inshore waters, a great deal of effort has gone into improving the siting and layout of fish farms and location factors (Cobham Resource Consultants, 1987), not only by the predecessor agencies of SNH but also by the industry itself, and controlling authorities. Rapid expansion of ocean-based aquaculture may result in demands for expansion from quiet sheltered areas to exposed sea locations. Prototype giant fish cages are now being developed to withstand the rigours of more exposed conditions. These larger cages – up to 50 m across and 15 m high – will be conspicuous objects in more open waters and will be more difficult to relate to landform than smaller inshore cages. In inter-island waters or outside the mouths of inlets, they may well have the effect of subtly altering scale and changing the character of seascape.

We have perhaps the greatest experience of oil and gas installations in our Scottish coastal waters. Apart from the impact of oil-spills, whether of fuel oil from ships or loading bays, or crude oil from production platforms, the location siting and design of pipeline landfalls, processing plant and service bases, not to mention platform construction yards all tend to require coastal locations. So far with the exception of Sullom Voe and Scapa Flow, such installations have not impacted upon island seascapes and their siting has been well chosen in its minimal impact upon the wider seascapes. As the search for resources turns from the North Sea to the Western seas the demand for additional processing plant is not perhaps likely to be great, but the impact of pipelines in the harder geology of our western archipelagoes and the more vertical and intimate scale of the topography may make the integration of installations into our island seascapes very much more difficult than has been the case among the softer outlines of Sullom Voe and Scapa Flow.

Potentially the most dramatic alteration to the nature and appearance of inshore and offshore waters comes from alternative energy installations. Although the concept of harnessing the renewable energy of the ocean is attractive in terms of its apparent sustainability, the scale of such installations as tidal barrages, wave power converters, surge power converters and wind turbines is such that the visual changes associated with their construction would always be considerable. Not only would the dynamics of the coastal waters be changed, but so would the ecology of its communities at least by the water-based devices. Prototype proposals, if developed commercially, appear to lead to extensive local change involving installations extending for some kilometres. Wind-based installations are essentially landward in character, but in an island context could greatly alter apparent scale and distance and impair such qualities as remoteness. More conventional generating stations frequently require coastal locations for cooling water, and desalination plants may be required on islands where fresh water is scarce. Although subject to planning control such installations change not only the marine ecosystems affected by their thermal discharges, but also the relativities of scale and mass of their sites.

3.4 Towards a Better Framework for Care of Seascape

This incomplete catalogue of changes which could alter and impair the quality of our superb heritage of seascape is intended to underline the need for better and more integrated management. Just as the creation of Scottish Natural Heritage has been heralded as a welcome step towards more integrated approaches to the planning and management of land, similar consideration needs to be given to the conservation and management of the seas around our shores. Traditionally we have viewed the coast as a boundary where the land meets the sea. It should be seen as a zone of transition between the terrestrial and the marine, a continuum of rich resources and assets, important both materially and spiritually to man, change to one part of which is likely to affect other parts of an extremely dynamic system (Watson, unpublished).

One of the major differences between the land and the sea is that the sea belongs to everyone and no one. Lack of individual ownership may be welcome but it inhibits the introduction of traditional incentive-led measures to encourage its better management. New kinds of cooperative planning and management are therefore needed if we are to give the sea the same kind of consideration that we give to the land, and indeed treat it as part of a recognized continuum.

Government has been reluctant to extend the jurisdiction of the Town and Country Planning Acts (Anon., 1992b), which currently ceases at Low Water Mean of Spring Tides (LWMOST), to either the three-mile limit or the 12-mile limit. While this may be understandable because of the complexity of legislation (it is estimated that over 80 Acts of Parliament govern the protection of the sea (Eno, 1991)) it might provide an interim means of control of some elements while some more comprehensive system was developed.

Through the Natural Heritage (Scotland) Act, Scottish Natural Heritage inherits powers to notify Sites of Special Scientific Interest to mean low water mark, and to propose to the Secretary of State sites for designation as Marine

Nature Reserves to the 12-mile limit. International legislation empowers SNH together with the Joint Nature Conservation Committee (JNCC) to designate Special Protection Areas to 12 miles and Ramsar sites to 6 miles offshore. Since such sites must also be SSSI, offshore Special Protection Areas and Ramsar sites cannot be designated in the present circumstances. It is interesting to note that protection of an offshore bird breeding island would also oblige the government to protect the food supplies of the birds that breed there.

Scottish Natural Heritage has also inherited responsibility for advising the government about developments in National Scenic Areas. It seems likely that National Scenic Areas will ultimately be replaced by a more integrated form of designation provided for in the Natural Heritage (Scotland) Act – the Natural Heritage Area. While the concept of NHAs is still being considered in detail, their more comprehensive nature may provide for them also to embrace consideration of marine heritage, especially relevant in the Highlands and Islands where land and sea are so interlocked, and so locked into the way of life of the people.

Scottish Natural Heritage may give advice anywhere in the marine environment on aspects of the natural heritage and its sustainable use. The opportunity must be taken to influence the development of strategic thinking of the plethora of agencies and bodies that control or exploit the sea, such as the Scottish Office Agriculture and Fisheries Department, Highlands and Islands Enterprise, Highland Regional Council, the Islands Councils, the Crown Estate Commissioners and the fishermen's associations. It has sometimes been recognized that the promotion of the conservation of the natural heritage through the formation of Natural Heritage Areas would need some kind of forum for coordination of different agencies objectives and subscribing to common goals. Ought not the same principle to be extended to offshore waters?

The House of Commons Environment Committee, in its report *Coastal Zone Protection and Planning* (Anon., 1992a), recognized that the present divide between the landward and seaward planning systems obstructs any attempt at integrated planning of the coastal zone, and recommended that Government address the issue of harmonizing landward planning control and seaward planning control as far as the 12-mile nautical limit. They also concluded that definitions of the coastal zone may vary from area to area and from issue to issue and that a pragmatic approach must therefore be taken at appropriate national, regional and local levels.

The Committee also endorsed an approach favoured by the European Commission which is expected to advocate the adoption of Coastal Zone Management (CZM). Definitions of CZM vary from country to country, but in common with Natural Heritage Areas, they can be based on environmental principles. The importance of Coastal Zone Management is that it aims to integrate *all* uses and activities on the coastal zone (see Gubbay, 1990). Its main objectives are to promote sustainable use of the coast; balance demands for coastal zone resources; resolve conflicts of use; promote environmentally sensitive use of the coastal zone; and treat the coastal zone as a unit for strategic planning. In short, one may draw two conclusions: Coastal Zone Management is based on the same principles as the Natural Heritage (Scotland) Act, and would assist SNH in promoting sustainable use of resources, promoting restoration and enhancement of depleted resources, and maintaining and enhancing genetic and scenic diversity and their enjoyment by mankind. In regard to seascape we need to educate people to realize how important seascape and coastal landscape are in their experience of the sea and its shore. At present this is but poorly appreciated and the value of a planning approach that recognizes visual integration of our inshore waters and coastal fringe poorly realized. An analysis of coastal landscapes is needed which defines what qualities and components are essential to their character and how they vary in different types of coastal landscape and inter-island seascape. Such an assessment could provide a basis for strategic planning to direct appropriate development to areas where it can be assimilated or even enhance character. It could recognize heritage areas where change is inimical. Such areas are usually those with strong 'natural' or 'cultural' characteristics. In Scotland they are likely to include coastal and island locations, which because they cross local political boundaries may require a second level of analysis incorporating political considerations as well as the initial systematic assessment. While such a process has not yet occurred in Scotland, it is a badly needed prerequisite to any strategic planning or conservation measures for coastal landscapes and seascapes near our shores.

References

Anon. 1988a. *Marine Fish Farms in Scotland: Development Strategy and Area Guidelines*. The Crown Estate, Edinburgh.

Anon. 1988b. *The Reduction of the Impact of Fish Farming in the Natural Marine Environment*. Report for the Nature Conservancy Council by the Institute of Aquaculture, University of Stirling.

Anon. 1992a. House of Commons Environment Committee: Coastal Zone Protection and Planning; HMSO HC (1991–92) Paper 17–I.

Anon. 1992b. Department of the Environment: Coastal Zone Protection and Planning. The Government's Response to the Second Report from the House of Commons Select Committee on the Environment HMSO, Cm20ll.

CCS 1978. *Scotland's Scenic Heritage*. Countryside Commission for Scotland, Perth.

Cobham Resource Consultants 1987. An Environmental Assessment of Fish Farming. Countryside Commission for Scotland, Perth.

Dasman, R. F. 1973. Classification and use of protected natural and cultural areas. *IUCN Occasional Paper No 4*, Morges, Switzerland.

Eno, N. C. (Ed) 1991. *Marine Conservation Handbook*. Nature Conservancy Council, Peterborough.

Gubbay, S. 1990. *A Future for the Coast? Proposals for a UK Coastal Zone Management Plan*. Worldwide Fund for Nature and Marine Conservation Society.

Nature Conservancy Council 1990. *Marine Consultation Areas: Scotland*. Nature Conservancy Council, Edinburgh.

Watson, A. J. *The Marine Environment – a North West Regional Perspective*. Scottish Natural Heritage, North West Region, Inverness (unpublished).

4 THE GENETIC STRUCTURE OF INTERTIDAL POPULATIONS OF TWO SPECIES OF MOLLUSC ON THE SCOTTISH WEST COAST: SOME BIOGEOGRAPHIC CONSIDERATIONS AND AN ASSESSMENT OF REALIZED LARVAL DISPERSAL

C. D. Todd, W. J. Lambert and J. P. Thorpe

Summary

1. Most marine benthic invertebrates reproduce by means of planktonic larval stages and thus dispersal ability from the parental source, and subsequent colonization of new habitats, is generally assumed to be a consequence of the pelagic larval period.

2. We have studied the genetic structure of intertidal populations of two species of molluscs, *Goniodoris nodosa (planktotrophic)* and *Adalaria proxima (pelagic lecithotrophic)*, around the northern British Isles between north Wales and northeastern England.

3. Our expectations are that dispersal potential of *G. nodosa* and *A. proxima* will be on a scale of 10^2–10^3 km and 10^1–10^2 km respectively. Accordingly, we expected that populations of these two species would be genetically differentiated on scales of 10^3–10^4 km (*G. nodosa*) and 10^2–10^3 km (*A. proxima*).

4. For *G. nodosa*, no significant genetic differentiation of the 12 sub-populations was found throughout the geographic range sampled (approximately 1500 km), conforming to expectations.

5. For *A. proxima* we found extraordinarily high levels of genetic differentiation of all populations at all genetic loci, and no evidence of inbreeding within any one population. Significant genetic differentiation

occurring on so small a scale (<100m) strongly implies that the larvae are subject to minimal dispersal away from the parental source despite local tidal currents >6 knots.

6. Dispersal is an unavoidable consequence of pelagic larval development and not a uniformly selective advantage for all species. We question the applicability of classical island biogeography theory to shallow water marine systems.

4.1   Island Biogeography in the Marine Context

By definition, marine islands are discrete and disjunct entities, but they should not be considered to be physically or biologically isolated: all islands are connected by the atmosphere, water and the substratum or seabed. The theory of island biogeography stems from the pioneering work of MacArthur and Wilson (1963, 1967) and concerns the analysis of the biotic patterns of species distribution observed on given islands. The theory seeks to explain patterns of species presence or absence and in this respect is primarily qualitative: island biogeography is less concerned with species abundance patterns and the associated concepts concerning ecological diversity and community structure. Island biogeography theory predicts the species richness of a given island to be dependent upon essentially two independent sets of processes – those affecting species' arrival or colonization, and those affecting species' extinction.

Crucial to island biogeography theory is biotic migration between the source area(s) and the island(s) in question. In general terms the fauna on that island will be the resultant of the pattern (and rate) of species' colonization from the source, the pattern (and rate) of species' extinction on the island and the total number of different species that the island can support. It is important to emphasize that, while the theory predicts the equilibrium number of species, the identity of these may vary with time. Some, having successfully established, may subsequently become extinct and other new immigrant species may colonize (see, for example, Simberloff and Wilson, 1970). Especially if colonization rates are low species will, over ecological time and on particularly isolated islands, evolve and become quite distinct from the source area ancestors: additionally, colonists may occupy niches on islands that are occupied by other (competitor) species in the source area, such as fruitflies on the Hawaiian islands (Carlquist, 1980).

The original MacArthur and Wilson theory predicts species numbers simply in relation to the physical attributes of the island and ignores such biotic interactions as competition, predation and co-evolution as well as the absolute levels of, and variation in, primary and secondary productivity; these are all implicated in determining community structure and species richness. Moreover, it explicitly equates all species, and ignores their ecological impact on the community in total and other species' populations. A recent appraisal of island biogeographic data by Case and Cody (1987) has highlighted the differing colonizing and persistence ability of a range of taxa and the varying 'goodness of fit' of the data to the model. Thus, while as expected, they found that birds and mammals are respectively good and poor colonizers, they also found that both have poor persistence abilities. Among the reptiles, they found that lizards tend to show strong persistence, but poor colonizing ability. Importantly, therefore, in generating predictions of species richness patterns on islands in relation to even simple parameters, such as island size or remoteness, one has to acknowledge that contrasting taxa will behave quite differently.

4.1.1 Means of dispersal

Biogeographers now recognize various types of pathways allowing the spread of organisms (Cox and Moore, 1985). *Corridor* pathways refer particularly to continental landmasses, in that organisms may spread from one side of a continent to another along a route characterized by a wide range of habitat types. The species concerned may differ little at either end of such a corridor. The notion of a *filter* arises from a narrow range of habitat types along the corridor, such that only few species successfully traverse the corridor. The *sweepstakes route*, which is particularly relevant to island faunas, can hypothetically be illustrated by freshwater organisms on tropical islands: such a habitat type is rare among islands and there is, therefore, a considerable element of chance as to whether or not a particular species successfully colonizes a given island.

4.1.2 Marine islands and colonization problems for shallow-water, hard substratum organisms

For many shallow water, or intertidal, marine invertebrates the sweepstakes route of colonization is very much applicable. Consider, for example, a specialist Pacific intertidal tropical barnacle or bivalve species: not only would the planktonic larvae of such a species have to traverse the possibly huge distances (10^2–10^3 km) between islands, but they require to encounter hard rock substrata on the shoreline. Given the isolation of many of the Pacific islands, and the prevalence of sand on tropical shorelines of volcanic islands and atolls, it is likely that considerable elements of chance will determine the colonization success of such organisms. Assuming a planktonic mortality rate of 99% Scheltema (1986), for example, has estimated a probability only of 3×10^{-4} for a larva entrained in the Pacific South Equatorial Current actually encountering an island (let alone the correct substratum).

The case of the Scottish west coast islands is not, however, so extreme. All are close together, with St. Kilda and North Rona perhaps being the most removed. With the exception of the Outer Hebrides and North Rona (Lewisian gneiss;

perhaps >2700 million years (m.y.) the Scottish west coast islands (including St. Kilda and Rockall) are of similar climate and geological age (Tertiary granites, 52–63 m.y.; Emeleus, 1991): the Pleistocene glaciations affected all of the Scottish islands (Peacock, 1983) except Rockall, and there is no evidence of post-glacial land bridges which, if present, would have exerted important influences on post-Pleistocene colonization (Berry, 1992). Intertidal and shallow water substrata do, however, vary greatly, from silt muds in sheltered channels and the heads of sealochs, to sandy sediments and hard rock substrata both on sheltered coasts and shores exposed to oceanic wave action. Such substratum discontinuities do, therefore, present considerable potential barriers to dispersal for intertidal organisms with specialist substratum requirements (e.g. rock, for macroalgae and barnacles), but as described below, these are probably on too small a scale to confer colonization problems to most marine invertebrates or algae.

Approximately 71% of the earth's surface is covered by seawater, with an average depth of 3900 m. Whereas one can readily recognize and distinguish obvious terrestrial biomes (such as deserts, savannahs, tropical rainforests) the same does not extend to the marine environment. Invertebrates inhabiting shallow water soft sediments, for example, may be ecologically very similar across polar, temperate and tropical latitudes. The ocean surface may show little fluctuation in temperature, salinity and oxygen concentration over distances of hundreds of kilometres, and yet these same parameters may change rapidly with depth. Importantly, the deep ocean floor is primarily mud. For hard substratum, shallow water or intertidal organisms (such as limpets, barnacles or corals), oceanic islands are truly remote and isolated: such islands are surrounded by totally unsuitable substrata and water depths. Benthic marine invertebrates may disperse to disjunct islands by three distinct means: direct swimming, rafting on floating debris and transport of planktonic larvae by surface ocean currents. The swimming powers of most benthic invertebrates are limited, and rafting would appear to be the exception rather than the rule, although pumice is a frequently colonized substratum in areas of the Pacific (Jokiel, 1987, 1989). The planktonic larval stages of otherwise benthic invertebrates are, however, commonly held to provide the major dispersal and colonization potential.

Most benthic marine invertebrates reproduce by means of planktonic larval stages. Larvae which hatch from small eggs, and require extended periods (weeks or months) drifting and feeding, growing and developing in the plankton to a size and state at which settlement and metamorphosis to the adult form is possible, are termed planktotrophic. Other species lay fewer, larger eggs and provide the offspring with all the reserves that they require to complete development to the adult form. Such development is termed lecithotrophic and may result in the hatching of a fully-formed benthic juvenile (non-pelagic lecithotrophy) or a briefly planktonic larval stage which settles to the substratum within a few hours or days (pelagic lecithotrophy). If possession of a drifting planktonic larval stage for an otherwise sedentary or sessile adult can be viewed as a means of genetic dispersal and colonization ability, it is apparent that species displaying the above contrasting larval types will show markedly different population dynamics.

4.2 Terrestrial/Marine Contrasts in Island Biogeography – the Hawaiian Islands

The Hawaiian islands are remote and, as a whole, comprise almost a linear chain in the tropical north Pacific, spanning a distance of approximately 2650 km. Hawaii is 3200 km distant from North America and 5500 km from Japan. The islands are all volcanic in origin, arising from the deep ocean floor at approximately 5000 m depth, and forming as the Pacific plate passes over a stationary mantle plume. Kure is the westernmost and oldest island (approx. 15 m.y.) and Hawaii the easternmost, largest and youngest (approx. 0.4 m.y.) (Carson, 1984). Biogeographers have discerned a pattern of repeated colonizations from continental and other remote island sources and proximity within the chain has facilitated the spreading of species between the islands. However, the biogeographic feature which characterizes the Hawaiian flora and fauna is the extraordinary extent of adaptive radiation and speciation, as exemplified by the lobeliad plants, honeycreeper birds, tree snails and fruit flies. However, as Carson (1987) has emphasized, not all colonists gave rise to speciose lineages: many gave rise to just the one endemic species. Notwithstanding four species of anadromous gobioids there are no endemic freshwater fish species, no endemic reptiles or amphibians, and only one native species of mammal (a bat). It has been estimated that the entire Hawaiian avifauna arose from as few as 15 colonizations, which subsequently underwent extreme levels of differentiation and radiation (Freed, *et al.*, 1987), with the 25 species of honeycreepers arising from a single colonization (Carson, 1987).

Paradoxically, most of the endemic Hawaiian plant species have large fleshy fruits instead of dispersive dry seeds. It seems likely that many plant colonists arrived in the guts of birds rather than as wind-blown or water-borne seeds. Indeed, dispersal by sea accounts for only about 5% of the non-endemic Hawaiian seed plants (Cox and Moore, 1985). The extraordinary levels of divergence and radiation of the terrestrial flora and fauna are in sharp contrast to the shallow water marine fish and invertebrate fauna. Species endemism of the terrestrial biota of the Hawaiian islands is >90% of the species (species : genus ratio >10 : 1): this differs strikingly from the marine fauna, of which only approximately 32% of species are endemic (species : genus ratio 1–2 : 1) (Kay and Palumbi, 1987). Nonetheless, such a level of endemism is high for marine systems (see, for example, Scheltema, 1986). A similar overall pattern is shown by inshore fish of which, again, approximately 30% are endemic species (Hourigan and Reese, 1987). Importantly, and in marked contrast to the terrestrial habitat, there appear to be no island-specific endemic marine species within the Hawaiian chain (Kay and Palumbi, 1987):

the likelihood is that distance is less of a barrier in the marine environment and that dispersal between islands (by rafting or, more probably, larval transport) is a sufficiently frequent occurrence to preclude isolation and divergence of gene pools.

This example of the contrasting broader patterns of species colonization/extinction and speciation of the Hawaiian chain serves to illustrate that a theory which was developed explicitly for the analysis of terrestrial biota cannot necessarily be extrapolated to the marine environment.

4.3   The Islands of the Scottish West Coast

Berry (1992) reviewed several studies of the terrestrial biota of the Hebridean islands and showed generally decreasing numbers of species of plants, birds and land vertebrates with distance from the mainland. Importantly, however, the effects of island size are not considered in that presentation. With specific regard to the terrestrial mammals, Berry (1992) has emphasized the importance of inadvertent introductions of mice by humans and of founder effects underlying the patterns of genetic differentiation between islands. Regrettably there appear to be no adequate databases available to assess the biogeography of the intertidal or shallow water marine biota of these islands but our interest lies in assessing the extent to which two geographically widespread marine molluscs, with differing planktonic developmental periods, display genetic continuity of populations (i.e. gene flow) around the northern British Isles.

Between Islay and Lewis there are approximately 100 major islands along the Scottish west coast, spanning a distance of approximately 330 km. Importantly, none are separated by more than a few kilometres and the Outer Hebrides, as a group, are separated from Skye only by the 24 km wide Little Minch. The residual tidal flow of water around the northern British Isles is northwards from the Irish Sea and open Atlantic Ocean, passing through the Minch and also around the western coasts of the Outer Hebrides (Anon., 1974; Ellett, this volume). The flow then is eastwards around northern Scotland through the Pentland Firth and down the east coast of Scotland into the central North Sea. White *et al.* (1988) investigated larval transport of *Nephrops norvegicus* in the western Irish Sea and noted residual tidal flow of the order of 1.7–5.2 km·d^{-1}. Northward residual flow rates of approximately 5 km·d^{-1} were recorded by McKinley *et al.* (1981) in the region of Islay and the Small Isles, whereas Ellett and Edwards (1983) have recorded maximal northward residual flow rates of 11.8 km·d^{-1} in the Tiree Passage. Accordingly, for the purposes of estimating potential larval transport in the present study, we have chosen the possibly conservative estimate of an average residual tidal flow of 5 km·d^{-1} around the coasts of Scotland.

We have studied the genetic structure of intertidal populations of two species of mollusc around the northern British Isles over the past eight years: the study sites included north Wales, Northern Ireland, western, northern, and eastern Scotland and northeast England. Because of its complex indented coastline, most of our sample sites do, however, concern numerous mainland (sealoch) and island locations on the Scottish west coast. Our overall objective has been to assess the realized dispersal of the pelagic larvae of two species of mollusc with planktonic reproductive phases of different duration. Analysis of the scale of genetic differentiation among local populations will (1) permit the assessment of the utility of such approaches as island biogeography theory in quantifying the connectedness of populations, (2) allow informed judgement of the validity of the extrapolation of culture data to actual dispersal potential for given species from knowledge of their larval development times in the laboratory, and (3) provide empirical data to allow appraisal of the ecological consequences of contrasting larval types among benthic marine invertebrates.

4.3.1 Goniodoris nodosa *and* Adalaria proxima

The two species of nudibranch mollusc (*Goniodoris nodosa* Montagu and *Adalaria proxima* (Alder and Hancock)) occur intertidally on a variety of substrata. Both prey upon various species of bryozoans, which may themselves occur either epiphytically (on *Fucus* spp. and *Laminaria* spp.) or on the undersurfaces of boulders. In principle, both the bryozoan prey species and the nudibranchs are found either epiphytically on shores sheltered from wave action or beneath boulders on more exposed coasts. All of the western Scottish sample sites are within sealochs or on sheltered island coasts and the animals are thus algal-associated. *Goniodoris nodosa* is unusual among nudibranchs in preying both upon bryozoans (e.g. *Alcyonidium* spp., *Flustrellidra hispida* (Fabricius) and ascidian sea squirts (e.g. *Botryllus schlosseri* (Pallas), *Dendrodoa grossularia* (van Beneden)). *Adalaria proxima* preys upon a variety of bryozoans (including the ctenostome *Alcyonidium* spp.) but preferentially takes the cheilostome *Electra pilosa* (L.). Spawning of *G. nodosa* occurs between January and May and between March and May for *A. proxima*. Both species are annual in their life cycle and strictly semelparous – that is, following the completion of spawning, all adults die. Populations of both species are, therefore, turned over every year and there is no generation overlap. Recruitment and establishment of the offspring generation arises from settlement and metamorphosis of the planktonic larval stage for both species.

Importantly, however, there are major contrasts in the two species' reproductive strategy: *G. nodosa* lays large quantities (up to 10^4–10^5) of small eggs (106 ± 0.8 μm [s.e.] diameter) in gelatinous attached spawn masses, and these hatch as poorly developed larvae which themselves require an extended period of feeding, growth and development in the obligatory planktonic phase prior to the larva attaining competence to settle. Once development is complete the larva is capable of metamorphosis to the adult form: metamorphosis is triggered by the larvae encountering the adult prey bryozoans or ascidians. Complete development in the plankton requires approximately 10 to 13 weeks at ambient field temperatures (unpubl. data) and during this period the larva will be subject to transport by tidal currents. Note that dispersal is apparently *enforced*, because during the obligatory pre-competent pelagic phase the larvae are incapable of metamorphosis, even if they encounter the live prey bryozoans or ascidians. We expect, therefore, that larvae of *G. nodosa* will be dispersed over distances of 10^2–10^3 km.

By contrast spawn masses of *Adalaria proxima* contain fewer (10^2–10^3), larger eggs (180 ± 0.4 μm diameter) which hatch at a more advanced larval state and do not require extrinsic planktonic nutrition to complete their development. They do, however, require minimally 1–2 days to attain competence, and some larvae may not metamorphose for several days after encountering the inductive cue (the live bryozoan prey): importantly, most marine invertebrate larvae have the capacity, once competence has been attained, to delay metamorphosis until the appropriate inductive cue or trigger is encountered (for review see Pechenik, 1990). We have no data on the duration of the delay phase for *G. nodosa*, but in the laboratory fed larvae of *A. proxima* may delay metamorphosis for several weeks (Kempf and Todd, 1989; unpubl. data). Thus, although the larvae of *A. proxima* are likely to be subject to limited planktonic dispersal during the 1–2 day obligatory pelagic phase, their dispersal potential during the delay phase should not be underestimated (see also Pechenik, 1990). Accordingly, our expectation was that larval dispersal of *A. proxima* would be on the scale of 10^1–10^2 km.

The distributions of populations of *G. nodosa* and *A. proxima* are markedly heterogeneous even along the Scottish west coasts. The prey bryozoans vary spatially in their abundance – with populations especially well-developed along shorelines subject to marked tidal flow – and the nudibranchs are even more heterogeneous in their dispersion. Nonetheless, particular sites consistently support populations of both of these molluscs, and we have continuous genetic data for up to eight successive generations from repeatedly sampled areas in Argyll (see, for example, Todd *et al.*, 1988). For sedentary, annual and semelparous organisms such as these two species of mollusc, there are only two means of migration of genes between geographically isolated sites or islands which may support populations – 'rafting' of adults on detached algal fronds and dispersal of larvae in the plankton. We have no data on rafting of adults, but accept that there is a distinct possibility that on very rare occasions such detached fronds may become stranded among other fucoids bearing the prey bryozoans on a suitable shoreline (see, for example, Jokiel, 1987, 1989 for rafting and stranding of Pacific corals). From the foregoing it is clear that the larval stage confers markedly differing dispersal potential for these two species.

Mathematical models of gene flow (i.e. migration) between populations (or sites) vary greatly in their assumptions, but almost irrespective of these – and in the absence of any abnormal selective forces – it is apparent that almost any level of migration, however small, will prevent populations from diverging genetically (for a general discussion see, for example, Slatkin, 1985; Maynard Smith, 1987). Accordingly, our expectations on the strength of the foregoing were that populations of G. *nodosa* would show significant genetic differentiation on a scale of 10^3–10^4 km, whereas A. *proxima* would display differentiation only on a scale of perhaps 10^2–10^3 km. This latter expectation appeared all the more likely in view of the incidence of a simple colour polymorphism in A. *proxima*. Individuals from the east coast of England and the east, north and northwest coasts of Scotland are invariably white: those from the west coasts of Scotland and from north Wales and Northern Ireland are almost exclusively yellow. In the knowledge of the residual tidal flow patterns, it would appear that the yellow morph of A. *proxma* has spread as far north as northwest Sutherland, but then is replaced by the white morph.

4.3.2 Experimental methods

We have used standard starch gel electrophoresis methods to obtain estimates of allele frequencies at certain polymorphic genetic loci for both species (Havenhand *et al.*, 1986; Todd *et al.*, 1988, 1991 for methods). Individuals are scored for up to six polymorphic loci and population estimates of allele frequencies have been obtained for numerous sites around the northern British Isles (see below). The detailed data are published elsewhere (Todd *et al.*, in prep.): here we present only summary examples of the geographic databases for both species, but include more detailed data for certain island populations of *Adalaria proxima* which serve to illustrate some of the more striking results to derive from these studies. The genetic data for individuals and the various samples have been analysed using *F*-statistics (Weir, 1990). In principle, the *F*-statistics analysis initially considers all the samples to be sub-populations of a single panmictic breeding population (Wright, 1951). All the individuals' allele frequencies for all sites are combined and these totals tested for departure from Hardy–Weinberg equilibrium. A value of approximately zero for F_{IT} indicates that overall there is no departure from Hardy–Weinberg expectations and that the data can be considered to have been drawn from a single breeding population. F_{IS} (the 'inbreeding coefficient') assesses the degree of departure from Hardy–Weinberg expectations, attributable to inbreeding, for individuals within the sub-populations, and F_{ST} (the 'fixation index') assesses the degree of differentiation between the sub-populations.

4.3.3 Geographic results for Goniodoris nodosa

Data are available for four polymorphic loci (6-*Pgdh*, *Acon*, *Mpi*, *Sordh*) from 12 populations of the 1988/89 generation of *Goniodoris nodosa* sampled at Robin Hood's Bay (Beck Scar = 1; Cowling Scar = 2) (North Yorkshire, England), Kingsbarns (3) (Fife), Kylesku (8) and Oldany island (9) (Sutherland), Shieldaig (10) (Wester Ross), Loch Sligachan (11) (Skye), Loch Ailort (13), Clachan Seil (16), Balvicar (17), (Argyll, Scotland), The Dorn (21) and Portaferry (22) (N. Ireland) and Menai Bridge (23) (Wales). The shortest linear distance around the coasts of Scotland, and ignoring the convolutions of the shoreline, is approximately 1500 km between Menai Bridge and Robin

Hood's Bay. Table 4.1 shows the summary *F*-statistics for the four loci and over all loci: these conclusively show that there is no significant differentiation of the 12 sub-populations throughout the geographic range sampled. Neither is there any evidence of inbreeding within any of the 12 sub-populations. The data for 6-*Pgdh* are an example of the similarity in allele frequencies among these 12 sub-populations (Figure 4.1). These data are, therefore, in close agreement with our expectation of genetic differentiation of populations of *G. nodosa* likely to occur only on scales in excess of 10^3 km.

Table 4.1. *F*-statistics of loci from sub-populations of *Goniodoris nodosa* collected at 12 sites around the British Isles (1988–89). 6-*Pgdh* = 6-Phosphogluconate dehydrogenase, *Sordh* = Sorbitol dehydrogenase, *Mpi* = Mannose phosphate isomerase, *Acon* = Aconitase

	6-*Pgdh*	*Sordh*	*Mpi*	*Acon*	Over all loci
F_{IT}	−0.0128	−0.0090	−0.0047	−0.0056	−0.0097
F_{ST}	0.0023	−0.0020	−0.0034	0.0111	−0.0008
F_{IS}	−0.0151	−0.0070	−0.0013	−0.0169	−0.0089

Sub-populations with values of:
  F_{ST} <0.05 indicate 'little' genetic differentiation;
  F_{ST} ranging between 0.05–0.15 indicates 'moderate' genetic differentiation;
  F_{ST} ranging between 0.15–0.25 indicates 'great' genetic differentiation;
  F_{ST} >0.25 indicate 'very great' genetic differentiation among sub-populations (Wright, 1978).

4.3.4 *Geographic results for* Adalaria proxima

Data are available for five loci (*Fum, Mdh-2, α-Gpdh, Mpi* and *Acon*) from 19 populations of the 1988/89 generation of *Adalaria proxima* sampled at Robin Hood's Bay (Beck Scar = 1; Cowling Scar = 2) (North Yorkshire), Loch Eriboll (6), Loch Inchard (7), Kylesku (8) and Oldany island (9) (Sutherland), Shieldaig (10) (Wester Ross), Loch Sligachan (11) and Loch Ainort (12) (Skye), Loch Ailort (13), Loch Sunart (14), Loch Creran (15), Clachan Seil (16), Balvicar (17), Cuan Ferry (18), and Loch Sween (20) (Argyll, Scotland), The Dorn (21) and Portaferry (22) (N. Ireland) and Menai Bridge (23) (Wales). From the summary *F*-statistics in Table 4.2 it is clear that there is no single panmictic population and that there are major contrasts in the genetic structure of the 19 populations sampled for *A. proxima*. F_{IS} clearly shows that there is no inbreeding within any one population, and the F_{ST} value is indicative of extraordinarily high levels of genetic differentiation of all populations at all genetic loci. The values for *Acon* are low because this locus showed polymorphism at only three of the sites, with the remainder being fixed for the one allele. There is no geographic clinal structure to the genetic variation seen and no linkage disequilibrium (Todd *et al.*, in prep.) although certain

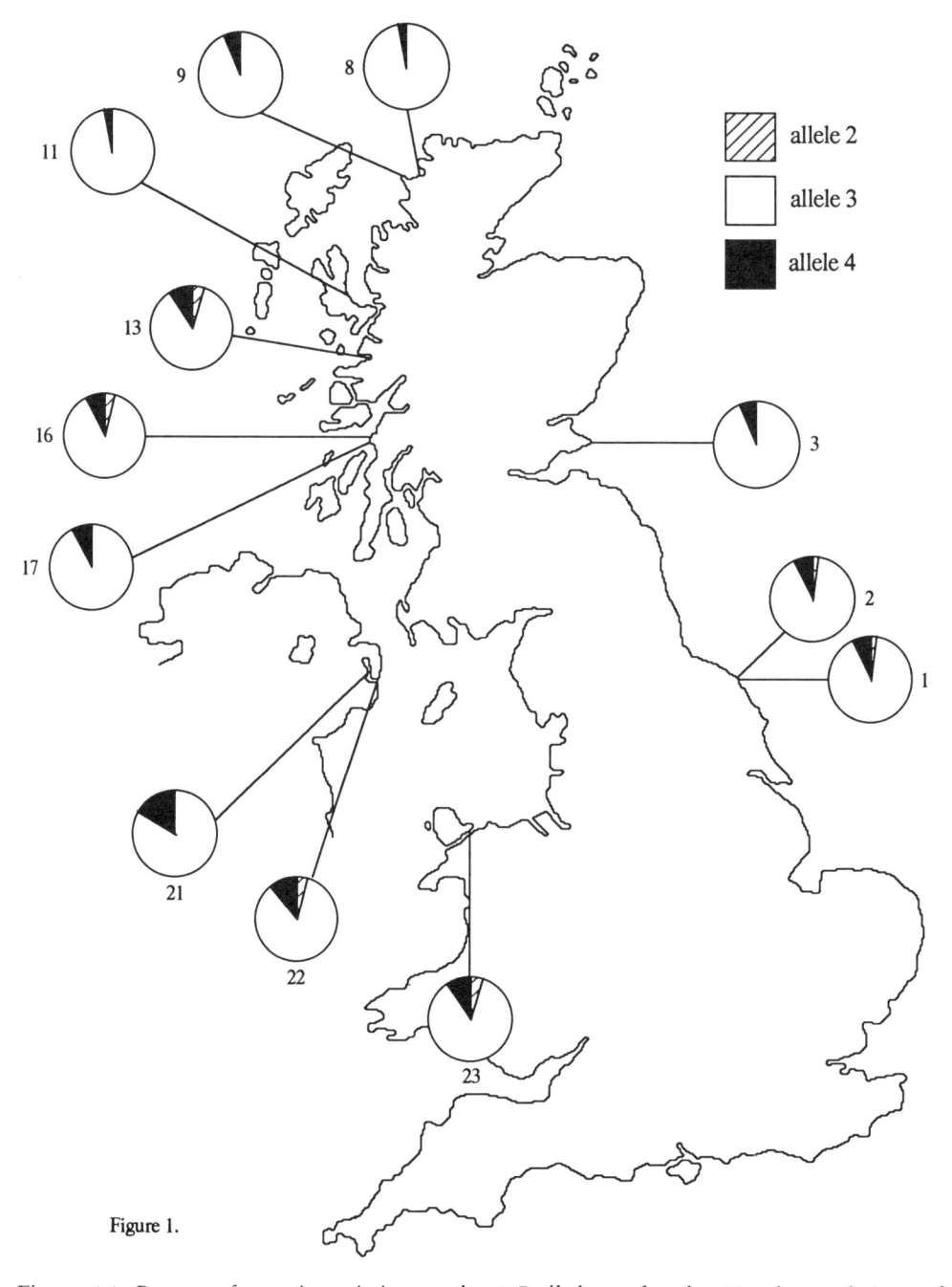

Figure 1.

Figure 4.1. Pattern of genetic variation at the 6-*Pgdh* locus for the 12 sub-populations of *Goniodoris nodosa* around the British Isles. There is marked similarity in the frequency of the common allele (allele 3) among all sub-populations. Allele 1 was not present during this census.

Table 4.2. *F*-statistics of loci from populations of *Adalaria proxima* collected at 19 sites around the British Isles (1988–89). *Mdh-2* = Malate dehydrogenase, *Fum* = Fumarate hydratase, α-*Gpdh* = α-Glycerophosphate dehydrogenase, *Mpi* = Mannose phosphate isomerase, *Acon* = Aconitase

	Mdh-2	*Fum*	*Mpi*	α-*Gpdh*	*Acon*	Over all loci
F_{IT}	0.3637	0.2694	0.2272	0.1447	−0.0038	0.3004
F_{ST}	0.3357	0.2928	0.2244	0.1307	0.0401	0.2990
F_{IS}	0.0421	−0.0332	0.0036	0.0161	−0.0456	0.0020

See Table 4.1 for key to F_{ST}.

areas are characterized by unique alleles at certain loci. Thus, for example, a private allele at the *Mpi* locus occurs in northeastern England and eastern Scotland, with another in N. Ireland only. Similarly, a private allele at the α-*Gpdh* locus is recorded for only certain populations in Argyll (see below). The data for *Fum* are an example of the differentiation in allele frequency among populations of *A. proxima* (Figure 4.2). All the evidence therefore points to extreme levels of differentiation of populations of *A. proxima*: a previous analysis of three populations (Clachan Seil, Balvicar, Cuan Ferry) of *A. proxima* at Seil island, Argyll (Todd, *et al.*, 1988) had indicated marked differentiation of populations separated by as little as 3 km, despite the fact that all three sites are in direct tidal contact and that local tidal currents may attain 6 knots (2.5 m·s^{-1}). The deduction from these data is that dispersal of larvae simply does not occur, despite the above expectations derived from knowledge of the duration of the pelagic larval phase. In an attempt to define more closely the scale of differentiation of these populations, we have recently re-examined the Seil island populations and include here further comparative data from the adjacent island of Luing.

4.3.5 *Small-scale population genetic analysis of* Adalaria proxima: *Seil and Luing islands, 1991–92*

Figure 4.3 illustrates the nine sample sites for which population samples of *Adalaria proxima* were obtained: the genetic data are presented in Table 4.3. For completeness we include all alleles that are known for all loci, although some are absent from these particular samples (see above). Note that in this analysis we include data for an additional locus (*Tpi*) which was not previously screened in the 1988/89 sampling. Inspection of the data in Table 4.3, and the summary *F*-statistics in Table 4.4, demonstrates the exceptional levels of genetic differentiation of all of these populations. Even for populations separated by as little as 90 m (at Ardinamar and Lachlainn) or 150 m (at Balvicar and Winterton) there are marked genetic differences.

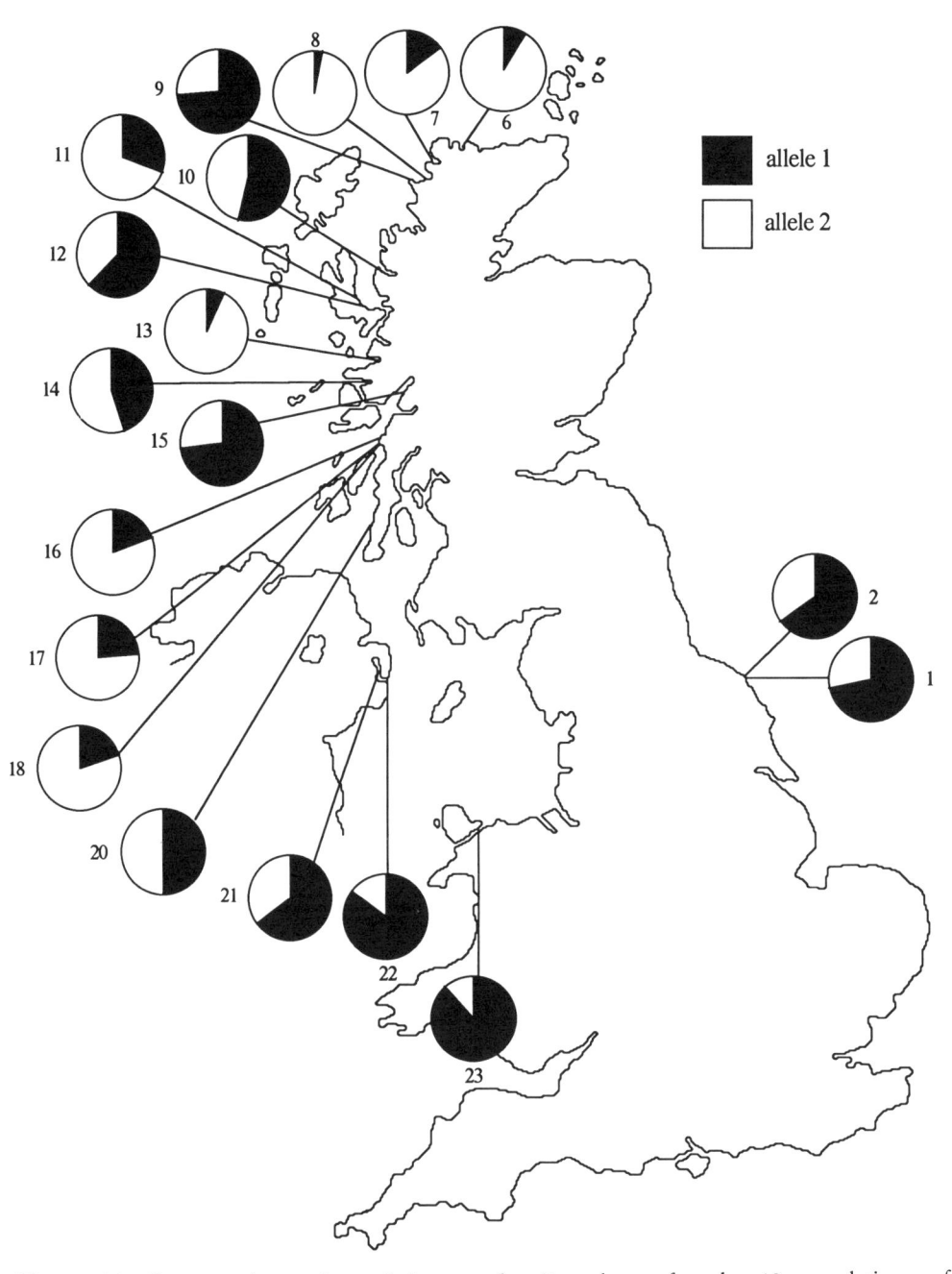

Figure 4.2. Pattern of genetic variation at the *Fum* locus for the 19 populations of *Adalaria proxima* around the British Isles. These data show marked differentiation among the populations at the common allele (allele 2).

Table 4.3. Allele frequencies of populations of *Adalaria proxima* at locations around Argyll (islands of Seil and Luing, 1991–1992). *Fum* = Fumarate Hydratase, *Mdh* = Malate Dehydrogenase, α-*Gpdh* = α-Glycerophosphate Dehydrogenase, *Mpi* = Mannose phosphate isomerase, *Acon* = Aconitase, *Tpi* = Triose phosphate isomerase. (*n* = number of individuals screened for each enzyme)

SITE		Clachan north	Clachan Seil	Clachan south	Balvicar	Winterton	Cuan ferry	Ardina-mar	Lach-lainn	Cullipool
Fum										
	n	33	46	33	34	33	31	31	32	32
	1	0.061	0.065	0.182	0.412	0.348	0.097	0.419	0.359	0.828
	2	0.939	0.935	0.818	0.588	0.652	0.903	0.581	0.641	0.172
Mdh										
	n	33	46	34	34	33	31	31	32	32
	1	0.455	0.424	0.368	0.191	0.288	0.032	0.048	0.078	0.000
	2	0.545	0.576	0.632	0.809	0.712	0.968	0.952	0.922	1.000
	3	0.000	0.000	0.000	0.000	0.000	0.000	0.000	0.000	0.000
α-*Gpdh*										
	n	33	46	33	34	33	28	25	26	32
	1	0.000	0.000	0.000	0.000	0.000	0.000	0.000	0.000	0.000
	2	0.000	0.000	0.000	0.000	0.000	0.000	0.000	0.000	0.000
	3	1.000	1.000	1.000	0.941	0.955	0.806	0.820	0.615	1.000
	4	0.000	0.000	0.000	0.059	0.045	0.194	0.180	0.385	0.000
Mpi										
	n	33	29	19	14	19	28	31	32	32
	1	0.000	0.000	0.000	0.000	0.000	0.000	0.000	0.000	0.000
	2	0.000	0.000	0.000	0.000	0.000	0.000	0.000	0.000	0.000
	3	1.000	1.000	1.000	1.000	1.000	1.000	1.000	1.000	1.000
	4	0.000	0.000	0.000	0.000	0.000	0.000	0.000	0.000	0.000
	5	0.000	0.000	0.000	0.000	0.000	0.000	0.000	0.000	0.000
Acon										
	n	33	35	29	34	33	28	20	19	32
	1	0.026	0.043	0.086	0.000	0.000	0.000	0.000	0.000	0.000
	2	0.974	0.957	0.914	1.000	1.000	1.000	1.000	1.000	1.000
Tpi										
	n	27	–	34	28	27	13	31	32	32
	1	0.056	–	0.000	0.000	0.000	0.000	0.000	0.000	0.000
	2	0.944	–	1.000	1.000	1.000	0.885	1.000	1.000	0.953
	3	0.000	–	0.000	0.000	0.000	0.115	0.000	0.000	0.047
COLOUR MORPH										
White		1	5	0	0	0	0	0	0	6
Yellow		32	41	34	34	33	31	31	32	26

4.4 Discussion

Isolation of populations is one of the major driving forces in evolution because it may result in genetic divergence and speciation. In contrast to continental land masses, islands show extreme levels of isolation; this isolation presents barriers to potential colonist species which will in all probability show common features of dispersal capacity. It is of interest, therefore, that the rocky shores of the remote oceanic island of Rockall (which is located some 360 km west of the Outer Hebrides) are characterised not by mussels, barnacles and limpets –

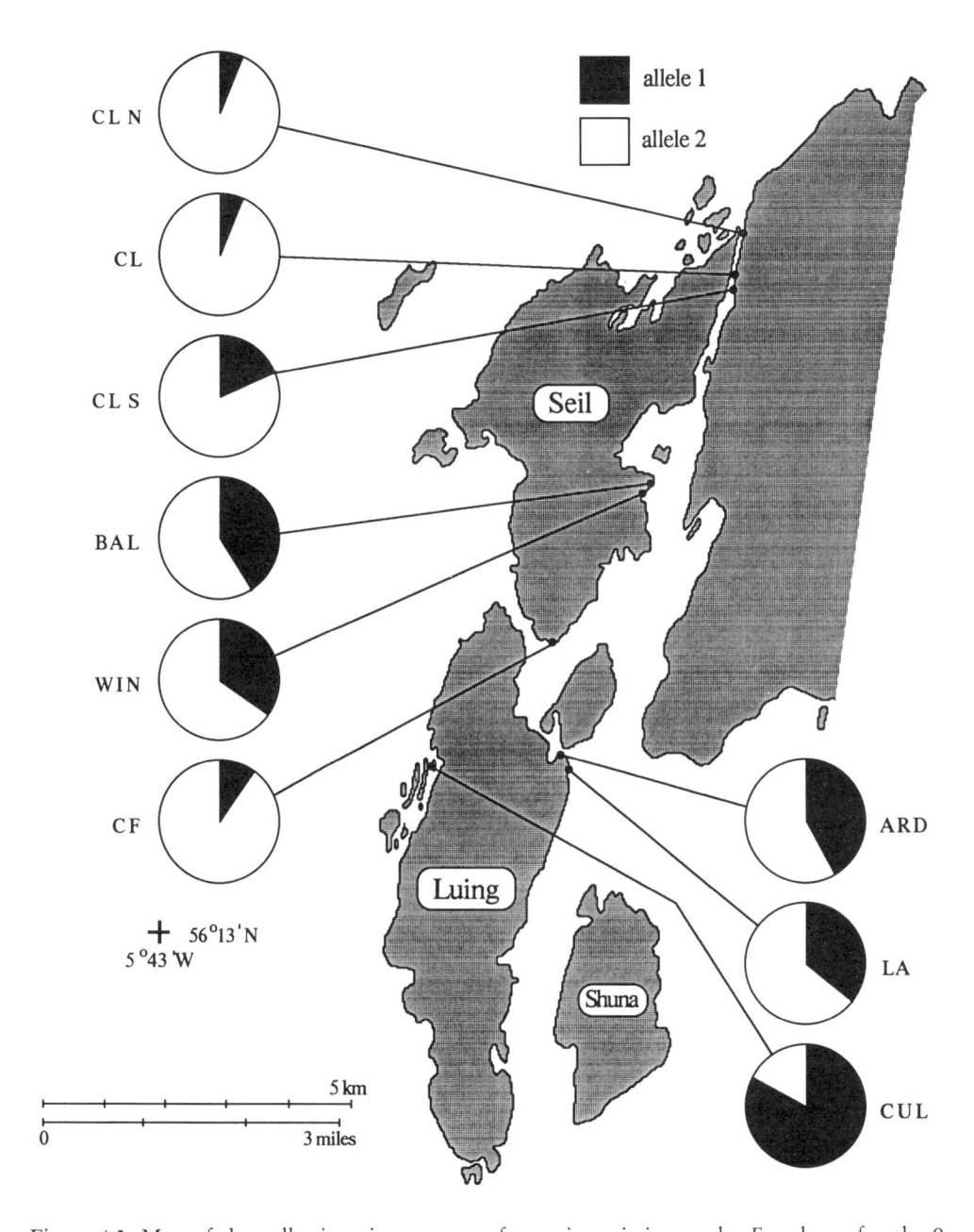

Figure 4.3. Map of the collection sites pattern of genetic variation at the *Fum* locus for the 9 populations of *Adalaria proxima* around the islands of Seil and Luing, Argyll, western Scotland. (CL N = Clachan North, CL = Clachan Seil, CL S = Clachan South, BAL = Balavicar, WIN = Winterton, CF = Cuan Ferry, ARD = Ardinamar, CUL = Cullipool, LA = Lachlainn).

Table 4.4. *F*-statistics of loci from populations of *Adalaria proxima* collected at 8 sites around the islands of Seil and Luing, Argyll, western Scotland (1991–92). *Mdh-2* = Malate dehydrogenase, *Fum* = Fumarate hydratase, α-*Gpdh* = α-Glycerophosphate dehydrogenase, *Acon* = Aconitase, *Tpi* = Triose phosphate isomerase. *Mpi* was monomorphic at all sites. Data for Clachan Seil are omitted because animals were not screened for *Tpi*; the F_{ST} over all loci including Clachan Seil is 0.2119

	Mdh-2	*Fum*	α-*Gpdh*	*Acon*	*Tpi*	Over all loci
F_{IT}	0.1662	0.2730	0.1891	−0.0057	−0.0072	0.2076
F_{ST}	0.1768	0.2408	0.1757	0.0532	0.0500	0.1974
F_{IS}	−0.0129	0.0424	0.0163	−0.0623	-0.0602	0.0127

See Table 4.1 for key to F_{ST}.

as would be typical of adjacent mainland shores exposed to wave crash – but by algal species. The intertidal and shallow subtidal zones have a luxuriant cover of *Alaria esculenta* (L.) Grev., which is characteristic of shores with extreme wave exposure. This blanket of algae could effectively screen the substratum from settling larvae of sedentary and sessile invertebrates. Mussels, barnacles and limpets all have long-lived planktotrophic larvae which might be presumed to confer dispersal advantage to the reproductive adult: the colonization abilities of such larvae are presumably maximal and it might therefore be expected that such species should characterize islands such as Rockall. This latter expectation is, however, counter-intuitive – certainly barnacles, mussels and limpets might well display maximal *colonization* potential, but the *persistence* of established individuals (and thence populations) is minimal because any offspring from these invertebrates will surely be taken away from Rockall and have minimal probability of return after completion of larval development. In much the same way that Case and Cody (1987) distinguished colonization and persistence abilities for terrestrial plants and vertebrates, so too can one extend the argument to the benthic intertidal invertebrates of Rockall. The invertebrates one expects to observe are a limited number of species with non-pelagic development; i.e. species which, by chance, do establish and persist on the island due to their lack of dispersal *away* from the habitat. Importantly, therefore, the one intertidal grazing mollusc which is present at Rockall is *Littorina saxatilis* (Moore, 1977). Notwithstanding the taxonomic controversy which still surrounds certain species of this genus, the occurrence of that mollusc on Rockall is relevant because females brood their eggs and these hatch as fully-formed benthic juveniles. There is no dispersive phase in the life cycle of *Littorina saxatilis*. This, admittedly, begs the question as to how *Littorina saxatilis*, and also, the other 15 species of (meiofaunal) invertebrates recorded from this very small and remote island (Moore, 1977; Johannesson, 1988), actually succeeded in colonizing. Detailed survey of the intertidal might reveal the incidence of a very few individuals of planktotrophic species, but these would not be predicted to be abundant or persistent because of the improbability both of colonization from remote sources and from offspring released by adults on Rockall itself. Indeed, individual barnacles must copulate with adjacent mature adults in order to fertilize their broods and both mussels and limpets are dioecious and release gametes to the water column. Successful colonization and establishment of an individual mussel, barnacle or limpet does not, therefore, necessarily even guarantee the future production of fertile offspring; this, plus the improbability of larval return to isolated islands such as Rockall, markedly increases the improbability of such species characterizing remote islands.

The fact that the majority of temperate and tropical shallow water benthic marine invertebrates reproduce by means of planktotrophic larvae (Thorson, 1946, 1950) might indicate that there is considerable advantage to the individual adult in dispersing its offspring. Certainly, the deduction that dispersal is the major rôle or function of marine invertebrate larvae has often been drawn, either explicitly, or implicitly (see reviews by, for example, Strathmann, 1980; Jablonski and Lutz, 1983; Day and McEdward, 1984; Grahame and Branch, 1985; Todd, 1985; Pechenik, 1990). Strathmann (1974), Strathmann *et al.* (1981) and Palmer and Strathmann (1981) have, however, been more cautious in this regard. The persuasive evidence that planktotrophy is the primitive or ancestral larval strategy in many phyla, and that (pelagic and non-pelagic) lecithotrophy is the more advanced derivative (Strathmann, 1978), counters simplistic arguments attributing dispersal advantage to all planktonic larvae. Rather, as has been argued elsewhere (Strathmann, 1974, 1985; Palmer and Strathmann, 1981; Kempf and Todd, 1989; Todd *et al.*, 1988), dispersal should be viewed as a potentially unavoidable *consequence*, even an evolutionary constraint, of the pelagic larval development strategy. Undoubtedly many abundant and widespread species with planktotrophic larvae have overcome these constraints of larval mortality and recruitment failure, and are consistently successful: to these there will be adaptive benefits in larval dispersal and colonization, but to uniformly ascribe selective advantage to supposedly dispersive larvae is fallacious.

That there should be significant genetic differentiation of *Adalaria proxima* populations on so small a scale implies strongly that the larvae generally are not actually entering the water column, and hence are precluded from being subject to pelagic dispersal. Dispersal is likely to be strongly leptokurtic and skewed to the right (Todd *et al.*, 1988) and those larvae of *A. proxima* that do become pelagic in non-residual tidal flows of up to 2.5 m.s^{-1} are likely to be subject to rapid and complete removal from the adult microhabitat. Minimum dispersal distances in this species are presently being investigated experimentally in the field by transplanting populations of known genetic structure between different sites.

The striking genetic contrasts among and between populations of these two species of mollusc are dominated by the high levels of heterogeneity between populations, but conformity to Hardy–Weinberg expectations within populations, for *Adalaria proxima*. Moreover, these large differences are detectable over very short distances (<100 m). The efforts of many workers over the past 25 years have provided a very large literature concerning the putative effects of selection on allozyme loci (reviewed by Nei, 1987; early studies comprehensively discussed by Lewontin, 1974). Despite all this work, it remains a subject of debate whether selection generally does have any discernible effect on allozyme loci (but see Gillespie, 1991). The only clear idea is that if there are any effects of selection, they are extremely small and subtle; large selective effects are either very rare or do not occur. Thus it is most improbable that the large interpopulation differences observed in *A. proxima* are a consequence of different selective regimes. Either selection or drift on any scale would be expected to disrupt Hardy–Weinberg equilibrium, but it should be noted that tests of fit to Hardy–Weinberg equilibrium are statistically weak (Fairbairn and Roff, 1980; Lessios, 1992). It is possible that a major determinant of the interpopulation variation observed here has been founder effect or past population bottlenecks.

The marked 'marine/terrestrial' contrasts in levels of species endemism amongst the biota of the Hawaiian island chain discussed above possibly reflect fundamentally different patterns of species colonization/extinction and adaptive radiation. Moreover, the incidence (or lack thereof) of island-specific taxa perhaps lends weight to the argument that the classical theory of island biogeography is less applicable to marine island communities than it is to terrestrial systems. This appears to be due largely to the greater transport potential of reproductive and adult stages of marine species on ocean currents and the greater physical uniformity of the marine environment over geographic distances. Nevertheless, it is important to stress that the overall 30% level of endemism of Hawaiian reef fishes is not shared by all families (Hourigan and Reese, 1987). These authors have shown that species endemism among Hawaiian reef fishes ranges from 0% among Ballistidae (triggerfishes) to 64% for the Serranidae (groupers). Well-represented families tend to have more extended pelagic larval phases. With regard to speciation, however, there is no clear pattern of endemism in relation to larval development strategy (pelagic *versus* demersal spawning) and, as mentioned above, there are no island-specific endemics with the exception of anadromous stream gobioids. Their conclusion is that, for the established species, there is little evidence of inter-island differentiation or adaptive radiation because of the dispersal potential of pelagic larval fish.

Nonetheless, for shallow water hard substratum benthic species of invertebrates, oceanic islands truly are isolated because they are essentially surrounded by water of uninhabitable depth and/or unsuitable mud substratum. On a smaller scale, the islands of the western coasts of Scotland should not be considered isolated within the context of the reproductive and colonizing potential of most marine species. However, our studies have convincingly shown that closely adjacent populations of molluscs on the shores of the same island may be essentially genetically isolated from one another. This, in itself, must raise questions about the approach that conservationists may take in protecting selected species, localities, islands, or habitat types.

A final cautionary note. The overwhelming majority of oceanic islands are located within the tropics. For a wide range of invertebrate phyla there are clear latitudinal biogeographic trends in the incidence of planktotrophy and lecithotrophy among shallow water benthic marine species. Specifically, high-latitude polar biotopes are characterized by almost exclusively non-pelagic lecithotrophic species, while tropical communities are typified by a preponderance of planktotrophic species: temperate mid-latitude communities show mixed strategies. With this in mind, and the above discussion of larval transport potential among both fish and invertebrates, it is clear that any biogeographic principles or paradigms based upon tropical island communities cannot be uncritically applied to higher latitudes.

Acknowledgements

Financial support for the bulk of this work was from NERC (grant numbers GR3/6334; GR3/8167). Additional funding for work in Hawaii (CDT) was generously provided by the Royal Society and the Nuffield Foundation. To all we are grateful.

References

Anon., 1974. *West coast of Scotland pilot*. Ministry of Defence, Hydrographic Department, Somerset, England.

Berry, R. J. 1992. The significance of island biotas. *Biological Journal of the Linnaean Society*, **46**, 3–12.

Carlquist, S. 1980. *Hawaii, a Natural History. Geology, Climate, Native Flora and Fauna above the Shoreline*. Pacific Tropical Botanical Garden, Honolulu.

Carson, H. L. 1984. Speciation and the founder effect on a new oceanic island. In Giddings, L. V., P. H. Raven and S. H. Sohmer (Eds), *Biogeography of the tropical Pacific*. BP Bishop Museum, Honolulu, 43–54.

Carson, H. L. 1987. Colonization and speciation. In Gray, A. J., Crawley, M. J. and Edwards, P. J. (Eds), *Colonization, succession and stability*. Blackwell, Oxford, 187–206.

Case, T. J. and Cody, M. L. 1987. Testing theories of island biogeography. *American Scientist*, **75**, 402–11.

Cox, C. B. and Moore, P. D. 1985. *Biogeography. An Ecological and Evolutionary Approach*. Blackwell, Oxford.

Day, R. and McEdward, L. 1984. Aspects of the physiology and ecology of pelagic larvae of marine benthic invertebrates. In Steidinger, K. A. and Walker, L. M. (Eds), *Marine Plankton Life Cycle Strategies*. CRC Press, Inc., Boca Raton, FL, 93–120.

Ellett, D. L. and Edwards, A. 1983. Oceanography and inshore hydrography of the Inner Hebrides. *Proceedings of the Royal Society of Edinburgh*, **83B**, 143–60.

Emeleus, C. H. 1991. Tertiary igneous activity. In Craig, G. Y. (Ed), *The Geology of Scotland*, (3rd edition), The Geological Society, Bath, 455–502.

Fairbairn, D. J. and D. A. Roff, 1980. Testing genetic models of isozyme variability without breeding data: can we depend on the X^2? *Canadian Journal of Aquatic Sciences*, **37**, 1149–59.

Freed, L. A., Conant, S. and Fleischer, R. C. 1987. Evolutionary ecology and radiation of Hawaiian passerine birds. *Trends in Ecology and Evolution*, **2**, 196–203.

Gillespie, J. H. 1991. *The causes of molecular evolution*. Oxford University Press, Oxford.

Grahame, J. and Branch, G. M. 1985. Reproductive patterns of marine invertebrates. *Oceanography and Marine Biology, An Annual Review*, **23**, 373–98.

Havenhand, J. N., Thorpe, J. P. and Todd, C. D. 1986. Estimates of biochemical genetic diversity within and between the nudibranch molluscs *Adalaria proxima* (Alder and Hancock) and *Onchidoris muricata* (Müller) (Doridacea: Onchidorididae). *Journal of Experimental Marine Biology and Ecology*, **95**, 105–11.

Hourigan, T. F. and Reese, E. S. 1987. Mid-ocean isolation and the evolution of Hawaiian reef fishes. *Trends in Ecology and Evolution*, **2**, 187–91.

Jablonski, D. and Lutz, R. A. 1983. Larval ecology of marine invertebrates: paleobiological implications. *Biological Reviews*, **58**, 21–89.

Johannesson, K. 1988. The paradox of Rockall: why is a brooding gastropod (*Littorina saxatilis*) more widespread than one having a planktonic larval dispersal stage (*L. littorea*)? *Marine Biology*, **99**, 507–13.

Jokiel, P. L. 1987. Ecology, biogeography and evolution of corals in Hawaii. *Trends in Ecology and Evolution*, **2**, 179–82.

Jokiel, P. L. 1989. Rafting of reef corals and other organisms at Kwajalein Atoll. *Marine Biology*, **101**, 483–93.

Kay, E. A. and Palumbi, S. R. 1987. Endemism and evolution in Hawaiian marine invertebrates. *Trends in Ecology and Evolution*, **2**, 183–6.

Kempf, S. C. and Todd, C. D. 1989. Feeding potential in the lecithotropic larvae of *Adalaria proxima* and *Tritonia hombergi*: an evolutionary perspective. *Journal of the Marine Biological Association of the United Kingdom*, **69**, 659–82.

Lessios, H. A. 1992. Testing electrophoretic data for agreement with Hardy–Weinberg expectations. *Marine Biology*, **112**, 517–23.

Lewontin, R. C. 1974. *The Genetic Basis of Evolutionary Change*. Columbia University Press, New York.

MacArthur, R. H. and Wilson, E. O. 1963. An equilibrium theory of insular zoogeography. *Evolution*, **17**, 373–87.

MacArthur, R. H. and Wilson, E. O. 1967. *The Theory of Island Biogeography*. Princeton University Press, Princeton.

Maynard Smith, J. 1987. *Evolutionary Genetics*. Oxford University Press, Oxford.

McKinley, I. G., Baxter, M. S., Ellett, D. J. and Jack, W. 1981. Tracer applications of radiocaesium in the Sea of the Hebrides. *Estuarine, Coastal and Shelf Science*, **13**, 69–82.

Moore, P. G. 1977. Additions to the littoral fauna of Rockall, with a description of *Areolaimus penelope* sp. nov. (Nematoda: Axonolaimidae). *Journal of the Marine Biological Association of the United Kingdom*, **57**, 191–200.

Nei, M. 1987. *Molecular Evolutionary Genetics*. Columbia University Press, New York.

Palmer, A. R. and Strathmann, R. R. 1981. Scale of dispersal in varying environments and its implication for life history of marine invertebrates. *Oecologia*, **48**, 308–18.

Peacock, J. D. 1983. Quarternary geology of the Inner Hebrides. *Proceedings of the Royal Society of Edinburgh*, **83B**, 83–90.

Pechenik, J. A. 1990. Delayed metamorphosis by larvae of benthic marine invertebrates: does it occur? is there a price to pay? *Ophelia*, **32**, 63–94.

Scheltema, R. S. 1986. Long distance dispersal by planktonic larvae of shoal-water benthic invertebrates among central Pacific islands. *Bulletin of Marine Science*, **39**, 241–56.

(Top) Duncansby Stacks. A characteristic seascape of the northern and eastern coast and islands.

(Above) Machair at Loch Briste on South Uist: A six-spot burnet moth (Zygaena filipendula) *on red clover* (Trifolium pratense) *together with yellow rattle* (Rhinanthus minor).

(Right) An exposure of Old Red Sandstone at Dyke-end on Orkney.

(Above) The remote, wave-exposed, sandy beach at
Sandwood Bay, Sutherland.

(Right) Rugged, cliff coastline with off-lying stacks and skerries.

Simberloff, D. S. and Wilson, E. 1970. Experimental zoogeography of islands: a two-year record of colonization. *Ecology*, **51**, 934–7.

Slatkin, M. 1985. Gene flow in natural populations. *Annual Review of Ecology and Systematics*, **16**, 393–430.

Strathmann, R. 1974. The spread of sibling larvae of sedentary marine invertebrates. *American Naturalist*, **108**, 29–44.

Strathmann, R. R. 1978. The evolution and loss of feeding larval stages of marine invertebrates. *Evolution*, **32**, 894–906.

Strathmann, R. R. 1980. Why does a larva live so long? *Paleobiology*, **6**, 373–6.

Strathmann, R. R. 1985. Feeding and non-feeding larval development and life history evolution in marine invertebrates. *Annual Review of Ecology and Systematics*, **16**, 339–61.

Strathmann, R. R., Branscomb, E. S. and Vedder, K. 1981. Fatal errors in set as a cost of dispersal and the influence of intertidal flora on set of barnacles. *Oecologia*, **48**, 13–8.

Thorson, G. 1946. Reproduction and larval development of Danish marine bottom invertebrates. *Meddelelser fra Kommissionen for Danmarks fiskeri - og Havundersøgelser, Serie: Plankton*, **4**, 1–523.

Thorson, G. 1950. Reproductive and larval ecology of marine bottom invertebrates. *Biological Reviews*, **25**, 1–45.

Todd, C. D. 1985. Reproductive strategies of north-temperate rocky shore invertebrates. In Moore, P. G. and Seed, R. (Eds), *The Ecology of Rocky Coasts*. London: Hodder & Stoughton 203–19.

Todd, C. D., Havenhand, J. P. and Thorpe, J. P. 1988. Genetic differentiation, pelagic larval transport and gene flow between local populations of the intertidal marine mollusc *Adalaria proxima* (Alder and Hancock). *Functional Ecology*, **2**, 441–51.

Todd, C. D., Thorpe, J. P. and Hadfield, M. G. 1991. Genetic structure of populations of the aplysiid opisthobranch *Stylocheilus longicaudus* (Quoy and Gaimard) around the shores of O'ahu, Hawaii. *Journal of Molluscan Studies*, **57**, 153–66.

Weir, B. S. 1990. *Genetic Data Analysis: Methods for Discrete Population Genetic Data*. Sinauer Associates, Inc., Sunderland, MA.

White, R. G., Hill, A. E. and Jones, D. A. 1988. Distribution of *Nephrops norvegicus* (L.) larvae in the western Irish Sea: an example of advective control on recruitment. *Journal of Plankton Research*, **10**, 735–47.

Wright, S. 1951. The genetical structure of populations. *Annals of Eugenics*, **15**, 323–54.

PART TWO
WILDLIFE
AND THE MARINE HERITAGE

PART TWO
WILDLIFE AND THE MARINE HERITAGE

On all the Scottish islands which are dotted around the coast it is difficult to escape from the sea. The taste and smell of the salt spray, the sounds from the restless movements of the waves and the expansive, seemingly never-ending skies all serve to remind one of its dominating presence.

Inland, away from the coastal margins where water meets land, the flora and fauna is a relatively familiar one visually dominated by flowering plants, with insects, spiders and birds the most obvious and numerous animals. Compared with mainland Scotland there are differences, in particular the general lack of stands of tall trees. These have been replaced by smaller dwarf shrubs better equipped to survive the strong winds which are characteristic of the island climate. The islands are therefore often reminiscent of the Scottish uplands. The terrestrial fauna comprises much more than the readily recognizable insects, spiders and birds. Other groups such as annelids, nematodes, molluscs and mammals are all present but remain discreet. All these species, both plants and animals, are adapted to their preferred habitats, but as one nears the sea conditions begin to change and more specialized adaptations are required in order to survive.

The cliffs which border many of the islands, and the sand dunes, shingle and machair, for which the Western Isles are so famous, each support a much more limited but specialized flora. Because of the specialized conditions which many of these species require they are restricted in their distribution and thus relatively rare. The islands of Scotland represent one of the last safe bastions for some of these species such as the Scottish primrose (*Primula scotica*) found on the maritime heaths on the cliff tops in Orkney and the oyster plant (*Mertensia maritima*) on shingle shores. Even in the islands the numbers of these species are declining as land use practices change and specialized habitats disappear. Other species, while just as adept at surviving these rather harsher conditions, are more widespread and just as spectacular. The sight of thrift (*Armeria maritima*) in full flower with a backdrop of brightly coloured orange, yellow and green lichens is not easily forgotten. Of all these, perhaps the machair is most restricted in distribution, being largely confined to the Western Isles. Stewart Angus eloquently describes not only its biological and geomorphological importance but also its place in the cultural fabric of the islands of Scotland.

Despite the more specialized requirements of species living in the maritime fringe, the basic form of the plants is still recognizable and the change, when it occurs, is dramatic and sudden. Above high water mark the flowering plants are dominant, but below this mark they give way almost totally to the algae. Very few flowering plants have successfully made the transition to the truly marine environment. The three species of eelgrasses (*Zostera* spp.) and the two species of tasselweeds (*Ruppia* spp.) are the sole representatives, but they are very important in certain areas not only because their roots bind the sand and mud but also because they provide a valuable food source for visiting birds.

The diversity of intertidal habitats and their associated flora and fauna is discussed by Ian Fuller and John Baxter. On the rocky shores the brown fucoid algae are the dominant species and in a relatively short distance, both horizontally and vertically, a range of different algae are found, arranged in distinctly defined bands down the shore. This zonation of the large brown seaweeds is reflected by the various species of animals and other smaller algae.

The disappearance of the flowering plants in these communities is mirrored by the insects and spiders. The shores are home to a variety of animals including sponges, sea anemones, polychaete worms, molluscs of various forms, crustacea (which are the numerous arthropod species) and other, wholly marine phyla such as the echinoderms and tunicates. In the intertidal region the molluscs are generally the most numerous and conspicuous species. With their protective shells they are best able to survive the stresses of being alternately immersed in seawater and then exposed to air and rain. As with the flowering plants, however, there are the exceptions to the rule and a small number of species of non-crustacean arthropods, such as the sea spider and marine mites, as well as Collembola and both Mesostigmatid and Cryptostigmatid mites, have made the transition from land to sea.

The great length and diversity of shoreline around the islands of Scotland results in a rich flora and fauna which is further enhanced by the effects of the warmer waters of the North Atlantic Drift as they affect the Western Isles and Orkney and the influence of the colder Arctic waters around Shetland. Southern species, more characteristic of the English Channel, are found around the Western Isles and Orkney, while cold water species extend as far south as Shetland. The animals and plants of the shore are much less familiar to most people than those of the land but during the periods of low tide they are accessible to those who would spend some time hunting among the seaweed and turning over boulders.

Below low water mark the delights of the underwater life are directly available only to the privileged few who don SCUBA gear and brave the cold waters. Many of the islands, located as they are on the western and northern fringes of Scotland with the clear waters of the Atlantic ocean washing on their shores, are home to a spectacular range of animals and plants, some of which are described by David Connor.

As on the shores, in the more shallow reaches large macroalgae create a three-dimensional framework within which the various animals exist. In these clear waters the large kelps can extend to depths of over 30 m, but around the east coast islands they may grow no deeper than a few metres. At depths where the algae can no longer survive due to low light levels, the animals take over and dense carpets of sea anemones and sea squirts are found covering the rock faces, together with feather stars and brittle star beds. The dominance of the molluscs is reduced and the echinoderms and various soft-bodied filter-feeding organisms take over. In the deeper sheltered waters around the islands other strange and beautiful animals are to be found living in and on the sandy and muddy bottoms. These are species such as the sea pen *Funiculina quadrangularis* and the sea anemone *Pachycherianthus multiplicatus*. Algae are still the primary producers which serve these deeper water animal communities but it is the microscopic phytoplankton which have taken over.

Much of what has been described is distinctive of the marine environment but there are further important components of the ecosystem. The seas around the Scottish coast are rich in fish and Roger Bailey provides an insight into some of those populations which people have hunted for many years although there are many more which have not been subjected to direct exploitation.

The top marine predators are undoubtedly among the most high profile elements of the marine wildlife. Paul Thompson briefly reviews their distribution and past exploitation before highlighting the need for much more research essential to promote their management and thus ensure their conservation. The seals and cetaceans which frequent the coast rely to a very great degree on the relative tranquillity and isolation of many of the islands. Many of the smaller islands and skerries are important haul out and breeding sites for both grey (*Halichoerus grypus*) and common (*Phoca vitulina*) seals which also depend on the plentiful food supply to be gathered from the surrounding waters. The waters around the islands yield the sight of various species of cetacean including killer whales (*Orcinus orca*), minke whale (*Balaenoptera acutorostrata*), bottlenose dolphin (*Tursiops truncatus*) and harbour porpoise (*Phocoena phocoena*).

It is perhaps the birds which have, more than any other group, highlighted the importance of the Scottish islands. The Northern Isles in particular, but also others such as the Isle of May and the Bass Rock on the east coast together with Ailsa Craig and Islay on the west, are all vitally important as breeding and over-wintering areas for millions of seabirds. Pat Monaghan describes the importance of the islands of Scotland for marine birds in the wider contexts of the UK and Europe. Despite their great numbers, these birds are nonetheless vulnerable, and it is only through the maintenance of the complete ecosystem, and a recognition of the complexity of such an integrated system, that the marine natural heritage of the Scottish islands will be protected and assured for the generations to come.

The six chapters in this part of the book can, by necessity, only give a glimpse of what there is to be cherished and enjoyed. The marine environment is unyielding and often harsh, but the animals and plants have adapted to survive and in many cases thrive in such conditions.

5 THE CONSERVATION IMPORTANCE OF MACHAIR SYSTEMS OF THE SCOTTISH ISLANDS, WITH PARTICULAR REFERENCE TO THE OUTER HEBRIDES

S. Angus

Summary

1. Machair has a very limited world distribution, being restricted to the north and west of Scotland and the west of Ireland. Though traditionally defined solely in terms of the shell-rich coastal plain, this paper examines machair in its wider context. Machair is of conservation importance for its land-form, botany, zoology, archaeology and landscape, as well as for its transitional habitats. Machair is a living, cultural landscape, and its value for countryside conservation should be acknowledged not merely by the application· of designations but by meaningful dialogue with occupiers.

2. Though important and sometimes extensive machairs occur on the Scottish mainland the habitat is best developed on the islands, especially in the Outer Hebrides and on some of the islands of the Inner Hebrides and Orkney and Shetland. Machair demonstrates close relationships between climate, soils, landscape, vegetation, biota, and the history of human economic activity, settlement and culture.

3. This paper concentrates on the machair of the Outer Hebrides of Scotland, but refers to other island groups, to mainland Scotland and to Ireland, to establish the national and international context. While acknowledging its obvious importance, the subject of machair management is beyond the scope of this paper.

5.1 Introduction

Machair is the only major habitat universally known by a Gaelic name. The usage of the word in both Gaelic and English has been discussed by Angus (1993). Bassett and Curtis (1985) have highlighted the strong correlation between the distribution of machair and the Gaeltacht (Gaelic-speaking area) of Ireland: there would be an equally strong correlation between the present-day distribution of machair and Gaelic in Scotland were it not for the presence of machair in Orkney and Shetland, where Gaelic has never been a local language. There are certainly similarities in the land use histories of the different machair areas in addition to those of language, and it may be that cultural factors are as important as biotic and abiotic influences in determining machair distribution.

Ritchie (1976) defined machair (*sensu stricto*) solely in terms of the machair plain, excluding even the foredunes, with the boundary between the two marked by the disappearance of marram *Ammophila arenaria*. Even this rather strict definition demonstrates the complexity of machair, in that it embraces landform, shell content, grazing, human influence, and climate. Curtis (1991b) has expanded on Ritchie's definition.

1. Mature coastal sand-plane with almost level surface,

2. Significant proportion of shell fragments in the sand producing a lime-rich soil (> pH 7.0),

3. Grassland vegetation with low frequency of sand-binding species and with the following core species: red fescue *Festuca rubra*, white clover *Trifolium repens*, common bird's-foot-trefoil *Lotus corniculatus*, yarrow *Achillea millefolium*, lady's bedstraw *Galium verum*, ribwort plantain *Plantago lanceolata*, eyebright *Euphrasia* spp., daisy *Bellis perennis* and the moss *Rhytidiadelphus squarrosus*,

4. Human interference, principally by grazing, during the recent historical period,

5. A moist, cool, oceanic climate.

Conservationists are obliged to look at machair in an even wider context, including related habitats and transitions, for which the term 'machair systems' is suggested. For the machair plain (i.e. machair *sensu stricto*) the term 'machair grassland' suggested by Curtis (1991b) should be employed. Machair systems incorporate strandline, dune, machair grassland, coastal lochs and marshes within the machair area, saltmarsh, and transitions between these, including 'blackland' a transitional habitat between machair and moorland. Hebrideans use 'machair' loosely, often meaning the entire area from beach to blackland, but sometimes the machair plain alone (Ritchie, 1967).

Machair is found only in Scotland and Ireland, where it is restricted to areas having the combination of the factors listed by Curtis (1991b). In Scotland, the main areas are North and South Uist and Tiree, with significant areas in the other islands of the Outer Hebrides, in Orkney and Shetland, and on some of the Inner Hebrides, notably Coll, Colonsay, Mull, Islay and Iona. Though some of the 'links' of the east coast of Scotland may superficially resemble machair, they are distinguished primarily by the lower base status of the former (though some links have a high shell content) and always on the basis of flowering plants, climate, and history of land use. Shaw *et al.* (1983) have remarked upon the fact that the full range of variation from beach to landward habitats is largely retained in machair, in contrast to the east coast dune grasslands of the mainland which have been substantially altered on at least the landward margin. In Ireland machair occurs on the west coast in Counties Galway, Mayo, Sligo and Donegal (Curtis, 1991a).

Mather and Ritchie (1977) give a total machair (*sensu stricto*) area for Scotland of 14 500 ha, with a total beach complex area for the Highlands and Islands (including non-machair areas) of 26 700 ha. Of their machair, 2900 ha occurred on the mainland, but most of the habitat was on the islands: 6000 ha in the Western Isles, 1500 ha in Orkney, and 180 ha in Shetland. Of the Inner Hebrides, Tiree contains the highest proportion of machair, having 1830 ha (24% of total area of island) whereas neighbouring Coll has only 260 ha (4% of total area) (Shepherd, 1989). The area of machair in Ireland is in the order of 7500 ha (Curtis, personal communication, 1991). Thus the total area of the habitat, even in the form of machair systems, is probably in the order of 30 000–40 000 ha.

5.2 Geomorphology

Machair has geomorphological importance related to its origin and development, and Mather and Ritchie (1977) have argued that the dynamics of the land-forms are as worthy of conservation as the land-forms in their static sense. The same authors point out that the strong correlation between geomorphological and biological interest is not mere coincidence but a reflection of variety of land-form leading to variety of habitat. The importance of the water table in the evolution of machair surfaces and the dynamic aspects of machair has been widely emphasized (e.g. Ritchie, 1979), and must clearly be given the closest attention in the study of machair dynamics. Water is also important in the formation of aeolinite, or 'dune sandstone', of which there are examples in most machair areas (Ritchie and Mather, 1972), the most important of which are probably at the Bu, Burray, Orkney, where it underlies the upper beach (Mather *et al.*, 1975), Evie, Orkney (Mather *et al.*, 1974), Luskentyre, Harris (Ritchie and Mather, 1970) and at Dunloughan, Mannin Bay, Co. Galway.

Mather and Ritchie (1977) presented a graded list of Beach Complexes of Outstanding Geomorphological Importance, but this will shortly be updated by a section of the Joint Nature Conservation Committee's (JNCC) Geological Conservation Review (GCR) (in preparation). The importance of machair may be judged from the fact that out of 36 sites identified by the GCR as being of national importance for coastal geomorphology (including hard coasts), no less than twelve have machair as a major component, with another site, St. Ninian's Tombolo in Shetland, having machair as a feature of interest. Of the twelve, seven are located in the Outer Hebrides and another two in the Northern Isles, with only two on the mainland. The complete list is given in Table 5.1. Though Orkney has the largest machairs outside the Outer Hebrides, they tend to lack the diversity of forms developed in the Western Isles (Mather *et al.*, 1975). In a review of Orkney sites, the Nature Conservancy Council (1978) stated that the Bay of Newark on Sanday, Orkney, was the most complex and complete machair system on Orkney, and one of the most extensive outside the Outer Hebrides.

Table 5.1. Geological Conservation Review Sites in Scotland having machair as a major feature of interest:

1. Dunnet Bay, Caithness
2. Eoligarry, Barra
3. Luskentyre – Corran Seilebost, Harris
4. Machairs Robach and Newton, North Uist
5. Mangersta, Uig, Lewis
6. Pabbay, Sound of Harris
7. Traigh na Berie, Uig, Lewis
8. Ardivachar – Stoneybridge, South Uist
9. Central Sanday, Orkney
10. Balta, Shetland
11. Machir Bay, Islay
12. Sandwood, Sutherland

5.3 Biological Importance of Machair Ecosystems

Both Darling (1947) and Darling and Boyd (1964) state that the machair 'starts with the florally sterile zone of shell sand, then there is the bank of unstable dunes, on the seaward edge of which the marram grass begins to grow thinly'. The profile of the foreshore depends largely on the degree of exposure, and on open beaches the presence of a shingle band below the dunes may be vital in protecting the dunes and/or machair from storm surges. Dunes or sandhills may be extensive and high, reaching a maximum of 35 m at Luskentyre Banks in Harris. Often the dunes have been lost by coastal retreat or erosion, and the machair is fronted by an eroding scarp which may be fretted by blowouts. The dunes are often active and blown sand may be carried far inland over the machair plain, to form secondary depositional features, or to be deposited in the marsh or machair loch. Ritchie (1979) has indicated that the seaward margins of many machair lochs are the sites of active sand deposition. The machair plain slopes gently away from the sea, though this may be obscured by secondary deposition or by erosional features.

The lower lying machair floods in winter, often enlarging the permanent lochs and creating new, very shallow 'winter lochs'. Ritchie (1967) has pointed out that these sheets of winter water may play a very important role as agents of erosion, and has contrasted the role of water in winter with that of summer, when drought conditions may prevail. The permanent marsh or machair loch marks the landward boundary of the machair plain. This gives way to 'blackland', a zone where blown sand has ameliorated the acidity of the peat and forms a distinct agricultural zone in the Uists between machair plain and acid peatland. This sequence can also be seen in Tiree, where the machair (which is not cultivated) gives way to crofts and finally to the *sliabh* (acid moorland), with occasional machair lochs.

The machair is extremely low-lying, and man and the sea have both modified drainage patterns. Ritchie (1967) notes the widespread drainage of lochs by man, and the pre-eighteenth century network of coastal lochs in the Uists was certainly more extensive than it is today. Anderson (1785) noted with concern that blown sand was filling in the network of coastal lochs and threatening their viability as navigable links. The sea has also drowned some of this low-lying landscape, as is evident from the many deposits of intertidal peat which have been found throughout the machair areas (e.g. Ritchie, 1985). Some of the machair lochs have seawater incursions on every tide, some occasionally; at some sites saltmarsh has been created and, in extreme cases, intertidal sand flats such as the Baleshare, Kirkibost and Valley fords.

The presence of rivers adds more variation, as at Luskentyre, Gress and Howmore; these influence erosion and deposition, where the areas around the estuaries are often more active than other parts of these systems. The presence of offshore reefs, islands and spits may further complicate the picture.

Gimingham (1964) has shown that machair vegetation extends into areas where shell sand has blown over on to adjacent cliffs, slopes, or peat-covered land, and that these regions often provide the most fertile grazing or cultivated land in the area.

5.3.1 Botany

Tansley (1939) described machair vegetation from Dog's Bay, Co. Galway, but did not mention machair *per se*. It was not until the 1940s (e.g. Wilmott, 1945; Darling, 1947; Macleod, 1949) that the botanical interest of machair was realized and identified as a distinct habitat. Machair was described in some detail by Gimingham (1964) but was not widely highlighted until the 1970s, when a Machair Working Group was formed by the Coastal Ecology Research Station at Norwich, which held a seminar on machair which was stimulated by correspondence between Ranwell of CERS and Ritchie and Gimingham, both of the University of Aberdeen. The botanical distinction between machair and dune grasslands in other areas was more firmly established in the first of three such seminars by Ranwell (1974), who contrasted the relatively low number of species of flowering plants on machair (100–150) with the 400–500 on large mainland dune systems such as Culbin and Ainsdale, but pointed out that the richness of the mainland systems was partly attributable to introduced species whereas machair systems have a comparatively pure flora representative of the locality. It is possible that the number of species on island machair systems has been reduced by the 'island effect' (Macarthur and Wilson, 1967), but the machair of the Monach Isles, some 10 km west of North Uist, has over 180 species, with a further eleven which had apparently been lost in recent years because of the cessation of cultivation (Perring and Randall, 1972). Maturity of the machair vegetation could also determine species diversity though the example of the Monach Isles shows how recent cultivation can augment the total and, even without cultivation, recent machair surfaces may have high botanical diversity: half of one of the areas on Pabbay, Sound of Harris, identified as being of high botanical interest in a survey in 1983 (Nature Conservancy Council internal report) is shown on the 1857 Admiralty Chart as intertidal sand. Much of the area of this former inlet is identified as 'seasonal loch' by Ritchie (1981).

The Nature Conservancy Council (NCC) recognized the importance of machair in its *Nature Conservation Review* (Ratcliffe, 1977), though large areas were still poorly known at that time. Many of the gaps were filled by subsequent surveys by the NCC (Pitkin *et al.*, 1983), the Institute of Terrestrial Ecology (Shaw *et al.*, 1983) and the NCC's National Sand Dune Vegetation Survey. In Ireland, machair was not recognized until 1980 (Akeroyd and Curtis, 1980) and has been further described by Bassett and Curtis (1985) and Curtis (1991b).

The vegetation of the strandline and yellow dune consists for the most part of widespread communities and species (Pitkin *et al.*, 1983). A few rare species such as oyster plant *Mertensia maritima* are present while locally scarce species include viper's bugloss *Echium vulgare* (Taransay and Scarista, Harris), pyramidal orchid *Anacamptis pyramidalis* and sea bindweed *Calystegia soldanella* (Eriskay, Vatersay and South Ronaldsay).

Grazed machair grassland is notable for its orchids, including machair ecotypes such as *Dactylorhiza fuchsii hebridensis* (Wilmott). Of particular note are a number of cross-generic hybrids, e.g. *Coeloglossum viride X Dactylorhiza maculata* (Ferreira, 1987; Pankhurst and Mullin, 1991). Other Outer Hebrides rarities include Holy-grass *Hierochloë odorata*, bog hair-grass *Deschampsia setacea*, cowbane *Cicuta virosa* and hoary whitlowgrass *Draba incana* (Pitkin *et al.*, 1983). Marsh yellow-cress *Rorippa islandica* occurs in damp areas on the Monach Isles (Perring and Randall, 1972). Orkney machair has limestone bedstraw *Galium sterneri* and early marsh orchid *Dactylorhiza incarnata* (Bullard and Goode, 1975), while Shetland has northern autumn gentian *Gentianella amarella septentrionalis* (also in Outer Hebrides) and sea pea *Lathyrus japonicus* (A. Douse, personal communication, 1992); Tiree has *Draba incana* and purple milk-vetch *Astragalus danicus*.

Crawford (1991) has examined the vegetation of cultivated ground in the Uists and has identified a range of weed assemblages which seem to be determined by the crop type and by the stage of rotation, though there also seemed to be a difference between North and South Uist. Potato shades out annuals, especially the shorter ones. Cereals may be dominated earlier in the season by corn marigold *Chrysanthemum segetum*, bugloss *Anchusa arvensis*, field pansy *Viola arvensis*, common cornsalad *Valerianella locusta*, red dead-nettle *Lamium purpureum*, charlock *Sinapis arvensis* and sun spurge *Euphorbia helioscopa*. In the first year fallow, these are replaced to varying degrees by wild pansy *Viola tricolor*, creeping buttercup *Ranunculus repens*, common forget-me-not *Myosotis arvensis*, sea mouse-ear *Cerastium diffusum* and common stork's-bill *Erodium cicutarium*. In the second year fallow *Festuca rubra* and *Trifolium repens* predominate, and the transition from agriculture back to 'natural' machair is marked by the replacement of *Ranunculus repens* by meadow buttercup *R.acris*. Many of these species have been eliminated from agricultural land elsewhere by herbicides and chemical fertilizers, and Ranwell (1974) has suggested that the weed flora of cultivated machair could be of ancient origin. Ranwell (1981) has pointed out that Hebridean machairs provide one of the few areas where old field successions, up to a century or more old, can still be seen in the British Isles; he has suggested that the commoner marsh orchids take about 30 years to recolonize formerly cultivated machair while the full flora associated with uncultivated machair may take up to 100 years to return.

Blackland in the Outer Hebrides is generally of low botanical interest, and is important in nature conservation terms chiefly for its breeding birds and for its place in the machair-moorland transition (Nature Conservancy Council, 1986). Uist hay meadows, which often lie on blackland, were surveyed by Mackintosh and Urquhart (1983). The mean number of flowering plants was 7.7–11.7/m^2 depending on the type of hayfield. None was believed to be of outstanding botanical importance, though some types supported a range of orchids including *Dactylorhiza incarnata*.

Irish machairs have been described by Curtis (1991b). These are broadly similar to Scottish machair in terms of both communities and species, though there are some very obvious differences such as the abundance of squincancywort *Asperula cynanchica* on many Irish machairs. Ireland can match the best of Scotland for the profusion of orchids such as the frog orchid *Coeloglossum viride*, *Dactylorhiza incarnata* and for cross-generic hybrids, but only Irish systems have bee Orchid *Ophrys apifera*, Irish marsh orchid *Dactylorhiza traunsteineri* and the dense-flowered orchid *Neotinea maculata*, the last being a Mediterranean species found in Britain only on the Isle of Man.

5.3.2 Saltmarsh

There are about 500 ha of saltmarsh in the Outer Hebrides, almost all of which is associated with machair systems, though the largest saltmarsh, at Tong Saltings (96 ha), is part of a system which at best is 'machair-like' rather than machair proper (Ritchie and Mather, 1970). Saltmarsh is virtually absent from Tiree and Coll, except for a small area at the head of Loch Eatharna on Coll (P. Cashman, personal communication, 1992). The Northern Isles have many saltmarshes, but these are rarely part of the machair systems, though they occasionally lie close to machair. Linklet Bay on North Ronaldsay has curious depressions in the machair plain resembling saltmarsh pans; the water table lies very close to the surface and there is periodic drenching by salt spray so there may be some relationship (Mather *et al.*, 1974).

The botany of Outer Hebrides saltmarshes has been described in detail by Law and Gilbert (1986) and Ferreira (1987). All the islands have grazed saltings characteristic of northern Scotland (Adam, 1981) while Sheehy-Skeffington and Wymer (1991) have asserted that the closely cropped saltmarshes of western Ireland are almost as characteristic of the area as the machair. Adam (1987) has likened these western Irish saltings to those of northern Scotland, and the predominance of turf fucoids – turf-like growths of algae such as channel wrack *Pelvetia canaliculata* (L.) – is notable in both areas. Examples of Irish saltmarsh in machair systems may be found at Carnboy, Co. Donegal (Bassett and Curtis, 1985) and in the extensive machair system at Dooaghtry, Co. Mayo.

5.3.3 *Aquatic habitats*

The typical Uist machair loch may lie partially or wholly on shell sand, and the chemistry may be affected by inflow of water from peatland areas or from the sea. Water entering the machair with a pH of 4.5 may acquire a pH of up to 8.1 as it passes through the machair (Ritchie, 1974). Similar lochs occur elsewhere in the Outer Hebrides on Barra (Loch na Doirlinn and Loch Tangusdale) and on Lewis (Loch na Cartach and Loch na Cuilc) where both are being affected by blown sand and the latter shows signs of succumbing. On Tiree, Loch a'Phuill and Loch Bhasapol are fine examples of machair lochs. Shetland has only one loch which lies completely on shell sand, the Loch of Hillwell at Quendale, which is Shetland's largest machair system, though the Loch of Norby and the Loch of Melby at the Crook of Sandness, Kirk Loch at Breckon, Papil Water on Fetlar and Loch Spiggie on Mainland lie partly on machair (A. Douse, personal communication, 1992). Orkney has several machair lochs, notably on Sanday (North Loch, Loch of Riv, Loch of Langamay and Loch of Brue), Egilsay (Manse Loch, Loch of Welland and Loch Watten), and North Ronaldsay (Loch of Garso).

North-west Lewis machair systems tend to be small, with the exception of the now much-eroded Barvas, but there is a sequence of machair-related lochs impounded by shingle on this coast from Loch Dalbeg to Loch Mor Barvas. These lochs are subject to considerable salt spray input and, in the case of Loch Ordais, regular input of saline water on high tides. Loch Mor on Boreray in the Sound of Harris and Loch Ardvule in South Uist are also impounded by shingle and are subject to saline input from sea spray. Orkney has a very large number of lochs impounded by shingle, but only a small number of these are

(Top) A duck nest secreted in shore-line vegetation at Otterswick, Sanday, Orkney.

(Above) The sea urchin, Strongylocentrotus droebachiensis *on a boulder and cobble sea bed off Shetland.*

(Right) Serrated wrack, Fucus serratus.

(Above) Flotsam and jetsam on an exposed cobble shore on Canna together with a young gull chick.

(Left) Arachnanthus sarsi, a deep water species of sea anemone on the sea-bed east of the Garvellachs.

(Below) A mid shore community, comprising bladder wrack (Fucus vesiculosus) with an understorey including Leathesia difformis, thongweed (Himanthalia elongata), the encrusting pink alga, Lithothamnion sp. and the green alga Cladophora rupestris together with the barnacle (Semibalanus balanoides) and the limpet (Patella vulgata).

associated with machair, such as Lea Shun and Loch of Matpow on Stronsay.

Several lochs lying on shell sand have regular inputs of saline water: Oban Irpeig, North Uist; Oban a'Chlachain, North Uist and Loch Bee, South Uist. The brackish lochs have a high species diversity, attributed by Nicol (1936) to the large range of substrates and relatively stable salinities. These lochs display a salinity gradient which is reflected in successions of mysids, gammarids and hydrobiids. The hydrobiid sequence (in order of decreasing salinity) is: *Hydrobia ulvae* (Pennant), *Hydrobia neglecta* Muus, *H.ventrosa* (Montagu) and *Potamopyrgus jenkinsi* (Smith) (Waterston *et al.*, 1979). Species of note which occur in the brackish lochs include the lagoon cockle *Cerastoderma lamarcki* (Reeve) which has a very restricted distribution in the British Isles. An attempt was made to stop the sea flooding the machair at the north end of South Uist sometime prior to 1549, but this seems to have been rather ineffective, and it was not until 1842 that an effective sluice was installed in a causeway at the north-west end of Loch Bee. This loch has the distinction of being connected to both the Atlantic and the Minch, though the latter connection has been constructed by man (Waterston and Lyster, 1979). An Fhaodhail on Tiree was subject to occasional and perhaps regular incursion of saline water till a flap valve was installed recently (Wormell, 1989).

There are several examples of machair loughs in Ireland, notably Termoncarragh Lough and Cross Lough near Belmullet and Bunduff Lough, Co. Sligo, but there are none connected to the sea on even the highest tides, though there is probably a small input of sea spray at the most exposed sites.

Many machair lochs are characterized by a predominance of the *Chara aspera/Myriophyllum alterniflorum* (stonewort-milfoil) community and the influence of blown sand allows stoneworts to flourish at altitudes of up to 50 m in Lewis (Angus, 1991). The Loch of Hillwell supports Shetland's only population of spiked milfoil *Myriophyllum spicatum* (Berry and Johnston, 1980), a species which is frequent in machair lochs in the Western Isles (Pankhurst and Mullin, 1991). The Shetland pondweed *Potamogeton rutilus* occurs in machair lochs in North Uist, Tiree (Pankhurst and Mullin, 1991) and Coll (P. Cashman, personal communication, 1992), though it does not occur in this habitat in Shetland (A. Douse, personal communication, 1991).

One of the main features of interest of machair lochs is that a single loch may include not only a salinity transition going from almost completely saline to completely fresh, but there may be a similar gradation in the trophic status. Ratcliffe (1977) described lagoons as 'the rarest type of coastal habitat', adding that of these the most highly valued type is that showing markedly brackish conditions.

5.3.4 Birds

The environmental variability of machair systems provides exceptionally rich breeding and feeding areas for birds. Their numbers are doubtless considerably enhanced on the islands by the absence of native ground predators and in many cases by aspects of traditional land use. Though the machair is best known for the high densities of waders, important wildfowl may occur in suitable machair systems, and two nationally scarce species, corncrake (*Crex crex*) and corn bunting *(Emberiza calandra)*, are noted machair birds.

Though Shepherd and Stroud (1991) have claimed that virtually the entire machair habitat has been surveyed for breeding birds since 1983, this is true only of the Uists and some of their offshore islands (Fuller *et al.*, 1986), Coll and Tiree (Shepherd and Stroud, 1991) and Ireland (Nairn and Sheppard, 1985). Ornithological surveys of Shetland which included the machair but did not treat it separately suggest that densities of breeding waders are higher than in comparable mainland habitats but are rather lower than those of the Hebrides (A. Douse, personal communication, 1991). Lewis, Harris and Orkney, as well as the mainland machairs, remain largely unsurveyed for birds. Densities of breeding waders in the Uists and Tiree and Coll have been claimed to be among the most important breeding grounds for waders in the north-west Palaearctic (Fuller *et al.*, 1986).

Table 5.2. **Numbers of breeding waders.** The numbers given for Tiree refer to the whole island, only 24% of which is machair, but numbers on other habitats form only a small proportion. Sources: Uists & Barra, Fuller *et al* 1986; Tiree and Coll, Shepherd *et al* 1988; Ireland, Nairn & Sheppard, 1985. Percentages of the UK breeding population are given in the second column for the two best areas. Due to differences in techniques of survey and estimation, numbers may not be directly comparable between areas and are given here for indication only: reference should be made to the sources for more detailed information.

Area	Uists & Barra		Tiree		Coll	Irish Machair
Species						
Lapwing	4350	2.0%	3000	1.4%	500	312
Dunlin	3300	36.0%	350	3.8%	20	121
Redshank	2650	8.2%	600	1.8%	125	17
Snipe	1000–2000	3.3–6.6%	1200	4.0%	500	54
Ringed Plover	2250	26.8%	250	3.0%	30	64
Oystercatcher	2700	7.1%	620	1.6%	150	21

All studies show that the birds are not uniformly distributed over the habitat, and individual species show marked habitat preferences.

The most numerous breeding machair wader in all areas is the lapwing *(Vanellus vanellus)* (Table 5.2). In the Western Isles its most favoured habitat is dune slacks (85 prs/km²), with very high densities on damp grassland and fen (42 prs/km²) and wet cultivated machair (39 prs/km²). Hay meadows, blackland, and dry cultivated machair all have densities in excess of 30 prs/km². Densities are lower in Tiree, the maximum being 37.7 prs/km² on dry machair (compared with 29 prs/km² on dry machair in Uists) and 36.5 prs/km² on coarse wet pasture.

Dunlin *(Calidris alpina)* is the second most important wader in the Uists, which support over one-third of the UK breeding population. Damp grassland/fen is the optimum nesting habitat (66 prs/km²) followed by dune slacks (56 prs/km²), saltmarsh (53 prs/km²) and wet cultivated machair (45 prs/km²). Locally densities can be even higher: one area of approximately 1 km² of wet machair in the Uists had about 300 pairs. The highest numbers on Tiree are found on The Reef, with most of these contributing to the overall density for wet machair of 71.5 prs/km². The only other habitat of major significance is short wet heath (49.2 prs/km²).

In national terms the second most significant species is ringed plover *(Charadrius hiaticula)*, with more than a quarter of the UK population breeding in the Uists, where the highest densities (107 prs/km²) are found on wet cultivated machair. Dry cultivated machair supports 60 prs/km², dune slacks 50 prs/km² and saltmarsh 38 prs/km². On Tiree exceptional densities occur on disused runways (2400 prs/km²) whereas the second best habitat, ploughed areas, holds only 27.8 prs/km².

Large numbers of oystercatchers *(Haematopus ostralegus)* were recorded in the Uists with lower numbers on Tiree. In the Uists they show a preference for dry cultivated machair (27 prs/km²) followed by blackland (24 prs/km²) and dune slacks (21 prs/km²). Though a breeding density of 100 prs/km² was reported from the old runways this was based on a total of only two pairs. The highest numbers breed on dry machair on The Reef.

Redshanks *(Tringa totanus)* are particularly numerous in the Western Isles, nesting mainly in damp grassland and fen (73 prs/km²) and on wet cultivated machair (46 prs/km²). Hay meadows and blackland both support densities of 25 prs/km². Densities are even higher on Tiree, with 128.5 prs/km² on marsh/fen clearly preferred over other habitats where even the best have densities of only 10–20 prs/km².

No snipe *(Gallinago gallinago)* densities were calculated for habitats in the Uists due to difficulties of counting (Fuller *et al.*, 1986) though an earlier survey of Baleshare, North Uist (Fuller, 1981) estimated 14 prs/km² on wet machair and wet blackland. Densities of drumming snipe on Tiree reach 327/km², mainly on The Reef and on Loch an Eilein. Densities of 99/km² were found in reed beds, 61.5/km² on wet machair and 50.8/km² on wet acidic grassland, with several other habitats yielding densities comparable with that of Baleshare.

In terms of overall wader density, the most productive habitat in the Uists is wet cultivated machair (332 prs/km²), dominated by ringed plover. Fen supports 246 prs/km², dune slacks 220 prs/km², damp uncultivated machair 176 prs/km², cultivated machair 160 prs/km² and saltmarsh 140 prs/km². On Tiree the preferred habitat (excluding the old runways) is marsh and fen with 751 prs/km², half of which are snipe, followed by wet machair (221 prs/km²), reed beds (164 prs/km², mainly snipe) and coarse wet pasture (135.5 prs/km²).

The sequence of breeding waders from coast to peatland has been described and figured by Fuller (1982), and this sequence must be regarded as an integral and important aspect of the machair transition.

The machair coasts are frequented by waders during winter and passage, with different species preferring beach, strandline, flooded machair and croft land to different extents. Numbers of sanderling *(Calidris alba)*, ringed plover *(C. hiaticula)*, bar-tailed godwit *(Limosa lapponica)* and turnstone *(Arenaria interpres)* reach national or international levels in the Uists and/or Tiree and Coll, with lower numbers of redshank *(T. totanus)* and curlew *(Numenius arquata)* (Buxton, 1982; Madders and Moser, 1989).

Machair lochs in the Uists have locally important breeding populations of little grebe *(Tachybaptus ruficollis)*, mute swan *(Cygnus olor)*, shoveler *(Anas clypeata)*, tufted duck *(Aythya fuligula)* and, more rarely, scaup *(Aythya marila)*, pintail *(Anas acuta)* and gadwall *(Anas strepera)* (Hopkins and Coxon, 1979; Owen *et al.*, 1986; Cunningham, 1990). The mute swan breeding densities in the Uists are the highest in Britain (Spray, 1991). Wildfowl populations on Tiree often involve similar species, usually in slightly lower numbers (Stroud, 1979). Coot *(Fulica atra)* and moorhen *(Gallinula chloropus)* are important machair loch birds, but they have virtually disappeared from Lewis and Harris, possibly due to the depredations of mink. Shelduck *(Tadorna tadorna)* breed in the dunes of many machair systems.

The Uists are noted for their approximately 2000 indigenous greylags *(Anser anser)*; they tend to breed to the east of the machair systems and winter on the machair, though they frequent a range of habitats throughout the year (Paterson, 1987; Elliott, 1993). Similarly, the 3500 or so barnacle geese *(Branta leucopsis)* which winter in the Outer Hebrides, do so in a variety of habitats, with a significant proportion preferring uninhabited islands; in the case of the Monachs, where the wintering flock may exceed 1000, the islands' isolation may be more important than the machair feeding grounds. The wintering population of barnacle geese in Tiree is shared with Coll and may exceed 1400, with the main wintering grounds on machair and improved grassland (Newton and Percival, 1989; P. Cashman, personal communication, 1992).

The wintering flocks of Greenland white-fronted geese *(Anser albifrons flavirostris)* in the Outer Hebrides are currently insignificant compared with those of Islay, though this was not formerly the case. The steady reduction in numbers from perhaps 5000 in the 1950s to a maximum of 85 in 1987/88 is of concern (Cunningham, Stroud and Fox, 1990). Up to 1100 occur in Tiree and Coll (P. Cashman, personal communication, 1992).

South Uist is noted for its resident mute swans, which were introduced in the late nineteenth century. The population numbers about 830, breeding mainly on machair lochs, and the numbers wintering on Loch Bee may exceed 500 (M. Elliott, personal communication, 1992). Only 7–11 pairs breed on the machair lochs of Tiree, but wintering numbers may reach 100; a link with the Uists population has been established (Newton, 1989). On average, some 30–40 whooper swans *(Cygnus cygnus)* winter in Lewis and Harris, mainly on the coastal lochs of northwest Lewis such as Loch Ordais and on Coll Saltings, though some haunts are outside the machair areas. The machair lochs of the

Uists and Barra also support wintering whooper swans, and there have been reports of sporadic breeding (Cunningham, 1990).

The Outer Hebrides now form the main breeding stronghold of the corncrake, which has declined dramatically elsewhere in Britain over the last century. The total number of singing males in the Outer Hebrides has increased from 260–269 in 1978–79 to 300–324 in 1988, giving these islands 54% of the UK breeding population. Over the same period the Tiree numbers increased from 85 to 99–103 (Hudson *et al.*, 1990). Corncrakes require iris *Iris pseudacorus* beds or other tall vegetation for cover in late May and early June, when the machair vegetation is still very short, and they move to hayfields from July onwards, often moving to cereal crops once the hay is harvested. The home range is in the order of 30 ha, exceptionally 100 ha (RSPB, unpublished report 1992).

The corn bunting differs from the corncrake in that it has undergone a decline within the machair areas as well as nationally. In 1983 there were thought to be 275–365 pairs in the Western Isles, mainly in the Uists (Williams *et al.*, 1986) while there were believed to be 60–100 on Tiree so that the Outer Hebrides and Tiree together hold the greater part of the UK breeding population (Cadbury, 1989). Corn buntings tend to thrive on the low input agriculture which favours corncrakes but are more heavily dependent on arable weeds, which could explain their recent disappearance from Lewis and Harris, where there is now very little machair cultivation.

The red-necked phalarope *(Phalaropus lobatus)* has bred in very small numbers on machair lochs in the Outer Hebrides but prefers other lochs in the Northern Isles. Its sole Irish breeding station is on a machair loch in the Belmullet area, but it is not thought to have bred there recently.

Terns breed in significant numbers on machair in the Northern Isles and, to a lesser extent, in the Hebrides, including the Arctic *(Sterna paradisaea)*, common *(Sterna hirundo)* and little *(Sterna albifrons)* terns, the last being a Schedule 1 species (Species which receive protection at all times under the Wildlife and Countryside Act, 1981). Unlike the other birds of the machair, the terns use the habitat for nesting only, and all feeding is done away from the machair systems.

In parts of Ireland (Merne, 1991) and Islay (R. Macdonald, personal communication, 1992) significant numbers of the scarce chough feed on machair and breed on nearby cliffs.

The work of Nairn and Sheppard (1985, Table 5.1) establishes that Irish machair does not compare with that of Tiree or the Western Isles for breeding birds. Though many of the species listed above for machair breed in the Northern Isles, they do not do so in significant numbers on machair (e.g. Lea and Bourne, 1975). Though the high densities noted for North and South Uist and Benbecula extend to some of the larger islands in the Sound of Harris, neither Barra nor Lewis and Harris supports comparable numbers of waders or wildfowl, though both have significant numbers of corncrakes.

Wilson (1978) has shown that generally waders breeding on machair prefer to nest on cultivated or recently cultivated ground, but require longer established vegetation for feeding. Oystercatcher and ringed plover particularly preferred open areas on ploughed land or in poor growth of cereals, but dunlin nesting habitat could be destroyed by ploughing. The strip cultivation was thought to be of major benefit to waders in that the habitat diversity enabled birds to breed at higher densities.

5.3.4 Mammals

Machair is not particularly noted for its mammals, though species (e.g. Orkney vole *Microtus arvalis*) and subspecies of mice and voles confined to the Hebrides or Northern Isles are found on machair but are not restricted to it. Tiree and Pabbay (Sound of Harris) lack rabbits and thus provide valuable sites for comparison in studies of the effects of grazing on vegetation and erosion. Widespread introductions of hedgehogs to islands and of mink and polecat to Lewis and Harris pose a considerable threat to ground-nesting birds in areas with no native ground predators. Tiree machair has introduced brown hares while Pabbay has introduced red deer which frequent the machair.

Though grey seals breed mainly on rocky islets, the colony on the Monach Isles has expanded dramatically in recent times, so that it is now the largest grey seal colony in the UK in terms of pup production, and probably the second largest in the world. It has been suggested that grey seals would prefer sandy beaches for breeding but there are very few areas so undisturbed as the Monachs, where the seals utilize not only the beaches but the adjoining machair (D. Thompson, Sea Mammal Research Unit, personal communication, 1992).

5.3.5 Invertebrates

Much of the work done on the invertebrates of the Outer Hebrides has been confined to species recording, usually at the level of island groups rather than by habitat or precise location, summarized by Waterston (1981). One of the most interesting species is the moth the belted beauty *Lycia zonaria* (D. and S.) which occurs in western Ireland, northern England and Ardnamurchan, and in the Inner and Outer Hebrides. This distribution is difficult to explain, as the females are flightless (Waterston, 1981). Many other noteworthy insects including several Red Data Book species were recorded in machair systems in Lewis and Harris by MacGowan (1986).

A survey by the Institute of Terrestrial Ecology revealed distinct communities of invertebrates in the Outer Hebrides compared with dune sites elsewhere in Scotland, possibly due to shelter, but it could be the 'island effect' (Nature Conservancy Counil, 1986). The fossorial bee *Colletes floralis* Evers. lives on south-facing banks of sand in the Outer Hebrides, Tiree and Donegal (Waterston, 1981).

Snail numbers decrease towards the moorland, and numbers are clearly related to the calcium content of the machair (M. Elliott, personal communication, 1992). In damp weather vast numbers of helicid snails may be seen on dunes and machair, mainly the heath snail *Helicella itala* (L.) and the pointed snail *Cochlicella acuta* (Müller), but locally *Cepaea hortensis* (Müller) and the so-called common snail *Helix aspersa* (Müller) occur. In Tiree *Cepaea hortensis* (Müller) occurs with the related *C.nemoralis* (L.), and the latter is the commoner species on Irish machairs. The moss bladder snail *Aplexa hypnorum* (L.) which has a very restricted distribution in Scotland has been reported from the Monachs, the Uists and Tiree (Nature Conservancy Council, 1986).

Boyd (1960) noted profound differences between the invertebrate fauna of grazed machair and adjacent ungrazed machair.

The rare saltmarsh beetle *Dicheirotrichus gustavi* has recently been recorded from the Outer Hebrides (Nature Conservancy Council, 1986).

The distinctive invertebrate fauna of Irish machair, which has elements in common with the fauna of the Scottish island machairs, is described by Speight (1991).

5.4   Man and Machair

Machair is rich in archaeological remains: man's association with machair goes back at least 5000 years in Scotland (Crawford, 1981) and possibly as much as 8000 years in Ireland (Bassett and Curtis, 1985). Important digs have been carried out at Northton (Simpson, 1976), the Udal (Crawford, 1963–90) and at Rosinish, Benbecula (Shepherd, 1976). Armit (1992) has drawn attention to the huge number of archaeological remains at Traigh na Berie in Uig, Lewis, where over 50 monuments (excluding blackhouses and associated structures) have been identified in a study area of approximately 3 km by 4 km. In Orkney, Skara Brae is on machair, as are Jarlshof and St. Ninian's Chapel on Shetland. Irish machair also has large numbers of archaeological remains, though not so many of these have been excavated (T. Curtis, personal communication, 1992). Ireland has also yielded traces of cultivation ridges, the 'feannagan' which still survive in the Hebrides. In addition to buried buildings and walls, machair preserves a historic landscape. This rich heritage is threatened throughout the machair areas by marine and anthropogenic erosion.

There are similarities in the human history and usage of machair in Ireland and Scotland up until the end of the nineteenth century, and it may be that the crofting act of 1886 was instrumental in retaining the high level of cultivation in parts of the Scottish machair which have now virtually vanished from Ireland, where even hay crops are rare on machair, though local cultivation persists in parts of Donegal (Curtis, 1984). The near-absence of cultivation in Ireland has been attributed to the post-famine population collapse (T. Curtis, personal communication, 1992).

The main crops in the Uists are hay and cereals – rye *Secale cereale* and the short black oat *Avena strigosa*. The distinguishing aspects of this cultivation are that it is rotational and is in unfenced plots rather than fields, with patches left fallow for two years or more. Though traditional practices are still followed there is an increasing tendency to make silage, mainly from cereals (M. Elliott, personal communication, 1992) and to store the silage in black 'big bale' bags; this may give rise to the sort of litter and erosion problem which has been associated with bagged silage on Irish machair. Cultivation of the machair in Lewis and Harris is now virtually confined to a few patches of potatoes (which are also grown in the Uists).

Significant areas of Orkney and Tiree and some Irish machair systems have been undersown with grasses such as perennial rye-grass *Lolium perenne* leading to a decline in flowering plant diversity.

All machair is grazed by sheep or cattle, or both. Sheep are the main grazing animal on most machairs, but the grazing density and the sheep : cattle ratios are all-important in determining the quality of machair for wildlife and for the long-term interest of grazing. In Orkney, cattle predominate (Bullard, 1975). The ratio of cattle to sheep in Tiree is about 1 : 3, in the Uists 1 : 20, in Lewis and Harris 1 : 264 though these figures apply to the whole island groups and the situation on machair may be very different. In Lewis and Harris, however, most of the cattle are in dairy herds on Stornoway farms, and there is little cattle grazing on machair. This has implications for erosion, as described by Angus and Elliott (1992). There is a traditional pattern of grazing cattle only in the winter, allowing crops to be grown; the stock is summered on the hill land (or on the *sliabh* in Tiree) so that they do not suffer from the cobalt deficiencies associated with machair. With mineral supplements now available, this practice is decreasing, and cattle may be grazed all year round, as they are at some sites of outstanding botanical interest in Ireland.

Seaweed has traditionally been spread on the machair prior to cultivation to add valuable nutrients (the soil is deficient in manganese and cobalt) and help prevent erosion, but between 1735 and 1822 it was burned for kelp ash for the proprietors. Angus and Elliott (1992) have described how the land came to be neglected during this period not merely due to the lack of seaweed application, but also due to physical damage from the horses and carts used for transport in connection with the kelp manufacture. By the time the kelp market collapsed in 1822, the human population had risen enormously, but the land was unable to cope with the increased numbers. The people who had been required to make kelp (and money) for the landlords were now surplus to requirements, and the decline in the kelp industry, which had often been closely associated with machair, played a key role in the clearances which followed its collapse.

As previously noted, machair is the only major habitat type to have been named in Gaelic. There are songs and stories about the machair in Gaelic (Angus, 1993), and the language and its more obscure vocabulary are as worthy of conservation as its wildlife. The cultural links between man and machair could hardly be stronger, and the human story is inextricably linked with that of machair.

The early association between Man and machair is demonstrated in the numerous, well-preserved archaeological remains which occur throughout the machair areas, and it should be remembered that the study of these remains reveals information not only about the former human inhabitants and their way of life, but also of the history of the natural environment and machair development and sand mobility in particular.

Today the machair systems are extensively used for recreation, from widespread pastimes such as walking and bird watching to sand yachting and access for swimming and windsurfing; indeed, Tiree is said to represent one of the finest locations for windsurfing in the UK because it offers easy access and superb surfing conditions no matter what the wind direction. Evidence of other recreational activity can often be seen in the form of goal posts, whether they be for soccer in Scotland or Gaelic Football in Ireland.

Tourists are attracted to the machair of the Scottish islands for scenery and wildlife, and interest in a different human lifestyle. A shortage of car parking near some favoured sites encourages visitors to drive on the machair, and car-bound picnickers cause particular damage by driving close to the eroding machair front to obtain a sea view thus adding to the instability of the edge.

An analysis of management problems is beyond the scope of this paper: those associated with erosion have already been described by Angus and Elliott (1992); but the role of recreation and grazing should also be considered.

5.5 Landscape

Seen in summer, machair is spectacular: the combination of landform, machair lochs, agricultural mosaic, and expanses of wild flowers which change as the season progresses, gives a rich variety of colour. The mountain backdrop and the intense colour of offshore sand often contrasting with scattered, dark, seaweed-covered rocks, greatly enhances the experience, as do the changing light patterns and, in parts of the Uists and Tiree, a near 180° vista. The view from the sea should also be considered in these maritime communities, where boats are regularly used for work and leisure by local people. The machair makes a major contribution to Hebrideans' 'sense of place', even for people who live some distance away from machair systems. Traditional forms of agriculture and architecture contribute to the landscape experience, and it is interesting to note that Tiree seems to have retained more of its older traditional buildings than the Outer Hebrides.

The importance of flowers to the visual experience of the Uists has been stressed by the Countryside Commission for Scotland in their description of the National Scenic Area, referring to the impression, so easily gained early in the season, that the cultivated areas of the machair appear to grow crops of wild flowers rather than grain. Murray (1973) has described in graphic terms how the humble daisy had provided him with a splendid display of white on his ascent of Chaipaval, above Northton, only for this to be exchanged for pink as the flowers closed during his evening descent. Likewise the birds are an essential part of the machair landscape.

5.6 Designations

The conservation importance of machair has been recognized throughout its range by the designation at both national and international level of a substantial proportion of its area for a variety of purposes.

Most of the Outer Hebridean machair falls within two National Scenic Areas: only the machairs of Broad Bay and some small systems on the north-west coast of Lewis are omitted.

The only machair National Nature Reserves are in the Outer Hebrides: the Monach Isles, off North Uist, and Loch Druidibeg in South Uist. Approximately 30 Sites of Special Scientific Interest (SSSI) have been notified on machair, almost all in the islands. Of these, Balranald in North Uist is a Royal Society for the Protection of Birds Reserve. Termoncarragh Lough in Belmullet, Co. Mayo, is a reserve administered by the Irish Wild Bird Conservancy.

Of the 50 machair sites listed for Ireland by Curtis (1991a) 29 have been designated as Areas of Scientific Interest by the National Parks and Wildlife Service of the Office of Public Works. Five of these sites are believed to be of international importance (Table 5.3).

In 1988 the machair of the Uists, Benbecula, Barra and Vatersay, comprising about 7500 ha in total, was designated an Environmentally Sensitive Area (ESA) under Section 18 of the Agriculture Act 1986 (Department of Agriculture and Fisheries for Scotland, 1989). Crofters are offered incentives (on a purely voluntary basis) to manage their crofts and common grazings on a traditional basis. The objectives may be summarized as: limiting the use of chemicals, encouraging late cutting of hay and silage; encouraging the use of organic fertilizers and rotational cropping; and encouraging positive conservation measures. ESAs have been announced by the Secretary of State for Scotland covering the whole of Shetland and the Argyll Islands which will include significant areas of machair. The Mannin Bay area of Co. Galway in Ireland has been similarly designated.

Though few machair sites have yet been designated as Special Protection Areas as part of the EC Council Directive on the Conservation of Wild Birds 1979 (Stroud *et al.*, 1990) a substantial proportion of the habitat is a candidate for such designation, reflecting the scale of importance of machair for birds alone. Machair has been listed on the 1992 EC Species and Habitats Directive, though it is too early to predict the proportion which will be designated. Irish machair and the saline machair lochs of the Outer Hebrides and Northern Isles have been given priority status under this directive.

The only machair site designated under the Unesco Man and the Biosphere Reserve Programme is Loch Druidibeg, South Uist. There are no machair World Heritage Sites.

5.7 Discussion

The role of man in enhancing the conservation value of machair has been highlighted in this paper, but the positive influence of cultivation on the

Table 5.3. Designated areas of machair systems on Scottish islands. Measurements of areas are not given as the sites often include substantial areas of other habitats. The entries signifying "candidate" for candidate SPA and Ramsar have been taken from "List A" in Stroud *et al* 1990 which has been superseded but not finalised.

Loch na Cartach, Lewis	SSSI
Gress Saltings, Lewis	SSSI
Tong Saltings, Lewis	SSSI
Loch Dalbeg	SSSI
Traigh na Berie	cSSSI, NSA
Mangersta, Lewis	SSSI
Luskentyre Banks & Saltings, Harris	SSSI*, NSA
Northton Bay, Harris	SSSI*, NSA
Pabbay, Harris	cSSSI*, NSA, cSPA
Berneray, Harris	cSSSI, cSPA
Machairs Robach & Newton, North Uist	SSSI, NSA, ESA
Vallay, North Uist	SSSI, NSA, ESA
Baleshare & Kirkibost, North Uist	SSSI*, ESA, cSPA, cRamsar
Balranald & Loch nam Feithean Bogs	SSSI*, ESA, RSPB Reserve, cSPA, cRamsar
Monach Isles, North Uist	SSSI*, NNR, cSPA
Loch Bee, South Uist	SSSI, ESA, cSPA, cRamsar
Loch Bee Machair, South Uist	SSSI, ESA, cSPA, cRamsar
Bornish – Ormiclate Machair, South Uist	SSSI, NSA, ESA, cSPA, cRamsar
Loch Druidibeg, South Uist	SSSI*, NNR, NSA, ESA, SPA, Ramsar, Man & Biosphere Reserve
Howmore Estuary, Lochs Roag & Fada, S.Uist	SSSI, NSA, ESA, cSPA, cRamsar
Loch Hallan, South Uist	SSSI, NSA, ESA, cSPA, cRamsar
Eoligarry, Barra	SSSI, ESA
Central Sanday, Orkney	SSSI
Northwall, Sanday, Orkney	SSSI, cSPA, cRamsar
North Ronaldsay Coast	cSPA, cRamsar
Burrafirth, Unst	NSA cESA
Balta, Unst, Shetland	SSSI, cESA
Quendale, Shetland	SSSI, cESA
Breckon, Yell, Shetland	SSSI, cESA
Lochs of Spiggie & Brow, Shetland	SSSI*, NSA, cSPA, cRamsar, cESA
Sandwick, Unst, Shetland	cESA
St Ninian's Tombolo, Shetland	SSSI, NSA, cESA
Ceann a'Mhara – Loch a'Phuill, Tiree	SSSI*
An Fhaodhail & The Reef, Tiree	SSSI, cSPA, cESA
Hough Bay-Balevullin Machair, Tiree	SSSI, cSPA, cESA
Totamore Dunes, Coll	SSSI, cSPA, cESA
Crossapol and Gunna, Coll	SSSI, cSPA, cESA
The Rhinns, Islay (includes Machir Bay)	SSSI, cESA, part is cSPA and cRamsar
North Colonsay	SSSI, cSPA, cESA
Oronsay	SSSI, cESA
Calgary Bay, Mull	SSSI, cESA

Key: SSSI = Site of Special Scientific Interest, asterisk denotes Key Site; NSA = National Scenic Area; ESA = Environmentally Sensitive Area; SPA = Special Protection Area. The prefix "c" against any of these designations denotes a candidacy for (but not necessarily an intention of) designation.

countryside conservation interest of machair is restricted to traditional forms of agriculture as still practised in the Uists; the increasingly widespread 'improvement' of machair to bring it into more intensive agricultural production has a correspondingly negative effect on the wildlife and scenic value.

In the absence of grazing, as demonstrated by a fenced area on the Reef (Boyd, 1960) *Festuca rubra* forms a dense mat to the exclusion of other species. Boyd believed, as did Vose *et al.* (1956) that machair is a plagioclimax, and that if grazing was removed permanently it would become a heather *Calluna vulgaris* or purple moor-grass *Molinia caerulea* heath, depending on drainage, with rank *Festuca* as a stage in this succession. There are patches of *Calluna* on sand (not blackland) on the Loch Bee SSSI in South Uist, (M. Elliott, personal communication, 1990) while machair at the Bay of London on Eday, Orkney, is dominated by *Calluna* and *Erica* (Mather *et al.*, 1974). The introduction of seasonal grazing on Colonsay has resulted in greater prominence of ragwort *Senecio jacobaea* and burnet rose *Rosa pimpinellifolia* (R. Macdonald, personal communication, 1990).

In formulating any conservation policy for machair, the sand supply must be afforded a very high priority. Ritchie (1979) suggests that the volume of sand in the Uists is roughly constant, so that removal of significant quantities of sediment from any part of a dynamic system could have an adverse effect throughout that system. Mate (1991) has questioned this conclusion, indicating that the sand supply is not so limiting, but until the question is resolved it is advisable to adopt a cautious approach to exploitation of any sand from a machair system.

Machair is such a restricted and valuable habitat that any attempt to prioritize areas for conservation is almost invidious. It must be stressed, however, that the people who live on the machair, and who are largely responsible for the value of the habitat today, have certain expectations, such as traditional sand and gravel extraction and exploitation for tourism, which must in some isolated cases be regarded as threats. There are also natural threats, notably that of coastal retreat, to which must be added the anthropogenic 'biological' threats in the form of rabbits and introduced ground predators; if mink establish themselves in the Uists by crossing the Sound of Harris the consequences for the internationally important numbers of ground-nesting birds could be catastrophic. Resources can and should be allocated to alleviate these problems where it is possible to do so, and it is reasonable to prioritize the habitat in order to allocate resources most effectively. Even when applying funds which are exclusively environmental, the human perception of the nature and extent of problems should be incorporated, and local people should ideally be involved in decision-making in order to give a sense of ownership of the asset as well as the problem within the community.

Tiree lacks the geomorphology and landscape designations of the Outer Hebrides and parts of the Northern Isles, while the number and range of machair loch types in the Outer Hebrides is unrivalled. Only the Outer

Hebrides and Tiree have the internationally important breeding birds, while Ireland has geomorphology, botany and landscape interest. Additionally, many of the Orkney machairs have been agriculturally improved to such an extent that they no longer resemble the 'natural' habitat except in land-form. Mainland machairs tend to be small, and even the largest such as Sandwood tend not to have the high breeding bird numbers of the islands. This crude analysis points to the Outer Hebrides as being *the* outstanding machair area, and even a more localized analysis based on Table 5.3 would seem to point to the Outer Hebrides as the machair area of highest quality.

Machair is by any standards a habitat of outstanding value for wildlife, landscape and geomorphology interest. It is a habitat and landscape created by sea, climate, and man, with considerable cultural values, and is almost (but not quite) uniquely Scottish. There is a considerable literature in both Scottish and Irish Gaelic and a vast amount of information vital to the understanding of machair held in the heads of people who live there; conservationists must use this information.

The foregoing analysis identifies gaps in the survey information, if not on the part of the author. The conservation organizations require more base-level information on the habitat and its extent, and more study is needed of management problems aimed at solving these. Perceptions differ, and islanders must be full and active participants in any attempts by conservation bodies not only in addressing machair problems, but in identifying them. There are considerable advantages to be gained from sharing information between the various machair areas, particularly between Scotland and Ireland, and this again should not be confined to the academics but should involve those who live and work with the machair.

The beach reports commissioned from Aberdeen University Geography Department by one of Scottish Natural Heritage's predecessor bodies, the Countryside Commission for Scotland, are still of immense value for conservationists today, but a new survey of the beaches of Scotland, from the viewpoint of SNH's broader remit, and the social circumstances of the 1990s, would be an immensely valuable tool in the conservation of this valued habitat; modern techniques such as Geographical Information Systems are available to help in analyses, while the greater awareness of the value of machair systems on the part of local people would be a great advantage in formulating management policies for the future.

The SNH Peatland Management Schemes for the blanket bogs of Sutherland and Caithness have shown how it is possible for local people to benefit the environment and themselves through financial incentives. The Uists, Benbecula, Barra and Vatersay ESA has begun to tackle the problem in part of the machair area of Scotland, but it has not addressed all the problems or all the areas of machair, and there may be a case for a Machair Management Scheme analogous to the Peatland scheme.

Though interest in machair among the academic community was considerable in the 1970s, and there was intense survey activity in the Uists in the 1980s, the widespread study of machair has only recently been revived, and now incorporates the Irish element, which must be warmly welcomed, as it promotes an integrated trans-national approach. Until recently, however, there was a tendency on the part of academics to study only the habitat and biota, and discuss these only with other academics. Fortunately this attitude has virtually disappeared, and it is vital that local people be involved in any future studies and discussions: while designations have a necessary role in countryside conservation, the real world of the north of Scotland and the north-west of Ireland dictates that effective protection for this outstanding habitat should incorporate 'conservation by conversation'.

Acknowledgements

I would like to thank Dr M. M. Elliott (Lochaber), Dr A. S. MacLennan (Inverness), Dr Nigel Buxton (Inverness), Patrick Cashman (Argyll), Dr Andrew Douse (Shetland), Liz McTeague (Orkney) and Dr Ronald Macdonald (Islay) of Scottish Natural Heritage for their valuable comments on an earlier draft of this paper. Dr Tom Curtis of the Irish National Parks and Wildlife Service, Dublin, generously contributed comments on the Irish situation. Dr John Miles of the Scottish Office and an anonymous referee gave helpful comments.

References

Adam, P. 1981. The vegetation of British salt marshes. *New Phytologist*, **88**, 143–96.

Adam, P. 1987. Some observations on Irish saltmarsh vegetation. *Bulletin of the Irish Biogeographical Society*, **10**, 42–55.

Akeroyd, J. R. and Curtis, T. G. F. 1980. Some observations on the occurrence of machair in western Ireland. *Bulletin of the Irish Biogeographical Society*, **4**, 1–12.

Anderson, J. 1785 *An Account of the Present State of the Hebrides and west coast of Scotland.* Report to the Lords of the Treasury.

Angus, S. 1991. Climate and vegetation of the Outer Hebrides. In Pankhurst, R. J. and Mullin, J. M. (Eds), *Flora of the Outer Hebrides*, Natural History Museum Publications, London, 28–31.

Angus, S. 1993. The meaning and use of the word machair in Gaelic and English. *Hebridean Naturalist*, **11**, 41–9.

Angus, S. and Elliott, M. M. 1992. Erosion in Scottish machair with particular reference to the Outer Hebrides. In Carter, R. W. G., Curtis, T. G. F. and Sheehy-Skeffington, M. J. (Eds), *Coastal Dunes: Geomorphology, Ecology and Management for Conservation*, A. A. Balkema, Rotterdam, 93–112.

Armit, I. 1992. *Archaeological Field Survey of the Bhaltos (Valtos) Peninsula, Lewis.* Unpublished report to Historic Scotland.

Bassett, J. A. and Curtis, T. G. F. 1985. The nature and occurrence of sand dune machair in Ireland. *Proceedings of the Royal Irish Academy*, **85B**, 1–20.

Berry, R. J. and Johnston, J. L. 1980. *The Natural History of Shetland*. Collins, London.

Boyd, J. M. 1960. Studies of the differences between the fauna of grazed and ungrazed grassland in Tiree, Argyll. *Proceedings of the Zoological Society of London*, **135**, 33–54.

Bullard, E. R. 1975. Orkney habitats: an outline ecological framework. In *The Natural Environment of Orkney: Proceedings of the Nature Conservancy Council Symposium* held in Edinburgh 26–27 November 1974, Nature Conservancy Council, Edinburgh, 19–28.

Bullard, E. R. and Goode, D. A. 1975. The vegetation of Orkney. In *The Natural Environment of Orkney: Proceedings of the Nature Conservancy Council Symposium* held in Edinburgh 26–27 November 1974, Nature Conservancy Council, Edinburgh, 31–46.

Buxton, N. E. 1982. Wintering waders on the Atlantic shores of the Uists and Benbecula. *Scottish Birds,* **12,** 106–13.

Cadbury 1989. Corncrake and corn bunting status and habitats on Tiree and Coll, Inner Hebrides. In Stroud, D. A. (Ed), *Birds on Coll and Tiree,* 51–66.

Clapham, A. R., Tutin, T. G. and Moore, D. M. 1987. *Flora of the British Isles* (Third Edition). Cambridge University Press, Cambridge.

Crawford, I. A., 1963–90. Series of interim and unpublished reports on the excavations at Udal, North Uist (as cited in Ritchie, 1979).

Crawford, I. A. 1981. Towards an integrated general knowledge of machair – the need for intimate field observation and the real demands of the inter-disciplinary approach. In Ranwell, D. S. (Ed.), 1978. *Sand Dune Machair,* **3,** 20–4. Institute of Terrestrial Ecology, Norwich.

Crawford, I. 1991. Agriculture, weeds and the Western Isles machair. *Transactions of the Botanical Society of Edinburgh,* **45,** 483–92.

Cunningham, P. 1990. *Birds of the Outer Hebrides.* (Second Edition). Mercat Press, Edinburgh.

Cunningham, P., Stroud, D. A. and Fox, A. D. 1990. Greenland white-fronted geese in the Outer Hebrides. *Hebridean Naturalist,* **10,** 64–8.

Curtis, T. G. F. 1984. Sand dune machair in Ireland. *The Badger,* **18,** 12–13.

Curtis, T. G. F. 1991a. A site inventory of the sandy coasts of Ireland: their types and distribution. In Quigley, M. B. (Ed), 1991. *A Guide to the Sand Dunes of Ireland.* Compiled for the Third Congress of the European Union for Dune Conservation and Coastal Management. Galway, 6–17.

Curtis, T. G. F. 1991b. The flora and vegetation of sand dunes in Ireland. In Quigley, M. B. (Ed), 1991. *A Guide to the Sand Dunes of Ireland.* (Compiled for the Third Congress of the European Union for Dune Conservation and Coastal Management). Galway, 42–66.

Darling, F. F. 1947. *Natural History in the Highlands and Islands.* Collins, London.

Darling, F. F. and Boyd, J. M. 1964. *The Highlands and Islands.* Collins, London.

Department of Agriculture and Fisheries for Scotland. 1989. *Environmentally Sensitive Areas in Scotland: A First Report.* DAFS, Edinburgh.

Elliott, M. M. 1993. Greylag goose counts in the Uists from 1986 to 1991. *Hebridean Naturalist,* **11,** 56–60.

Ferreira, R. E. C. 1987. *Uig, Isle of Lewis: Coastal Vegetation Survey.* (Unpublished report to Nature Conservancy Council, Inverness).

Fuller, R. J. 1981. The breeding habitats of waders on North Uist machair. *Scottish Birds,* **11,** 142–52.

Fuller, R. J. 1982. *Bird Habitats in Britain.* Poyser, Calton.

Fuller, R. J., Reed, T. M., Buxton, N. E., Webb, A., Williams, T. D. and Pienkowski, M. W. 1986. Populations of breeding waders Charadriidae and their habitats on the crofting lands of the Outer Hebrides, Scotland. *Biological Conservation,* **37,** 333–61.

Gimingham, C. H. 1964. Maritime and sub-maritime communities. In Burnett, J. H. (Ed), *The Vegetation of Scotland,* Oliver & Boyd, Edinburgh, 67–142.

Hopkins, P. G. and Coxon, P. 1979. Birds of the Outer Hebrides: waterfowl. *Proceedings of the Royal Society of Edinburgh,* **77B,** 431–44.

Hudson, A. V., Stowe, T. J. and Aspinall, S. J. 1990. Status and distribution of corncrakes in Britain in 1988. *Scottish Birds,* **83,** 173–87.

Law, D. and Gilbert, D. 1986. *Saltmarsh Survey – NW Scotland: The Western Isles.* (Unpublished report to Nature Conservancy Council, Inverness).

Lea, D. and Bourne, W. R. P. 1975. The birds of Orkney. In *The Natural Environment of Orkney: Proceedings of the Nature Conservancy Council Symposium* held in Edinburgh 26–27 November 1974, Nature Conservancy Council, Edinburgh, 98–121.

MacArthur, R. H. and Wilson, E. O. 1967. *The Theory of Island Biogeography*. Princeton University Press, Princeton.

MacGowan, I. 1986. *Invertebrate Survey, Lewis and Harris, July 1986*. (Unpublished report to Nature Conservancy Council, Inverness).

MacKintosh, J. and Urquhart, A. 1983. *Survey of the Haymeadows of the Uists*. (Unpublished report to Nature Conservancy Council, Edinburgh).

MacLeod, A. M. 1949. Some aspects of the plant ecology of the Island of Barra. *Transactions of the Botanical Society of Edinburgh*, **35**, 67–81.

Madders, M. and Moser, M. 1989. Coastal waders in winter on Tiree and Coll. In Stroud, D. A. (Ed.), *Birds on Coll and Tiree*, Scottish Ornithologists' Club / Nature Conservancy Council, Edinburgh, 67–74.

Mate, I. D. 1991. The theoretical development of machair in the Hebrides. *Scottish Geographical Magazine*, **108**, 35–8.

Mather, A. S. and Ritchie, W. 1977. *The Beaches of the Highlands and Islands of Scotland*. Countryside Commission for Scotland, Battleby.

Mather, A. S., Smith, J. S. and Ritchie, W. 1974. *Beaches of Orkney*. (Unpublished report to Countryside Commission for Scotland by Geography Department, University of Aberdeen).

Mather, A. S., Ritchie, W. and Smith, J. S. 1975. An introduction to the morphology of the Orkney coastline. In *The Natural Environment of Orkney: Proceedings of the Nature Conservancy Council Symposium* held in Edinburgh 26–27 November 1974, Nature Conservancy Council, Edinburgh, 10–18.

Merne, O. J. 1991. Birds of Irish dunes – a review. In Quigley, M. B. (Ed), *A Guide to the Sand Dunes of Ireland*. Compiled for the Third Congress of the European Union for Dune Conservation and Coastal Management. Galway, 72–6.

Murray, W. H. 1973. *The Islands of Western Scotland*. Eyre Methuen, London.

Nairn, R. G. W. and Sheppard, J. R. 1985. Breeding waders of sand dune machair in north-west Ireland. *Irish Birds*, **3**, 53–70.

Nature Conservancy Council. 1978. *Orkney: Localities of Geological and Geomorphological Importance*. Geology and Physiography Section, Nature Conservancy Council, Newbury, Berkshire.

Nature Conservancy Council. 1986. *Agriculture and Environment in the Outer Hebrides*. (Unpublished report, Nature Conservancy Council, Edinburgh).

Newton, S. F. 1989. Wintering wildfowl of Coll and Tiree. In Stroud, D. A. (Ed.), *Birds on Coll and Tiree*, Scottish Ornithologists' Club / Nature Conservancy Council, Edinburgh, 99–114.

Newton, S. F. and Percival, S. M. 1989. Barnacle geese on Coll and Tiree. In Stroud, D. A. (Ed.), *Birds on Coll and Tiree*, Scottish Ornithologists' Club / Nature Conservancy Council, Edinburgh, 115–28.

Nicol, E. A. T. 1936. The brackish-water lochs of North Uist. *Proceedings of the Royal Society of Edinburgh*, **56**, 169–95.

Owen, M., Atkinson-Willes, G. L. and Salmon, D. 1986. *Wildfowl in Great Britain*. Second Edition. Cambridge University Press, Cambridge.

Pankhurst, R. J. and Mullin, J. M. 1991. *Flora of the Outer Hebrides*. Natural History Museum Publications, London.

Paterson, I. W. 1987. The status and distribution of Greylag Geese *Anser anser* in the Uists, Scotland. *Bird Study*, **34**, 235–38.

Perring, F. H. and Randall, R. E. 1972. An annotated flora of the Monach Isles National Nature Reserve, Outer Hebrides. *Transactions of the Botanical Society of Edinburgh*, **41**, 431–44.

Pitkin, P., Barter, G., Curry, P., Mackintosh, J., Orange, A. and Urquhart, U. 1983. *A Botanical Review of the SSSIs of the N and W coasts of the Uists and Nearby Islands*. (Unpublished report, Scottish Field Unit, Nature Conservancy Council, Edinburgh).

Ranwell, D. S. 1974. Machair in relation to the British sand dune series. In Ranwell, D. S. (Ed.),

Sand Dune Machair: Report of a Seminar at Coastal Ecology Research Station, Norwich, Institute of Terrestrial Ecology, 4–5.

Ranwell, D. S. 1981. Biological influences in some units of sand dune landscapes. In Ranwell, D. S. (Ed.), *Sand Dune Machair*, Institute of Terrestrial Ecology, Norwich, **3**, 29–34.

Ratcliffe, D. A. 1977. *A Nature Conservation Review*. 2 vols. Cambridge University Press, Cambridge.

Ritchie, W. 1967. The machair of South Uist. *Scottish Geographical Magazine*, **83**, 161–73.

Ritchie, W. 1971. *The Beaches of Barra and the Uists*. Report to Countryside Commission for Scotland by Geography Department, University of Aberdeen.

Ritchie, W. 1974. Spatial variation of shell content between and within 'machair' systems. In Ranwell, D. S. (Ed.), *Sand Dune Machair: Report of a Seminar at Coastal Ecology Research Station, Norwich*, Institute of Terrestrial Ecology, 9–12.

Ritchie, W. 1976. The meaning and definition of machair. *Transactions and Proceedings of the Botanical Society of Edinburgh*, **42**, 431–40.

Ritchie, W. 1979. Machair development and chronology in the Uists and adjacent islands. *Proceedings of the Royal Society of Edinburgh*, **77B**, 107–22.

Ritchie, W. 1981. The beach, dunes and machair landforms of Pabbay, Sound of Harris. In Ranwell, D. S. (Ed.), *Sand Dune Machair*, **3**, 13–19. Institute of Terrestrial Ecology, Norwich.

Ritchie, W. 1985. Inter-tidal and sub-tidal organic deposits and sea level changes in the Uists, Outer Hebrides. *Scottish Journal of Geology*, **21**, 161–76.

Ritchie, W. and Mather, A. S. 1970. *The Beaches of Lewis and Harris*. Report to Countryside Commission for Scotland by Geography Department, University of Aberdeen.

Ritchie, W. and Mather, A. S. 1972. Cementation in high latitude dunes. *Coastal Studies Bulletin*, **7**, 95–112. H. H. Roberts Coastal Studies Institute, Louisiana State University, Technical Report No. 131.

Shaw, M. W., Hewett, D. G. and Pizzey, J. M. 1983. *Scottish Coastal Survey, Main Report: A Report on Selected Soft Coast Sites in Scotland*. (Unpublished report by Institute of Terrestrial Ecology, ITE Project No. 340, Bangor).

Sheehy-Skeffington, M. J. and Wymer, E. D. 1991. Irish salt marshes – an outline review. In Quigley, M. B. (Ed), *A Guide to the Sand Dunes of Ireland*. Compiled for the Third Congress of the European Union for Dune Conservation and Coastal Management, Galway, 77–91.

Shepherd, I. A. G. 1976. Preliminary results from the Beaker settlement at Rosinish, Benbecula. *British Archaeological Reports*, No. 33, 209–19.

Shepherd, K. B. 1989. Breeding wader distribution, ecology and numbers. In Stroud, D. A. (Ed.), *Birds on Coll and Tiree*, Scottish Ornithologists' Club / Nature Conservancy Council, Edinburgh, 25–41.

Shepherd, K. B. and Stroud, D. 1991. Breeding waders and their conservation on the wetlands of Tiree and Coll, Outer Hebrides. *Wildfowl*, **42**, 108–17.

Shepherd, K. B., Green, M., Knight, A. C. and Stroud, D. A. 1988. *The Breeding Birds of Tiree and Coll in 1987/88 with Special Emphasis on Breeding Waders*. NCC Chief Scientists Directorate commissioned research report No. 827 (unpublished). Nature Conservancy Council, Peterborough.

Simpson, D. D. A. 1976. The later Neolithic and Beaker settlement at Northton, Isle of Harris. *British Archaeolical Reports*, **33**, 221–31.

Speight, M. 1991. The fauna of Irish sand dunes. In Quigley, M. B. (Ed), *A Guide to the Sand Dunes of Ireland*. Compiled for the Third Congress of the European Union for Dune Conservation and Coastal Management. Galway, pp. 67–71.

Spray, C. J. 1991. Population dynamics of mute swans *Cygnus olor* in the Outer Hebrides, Scotland. *Wildfowl Supplement*, No. 1, 143.

Stroud, D. A. 1979. Breeding waterfowl on Coll and Tiree. In Stroud, D. A. (Ed.), *Birds on*

Coll and Tiree, Scottish Ornithologists' Club / Nature Conservancy Council, Edinburgh, 43–50.

Stroud, D. A., Mudge, G. P. and Pienkowski, M. W. 1990. *Protecting Internationally Important Bird Sites: A Review of the EEC Special Protection Area Network in Great Britain.* Nature Conservancy Council, Peterborough.

Tansley, A. G. 1939. *The British Islands and their Vegetation.* 2 vols. Cambridge University Press, Cambridge.

Vose, P. B., Powell, H. G. and Spence, J. B. 1956. The machair grazings of Tiree, Inner Hebrides. *Transactions and Proceedings of the Botanical Society of Edinburgh,* **37,** 89–110.

Waterston, A. R. 1981. Present knowledge of the non-marine invertebrate fauna of the Outer Hebrides. *Proceedings of the Royal Society of Edinburgh,* **79B,** 215–321.

Waterston, A. R., Holden, A. V., Campbell, R. N. and Maitland, P. S. 1979. The inland waters of the Outer Hebrides. *Proceedings of the Royal Society of Edinburgh,* **77B,** 329–51.

Waterston, A. R. and Lyster, I. H. J. 1979. The macrofauna of brackish and fresh waters of the Loch Druidibeg National Nature Reserve and its neighbourhood, South Uist. *Proceedings of the Royal Society of Edinburgh,* **77B,** 353–76.

Williams, T. D., Reed, T. M. and Webb, A. 1986. Population size, distribution and habitat use of the corn bunting in the Uists and Benbecula. *Scottish Birds,* **14,** 57–60.

Wilmott, A. J. 1945. Vegetation. In Campbell, M. S. (Ed.), *The Flora of Uig,* Buncle, Arbroath, 20–43.

Wilson, J. R. 1978. Agricultural influences on waders nesting on the South Uist machair. *Bird Study,* **25,** 198–206.

Wormell, P. 1989. Bird habitats on Coll and Tiree. In Stroud, D. A. (Ed), *Birds on Coll and Tiree: Status, Habitats and Conservation,* Scottish Ornithologists' Club / Nature Conservancy Council, Edinburgh, 9–18.

Note: Nomenclature of flowering plants follows Clapham *et al.* (1987).

6 MARINE BIRDS

P. Monaghan

Summary

1. Marine birds are an important element of the Scottish marine heritage and are essential members of the wider marine ecosystem.

2. The islands of Scotland are very important to many species of seabird, but some in particular, such as the shearwater and the puffin are dependent on islands as safe nesting areas.

3. Seabird numbers have shown a general increase with only a few species showing a decline in recent years.

4. The continued success of the bird populations is dependent on a combination of factors, many of them directly or indirectly under the influence of anthropogenic factors.

6.1 Introduction

The marine birds that breed and feed around the Scottish coast are an important part of both our marine heritage and the marine ecosystem in general. It is not surprising that the large and conspicuous colonies of breeding birds served as an important source of food and raw materials for relatively isolated and impoverished island communities in historic times, nor that such colonies now attract wildlife enthusiasts (Cramp *et al.*, 1973; Nelson, 1980). More surprising is that, despite having been studied in some detail by professional biologists, conservationists and amateur ornithologists, it is only relatively recently that scientists modelling trophic interactions in marine food webs have attempted to incorporate seabirds as part of the spectrum of marine top predators. Yet an understanding of such trophic interactions is essential if the growing conflict between exploitation and conservation in the marine environment is to be resolved and, for example, our fisheries and oil industries are to be managed without detriment to marine birds (Furness and Monaghan, 1987).

In this paper, the diversity and biology of seabirds in Scotland is briefly described, with particular emphasis on the importance of islands, followed by a resume of their status and a consideration of the current threats to their conservation.

6.2 Species Diversity

In general, seabirds are long-lived, with low annual reproductive rates; they generally do not breed until several years old. Twenty-four species from seven families commonly breed in Scotland (see Lloyd *et al.*, 1991 for full details). There are four species of auk, the puffin (*Fratercula arctica*), the razorbill (*Alca torda*), the guillemot (*Uria aalge*) and the black guillemot or tystie (*Cepphus grylle*), all being wing-propelled diving birds that can pursue their prey underwater; two species of foot-propelled divers – the cormorant (*Phalacrocorax carbo*) and the shag (*Phalacrocorax aristotelis*); one sulid, the gannet (*Sula bassana*); eleven larids (six gulls and five terns), two skuas and four petrels. The majority breed in colonies and need safe nesting places and good food supplies relatively nearby. Scotland provides both these requirements. There is a concentration of pelagic fish species such as sandeels (*Ammodytes* spp.) and sprats (*Sprattus sprattus*) in the productive, shallow coastal waters; the rocky coastline and abundance of islands and stacks provide potentially safe nesting sites. Some species of seabird, such as guillemots and razorbills, gain protection against ground predators by nesting on sheer cliffs while others, such as most of the gulls and terns, defend their nest and young against predators by communal mobbing. Species that show neither of these anti-predator strategies, such as shearwaters and puffins, are particularly dependent on offshore islands for safe nesting (Figure 6.1), since these sites are, or at least were, generally free from predators such as foxes and rats.

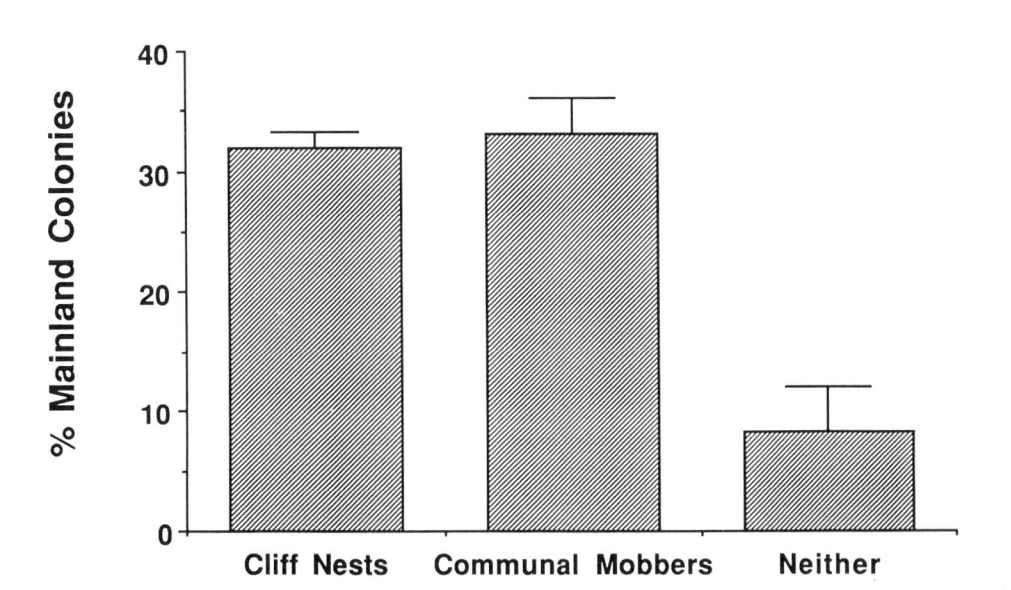

Figure 6.1. The proportion of colonies that are on the Scottish mainland rather than on islands for seabirds having different anti-predator strategies. The majority of colonies of those species that do not breed on cliffs or show communal mobbing are located on islands. (Data extracted from Lloyd *et al.*, 1991).

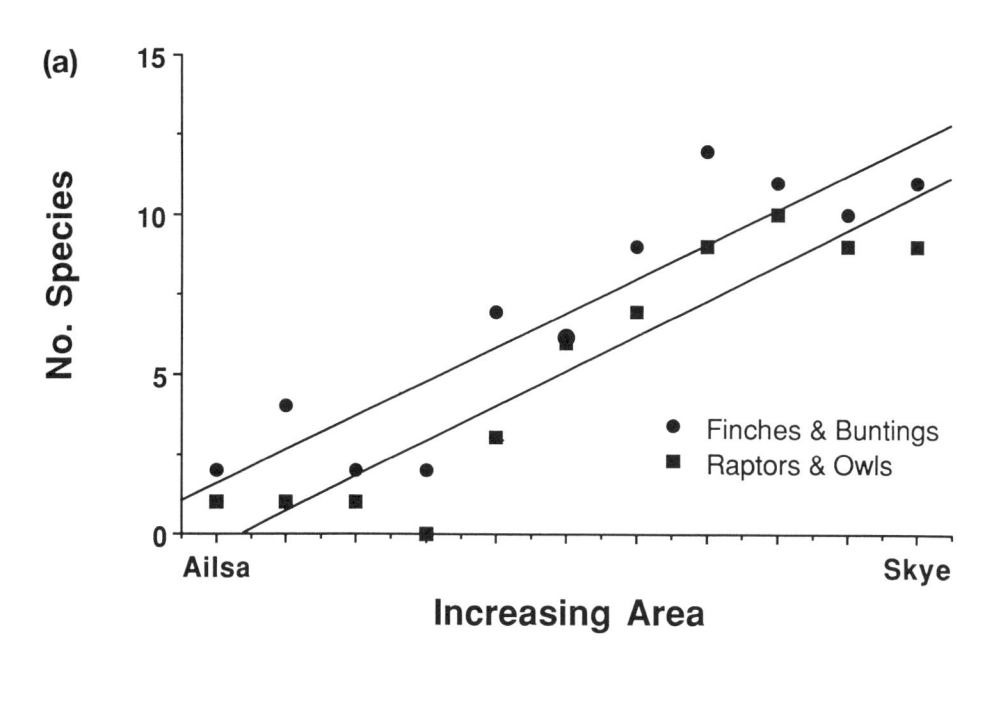

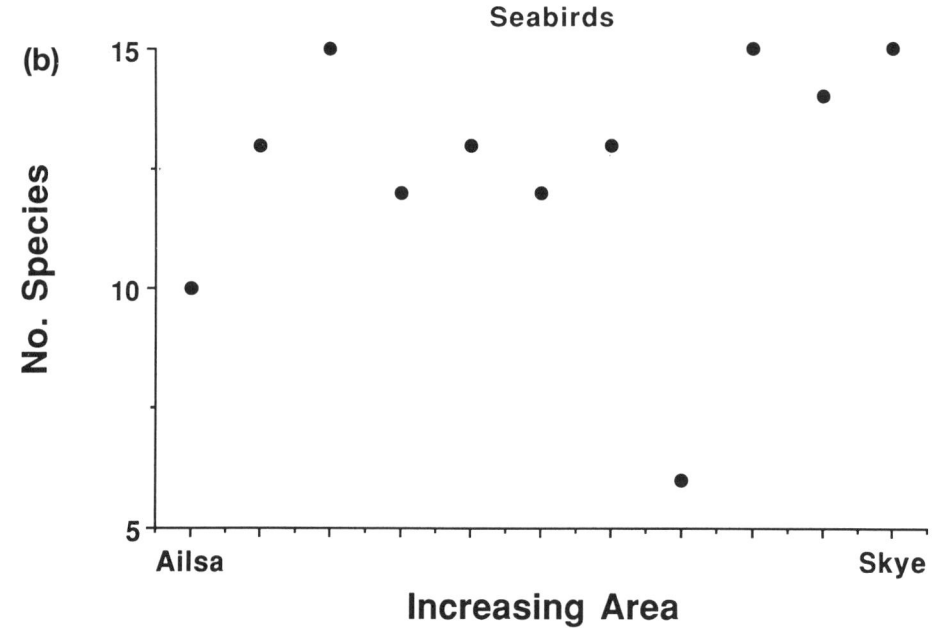

Figure 6.2. a) The number of species of raptors and owls, and finches and buntings that breed on eleven islands on the west coast of Scotland in relation to island area. There is a good correlation between island area and species number in both groups. (P<0.0l in both cases: data taken from Sharrock, 1976). b) The number of seabird species breeding on the same eleven islands (data extracted from Lloyd *et al.*, 1991). Here there is no significant relationship between island area and species number.

A traditional tenet of island biogeography is that the number of species breeding increases with island area. This is well illustrated by the islands of Scotland if we take terrestrial birds such as finches and buntings or raptors and owls (Figure 6.2a). However, no such relationship holds for seabirds (Figure 6.2b). This is of course because island area *per se* does not determine species diversity in seabirds, since the islands provide only breeding sites, the birds obtaining their food from the sea and intertidal areas. The area of sea available for a seabird to forage is unlikely to be determined by the area of the island on which it nests. The factors that do determine species diversity in seabirds are poorly understood but are likely to include the availability and diversity of breeding sites and the risk of predation together with the spectrum of available prey and foraging habitats. However an understanding of these factors is very important if we are to conserve as wide a variety of birds as possible within particular localities.

6.3 Population Status

There have been two national censuses of seabirds breeding in Britain, carried out by a combination of amateur and professional ornithologists and conservationists. The first was in 1969–70 and the second in 1985–87. Both censuses have been published as books (Cramp *et al.*, 1973; Lloyd *et al.*, 1991).

Table 6.1   The numbers of pairs of different seabirds breeding in Scotland and the proportion these represent of the British and European Populations. (Data from Lloyd *et al.*, 1991.)

Species	No. in Scotland (prs)	% British Isles	% Europe
Great Skua	7900	100	58
Gannet	127 868	68	57
Arctic Tern	72 400	89	26
Shag	32 100	68	26
Guillemot	638 443	79	21
GBB Gull	16 300	70	20
Kittiwake	356 600	66	20
Arctic Skua	3350	100	19
B. Guillemot	17 500	87	18
Razorbill	85 023	70	14
Herring Gull	96 000	50	10
LBB Gull	18 800	29	10
Fulmar	525 200	92	9
Common Tern	6200	38	7
Puffin	410 700	88	6
Sandwich Tern	2300	12	4
Cormorant	2900	25	3
Roseate tern	23	4	3

Prior to these counts numerical information was patchy and generally rather poor. Scotland currently holds the majority of most British breeding species and important European (and in some cases world) populations of several species (see Table 6.1 and Lloyd *et al.*, 1991). Between the two censuses, the majority of species have increased in numbers, and only three species have recently shown marked declines (Table 6.2). A computerized seabird colony register has now been set up, held by the JNCC Offshore Animals Branch in Aberdeen, which is continually updated to include data from a variety of monitoring programmes. A summary of each year's monitoring is published annually by JNCC (JNCC, RSPB and SOTEAG, '*Seabird Numbers* and *Breeding Success in Britain and Ireland*', obtainable from JNCC, Peterborough). Future population trends should therefore be comparatively well documented. While the recent increases are encouraging to conservationists, the actual reasons for the population changes are in many cases not well understood. This is particularly so in the case of one of our most abundant seabirds, the herring gull (*Larus argentatus*), considered for so long to be undergoing something of a population explosion, but now very much in decline. While this involves a increase in adult mortality rates (Jackson *et al.*, in preparation), there are considerable regional differences and at this stage the underlying causes are unclear.

Table 6.2 The recent population trends in seabirds breeding in Scotland. (Data from Lloyd *et al.*, 1991.)

Increasing	Decreasing	Unchanged
Fulmar	Herring Gull	GBB Gull
Gannet	Roseate Tern	Common Gull
Cormorant	Arctic Tern	Puffin
Shag		
Great Skua		
Arctic Skua		
LBB Gull		
Kittiwake		
Sandwich Tern		
Little Tern		
Guillemot		
Razorbill		
Black Guillemot		

6.4 Threats to Seabirds

The harvesting of eggs, chicks and immatures from seabird colonies by local people has rarely caused major population declines. Killing the adults is more detrimental, and indeed may have caused the extinction of the great auk. The large-scale shooting that occurred in the nineteenth century for sport and the millinery trade caused considerable population declines in some areas, and it was concern over such shooting that led to the formation of the precursor of the Royal Society for the Protection of Birds and the first legislation to protect birds in Britain towards the end of the nineteenth century. Pollutants such as toxic chemicals, plastic, heavy metals and oil can all kill seabirds. The increasing oil tanker traffic in the North Sea and on part of the west coast of Scotland is a considerable threat to some seabird populations, as tragically demonstrated by the recent wreck of the tanker *MV Braer* off Southern Shetland early in 1993. Until relatively recently, our knowledge of the distribution of seabirds at sea was scant, but the work of the Seabirds at Sea Team, organized under the former Nature Conservancy Council (now Offshore Animals Branch, JNCC), means that we now have much better information that can be used to highlight particularly important areas (Tasker *et al.*, 1987; Webb *et al.*, 1990). For some species, particularly ground nesters such as terns, disturbance caused by humans or domestic livestock can be a problem. These species are also at risk from ground predators such as hedgehogs, mink, foxes, ferrets and rats, though communal mobbing can be an effective deterrent in large colonies. These ground predators can be particularly serious when introduced to islands that previously constituted a safe haven for the more vulnerable seabird species, especially the burrow nesters that lack any communal defence. A good example of such a problem is Ailsa Craig, a major seabird island in south-west Scotland. The brown rat was accidentally introduced to the island following a shipwreck in 1889; since that time the number of rats has increased rapidly. This has been accompanied by a dramatic decline in the previously large puffin colony, and until recently the island held no burrow nesting seabirds. A rat control programme begun in 1991 appears to have met with some considerable success. The burrow nesting black guillemot and shelduck nested successfully on Ailsa Craig in 1991 and 1992, and there is currently no evidence of rat activity.

Both competitive and predatory interactions can occur between seabird species, as for example between gulls and terns. Gulls prey upon the eggs and young of terns and may take over areas on which terns formerly nested. On some islands, such as the Isle of May, expansion of the gull population was accompanied by a decline in tern numbers. To what extent this decline in breeding terns was a result of competition for nesting space, gull predation or changes in food availability is unclear and probably all three factors were involved to some degree.

Safe nesting sites are of little avail if not accompanied by good food supplies. Interactions between seabirds, fish stocks and fisheries are complex. While some seabirds may benefit from local fisheries due to increased availability of food via offal and discards, over-exploitation of local fish stocks can lead to very poor breeding success in seabird colonies (for examples see Furness and Monaghan, 1987). These relationships are difficult to study, since accurate data on the local abundance of important seabird prey such as sand eels are usually lacking (e.g. Monaghan, 1992). In Scotland, the decline in the population of sand eels around

Shetland in the 1980s resulted in very poor breeding success in several species of seabird, particularly the surface feeding kittiwakes (*Rissa tridactyla*) and Arctic terns (*Sterna paradisaea*). Subsequent studies have shown that diving seabirds, such as guillemots, were less adversely affected since they were able to increase their foraging effort considerably under the poor food conditions (Monaghan *et al.*, in press). Considerable controversy arose over the extent to which the local sand eel fishery had contributed to the seabird breeding failures in Shetland, and this whole issue highlighted our lack of understanding of sand eel population dynamics and the interactions between seabirds and their prey and the need for fishery managers to consider the ecological impact of a fishery (Monaghan, 1992). Conservationists also need to address the issue of the optimum size of seabird populations.

While seabirds themselves may provide useful indicators of the quality of the marine environment, very detailed information on prey preferences, foraging behaviour and on how different species respond to changes in food supplies are essential.

References

Cramp, S., Bourne, W. R. P. and Saunders, D. 1973, *The Seabirds of Britain and Ireland*. Collins, London.

Furness, R. W. and Monaghan, P. 1987. *Seabird Ecology*, Blackie, London.

Lloyd, C., Tasker, M. L. and Partridge, K. 1991. *The Status of Seabirds in Britain and Ireland*, T. and A. D. Poyser, London.

Monaghan, P. 1992. Seabirds and sand eels: the conflict between exploitation and conservation in the northern North Sea, *Biodiversity and Conservation*, **1**, 98–111.

Monaghan, P., Wright, P., Bailey, M., Uttley, J. D., Walton, P. and Burns, M. D. (in press). The influence of changes in food abundance on diving and surface feeding seabirds, *Canadian Wildlife Service Occasional papers*.

Nelson, B. 1980. *Seabirds*. Hamlyn, London.

Sharrock, J. T. R. 1976. *The Atlas of Breeding Birds in Britain and Ireland*, T. & A. D. Poyser, London.

Tasker, M. L., Webb, A. A., Hall, A. J., Pienkowski, M. W., and Langslow, D. R. 1987. *Seabirds in the North Sea*, Nature Conservancy Council, Peterborough.

Webb, A., Harrison, N., Leaper, G., Steele, R. D., Tasker, M. L. and Pienkowski, M. W. 1990. *Seabird Distribution West of Britain*. Nature Conservancy Council, Peterborough.

7 THE BIOLOGY OF ROCKY AND SEDIMENTARY SHORES AROUND THE SCOTTISH ISLANDS

I. Fuller and J. M. Baxter

Summary

1. The biological species assemblages which exist on and in the rocky and sedimentary shores around Scottish islands are described.

2. The environmental factors which influence the distribution of species assemblages are outlined.

3. The littoral biology of the three major archipelagoes – Shetland, Orkney and the Outer Hebrides – is compared and contrasted.

7.1 Introduction

There are three major island groups around the Scottish coast. From north to south these are Shetland, Orkney and the Western Isles, which may be subdivided into the Inner and Outer Hebrides. Smaller groups include St. Kilda and the islands of the Firth of Clyde together with the numerous islets dotted throughout the west coast sealochs. Islands are uncommon on the east coast of Scotland, however several do occur particularly in and around the Firth of Forth.

The coastline of Scotland measures approximately 11 800 km, while that of Shetland, Orkney, and the Outer Hebrides combined is about 4400 km, well over a third of the total. When all the Scottish islands are included they represent around 50% of the coastline, highlighting the significance of the islands as part of our marine heritage.

The aim of this paper is to describe and compare the range of intertidal habitats and associated biological assemblages which occur around the Scottish islands. The discussion will concentrate largely on Shetland, Orkney and the Outer Hebrides for which most information is known.

A large number of surveys based on specific taxonomic groups or designated localities have been carried out and provided much useful information. However, there is as yet no comprehensive survey information on the intertidal habitats and species around the Scottish islands.

Specific surveys include Lewis (1957) on the intertidal populations of North Uist, Price and Tittley (1978) on the seaweeds and rocky shores of the Island of Mull, Wilkinson (1975) on the marine algae of Orkney and Smith (1983) on the marine flora and fauna of Luing and the Garvellachs. The number and diversity of studies are such as to preclude mentioning them all in this paper.

Surveys have been carried out by River Purification Authorities in compliance with their statutory duties, and by university staff and individual marine biologists, often under contract to the Nature Conservancy Council (NCC). The Countryside Commission for Scotland commissioned reports to provide basic information on sandy beaches (for example, Mather *et al.*, 1974) as an aid to conservation and recreation planning. These described the physical characteristics of each beach, including rates of physiographical change, land use and accessibility, but did not include any sampling of the infauna on the beaches. More recently the University Marine Biological Station at Millport has been contracted to carry out surveys of many of the Scottish sealochs as part of the Marine Nature Conservation Review (MNCR) programme.

In recent years various aspects of the marine biology of the Northern Isles have received considerable attention associated with the development of the North Sea oil industry. The Shetland Oil Terminal Environmental Advisory Group (SOTEAG) has been carrying out intertidal biological monitoring since 1976 centred on the activities of the Sullom Voe terminal in addition to chemical and sublittoral biological monitoring. In Orkney between 1974 and 1990 the Marine Biology Unit of Dundee University carried out a programme of biological monitoring of both rocky and sandy shores in Scapa Flow in response to the development of the Flotta oil handling facility. These studies have not only provided valuable data on species present on the various shores but also on the long-term dynamics of various populations and species assemblages.

The MNCR at present is embarked on a long-term programme of work which aims to provide a complete and comprehensive survey of both the intertidal and shallow sublittoral habitats around the whole coastline of Great Britain. To date the MNCR has completed field surveys of Shetland and the sealochs including those of the Inner and Outer Hebrides, although the outer coast of the Hebrides remains unstudied.

It has also looked at a number of the smaller islands, including the Isle of May in the Firth of Forth but much marine survey work remains to be done on Scottish islands.

Rocky shores and sedimentary shores will be discussed separately in this paper. Sedimentary shore surveys usually take the form of quantitative transect studies. Rocky shore survey reports in contrast are most frequently qualitative or semi-quantitative descriptions of the range of shores which may be encountered within a particular study area. This dichotomy in approach is reflected in the format of sections 7.2 and 7.3: the discussion on rocky shores is qualitative in nature while the sandy shore discussion contains more quantitative information.

7.2   Rocky Shores

Lewis (1964) identified wave exposure as the predominant physical factor influencing species composition and zonation on rocky shores. The species assemblages, and their distribution around the islands, will therefore be described with respect to a wave exposure gradient. The biogeographical distribution of intertidal organisms will then be briefly discussed, followed by a comparison of the intertidal habitats and species assemblages found on Shetland, Orkney and the Outer Hebrides.

7.2.1   Extremely exposed shores

The unprotected western coasts of Shetland, Orkney and the Outer Hebrides are exposed to the full force of Atlantic waves as are those of Islay, Jura, Coll and Colonsay in the southern Inner Hebrides. The Outer Hebrides provide some shelter to the northern Inner Hebrides.

On the smooth, steep slopes and vertical faces which are often found at the foot of cliffs, the intertidal flora and fauna are limited to a relatively small number of species adapted to survive in the harsh conditions.

The sublittoral fringe is dominated by *Alaria esculenta* with an understorey of encrusting coralline red algae and, sometimes, mussels (*Mytilus edulis*). Limpets (*Patella ulyssiponensis* and *Patella vulgata*) and barnacles (*Semibalanus balanoides* and *Chthamalus* spp.) are the dominant species of the mid-tide region. In the lower regions of this zone tufts of filamentous red algae such as *Ceramium shuttleworthianum* and *Callithamnion* spp. grow in crevices, and dense carpets of small mussels are sometimes also present.

The upper littoral fringe is composed of a very wide zone covered by the black lichen *Verrucaria maura*, with small littorinid snails (including *Littorina neritoides*) living in crevices, and patches of the membranous red alga *Porphyra umbilicalis*. The relative heights of the zones are extended higher than is the case at less exposed sites due to the effects of the almost constant wave splash. The *V. maura* zone in particular extends in some cases for tens of metres up cliff faces.

One species which is found almost exclusively on these extremely exposed shores of the islands is *Fucus distichus* ssp. *anceps*. In general, fucoids characterize less exposed shores. This species however is adapted to extremely exposed shores; it has a stiff, stout stipe and the plants stand erect with over-arching fronds.

Fucus distichus ssp. *anceps* is essentially a northern taxon recorded from the shores of Shetland, Orkney, the Butt of Lewis and the west coast of Islay; it is recorded from the mainland of Scotland only in northern Caithness (Lewis, 1964).

7.2.2   Exposed and moderately exposed shores

While the vertical faces and steeply shelving shores open to Atlantic swells are exposed to the most extreme levels of wave action, the other rocky shores around the Scottish islands are sheltered to a greater or lesser degree.

Shores in the lee of most islands experience less wave action. Flinn (1974) described Shetland as a range of hills rising above the flat plains of the North Sea floor, with an outer and inner coast. The outer coast is composed of steep cliffs which have been eroded by Atlantic waves over millennia, but the inner coast is protected from such extreme wave action by the indented nature of the coastline which breaks the force of the prevailing westerly winds. In Orkney the shores around Scapa Flow are relatively sheltered compared with the outer shores of Hoy, the mainland and the northern isles. The eastern shoreline of the Outer Hebrides is considerably more sheltered than the western.

The physical nature of the shore can also modify the effects of wave action. The broken topography and wide horizontal extent of many rocky shores absorbs the force of the waves to varying degrees, resulting in a mosaic of wave exposure conditions. Under these circumstances, the linear, well-defined zonation pattern as found on extremely exposed bedrock shores is obscured.

A slight decrease in wave exposure results in a change in the characteristic species of the intertidal region.

Laminaria digitata replaces *A. esculenta* in the lower littoral fringe, and is usually associated with an increasingly diverse understorey of red algae including *Palmaria palmata*, *Corallina officinalis* and *Cryptopleura ramosa* and fauna such as the anemones *Sagartia elegans* and *Urticina felina* and the blue-rayed limpet *Helcion pellucidum*.

The increase in species diversity with reduced wave exposure is also manifest higher up the shore. The lower shore supports a variety of algal species, with occasional plants of *Fucus serratus* and sometimes *Himanthalia elongata* interspersed with various algae including *Mastocarpus stellatus*, *Laurencia* spp. and *Leathesia difformis*. The dominance of limpets and barnacles in the mid-shore is reduced, as patches of the evesiculate form of *Fucus vesiculosus* – *F. vesiculosus f. linearis* – appear.

On shores which are even more sheltered from wave exposure, the cover and diversity of fucoid species increases at all levels, producing a characteristic pattern of seaweed zonation. On the upper shore a narrow belt of *Pelvetia canaliculata* lies above a slightly wider band dominated by *Fucus spiralis*. The dominant alga of the mid-tide region is *Fucus vesiculosus*, which gives way to *F. serratus* on the lower shore, with the sublittoral fringe dominated by *L. digitata*.

The increase in fucoid cover is generally marked by a corresponding increase in the abundance and diversity of associated animals and algae. The *F. vesiculosus* canopy shelters a number of prosobranch mollusc species such as *Littorina littorea*, *Littorina obtusata* and *Littorina mariae*, and crustaceans including the isopod *Idotea granulosa* and several amphipod species. On the lower shore the hydroids *Dynamena pumila* and *Laomedea flexuosa* are epiphytic on *F. serratus*, and the molluscs *Tectura virginea*, *Tectura testudinalis* and *Calliostoma zizyphinum* may be present.

Exposed and moderately exposed shores are common round the islands of

Scotland. Baxter *et al* (1985) estimated that shores with either a barnacle/fucoid patchwork or complete fucoid coverage made up about 32% of the Orkney coastline. Although quantitative information is not available for the other islands, such shores have been reported by many authors, including Irvine (1974) from Shetland, and Norton and Powell (1979) and Smith (1979) from the Outer Hebrides.

7.2.3   Sheltered shores

Sheltered shores occur where wave action is markedly reduced by coastal topography. This can occur on the open coast where shelter is provided by offshore islands or deeply cut bays, but most sheltered shores on Scottish islands are found in sea water inlets, including the voes of Shetland, the bays of Orkney and the sealochs of the Outer Hebrides.

The mid-shore is dominated by *Ascophyllum nodosum*, and overall can be particularly species rich.

The long-lived *A. nodosum* fronds develop a greater diversity of epifauna than other fucoids, especially towards the lower part of the zone where length of exposure to air is reduced. Epifaunal species include *Alcyonidium gelatinosum*, *Flustrellidra hispida* and *Bowerbankia* spp. Coverage by *Ascophyllum* fronds on sheltered shores is generally denser than that of fucoid coverage on semi-exposed shores, providing greater protection from desiccation for organisms living under the canopy during low tide periods. Algal species richness is usually reduced by low light levels under the canopy, and is limited to a small number of species, including *Membranoptera alata*, *Plumaria elegans* and *Cladophora rupestris*.

Invertebrate species diversity can be particularly high with several species of amphipods, polychaetes including the scale worms *Lepidonotus squamatus* and *Harmothoe imbricata*, sponges such as *Halichondria panicea*, *Hymeniacidon perleve*, *Grantia compressa* and *Sycon coronatum*, and the ascidians *Dendrodoa grossularia*, *Botryllus schlosseri* and *Botrylloides leachii*.

The zonation pattern at these sites is similar to that found on semi-exposed shores. *Pelvetia canaliculata* and *F. spiralis* belts are present on the upper shore and a dense *F. serratus* belt exists below the *A. nodosum* zone. *L. digitata* is replaced on the lower littoral fringe by *Laminaria saccharina*.

The *F. serratus* and *L. saccharina* zones support a wide diversity of invertebrate species, particularly in areas which are not smothered by silt. These include the strawberry worm, *Eupolymnia nebulosa* and the fan worm *Sabella pavonina*, ascidians (*Ascidia conchilega*, *Ascidia mentula*, *Trididemnum tenerum* and *Ascidiella aspersa*), sponges (*Leuconia nivea*, *Leucosolenia* spp.) and large numbers of epiphytic and epilithic hydroids and bryozoans.

Irvine (1974) and Hiscock and Johnston (1990) noted that *A. nodosum* occurred in the mid-tide area at the heads of many of the voes in Shetland. Baxter *et al.* (1985) estimated that sheltered shores, dominated in the mid-shore by *A. nodosum*, formed 21% of the total Orkney coastline mainly as localized areas at the heads of inlets – often fringing sandy bays. The eastern side of the Outer Hebrides is much more sheltered in general than the western side and the numerous sealochs have substantial lengths of very sheltered *A. nodosum* dominated rocky shore (Norton and Powell, 1979).

7.2.4   Biogeography

The biogeographic range of intertidal organisms is influenced by sea temperature, climate and latitude among other factors.

There are, however, no simple relationships between these factors and the faunal or floral distributions around Scottish islands. The ranges of northern and southern species tend to overlap.

7.2.4.1   Southern species

Southern species in general tend to live further north on the west coast of the UK than on the east, due to the ameliorating influence of the North Atlantic Drift. Several southern species reach their northern limit at the Inner and Outer Hebrides, for example the brown alga *Cystoseira tamariscifolia* and the anemone *Bunodactis verrucosa*, while others reach their limit in Orkney.

Irvine (1974) noted two species of exposed shore algae, *Nemalion helminthoides* and *Cylindrocarpus berkleyi*, and two species of sheltered shore algae, *Arthrocladia villosa* and *Tilopteris mertensii* which are present in Orkney but absent from Shetland. Wilkinson (1975) also noted several species of algae which reach their northern limit in Orkney, including *Acrosorium uncinatum*, *Ceramium echionotum* and *Mesophyllum lichenoides*.

Hiscock (1981) described the absence or very restricted distribution in Shetland of some littoral animals which are present in abundance on shores in south-west Britain; these include *Gibbula umbilicalis*, *Patella depressa* and *P. ulyssiponensis*.

7.2.4.2   Northern species

Species with a northern distribution include *Fucus distichus* subspecies, one of which, *F. distichus* ssp. *anceps*, is characteristic of exposed northerly shores in the islands. There are two other subspecies of *F. distichus* which also have a northern distribution (Powell, 1957). One of these, *F. distichus* ssp. *distichus*, which is found in rock pools high in the intertidal region, extends no further south than Shetland, while *F. distichus* ssp. *edentatus* has a southern limit in Orkney.

Hiscock (1981) identified a small group of intertidal species which are present in Shetland but are absent or rarely recorded in the south of England, including *Lichina pygmaea*, *Margarites helicinus*, *Lacuna pallidula* and *Tectura testudinalis*. These are, however, not uncommon on most Scottish shores.

Both Hiscock (1981) and Irvine (1974) noted differences between species compositions of Shetland and Orkney. Shetland shores contain a more restricted range of species due to the presence of a number of southern species on Orkney which are absent on Shetland. The component of northern species which are found on Shetland but are not found on Orkney is relatively small.

A full review of the biogeographic distribution of intertidal animal and algal species is beyond the scope of this paper. Maggs (1986) described and discussed the distribution of Scottish marine macroalgae. No equivalent review has been carried out for invertebrate species.

7.2.5 Comparison between Shetland, Orkney and Outer Hebrides shores

Differences in species composition and richness on shores affected by similar levels of wave exposure are the result of a combination of environmental factors. These include the geographical distribution of species, extent of the intertidal region, and the diversity of sub-habitats such as rock pools and under-boulder areas.

The geology of the substratum is also an important factor. Hard igneous or metamorphic rocks are smoother and contain fewer cracks and crevices than sedimentary rocks.

7.2.5.1 Extremely exposed shores

The constant wave-splash on these steeply sloping shores serves to extend the upper limits of intertidal zones reducing the impact of differences in tidal range between the island groups. No comparative studies have been made between the extremely exposed shores of the three island groups, however there may be biogeographic differences in species composition.

The flora and fauna of Shetland is relatively impoverished in comparison to Orkney and the Outer Hebrides. This impoverishment was noted both by Irvine (1974) and Hiscock (1981) and is in part a reflection of the northern location and cold waters surrounding Shetland.

7.2.5.2 Exposed and moderately exposed shores

The shores of the outer coast of Shetland are mainly composed of impervious igneous and metamorphic rocks which slope steeply down to the sea. Along the margins of the voes this type of substrate is interspersed with narrow cobble and small boulder shores. The tidal range is narrow (the mean spring tidal range at Lerwick is 1.7 m).

In addition, the diversity of the intertidal fauna and flora is reduced by the relative scarcity of southern species which is not wholly counter-balanced by the addition of a small number of northern species. These factors result in the exposed and moderately exposed hard substrate shores of Shetland having species poor intertidal assemblages compared with Orkney and the Outer Hebrides.

Institute of Terrestrial Ecology (1975) noted a low frequency of rock pools and crevices on Shetland shores whereas the more gently sloping Orkney shores are composed of old red sandstone, which provides a network of cracks and crevices and thus a greater range of sub-habitats.

In addition the tidal range is wider than that of Shetland (the mean spring tidal range at Stromness is 2.9 m), and a number of southern species reach their northern limit in Orkney. All these factors result in richer intertidal species assemblages than are found on Shetland.

It is not possible to make a general comparison of species composition between Orkney and the Outer Hebrides on the basis of presently available information. No directly comparable quantitative studies have been made of the species assemblages of the two island groups. The Orkney sandstone shores provide more sub-habitats than the hard Lewissian Gneiss of the Outer Hebrides, but the tidal range around the Outer Hebrides is greater than that around Orkney (the mean spring tidal range at Stornoway is 4.1 m).

Norton and Powell (1979) noted that around most of Lewis and Harris the coastline is relatively steep and the littoral zone narrow and rocky. Smith (1979) described a conglomerate shore at Melbost Point on the east coast of Lewis which takes the form of a wide rock platform 1 km long extending over 500 m seawards to low water of spring tides. Sheltered niches were provided by vertical sided gullies and overhangs and rock pools were present.

These sub-habitats are more common on conglomerate shores than on the Lewisian gneiss which forms the majority of the hard substrate shores around the Outer Hebrides. It is probable that the conglomerate shores with their various sub-habitats are more species rich than the gneiss shores, but again no comparative studies have been made.

7.2.5.3 Sheltered shores

Ascophyllum nodosum dominated shores, fringed at low water by *Laminaria saccharina*, occur on sheltered hard substrate sites of all three island groups, however, they reach their greatest extent in the sealochs of the Outer Hebrides.

The large tidal range produces extensive intertidal areas in the sealochs. The sinuous, indented nature of their shorelines, together with the large number of islands in some lochs, results in a vastly greater length of coastline than is present in the marine inlets of the Northern Isles. For example, Lewis (1957) estimated that the shore of Loch Maddy is between 200 and 300 miles long, and identified it as having one of the richest rocky shore faunas of the British Isles.

There is wide variation in the *Ascophyllum* dominated habitats within the loch associated with degree of sedimentation, level of turbidity, rate of water movement and salinity fluctuations. In some of the smaller bays, the boulders under the algal canopy are covered by mud, and the rock fauna is greatly depleted. In contrast the tidal rapids within the loch support particularly rich faunas, including various species of hydroid, bryozoan and ascidians.

Differences in faunal and floral composition both along the length of each rapid, and between different rapids were noted. There were also wide variations in the biota of the sublittoral fringe within the loch.

The inner branches of Loch Maddy communicate with a system of brackish-water lochs. This has resulted in the development of species assemblages characteristic of sheltered brackish-water habitats, including the presence of *Fucus ceranoides* and *Ascophyllum nodosum f. mackaii*.

A wide range of sheltered habitats and species has also been reported for Loch Roag on Lewis (Scottish Marine Biological Association and Marine Biological Association, 1979), which is the largest loch system in the Outer Hebrides. The loch contains many narrow tidal channels with a range of current strengths and variety of sedimentary and rocky shore types which are rich in species.

The range of sheltered rocky shore intertidal habitats found in Outer Hebrides sealochs has not been reported from Orkney or Shetland. Small tidal rapids do occur at the entrance to some tidal basins in Shetland for example at Swinster Voe, which contain a rich fauna of prosobranch and opistobranch molluscs, echinoderms and ascidians (Hiscock and Johnston, 1990). However the number of rapids are small compared with the Outer Hebrides. In addition Hiscock and Johnston (1990) noted that, although these mollusc populations were richer than at other Shetland sites they were impoverished compared with those found on the west coast of Scotland. No significant tidal rapids occur on Orkney.

Localized freshwater inflows affect some of the marine inlets of Orkney and Shetland. *Fucus ceranoides* and dense green algae including *Enteromorpha* spp. are present; the extensive brackish habitats as found in the Outer Hebrides however are lacking. *Ascophyllum nodosum* f. *mackaii*, which is found in the sheltered inlets of Outer Hebrides sealochs under brackish conditions, is absent from Orkney and has been reported from only one site in Shetland, at Brindister Voe.

The wider tidal range, greater intertidal extent and variety of sub-habitats on the Orkney shores make it likely that they are more species rich than the Shetland shores.

Jones (1975) noted that very diverse populations of littoral organisms were often present on Orkney *Ascophyllum* shores. Many of the sheltered shores in the Shetland voes are composed of cobbles or small boulders (Hiscock and Johnston, 1990). These conditions do not favour the development of an extensive *A. nodosum* canopy, and cover may be scattered depending on the mobility of the substratum.

7.3   Sedimentary Shores

The sediment characteristics and fauna of shores on the three major Scottish archipelagoes – Shetland, Orkney and the Outer Hebrides – are distinctive.

7.3.1   Shetland

In Shetland the coastline is dominated by rock with sedimentary shores making up less than 2% of the total length (Mather and Smith, 1974). Soft sediments on both the exposed outer and sheltered inner coasts generally occur in small localized patches. Wave exposure on the open west coast of Shetland is too great to allow the existence of sandy beaches and even at the heads of inlets cobble beaches are predominant. Small, exposed steeply sloping sandy beaches occur infrequently in the bays and inlets on the south-west and eastern open coasts of Shetland (Douse, personal communication, 1992).

With increasing shelter, intertidal sediment accumulations occur, particularly at the heads of voes where sand flats, often with admixtures of gravel, are found. These deposits often contain considerable quantities of particulate peat which has either been deposited by freshwater streams or has been eroded from peat beds on the shore (Institute of Terrestrial Ecology, 1975).

The wave exposed beaches of South Mainland have a very low diversity of macrofauna characterized by the amphipods *Eurydice pulchra*, *Talitrus saltator* and *Eulimnogammarus pirloti* (Hiscock and Johnston, 1990).

The ITE study identified two main species assemblages in the voes, one found in muddy sand, containing *Macoma balthica*, *Arenicola marina*, *Cerastoderma edule* and *Mya arenaria*, and the other found in clean sand, with *Angulus tenuis*, *Arenicola marina* and *Ensis* spp; amphipods were not included in the study. They noted considerable intergrading between the two assemblages.

In gravel the fauna is generally sparse although *Cerastoderma edule* and *Venerupis pullastra* do occur (Hiscock and Johnston, 1990).

At Dales Voe and Gluss Voe, localized areas of fine and medium sand were found to support particularly rich but contrasting invertebrate infaunas. The infauna of Dales Voe was dominated by several species of annelids, including *Pygospio elegans* (up to 12 560 m^{-2}), *Fabricia sabella* (up to 1430 m^{-2}), various capitellids and molluscs, *Hydrobia ulvae* (up to 5810 m^{-2}), *C. edule* (up to 290 m^{-2}) and *M. balthica* (up to 2570 m^{-2}). Gluss Voe was dominated by crustaceans, especially *Corophium crassicorne* (up to 8090 m^{-2}) and tanaids (up to 5190 m^{-2}) but included significant mollusc and annelid populations. The striking differences between the fauna of Dales Voe and Gluss Voe were attributed to differences in sediment compositions of the two sites; Gluss Voe sediments were coarser, containing less silt, clay and organic matter and had a well-oxygenated interstitial circulation (Jones *et al.*, 1981).

During the course of these investigations high rates of infection of *C. edule* by the nemertine *Malacobdella grossa* were discovered. This association appears to be confined to the Shetland Isles (Jones *et al.*, 1979).

7.3.2   Orkney

Orkney has considerably more soft sediment areas around its coastline than Shetland. Baxter *et al.* (1985) estimated that 12% of the coastline of Orkney comprises soft, mainly sandy sediments, compared with a figure of 2% for Shetland.

A small number of pocket beaches occur on the exposed open coast, as at Rackwick and Bay of Skaill, but the majority of the sedimentary shores are protected from strong wave action by the coastal topography. Mather *et al.* (1974) noted a wealth of variety in types and characteristics of beach complexes on Orkney. In general the North Isles of Orkney, such as Sanday and Westray, have numerous, relatively large sandy beaches, while the mainland has fewer smaller units.

Atkins *et al.* (1985) described in detail the sediment composition and macrofauna of 14 of the principal moderately exposed and sheltered Orkney soft sediment beaches. The sediments were mainly very clean, fine to medium grain sands reflecting the lack of alluvial input to the beaches. Physically, many of the shores could be divided into three, with a steep upper section, a wide flat central region and a steepening lower section. The intertidal ranged from 80 to 1200 m wide.

Three faunistic zones reflected these three physical zones. The steep upper sections usually comprised coarse gravel or shingle containing little or no infauna. Where this coarse sediment was replaced by sand, populations of oligochaetes and/or amphipods (*Bathyporeia* spp.) were found.

The midshore zones were dominated numerically by the spionid *P. elegans* (reaching densities of 90 000 m^{-2} at some sites) and other polychaetes. *Arenicola marina* was common on most shores and altered the physical nature of the habitat in the mid-shore zone due to the mosaic of micro-habitats formed by its feeding cones and faecal mounds. *Arenicola marina* densities (estimated by counting casts) were up to 15 m^{-2}.

The lower shore zones were dominated by polychaetes or amphipods, or both. Creeklands Bay and Scapa Bay were dominated by polychaetes while Swanbister Bay and Widewall Bay were dominated by *Bathyporeia* spp. and *Ampelisca brevicornis*.

The terebellid polychaete *Lanice conchilega* reached densities of more than 100 m^{-2} at Bay of Stove and was present on many beaches below mean low water of spring tides.

Total densities of animals ranged from 1000 to 150 000 individuals m^{-2} and were greatest on the three Hoy beaches surveyed and lowest at Scapa Bay and Waulkmill Bay. In total 76 species were found comprising 31 polychaetes, 16 amphipods, 15 molluscs and 14 other groups.

The lower shore at Bay of Quoys on Hoy supported a unique and diverse assemblage of amphipods and polychaetes. Of particular note are the very high densities of two maldanid polychaetes on the lower shore; *Clymenura johnstoni* (9400 m^{-2}) and *Praxilella affinis* (595 m^{-2}); such exceptionally high densities have not been reported elsewhere. The tubes of these animals formed a stable structure which supported a rich assemblage of amphipods and polychaetes. The density of animals in this region reached a maximum of 125 000 m^{-2} comprising 32 species, including the spionids *Polydora antennata* and *Spiophanes bombyx* which were rare or absent at other sites but reached densities of 9500 and 3500 m^{-2} respectively at Bay of Quoys.

A striking feature of most Orkney shores was the relative insignificance of molluscs on the sandy beaches. Species such as *C. edule* and *Angulus tenuis* did occur but not in the numbers recorded by Eleftheriou and McIntyre (1976) on the Scottish mainland. A giant race of *C. edule* has been recorded in Scapa Flow

(Jones, 1975) and two other mollusc species, *Ensis siliqua* and *Ensis arcuatus* are important to local people. These animals which can only be collected by hand on the lowest spring tides – known as Spoot tides – are a highly prized delicacy.

In general Atkins *et al.* (1985) found very high abundances and diversities of amphipods and polychaetes in Orkney on moderately exposed and sheltered shores and attributed this to the fully marine conditions and good sediment circulation.

The faunistic differences between the shores were attributed to factors other than degree of exposure, including the influence of current, differences in sediment grades, shell sand content of the sediment and the influence of the underlying geology on the lengths and levels of the beaches.

Atkins *et al.* (1985) also compared species composition and densities of Orkney shores with those reported for Shetland by Jones and Jones (1981) and for the Scottish mainland by Eleftheriou and McIntyre (1976).

They considered that the two sheltered shores previously described for Shetland, at Dales Voe and Gluss Voe, showed animal abundances comparable with those found in Orkney, but a markedly different species composition. Mainland Scotland shores had a lower species diversity and density than Orkney shores.

7.3.3 *Outer Hebrides*

The sinuous sealochs and complex coastal topography result in a diverse range of sedimentary habitats around the outer Hebrides. In additional to fully marine sites, rivers of varying sizes enter the sea and sealochs and create brackish intertidal habitats with high silt contents to a far greater extent than occurs in either Orkney or Shetland.

Angus (1979) studied in detail the macrofauna of 20 intertidal sandy shores in Lewis and Harris and summarized the information available on the distribution of sandy shores around the whole of the Outer Hebrides.

The majority of the sandy beaches are on the western seaboard of the islands, and are exposed to strong wave action. Small pocket beaches occur around the coast of Lewis and Harris, while the entire western shoreline of South Uist is effectively one long, exposed sandy beach. This beach is maintained despite the extreme wave action because of a shallow rocky shelf which lies just offshore.

The waves break on this shelf before they reach the beach, and their energy is further reduced by extensive kelp forests in the shallow near-shore sublittoral.

Angus (1979) divided the infauna of the sandy shores of Lewis and Harris into four faunistically distinct types, associated with different conditions of exposure and salinity. These divisions correspond to those identified by Eleftheriou and McIntyre (1976) on the Scottish mainland, but contrast with the Orkney shores where wave exposure was not considered to be a major structuring factor. The four categories are as follows:

1. **Shores of high wave exposure.** These sites were characterized by a steep beach profile and coarse sand, with low biomass and very few species present. Crustacea were dominant by number, especially small amphipods such as *Bathyporeia* spp. and *Pontocrates norvegicus*. Larger crustaceans such as *Talitrus saltator* and *Eurydice pulchra* were usually present. A few polychaetes were also found, chiefly *Nephtys* spp., *Scololepis squamata* and capitellids. Molluscs were invariably absent.

2. **Moderately exposed shores.** These beaches usually had a flatter profile and finer sand than those found on the more exposed shores. In comparison to the most exposed shores the amphipod and polychaete fauna was more diverse and numerous. Molluscs, particularly *Angulus tenuis* and *Donax vittatus* were also usually present but occurred only at low densities. Other species frequently recorded included *Gammarus* spp, and *Travisia forbesii*.

The most sheltered sites were divided into two categories: fully marine sites and sites which are influenced by brackish water.

3. **Sheltered, fully marine shores.** On fully marine shores a wide diversity of infauna occured, including the species found on the moderately exposed beaches but at greater densities.

   Maximum reported densities included *D. vittatus*, 485 m^{-2}; *A. tenuis* 230 m^{-2}; Capitellidae, 175 m^{-2} and *Nephtys* spp. 50 m^{-2}. Some species which normally occur sublittorally were found at these sites, including *Ensis siliqua* and *Echinocardium cordatum*.

   This type of site is not confined to Lewis and Harris. A particularly rich sheltered marine shore was found at Oitir Bheag on Benbecula. Wide sand flats just above low tide level at this site were poorly drained and supported a rich infauna, including *Ensis siliqua*, *Echinocardium cordatum* and the burrowing anemone *Cerianthus lloydi* (Scottish Marine Biological Association and Marine Biological Association, 1979).

   Another particularly rich marine site was found at Teinish in Loch Roag. The principal species were *Mya truncata*, *Dosinia exolenta*, *Venerupis pullastra*, *Angulus tenuis*, *Echinocardium cordatum*, *Nephtys hombergi*, *Lanice conchilega* and an abundance of *Leptosynapta inhaerens* (10–100 m $^{-2}$).

4. **Sheltered shores influenced by brackish water.** Shores of this type have been described from Lewis and Harris. The fauna of these sandy beaches was influenced by small rivers crossing the intertidal region. Angus (1979) described these sites as 'semi-estuarine'. Species included the amphipod *Corophium volutator* found in abundances of up to 100 m^{-2}, the bivalve mollusc *Macoma balthica* with a maximum recorded density of 60 m^{-2}, the polychaete *Hediste diverscolor*, (790 m^{-2}) and the snail *Hydrobia ulvae* (1740 m^{-2}).

Within the Outer Hebrides there are a number of locations where sedimentary shores are influenced by tidal rapids. This has not been recorded from either Shetland or Orkney. These shores comprise particularly coarse, clean sediments and support several species which are normally found sublittorally.

In Loch Roag, a rapid which contains a shell and gravel shore was encountered; the burrowing fauna was dominated by bivalves and an echinoderm belonging to the genus *Leptosynapta* (Scottish Marine Biological Association and Marine Biological Association, 1979).

The maximum recorded population densities of infauna reported for Lewis and Harris shores are comparable to those found by Eleftheriou and McIntyre (1976) on mainland beaches, but are far lower than those reported by Atkins *et al.* (1985) for Orkney and Jones and Jones (1981) for Shetland. This may be partly explained by the fact that Angus was examining open coast sedimentary shores while Atkins *et al.* and Jones and Jones were studying shores in enclosed marine inlets. However comparative physical and biological studies would be required to determine the reasons for these real differences.

7.4   Conclusion

It is apparent from the studies reviewed here that each of the three major Scottish archipelagoes contain important intertidal biological sites. The sheltered sedimentary shores in Shetland voes are small, but contain distinctive species assemblages with high densities of infauna. These shores are important food sources for wader populations in Shetland (Jones and Jones, 1981). The small tidal rapid sites in Shetland also contain diverse biotas.

Some of the moderately exposed and sheltered sandy shores of Orkney contain exceptionally high densities of infauna (up to 125 000 animals m^{-2} at Bay of Quoys on Hoy), and species assemblages which have not been reported from elsewhere. Species richness of intertidal rocky sites in Orkney has not been assessed in detail, but the *Ascophyllum* dominated shores in particular are worth investigating.

The extensive sheltered rocky shores of the Outer Hebrides sealochs are likely to be the richest rocky shores of the three archipelagoes in terms of invertebrate species, although no comparative studies have been made. They may also be richer than many sealochs on the west coast of the Scottish mainland. The mainland sealochs are in general long and narrow, while the wide, shallow fjards of the Outer Hebrides are lined by convoluted coastlines and contain larger numbers of tidal rapids. It would be useful to carry out comparative studies between the sealochs in these two areas.

It would also be useful to extend the quantitative infaunal sandy shore sampling programme which was carried out by Angus (1979) around Lewis and Harris into the southern islands of the Outer Hebrides, and into the sealochs. Taken in conjunction with the work of Atkins *et al.* (1985) and Jones and Jones (1981), this would allow comparisons to be made between the sedimentary shore populations of the marine inlets of Shetland, Orkney and the Outer Hebrides.

The major statutory method available at present to protect intertidal sites of high conservation interest is through Sites of Special Scientific Interest (SSSI) designation. There are many intertidal SSSI sites extant at present, however they have mainly been designated because of their bird interest, or for geological reasons. The intertidal biota is protected only at a very limited number of sites.

It is doubtful whether SSSI legislation can be used to protect intertidal biota. This legislation is based on the terrestrial conservation concept of recompensing landowners for allowing part of their land to remain in a 'natural' or 'semi-natural' state. This concept is not relevant to the intertidal region in that the landowner is the Crown Estate, but any 'damage' is caused by outside agencies. The country conservation agencies and the Joint Nature Conservation Committee (JNCC) are at present investigating possible approaches towards protecting significant intertidal sites.

References

Angus, I. S. 1979. The macrofauna of intertidal sand in the Outer Hebrides. *Proceedings of the Royal Society of Edinburgh*, **77B**, 155–71.

Atkins, S. M., Jones, A. M. and Simpson, J. A. 1985. The fauna of sandy beaches in Orkney: a review. *Proceedings of the Royal Society of Edinburgh*, **87B**, 27–45.

Baxter, J. M., Jones, A. M. and Simpson, J. A. 1985. A study of long-term changes in some rocky shore communities in Orkney. *Proceedings of the Royal Society of Edinburgh*, **87B**, 47–63.

Eleftheriou, A. and McIntyre, A. D. 1976. The intertidal fauna of sandy beaches – a survey of the Scottish coast. *Scottish Fisheries Research Report No 6*. Aberdeen.

Flinn, D. 1974. The coastline of Shetland. In R. Goodier (Ed.), *The Natural Environment of Shetland: Proceedings of the Nature Conservancy Council Symposium*. NCC, Edinburgh, 13–23.

Hiscock, K., 1981. The rocky shore ecology of Sullom Voe. *Proceedings of the Royal Society of Edinburgh*, **80B**, 219–40.

Hiscock, K. and Johnston, C. M. 1990. Review of marine biological information for Shetland. *Nature Conservancy Council, CSD Report No 1000* (Marine Nature Conservation Review Report No MNCR/OR/01).

Institute of Terrestrial Ecology. 1975. *Report to the Nature Conservancy Council on some aspects of the ecology of Shetland, 6.2. Littoral biota of rocky shores. CSD Report 27, 6.3. Littoral biota of soft shores. CSD Report 28.*

Irvine, D. 1974. The marine vegetation of the Shetland Isles. In R. Goodier, (Ed.), *The Natural Environment of Shetland: Proceedings of the Nature Conservancy Council Symposium*, NCC, Edinburgh, 107–13.

Jones, A. M. 1975. The marine environment of Shetland. In R. Goodier, R. (Ed.), *The Natural Environment of Shetland: Proceedings of the Nature Conservancy Council Symposium*, NCC, Edinburgh, 85–94.

Jones, A. M., Jones, Y. M. and James, J. L. 1979. The incidence of the nemertine *Malacobdella grossa* in the bivalve *Cerastoderma edule* in Shetland. *Journal of the Marine Biological Association of the United Kingdom*, **59**, 373–75.

Jones, A. M. and Jones, Y. M. 1981. The soft shore environment of Sullom Voe and the north mainland of Shetland. *Proceedings of the Royal Society of Edinburgh*, **80B**, 203–18.

Lewis, J. R. 1957. An introduction to the intertidal ecology of the rocky shores of a hebridean island. *Oikos*, **8**(2), 130–60.

Lewis, J. R. 1964. *The Ecology of Rocky Shores*. English Universities Press, London.

Maggs, C. A. 1986. Scottish marine macroalgae: a distributional checklist, biogeographical analysis and literature abstract. *NCC CSD Report No 635*, Peterborough, 1–136.

Mather, A. S. and Smith, J. S. 1974. Beaches of Shetland. *Report to the Countryside Commission for Scotland*, Department of Geography, University of Aberdeen, 1–103.

Mather, A. S., Smith, J. S. and Ritchie, W 1974. Beaches of Orkney. *Report to the Countryside Commission for Scotland*, Department of Geography, University of Aberdeen, 1–168.

Norton, T. A. and Powell, H. T. 1979. Seaweeds and rocky shores of the Outer Hebrides. *Proceedings of the Royal Society of Edinburgh*, **77B**, 141–53.

Powell, H. T. 1957. Studies in the genus *Fucus* L. II. Distribution and ecology of forms of *Fucus distichus* L. emend. Powell in Britain and Ireland. *Journal of the Marine Biological Association of the United Kingdom*, **36**, 663–93.

Price, J. H. and Tittley, I. 1978. 'Marine ecosystems'. In E. C. Jermy and J. A. Crabbe (Eds), *The Island of Mull: A Survey of Its Flora and Environment*, British Museum (Natural History). London, 8.13–8.31.

Scottish Marine Biological Association and Marine Biological Association. 1979. Report on the shores of the Outer Hebrides: a biological survey of the littoral zone. *CSD Report No. 272*, NCC, Peterborough, 1–75.

Smith, S. M. 1979. Mollusca of rocky shores: Lewis and Harris, Outer Hebrides. *Proceedings of the Royal Society of Edinburgh*, **77B**, 173–87.

Smith, S. M. 1983. The shores of Luing and the Garvellachs: marine flora and fauna. *CSD Report No. 504*, NCC, Peterborough, 1–71.

Wilkinson, M. 1975. The marine algae of Orkney. *British Phycological Journal*, **10**, 387–97.

8 THE SUBLITTORAL ECOLOGY OF SCOTLAND'S ISLANDS

D. W. Connor

Summary

1. A combination of abiotic factors, both natural and man-induced, and biotic factors influence community structure and composition in the nearshore sublittoral zone. Of these, the natural abiotic factors are most well studied and can be used to distinguish different sublittoral habitats.

2. Sublittoral communities around Scottish islands are influenced by both boreal-arctic and boreal-lusitanean fauna and flora.

3. The sublittoral communities present around Scottish islands are discussed in relation to the physiographic features in which they occur; certain communities are characteristic of specific physiographic features, such as fjordic sealochs and submarine tunnels.

4. The wide variety of communities present is related to both the extent of island coastline and to the variety of physiographic features. The islands are considered most important for their brackish-water systems, for the fjardic lochs of the Uists, for the tunnel and cave systems at St. Kilda and Shetland and for the extremely wave exposed communities at Rockall.

8.1 Introduction

The seabed around Scotland's islands is the least well known of Scotland's extensive and diverse array of natural habitats, yet it encompasses an extremely varied and often very rich and beautiful variety of wildlife. The seabed is of high value for fisheries, recreation, education and research but requires conservation management to ensure its continued value, although much of it remains largely unspoilt at present.

An account is given here of the range of habitats which occur around Scotland's islands, and the main factors which influence the diversity of communities and species. Special attention is given to those features which are particularly important or interesting in the wider context of marine life throughout the British Isles and the north-east Atlantic.

The information on which this paper is based relies considerably on data collected during surveys undertaken or commissioned prior to 1987 by the Nature Conservancy Council (NCC) and, since that date, by the NCC's (now the Joint Nature Conservation Committee's (JNCC)) Marine Nature Conservation Review. Studies from other sources pertaining specifically to the description of sublittoral habitats around Scottish islands are limited, especially compared with the volume of information available for mainland Scotland. The considerable volume of work around Sullom Voe in Shetland (review by Hiscock and Johnston, 1990), descriptions of algal communities around Mull (Price and Tittley, 1978), Colonsay (Norton *et al.*, 1969) and the Firth of Lorne (Norton and Milburn, 1972), descriptions of brackish water flora and fauna in the Uists (Spence *et al.*, 1979; Waterston and Lyster, 1979) and studies undertaken from the University Marine Biological Station, Millport (reviewed by Connor, 1991a) are among the notable exceptions. Species referred to below are given according to the Marine Conservation Society Species Directory (Howson, 1987).

8.2   Extent of the Island Systems

Out of approximately 11,800 km of coastline around Scotland (JNCC Coastal Resources Database) over half is taken up by its islands and offshore rocks. The sheer extent of island coastline, comparable in the north-east Atlantic only to that of the Norwegian coast, yields an exceptionally wide range of physical conditions which are in turn reflected in the variety of habitats and species associated with these coasts. Although much of this resource lies to the west and north of Scotland, smaller islands and offshore rocks also occur within the Irish Sea (e.g. The Scares in Luce Bay) and the North Sea (e.g. the Isle of May and Bass Rock at the entrance to the Firth of Forth), providing additional habitat diversity on these coasts.

8.3   Environmental and Biological Influences

Benthic communities, considered here to be associations of species which recur in similar physical conditions and which are distinguishable by means of ecological survey (further discussed in Hiscock and Connor, 1991), are structured by a series of environmental and biological factors. The main abiotic factors which contribute to determining structure and composition in the sublittoral zone are well documented (Hiscock, 1983, 1985). To these natural factors, which are summarized in Table 8.1, can be added man-induced effects such as gross pollution, disturbance and deoxygenation, although such factors are generally limited in extent around Scotland's islands. Grazing pressures, recruitment, isolation and inter-species competition are among the

Table 8.1   Natural abiotic factors which determine community structure and composition in the nearshore sublittoral environment, together with an indication of the range of variation present around Scottish islands

Factor	Range or variation present
Substratum	Bedrock and boulder, through unstable stony ground and mixed sediments, to coarse and fine sediments; biological reefs (e.g. mussels).
Depth	0 to over 200 m within 5 km of the coast.
Illumination	Illustrated by the maximum depth to which kelp grows, which varies from a few metres to over 30 m depth.
Exposure to wave action	Extremely exposed to ultra sheltered, as defined by Hiscock (1990).
Strength of tidal streams	Very strong (8–10 knots or more) to negligible.
Salinity	Fully marine, through variable salinities, to estuarine and brackish conditions.
Temperature and stratification	Generally confined to moderate variations between about 6 and 14° C, but locally may vary from near freezing to 20° C in surface waters. Coastal waters may be fully mixed or thermally stratified, the latter occurring particularly in sealoch basins.
Oxygenation	Water column and the sediment-water interface predominantly fully oxygenated, although local deoxygenation occurs in isolated basins.
Geology	Range from hard igneous and metamorphic rocks, through sandstones to softer limestones and very soft talc.
Geomorphology	Bedrock habitats ranging from open rock surfaces to vertical walls and overhanging faces; gullies, tunnels and caves formed in some rock types. Boulders of highly variable size and shape creating different microhabitats such as boulder holes.

most important biological factors which additionally help structure community composition.

There is, then, a potentially complex array of factors controlling community composition at any particular site. Through ecological survey it is generally possible to indicate which are the principal physical factors structuring any specific community, although there is such variety at both a local and national level that detailed study is usually required to fully determine all the relevant factors.

The range of environmental factors, and hence habitat diversity, is limited to a large extent by the physiographic nature of the coastline, such that some of the factors listed above appear to be more significant than others in specific physiographic features. The sublittoral habitats and associated benthic

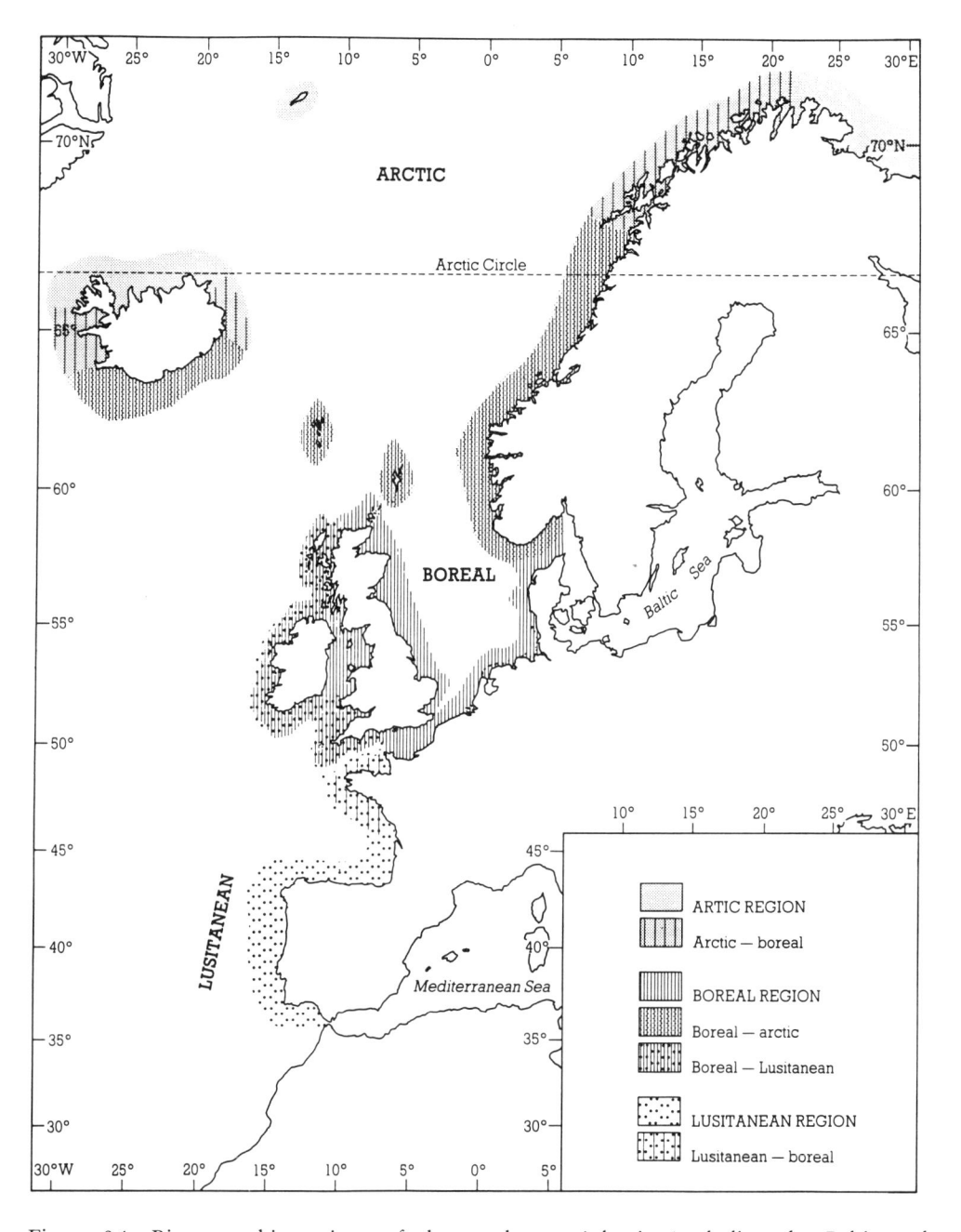

Figure 8.1. Biogeographic regions of the north-east Atlantic (excluding the Baltic and Mediterranean Seas) (from Hiscock, 1991)

communities of algae and animals around Scotland's islands are described later in relation to these physiographic features, after first discussing the wider topics of biogeography and island isolation.

8.4 Biogeography

The British Isles lie in a transition zone where cold-water boreal-arctic and warmer water boreal-lusitanean faunas and floras meet and merge (Figure 8.1 and further discussed in Hiscock, 1991). Elements of both these biogeographical zones are represented around Scotland's islands. To the west the Outer Hebrides lie in the path of the North Atlantic Drift which maintains sea temperatures, particularly during winter months, higher than more southerly latitudes in the Irish Sea. The outer isles and St. Kilda are bathed in Atlantic water of high salinity while the seas between the Outer Hebrides and the Scottish mainland receive less saline water which originates mainly from the Clyde and Irish Seas (Ellett, 1979). The differences in temperature are reflected in the considerable number of species of southern origin which occur commonly off western Ireland and reach their northern limits off western Scotland (see, for example, Maggs, 1986), but which are rare or absent from the northern basin of the Irish Sea. Some of these, for example the holothurian *Holothuria forskali* and the algae *Drachiella spectabilis* and *Dictyopteris membranacea*, appear to be confined (on the west coast of Scotland) to offshore island locations such as Coll, the Outer Hebrides and St. Kilda, where they most likely benefit from the warm water influence of the North Atlantic Drift.

Although the North Atlantic Drift continues around north-west Scotland to Shetland its influence decreases with increasing latitude; this is accompanied by a general reduction in species richness as more southern species are lost from the fauna and flora than are replaced by species of northern origin. This transition to a northern fauna and flora is considered to be most noticeable between Shetland and the rest of Scotland, with Shetland included in a separate biogeographic zone by many workers (e.g Alvarez *et al.*, 1988). Shetland supports populations of northern species, such as the urchin *Strongylocentrotus droebachiensis* and the holothurian *Cucumaria frondosa* (Howson, 1988), which are not found elsewhere in the British Isles. However it appears to lack other cold-water species such as the sea fan *Swiftia pallida* and the anemone *Protanthea simplex* (which occur frequently on Scotland's west coast) and supports very few individuals of the anemone *Bolocera tuediae* and the hydroid *Thuiaria thuja*, species which are much more common further south in the North Sea (Hiscock and Johnston, 1990). The latter two species occur around the Isle of May (Bennett, 1989) at the entrance to the Firth of Forth.

8.5 Isolation

The majority of Scotland's islands cannot be considered so isolated as to show significant effects of island biogeography, with community and species composition broadly similar in comparable island and mainland habitats.

However the restricted distribution of some species, as in the examples discussed above of northern species around Shetland, is likely evidence that widespread colonization by a species, despite the presence of suitable habitats, is not always commonplace and that island separation and chance recruitment may be restrictive factors in such a process. Other factors such as residual currents and water quality also play their part in restricting certain species to offshore island locations. In the sediment, for instance, the cerianthid anemone *Arachnanthus sarsi* is currently known from less than 10 sites in Scotland, Ireland and Norway (B. E. Picton, personal communication, 1991) and is confined, in Scotland, to island locations around Scarba, Coll, Harris and St. Kilda. The sea fan *Swiftia pallida* has not been recorded around Shetland (Hiscock and Johnston, 1990), and yet is common on the west coast of Scotland (e.g Connor, 1990) and present in Norway (Connor, 1991b).

Where such island isolation is likely to be much more significant is Rockall where 300 km of open sea and a 2000 m deep trough separate it from the nearest land (St. Kilda) and no doubt play a part in colonization both on the shore and in the shallow sublittoral zone. The shallow seabed around Rockall (to 50 m depth) is colonized by a restricted variety of species. From a comparison with St. Kilda and Foula, which lie much closer to the mainland, there appears to be between 40% and 60% fewer species recorded from Rockall (Laffoley and Hiscock, 1988) (although allowance must be made for differences in survey effort and the variety of habitats around each island). It is difficult to judge how much this is controlled by the extreme conditions of wave action and how much by Rockall's isolation. It is interesting to note that the infralittoral zone around Rockall itself is dominated to a depth of 33 m by the brown alga *Alaria esculenta*, a species normally confined to the sublittoral fringe, whereas Helens Reef, just 4 km away, supports a forest of kelp *Laminaria* spp. in the same

Table 8.2 Physiographic features represented within the islands of Scotland

Open coast (of large islands):
  Island complexes
  Offshore islands and rocks
  Surge gullies, caves and tunnels

Sounds or straits

Enclosed coast:
  Sealochs – Fjordic
             Fjardic
             Obs
  Voes – including vadills and houbs
  Estuaries
  Lagoons

zone. Such a dramatic difference in the predominant algae may indeed reflect the importance of chance recruitment and net current flow for survival of larvae and sporelings, even within areas so close together, although differences in wave surge conditions are also likely to be important in this instance.

8.6 Physiographic Features

The Scottish islands encompass a high proportion of the physiographic features represented in the British Isles and indeed include several that are best represented here (Table 8.2).

Most of the large islands (excepting Orkney) are highly dissected by a series of marine inlets, including the sealochs and obs of the Hebrides and the voes, vadills and houbs of Shetland. Of these, the fjardic lochs and obs are best represented within Scotland by those in the Hebrides, while the voes are the only examples of rias or drowned river valleys in Scotland.

8.6.1 Open coast

The open coast is fringed by a forest of the kelp *Laminaria hyperborea*. This forms a narrow strip around much of the coast as the rock shelves away steeply to animal dominated circalittoral communities, the rock eventually giving way to sediment plains of gravels and sands. The infaunal communities of these coarse sediments tend to include a high proportion of large bivalves, such as *Ensis* spp. and venerupids, together with heart urchins *Echinocardium* spp.

Around Orkney the kelp forests are particularly extensive where the seabed shelves less steeply, so much so that commercial harvesting of the kelp has often been considered (Institute of Offshore Engineering, 1986). In areas of moderate exposure to wave action the effects of grazing by urchins and other species can be marked, leaving both kelp stipes and the seabed beneath the kelp almost devoid of erect species. Large areas of the Inner Hebrides, particularly from Mull northwards, are so affected. With increased exposure to wave action, such as found around the western coasts of the Outer Hebrides, Orkney and Shetland, the dramatic effect of urchin grazing is reduced and both the kelp forests and the animal dominated circalittoral zone tend to be richer in erect species particularly of foliose algae, hydroids and sponges. Where wave action is particularly strong many of these erect species are confined to deeper water where the effects of wave action are ameliorated. In the shallow kelp zone this erect biota is largely replaced by more low-lying species of sponges, anemones and colonial ascidians. This shallow-water effect on the biota in strong wave action is most significant around Rockall, the most exposed island within the British Isles. Here, as already mentioned, *Alaria esculenta* extends from the shore down to over 30 m depth, and the rock beneath it is covered by a mosaic of low-lying cushion-forming species, which extend much deeper (to approximately 30 m) than on any other coast (Laffoley and Hiscock, 1988). Even at depths of 45 m, where the bedrock gives way to boulders, wave action is sufficiently strong to cause periodic movement of the rocks, with scour and abrasion affecting the communities at this depth.

8.6.2   Surge gullies, caves and tunnels

The geomorphology of many Scottish islands has led to the formation of numerous surge gullies in shallow water. Indeed these are so well developed around Islay that wave energy within them has been harnessed to generate electricity (Whittaker, 1991). These gullies characteristically support low lying 'cushions' of sponges, anemones, colonial ascidians, barnacles and mussels, species adapted to survive in the enormous surge action of these gullies. Around Papa Stour and Unst on Shetland and around Fair Isle these communities are more extensively developed in the long cave and tunnel systems of these islands. In these situations variations in conditions of wave surge promote a variety of communities from those typical of surge gullies to some, which are more subject to scour and abrasion, dominated by encrusting bryozoans and calcareous tube worms. Such communities are however best developed around St. Kilda which has the most extensive fully submerged cave and tunnel system in the British Isles. Here, in addition to communities typical of wave surge conditions elsewhere, there are species which are characteristic of the less turbulent conditions of submarine caves. Among these are the sponge *Dercitus bucklandi* and the anemone *Parazoanthus anguicomus* (Howson and Picton, 1985).

8.6.3   Sounds

Islands situated either close to the mainland or in island groups create sounds or straits which are most notable for the enhanced flow of tidal streams through them. The effect of these currents is usually most significant in the centre of the sounds, and much reduced among the kelp-dominated borders to the channels where tidal streams are typically much weaker. Among the largest examples in Scotland are the Sounds of Jura, Mull and Sleat, but there are numerous others between the island complexes of the Firth of Lorne, the Western Isles, Orkney and Shetland.

Many of the sounds are characterized by rocky tideswept seabeds with the centres of the channels often floored by coarse sediments, including beds of maerl, and mixtures of cobbles and boulders. Because of the enhanced tidal flow through them they often support a rich variety of species. This is likely to be related to the constant supply of food for filter feeding animals and to the strength of tidal streams which tends to reduce the grazing pressures of urchins compared with areas lacking strong water movement. Where tidal streams are exceptionally strong (reaching 8 knots or more), however, species richness tends to be reduced as fewer species appear to thrive under these more stressful conditions. A variety of different benthic communities develop in sounds, each related to the particular velocity of the currents present.

This variation can be illustrated by examples from sounds subject to differing maximum tidal flows.

In Bluemull Sound, between Yell and Unst on Shetland, which experiences tidal currents of up to 6 knots, the seabed supports extensive colonies of soft corals *Alcyonium digitatum* (Howson, 1988) and the calcareous tube worm *Salmacina dysteri*, with numerous anemones *Urticina felina* surviving in scoured pockets of shell gravel between the boulders. Where currents are less strong there are populations of the northern holothurian *Cucumaria frondosa* and more extensive plains of shell gravel, some supporting maerl *Phymatolithon calcareum* and other areas with dense aggregations of the normally cryptic brittlestar *Ophiopholis aculeata*.

In Kyle Rhea, between Skye and the mainland, where tidal streams reach 8 knots, rich tideswept algal communities occur including the growth of *Alaria esculenta* on unstable ground at 17 m depth (Hiscock and Covey, 1991). Bedrock ridges in the sound support a mixture of species highly characteristic of such strong currents, including the massive sponges *Pachymatisma johnstoni* and *Myxilla incrustans*, the anemone *Sagartia elegans*, hydroids such as *Tubularia indivisa* and *Eudendrium* spp., but lesser quantities of the soft coral *Alcyonium digitatum* than is present in Bluemull Sound.

In the exceptionally strong currents (>8 knots) generated through the Gulf of Corryvreckan, between Jura and Scarba, this association of sponges and anemones is occasionally confined to more 'sheltered' areas and replaced, at depths of 30 m, by a fauna of barnacles *Balanus* spp. and mussels *Mytilus edulis* (Picton *et al.*, 1982), which are more adapted to withstanding such strong water movement. Such variations in species composition have many parallels with those found in conditions of wave surge, as described above.

8.6.4 Sealochs

The majority of Hebridean islands have coastlines which are highly indented by sealochs. These can be divided into three types, namely fjordic lochs, fjardic lochs and obs.

The fjordic lochs are typically elongated steep-sided lochs which are divided into a series of deep basins separated by narrows or sills. They hold distinctive sublittoral communities, on both rock and sediment habitats, which develop in the very sheltered and still environment created behind the entrance sills. Shallow habitats tend to be dominated by a forest of the kelp *Laminaria saccharina*, which replaces the *Laminaria hyperborea* forest of more exposed open coasts. On deeper rock populations of the anemone *Protanthea simplex*, a species apparently confined to fjordic lochs, occur in association with the brachiopods *Neocrania anomala* and *Terebratulina retusa* (Figure 8.2). Occasionally these are accompanied by dense aggregations of the worms *Chaetopterus* sp. and *Sabella pavonina*, species which live in tubes attached to the rock. In contrast to the open coast, the sheltered nature of these fjordic basins leads to very stable sediments which often develop species rich epibiota

Figure 8.2. Sheltered circalittoral rock community including anemones *Protanthea simplex*, fanworms *Sabella pavonina*, and brachiopods *Neocrania anomala* which are typical components of this fjordic sealoch habitat. Scale: 25–30 cm across (drawing by Sue Scott)

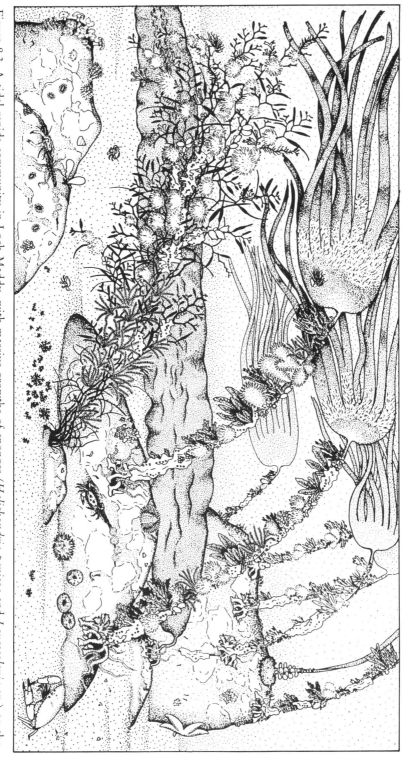

Figure 8.3. A tidal rapids community in Loch Maddy, with massive growths of sponges (*Halichondria panicea* and *Leucosolenia* sp.) on the stipes of the kelp *Laminaria hyperborea* and the podweed *Halidrys siliquosa*. Scale: 4–5 m across (drawing by Sue Scott)

and infaunal communities. The latter tend to be dominated by polychaete worms and small bivalves such as *Myrtea spinifera*, *Thyasira* spp., *Corbula gibba* and *Abra* spp., and there may be up to 100 species/m². The deep-sheltered basins are usually floored by fine undisturbed mud deposits in which a variety of large species, such as the prawn *Nephrops norvegicus*, shrimps such as *Calocaris macandreae*, the echiuran worm *Maxmuelleria lankesteri* and the fish *Lesueurigobius friesii*, excavate their burrows. Sitting erect from the mud surface are sea pens, for example *Funiculina quadrangularis*, and cerianthid anemones, such as *Pachycerianthus multiplicatus*, species which appear to be confined to fjordic sealochs in Scotland. Fjordic lochs, although best represented on the Scottish mainland, occur around the inner Hebridean islands of Mull and Skye and more rarely in the Western Isles, for example Loch Seaforth.

Fjardic lochs are generally much broader and shallower than fjordic lochs, typically lacking deep basins but broken into many shallow basins by numerous islands. In contrast to fjordic lochs, the fjards are best represented in the Western Isles, particularly the Uists. The many basins are separated by narrow channels through which tidal streams may be exceptionally strong, occasionally developing waterfalls as the tide ebbs from one basin to the next. Such strong currents give rise to algal communities possessing a rich variety of species and, in Loch Maddy, to unusual kelp formations (Fig. 8.3; Howson, 1991). The complexity of Loch Maddy, which has at least 22 sills, yields a wide variety of sublittoral habitats. In the upper reaches of the loch the basins become less saline and there is a transition to the brackish system of Loch an Duin (Nicol, 1936; Dipper *et al.*, 1981). The sublittoral zone complements that of the littoral which Lewis (1957) considered to be one of the richest and most interesting in the British Isles. Behind these channels are sheltered and shallow basins which are subject to greater fluctuations in both temperature and salinity than deeper fjordic basins. Many such basins in the Uists have extensive plains of very fine sediment at shallow depths of 2–4 m. These support species rarely encountered elsewhere, including dense populations of the synaptid holothurians *Labidoplax media* and *Leptosynapta bergensis* (Howson, 1991).

Obs are typically small ice-gouged basins connected to the open sea by narrow, often intertidal channels. As with fjards, most obs are situated in the Western Isles and range from small basins, no more than 0.2 km² (for example, Loch Obe, Barra) to larger more complex basins such as Loch Obisary in North Uist. Many of the obs are brackish in nature because of their restricted seawater input, supporting stands of the brackish-water grass *Ruppia* spp. and shoals of sticklebacks *Gasterosteus aculeatus*, as are found in Loch na h'Airde on Skye (Hiscock and Covey, 1991).

Perhaps the most intensively studied ob is Loch Obisary, which has attracted attention for both its benthic communities (Mitchell *et al.*, 1980; Dipper *et al.*, 1987) and its hydrography (Edwards, 1989). The hydrography of the loch appears to be unique in the British Isles, with a permanent halocline giving rise to a vertical separation of brackish and marine habitats.

8.6.4   Voes, vadills and houbs

These are features peculiar to the Shetland archipelago. The voes are all considered to be drowned river valleys or rias, excepting Ronas Voe which has an entrance sill and consequently fjordic characteristics. Off some voes lie almost enclosed bodies of water called vadills and houbs.

Unlike the fjords of western Scotland rocky habitats in the voes tend to be confined to shallow water, giving way at depths of 10–15 m to sediment plains, predominantly of muddy sands and gravels. Sediment plains in shallow water typically support algal communities which include a high proportion of brown algal species such as *Asperococcus turneri*, and more rarely in very shallow water stands of sea grass *Zostera marina*. Of particular note in Shetland are extensive sediment plains covered by thick loose-lying mats of algae such as *Phyllophora crispa* and populations of the snake blenny *Lumpenus lampretaeformis*, a species which is much less common further south.

Horse mussels *Modiolus modiolus* are particularly common in Shetland. They typically form clumps in a discrete band at about 20 m depth on the sediment plains. The horse-mussel clumps provide a rich habitat for other species of algae, hydroid and ascidian to grow and for mobile species to gain shelter. In addition to this clumped growth in the voes, *M. modiolus* forms denser beds where there are stronger tidal streams and also grows on bedrock on the open coast.

The vadills and houbs are essentially large brackish ponds cut off from the main body of the voe by a narrow bar or spit (Howson, 1988). They tend to be fringed by peat bog and saltmarsh and are very shallow (up to 2 m depth). Their brackish nature is reflected in the presence of stands of *Ruppia* spp., while the peaty sediment is dominated by oligochaetes, nematodes and *Corophium* spp. In some places there are large patches of phoronids and populations of holothurians such as *Leptosynapta inhaerens*. The sediment may be covered by filamentous algae, the chord weed *Chorda filum* and the red alga *Polyides rotundus*. In many respects the fauna and flora of these areas bears strong resemblance to the brackish obs of the Uists.

8.6.5   Estuaries and lagoons

Estuaries and lagoons are the least well-represented physiographic features around the Scottish islands although many of the sealochs and voes have estuarine habitats at their head and the obs, vadills and houbs are lagoonal in character but are not formed in the same manner as coastal lagoons, as defined by Barnes (1988). Barnes (1988) considers there to be only two proper lagoons on Scottish islands, namely Loch Ordais and Loch Arnol on Lewis. Both estuaries and lagoons are poorly developed in the Scottish islands. Where they do occur their habitats are primarily littoral.

8.7   Conclusion

The great extent of island coastline around Scotland gives rise to a wide range of physiographic features which in turn yield an exceptional variety of sublittoral habitats. Amongst these are a number of features which stand out for their uniqueness or importance within the context of the British Isles and north-west Europe. These include:

- the brackish habitats of the many obs, vadills and houbs of the Western Isles and Shetland;

- the fjardic lochs of the Uists;

- the extensive cave and tunnel systems of St. Kilda, Shetland and Fair Isle, and

- Rockall, because of its extreme exposure to wave action and its isolation.

As the Marine Nature Conservation Review continues its surveys around the rest of Great Britain the importance of particular communities and species both at a national and international level will become clearer and we will be able to identify those areas which best typify the communities which occur around our coast or which contain particularly unique or rare communities and species.

Acknowledgements

I am grateful to staff from the MNCR, particularly Keith Hiscock, for their helpful comments.

References

Alvarez, M., Gallardo, T., Ribera, M. A., and Garreta, G. 1988. A reassessment of northem Atlantic seaweed biogeography. *Phycologia*, **27**, 221–33.

Barnes, R. S. K. 1988. The coastal lagoons of Britain: an overview. (Contractor: University of Cambridge), *Nature Conservancy Council, CSD Report*, No. 933.

Bennett, T. L. 1989. Littoral and sublittoral survey of the Isle of May, Fife. *Nature Conservancy Council, CSD Report*, No. 907, (Marine Nature Conservation Review Report, No. MNCR/SR/2).

Connor, D. W. 1990. Survey of Lochs Linnhe, Eil, Creran and Aline. *Nature Conservancy Council, CSD Report*, No. 1073, (Marine Nature Conservation Review Report, No. MNCR/SR/12).

Connor, D. W. 1991a. Benthic marine ecosystems in Great Britain: a review of current knowledge. Clyde Sea, west Scotland, Outer Hebrides and north-west Scotland (MNCR Coastal sectors 12 to 15). *Nature Conservancy Council, CSD Report*, No. 1175, (Marine Nature Conservation Review Report, No. MNCR/OR/11).

Connor, D. W. 1991b. Norwegian fjords and Scottish sealochs: a comparative study. *Joint Nature Conservation Committee Report*, No. 12, (Marine Nature Conservation Review Report, No. MNCR/SR/18).

Dipper, F. A., Mitchell, R., and Earll, R. 1981. The survey and nature conservation evaluation of selected marine and brackish lochs in the Uists, Outer Hebrides. *Progress in Underwater Science*, **6**, 37–42.

Dipper, F. A., Lumb, C. M., and Palmer, M. A. 1987. A littoral, sublittoral and limnological survey of Loch Obisary, North Uist. 21st–29th June 1985, (Contractor: F. A. Dipper) *Nature Conservancy Council, CSD Report*, No. 807.

Edwards, A. 1989. The Loch Obisary surveys 1986/7, (Contractor: Scottish Marine Biological Association, Oban). *Nature Conservancy Council, CSD Report*, No. 952.

Ellett, D. J. 1979. Some oceanographic features of Hebridean waters. *Proceedings of the Royal Society of Edinburgh. Series B: Biological Sciences*, **77B**, 61–74.

Hiscock, K. 1983. Water movement. In R. Earll and D. G. Erwin (Eds), *Sublittoral Ecology. The Ecology of the Shallow Sublittoral Benthos*. Oxford University Press, Oxford, 58–96

Hiscock, K. 1985. Aspects of the ecology of rocky sublittoral areas. In P. G. Moore and R. Seed (Eds), *The Ecology of Rocky Coasts: Essays Presented to J. R. Lewis D.Sc*, Hodder and Stoughton, London, 290–328.

Hiscock, K. 1990. Marine Nature Conservation Review: methods. *Nature Conservancy Council, CSD Report*, No. 1072, (Marine Nature Conservation Review Report, No. MNCR/OR/5).

Hiscock, K. 1991. Benthic Marine ecosystems in Great Britain: a review of current knowledge. Introduction and Atlantic-European perspective. *Nature Conservancy Council, CSD Report*, No. 1170, (Marine Nature Conservation Review Report, No. MNCR/OR/6).

Hiscock, K., and Johnston, C. M. 1990. Review of marine biological information for Shetland. *Nature Conservancy Council, CSD Report*, No. 1000, (Marine Nature Conservation Review Report, No. MNCR/OR/1).

Hiscock, K., and Connor, D. W. 1991. Benthic marine habitats and communities in Great Britain: the development of an MNCR classification. *Joint Nature Conservation Committee Report*, No. 6, (Marine Nature Conservation Review report no. MNCR/OR/14).

Hiscock, S., and Covey, R. 1991. Marine biological surveys around Skye. *Nature Conservancy Council, CSD Report*, No. 1076, (Marine Nature Conservation Review Report, No. MNCR/SR/3).

Howson, C. M. (Ed.) 1987. *Directory of the British Marine Fauna and Flora. A Coded Checklist of the Marine Fauna and Flora of the British Isles and its Surrounding Seas*. Ross-on-Wye, Marine Conservation Society.

Howson, C. M. 1988. Marine Nature Conservation Review: survey of Shetland, Foula and Fair Isle, 1987. (Contractor: Field Studies Council Oil Pollution Research Unit, Pembroke). *Nature Conservancy Council, CSD Report*, No. 816.

Howson, C. M. 1991. Surveys of Scottish sealochs: the sealochs of North and South Uist and Benbecula. (Contractor: University Marine Biological Station, Millport). *Joint Nature Conservation Committee Report*, No. 3.

Howson, C. M. and Picton, B. E. 1985. A sublittoral survey of St. Kilda. (Contractor: British Sub-Aqua Club and Marine Conservation Society). *Nature Conservancy Council, CSD Report*, No. 595.

Institute of Offshore Engineering. 1986. *Redevelopment of an Orkney Seaweed Industry. A Market Appraisal and Suggested Development Strategy*. Edinburgh, Heriot-Watt University.

Laffoley, D. d'A., and Hiscock, K. 1988. *Marine Biological Survey of Rockall, 28 and 29 June 1988. Field Report*. Peterborough, Nature Conservancy Council.

Lewis, J. R. 1957. An introduction to the intertidal ecology of the rocky shores of a Hebridean island. *Oikos. Acta oecologia Scandinavica*, **8**, 130–60.

Maggs, C. A. 1986. Scottish marine macroalgae: a distributional checklist, biogeographical analysis and literature abstract. (Contractor: Queen's University, Belfast). *Nature Conservancy Council, CSD Report*, No. 635.

Mitchell, R., Dipper, F. A., Earll, R., and Rowe, S. 1980. A preliminary study of Loch Obisary: a brackish Hebridean loch. *Progress in Underwater Science*, **5**, 99–118.

Nicol, E. A. T. 1936. The brackish-water lochs of North Uist. *Proceedings of the Royal Society of Edinburgh. Series B: Biological sciences*, **56**, 169–95.

Norton, T. A., McAllister, H. A., Conway, E., and Irvine, L. M. 1969. The marine algae of the Hebridean Island of Colonsay. *British Phycological Journal*, **4**, 125–36.

Norton, T. A., and Milburn, J. A. 1972. Direct observations on the sublittoral marine algae of Argyll, Scotland. *Hydrobiologia*, **40**, 55–68.

Picton, B. E., Howson, C. M., Connor, D. W., and Williams, A. 1982. Sublittoral survey of Scarba, Lunga and the Garvellachs. (Contractor: B. E. Picton). *Nature Conservancy Council, CSD Report*, No. 436.

Price, J. H., and Tittley, I. 1978. Marine Algae. In A. C. Jermy and J. A. Crabbe (Eds), *The Island of Mull; A Survey of its Flora and Environment*. British Museum (Natural History), London, 19.1–19.37.

Spence, D. H. N., Allen, E. D., and Fraser, J. 1979. Macrophytic vegetation of fresh and brackish waters in and near the Loch Druidibeg National Nature Reserve, South Uist. *Proceedings of the Royal Society of Edinburgh. Series B: Biological Sciences,* **77B,** 307–28.

Waterston, A. R. and Lyster, I. H. J. 1979. The macrofauna of brackish and fresh waters of the Loch Druidibeg National Nature Reserve and its neighbourhood, South Uist. *Proceedings of the Royal Society of Edinburgh. Series B: Biological Sciences,* **77B,** 353–76.

Whittaker, T. 1991. *Islay. Wave Power in Action*. Review, Department of Energy, **17,** 10–11.

9 EXPLOITED FISH AND SHELLFISH STOCKS IN SEAS ADJACENT TO THE SCOTTISH ISLANDS

R. S. Bailey

Summary

1. Fish and shellfish species in the seas around Scotland have been exploited for many years. For some species much is known of the stocks, for others which have only recently been exploited, much less is known.

2. It is not possible to identify fish populations belonging to particular islands or even particular island groups. A much wider perspective than this must be taken in developing overall fisheries management.

3. Islands are important in shaping currents and increasing habitat diversity.

4. Of all the island groups, Shetland is by far the most important in terms of size of landings, mainly due to the presence of processing facilities.

9.1 Introduction

Commercially important fish and shellfish resources in the seas around Scotland have been the subject of research for over a century (Lucas, 1987). For some of the more traditional resources (haddock and herring, for example), the amount of quantitative information is considerable, whereas for others, and especially those that have only been exploited relatively recently, the available information is not so complete. What information is available about the fish and shellfish resources around the island groups is summarized in a number of earlier review papers (e.g. Bailey *et al.*, 1979, 1986; Hislop, 1986; Mason *et al.*, 1985), while a review of the biology of both exploited and unexploited species of fish found in the seas adjacent to the west coast of Scotland can be found in Gordon (1981) and Gordon and De Silva (1980). Poxton (1992) has also provided a review of the conservation of marine fish in Scottish waters. Scientific names of fish and shellfish used in this paper are given in Tables 9.3 and 9.4.

The population units considered by fishery scientists are termed 'stocks'. For present purposes the term 'stock' can be defined as all the fish of a given species occupying a particular sea area within which there is likely to be considerable mixing, and between which there is thought to be relatively little mixing. In the case of most exploited species, the stock units used for fishery assessment and management purposes are usually relatively large. Only in very few cases (for example, the Shetland population of the sand eel *Ammodytes marinus* and the Rockall stock of haddock) has a separate population been identified as belonging to a particular island or island group. Islands as such thus have little significance in a fisheries management context, although they may be very important in the sense that their physical presence and the associated submarine topography affects the hydrography and currents in the waters around them and creates a fragmentation which may affect the area and diversity of habitat suitable for inshore species. To inshore fishermen, they may also provide fishing opportunities during periods of severe weather.

The areas considered in this paper are those adjacent to the main island groups: the Orkney islands and Shetland islands, the Inner and Outer Hebrides, Rockall and the Clyde islands. Individual small islands along the Scottish east coast are not considered. After a brief survey of the importance of fish and shellfish to the island economies, the main commercially important stocks found in the seas adjacent to (within about 30 nautical miles) the islands are described. Where available, information is given on the level of exploitation of the stocks concerned.

9.2 Landings of Fish in the Scottish Islands

Landings of fish within each of the 20 fishery districts in Scotland are recorded by the Fisheries Statistics Unit of the Scottish Office Agriculture and Fisheries Department (Anon., 1992a,b). Within each district, landings are further subdivided by 'creek'. The landings of demersal fish, pelagic fish and shellfish in 1990 and 1991 are summarized in Table 9.1 for each of the main island groups. Landings in each of the 'creeks' associated with the islands are given in Table 9.2.

With the exception of Shetland, landings of fin fish into ports on the Scottish islands are relatively modest in scale. On most islands the landings are those needed to satisfy the small local markets. Rather more are landed where port facilities are available, for example the Outer Hebrides. Even then, however, the ports concerned compete for resources with mainland ports which have access to road or rail transport. In all island groups except the Shetland islands, landings are predominantly of shellfish which command a relatively high unit price. While some shellfish are processed locally, most go for export, many being shipped from the islands and transported live in 'vivier' lorries. Processing facilities for fin fish have been developed on some islands but are not of major importance at present except on Shetland. A reduction factory for production of fish-meal is in operation on Bressay, Shetland, but factories which were installed at two localities on the Outer Hebrides are no longer in operation.

Table 9.1 Weight and first sale value of fin fish and shellfish landings in each island group in 1990 and 1991
(Weight in thousand tonnes, value in millions of £; Source: Anon 1992a,b)

			Demersal fish	Pelagic fish	Shellfish	Total
Shetland	1990	Weight	21.48	93.33	1.13	115.94
		Value	13.25	10.21	1.33	24.79
	1991	Weight	18.86	84.96	1.00	104.82
		Value	12.26	9.05	1.40	22.71
Orkney	1990	Weight	0.68	–	0.93	1.61
		Value	0.62	–	2.05	2.68
	1991	Weight	0.21	–	0.88	1.09
		Value	0.23	–	1.71	1.94
Outer Isles	1990	Weight	2.11	0.13	3.92	6.16
		Value	1.05	0.04	7.65	8.73
	1991	Weight	1.54	0.02	4.42	5.98
		Value	1.35	0.02	8.20	9.57
Skye	1990	Weight	0.13	–	0.72	0.85
		Value	0.17	–	1.82	1.99
	1991	Weight	0.23	–	0.82	1.05
		Value	0.26	–	2.15	2.41
Luing,	1990	Weight	0.02	–	1.77	1.79
Mull, Coll		Value	0.02	–	2.77	2.79
and Tiree	1991	Weight	0.02	–	2.31	2.32
		Value	0.01	–	3.65	3.67
Gigha,	1990	Weight	0.04	–	0.52	0.56
Islay, Jura		Value	0.05	–	0.92	0.97
and Colonsay	1991	Weight	–	–	0.71	0.71
		Value	–	–	1.13	1.13
Clyde	1990	Weight	0.02	–	0.16	0.18
Islands		Value	0.02	–	0.60	0.62
	1991	Weight	0.03	0.03	0.14	0.21
		Value	0.03	0.01	0.38	0.42

The one exception to this overview is the Shetlands which accounted for 116 000 t of fish and shellfish landed in 1990 at a first-sale value of almost £25 million. There, processing facilities are well developed and, in addition, large numbers of foreign factory vessels (klondykers) assemble to convey supplies of pelagic fish (herring and mackerel) caught by Scottish fishing vessels to markets elsewhere. Of the fish and shellfish landed in Shetland, including those taken by the klondykers, pelagic fish are predominant in terms of weight (80%), but demersal fish are more important in terms of value (53%). Nevertheless, the importance of pelagic fish in the Shetlands is demonstrated by the fact that the islands accounted for almost 40% of all pelagic fish landed in Scottish ports in 1990.

Table 9.2   Weight and first sale value of fin fish and shellfish landings in each 'creek' in 1990 and 1991 (Weight in tonnes, value in thousands of £; Source: Anon 1992a,b)

Island group or Creek	Demersal fish		Pelagic fish		Shellfish		Total	
Orkney District	1990	1991	1990	1991	1990	1991	1990	1991
Sanday	–	–	–	–	47	26	47	26
	–	–	–	–	£151	£72	£151	£72
Westray	–	–	–	–	212	177	212	177
	–	–	–	–	£448	£308	£448	£308
Stronsay	–	–	–	–	46	27	46	27
	–	–	–	–	£96	£63	£96	£63
Rousay	–	–	–	–	58	25	58	25
	–	–	–	–	£135	£58	£135	£58
Kirkwall	601	163	–	–	263	327	864	490
	£567	£202	–	–	£583	£594	£1149	£795
Stromness	77	43	–	–	219	233	296	276
	£58	£30	–	–	£404	£461	£462	£492
South Ronaldsay	–	–	–	–	50	44	50	44
	–	–	–	–	£125	£107	£125	£107
Hoy	–	–	–	–	39	21	39	21
	–	–	–	–	£110	£47	£110	£47
Shetland District								
South Mainland and	–	8	–	–	4	8	4	17
Fair Isle	–	£14	–	–	£20	£15	£20	£28
Lerwick	16 195	13 321	93 320	84 958	199	160	109 714	98 439
	£7052	£5889	£10 203	£9047	£279	£265	£17 534	£15 201
Whalsay	98	85	–	–	41	41	139	125
	£62	£95	–	–	£24	£75	£86	£170
Skerries	–	–	–	–	–	15	–	15
	–	–	–	–	–	£27	–	£27
Yell, Fetlar and	362	539	–	–	262	220	624	759
Unst	£397	£603	–	–	£329	£355	£726	£958
Central Mainland	23	51	–	–	210	242	234	293
	£21	£49	–	–	£324	£304	£344	£353
Northmavine	214	157	–	–	64	73	278	230
	£186	£141	–	–	£47	£74	£233	£215
West Mainland	119	117	7	–	136	93	262	210
	£116	£101	£8	–	£154	£103	£278	£204
Scalloway	4472	4579	+	3	212	152	4685	4735
	£5416	£5370	+	£1	£157	£184	£5573	£5554

Table 9.2   (cont'd)

Island group or Creek	Demersal fish		Pelagic fish		Shellfish		Total	
Stornoway District								
Lochs	+	–	–	–	27	48	27	48
	+	–	–	–	£46	£95	£46	£95
Stornoway	1426	487	36	7	1479	1463	2941	1957
	£496	£448	£15	£6	£2198	£2086	£2709	£2540
Portnaguran and Ness	–	–	–	–	42	71	42	71
	–	–	–	–	£77	£165	£77	£165
Bernera (Lewis)	14	80	–	–	351	405	366	485
	£18	£110	–	–	£577	£772	£596	£882
North Harris	28	71	18	12	105	202	151	284
	£22	£56	£17	£10	£159	£242	£198	£308
Scalpay	–	–	–	–	16	21	16	21
	–	–	–	–	£91	£51	£91	£51
South Harris	–	95	–	+	86	245	86	340
	–	£78	–	+	£213	£493	£213	£572
Berneray (North Uist)	–	–	–	–	191	181	191	181
	–	–	–	–	£724	£398	£724	£398
North Uist	–	20	73	–	179	326	252	346
	–	£16	£11	–	£499	£939	£510	£955
Grimsay	–	–	–	–	82	109	82	109
	–	–	–	–	£326	£329	£326	£329
Benbecula	–	–	–	–	25	39	25	39
	–	–	–	–	£92	£99	£92	£99
South Uist and Eriksay	220	308	–	–	355	245	576	553
	£174	£236	–	–	£904	£540	£1077	£777
Barra	424	482	–	–	981	1067	1404	1549
	£335	£406	–	–	£1742	£1993	£2077	£2399
Mallaig District (Skye)								
Broadford	–	–	–	–	31	28	31	28
	–	–	–	–	£88	£49	£88	£49
Portree	3	22	–	–	213	293	216	316
	£3	£16	–	–	£512	£716	£515	£731
Snizort	128	206	–	–	258	247	386	453
	£170	£246	–	–	£592	£609	£762	£855
Dunvegan	–	–	–	–	34	60	34	60
	–	–	–	–	£69	£155	£69	£155
Bracadale	1	–	–	–	54	57	55	57
	£1	–	–	–	£179	£147	£179	£147
Strathaird	+	+	–	–	125	135	125	135
	+	+	–	–	£381	£477	£381	£477

Table 9.2   (cont'd)

Island group or Creek	Demersal fish		Pelagic fish		Shellfish		Total	
Oban District (Mull, Coll, Tiree etc)								
Luing	–	–	–	–	514	616	514	616
	–	–	–	–	£837	£1014	£837	£1014
Tobermory (Mull)	6	2	–	–	462	623	468	624
	£5	£2	–	–	£964	£1267	£968	£1269
Loch Scridain (Mull)	16	15	–	–	614	790	630	805
	£15	£12	–	–	£768	£1041	£783	£1054
Loch Buie (Mull)	–	–	–	–	13	55	13	55
	–	–	–	–	£11	£51	£11	£51
Coll	–	–	–	–	36	64	36	64
	–	–	–	–	£36	£70	£36	£70
Tiree	–	–	–	–	129	161	129	161
	–	–	–	–	£158	£212	£158	£212
Campbeltown District (Jura, Colonsay, Bute and Arran)								
Gigha	+	+	–	–	3	97	3	97
	+	£1	–	–	£6	£163	£6	£164
Port Ellen	36	1	+	–	517	529	553	530
	£47	£1	+	–	£915	£812	£962	£813
Port Askaig	–	+	–	–	–	82	–	82
	–	+	–	–	–	£143	–	£143
Jura	–	–	–	–	–	6	–	6
	–	–	–	–	–	£13	–	£13
Bute (Clyde)	21	31	4	23	129	97	153	151
	£22	£29	£2	£4	£563	£348	£587	£381
Arran (Clyde)	–	–	–	–	30	41	30	41
	–	–	–	–	£34	£30	£34	£30
Ayr District								
Cumbraes (Clyde)	+	2	–	10	2	6	2	18
	+	£4	–	£2	£8	£4	£8	£10

9.3   Fish and Shellfish Resources

Fish and shellfish caught by UK fishing vessels landing in Scottish ports are recorded by ICES (International Council for the Exploration of the Sea) statistical rectangles approximately 30 × 30 nautical miles in extent (Figure 9.1).

At this scale of recording, it is not possible to estimate the amounts landed, say, within a certain radius of each island or island group. Instead, in this paper the catches reported from those rectangles adjacent to the islands have been used, although some rectangles clearly include areas closer to the mainland than to any islands. To provide an indication of the landings of fish caught around the islands treated together, the area shown in Figure 9.1 has been chosen. For this purpose Rockall (not shown) is treated separately.

The amount of fishing by UK fishing vessels in each rectangle in the 'island area' in 1991 is shown in Figure 9.2 for towed demersal and pelagic gears. Creel fishing for lobsters and crab species also takes place and is particularly important around the coastlines of islands which offer extended opportunities of suitable ground and sheltered conditions. In some areas, grounds used by creel fishermen (static gear reserves) are protected from active fishing gears under the Scottish Inshore Fisheries Act.

In addition to fishing by UK vessels, there is a certain amount of fishing within the 12-mile limit (Figure 9.1) by vessels from other countries with historic fishing rights, although this is on a very small scale in most of the areas considered. Moreover, an area around Shetland is subject to controls under EC legislation on the number of non-UK vessels that may fish there. Certain other areas adjacent to some islands are protected from certain types of fishing by regulations under the EC conservation regulation. Examples are a herring spawning area closure to the north and west of the Outer Hebrides and the so-called 'Norway pout box' in the north-western North Sea adjacent to Orkney and Shetland in which fishing for Norway pout is prohibited with the objective of protecting haddock and whiting nursery areas.

The reported landings of fish and shellfish by rectangle within the 'island' area are shown for selected species in Figures 9.3 and 9.4. The species chosen are either representative of important groups of species (e.g. haddock representing the main stocks of roundfish) or species of particular interest or importance in the areas concerned. Landings of species of which on average more than 100 t were caught in the 'island' area in 1990–1991 are listed in Table 9.3. The main demersal species are haddock, cod and whiting, but some other species such as anglerfish and megrim have increased in importance in recent years because of their high value. Among pelagic species, herring and mackerel predominate, while the fisheries for sprats and sand eels have decreased in importance.

The most important shellfish are Norway lobster (*Nephrops norvegicus*), edible and velvet crabs and scallops. The distribution of each of the shellfish species tends to be patchy because of their association with particular types of substrate. Thus, *Nephrops* is found on clay and silt in which it can burrow, while edible crabs are found on gravelly sand and velvet crabs and lobsters on rocky inshore grounds. With the exception of squid, the distribution of shellfish generally follows the known distribution of sediment and rock types.

Owing to its isolation, landings of fish from Rockall Bank are given separately in Table 9.4. There, the main species exploited by UK fishing vessels are haddock

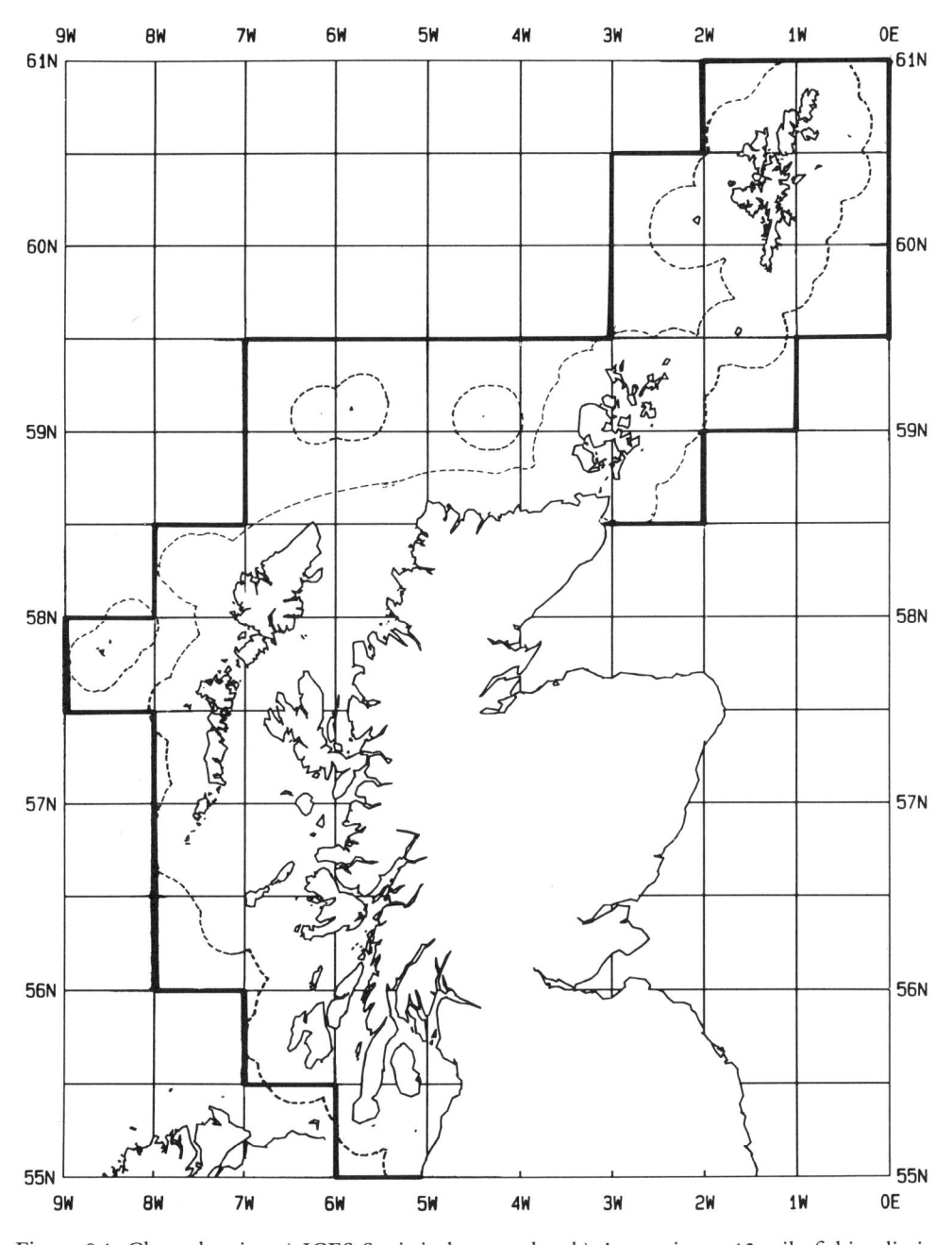

Figure 9.1. Chart showing a) ICES Statistical rectangles; b) Approximate 12-mile fishing limit (drawn by eye); c) Area chosen to represent 'island' seas (heavy bold line).

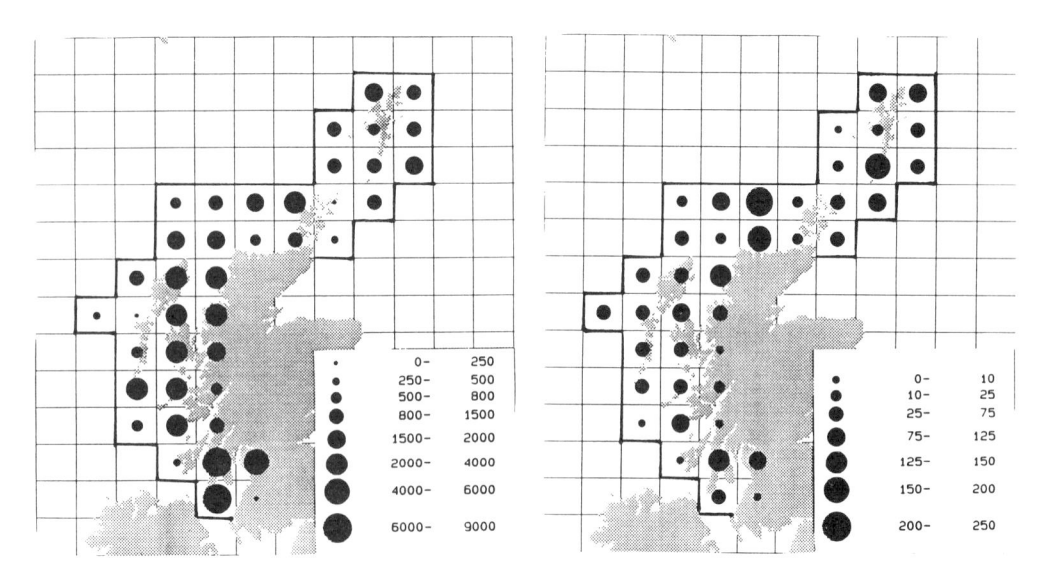

Figure 9.2. Reported fishing effort by UK fishing vessels in 1991. Left: days fishing by towed demersal gears (bottom trawl; Danish seine). Right: days fishing by pelagic gears (purse seine; midwater trawl).

and cod with, in some years, significant catches of squid. Vessels from other countries also fish in this area mainly using lines.

9.4   The State of the Stocks

Assessments of the state of the commercially important fish stocks in the northeast Atlantic are coordinated annually by ICES. For the area considered here, three of the ICES statistical areas are involved: the northern North Sea (Division IVa), the west of Scotland (Division VIa) and Rockall (Division VIb) (Figure 9.5). The units of stock assessment in general follow these statistical areas, but most stocks in the North Sea are assessed for the whole of the area (Divisions IVa, b and c combined).

For stocks that have been intensively investigated, full assessments are carried out of the historical development of the size of the stock, the incoming recruitment and the fishing mortality rate, the assessments being based on records and biological sampling of the commercial catches and fishing effort and regular research vessel surveys. For those stocks currently assessed by ICES, reports are published annually by the Advisory Committee on Fishery Management (ACFM) of ICES, together with management advice where required (Anon., 1993). An example of the type of information provided is shown in Figure 9.6 for the haddock stock west of Scotland. The results of recent assessments for all those fin fish stocks that have significant landings in the seas adjacent to the Scottish islands are summarized in Table 9.5. What information is available about shellfish stocks is summarized in Table 9.6.

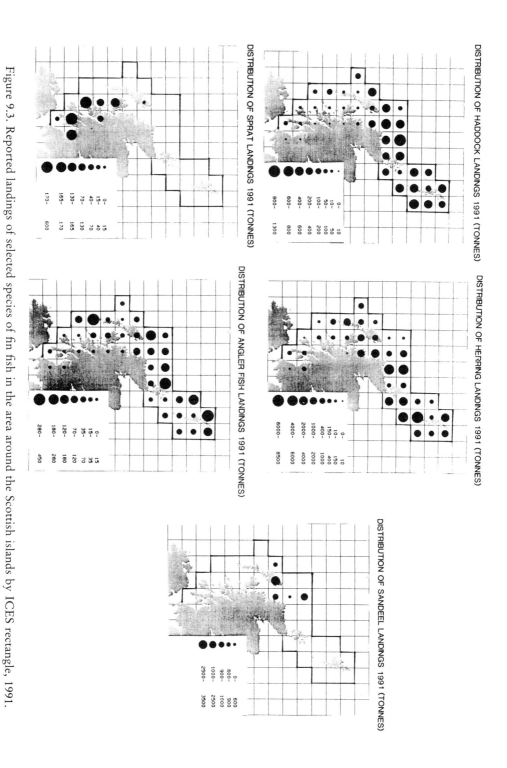

Figure 9.3. Reported landings of selected species of fin fish in the area around the Scottish islands by ICES rectangle, 1991.

DISTRIBUTION OF HADDOCK LANDINGS 1991 (TONNES)

DISTRIBUTION OF HERRING LANDINGS 1991 (TONNES)

DISTRIBUTION OF SPRAT LANDINGS 1991 (TONNES)

DISTRIBUTION OF ANGLER FISH LANDINGS 1991 (TONNES)

DISTRIBUTION OF SANDEEL LANDINGS 1991 (TONNES)

DISTRIBUTION OF NORWAY LOBSTER LANDINGS
1991 (TONNES)

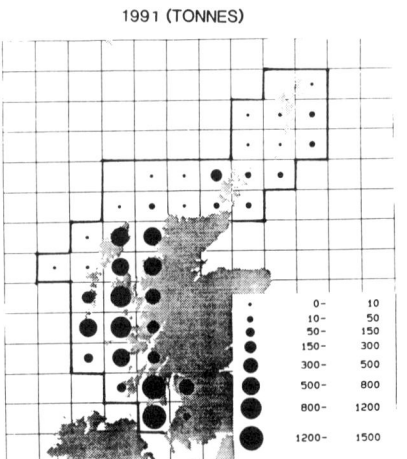

DISTRIBUTION OF VELVET CRAB LANDINGS 1991 (TONNES)

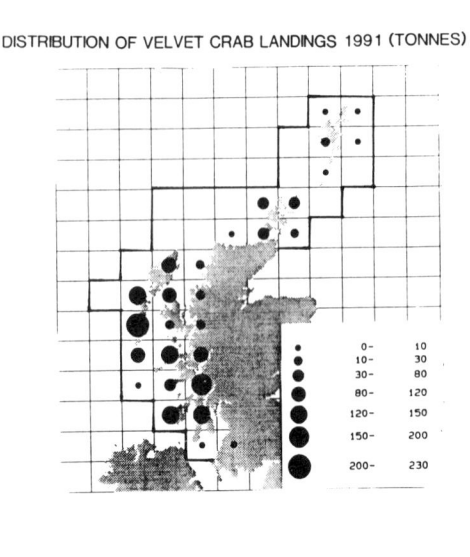

DISTRIBUTION OF SCALLOP LANDINGS 1991 (TONNES)

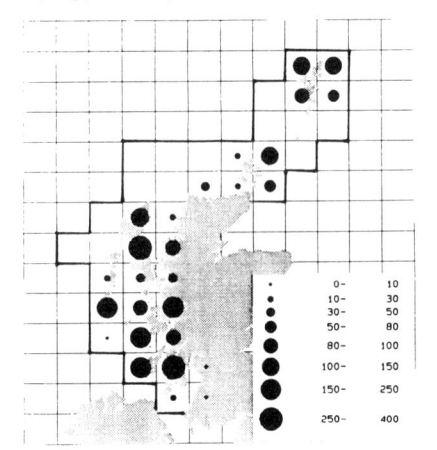

DISTRIBUTION OF QUEEN SCALLOP LANDINGS 1991 (TONNES)

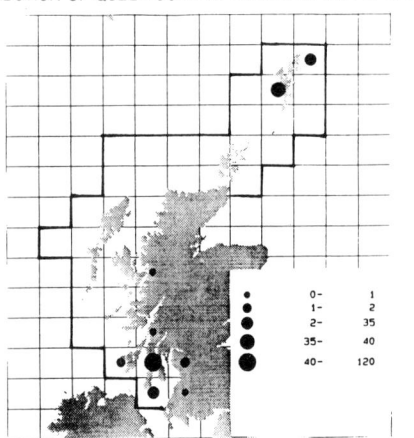

Figure 9.4. Reported landings of selected species of shellfish in the area around the Scottish islands by ICES rectangle, 1991.

In the case of the main demersal stocks in the North Sea and to the west of Scotland, the roundfish are all heavily exploited and the spawning stock sizes are in some cases close to their lowest recorded levels. In the case of North Sea haddock, the stock has recently increased as a result of improved recruitment by the year-classes spawned in 1990 and 1991, but the fishing mortality rate (a measure of the proportion of the stock removed by fishing each year) is still very high. For the mixed demersal fisheries in both the North Sea and Division VIa west of Scotland, ICES has for the last three years consistently advised a significant reduction in fishing effort. The stocks of anglerfish and megrim have not yet been estimated but what information is available indicates

Table 9.3   Reported landings in Scottish ports of fish and shellfish caught in the area shown in Figure 9.1.
(Values given are the mean for 1990 and 1991 in tonnes; Source: unpublished data from the Scottish Office Agriculture and Fisheries Department)

Demersal fish		*Pelagic fish*		*Shellfish*	
Haddock	10 600	Herring	57 300	Norway lobster	10 472
Melanogrammus aeglifinus		*Clupea harengus*		*Nephrops norvegicus*	
Cod	9100	Mackerel	32 900	Edible crab	4250
Gadus morhua		*Scomber scombrus*		*Cancer pagurus*	
Whiting	8600	Sand eel	12 300	Scallop	2888
Merlangius merlangus		Mainly *Ammodytes marinus*		*Pecten maximus*	
Spurdog	3700	Sprat	1200	Velvet crab	1681
Squalus acanthias		*Sprattus sprattus*		*Leocarcinus puber*	
Anglerfish	3100			Periwinkle	1425
Lophius piscatorius				*Littorina* spp	
Saithe	3100			Lobster	570
Pollachius virens				*Homarus gammarus*	
Skate	2100			Squid	375
Raja spp				mostly Loliginidae	
Plaice	1700			Green crab	308
Pleuronectes platessa				*Carcinus maenas*	
Hake	1300			Queen scallop	202
Merluccius merluccius				*Chlamys opercularis*	
Megrim	1300				
Lepidorhombus whiffiagonis					

Other species with landings of > 100 t (10 t for shellfish)

Ling	Horse mackerel	Whelk
Molva molva	*Trachurus trachurus*	*Buccinum undatum*
Witch		Octopus
Glyptocephalus cynoglossus		Octopodidae
Lemon sole		Crawfish
Microstomus kitt		Palinuridae
Common dab		
Limanda limanda		
Catfish		
Anarhichas lupus		
Pollack		
Pollachius pollachius		

Table 9.4 Reported landings in Scottish ports of fish and shellfish caught in the area around Rockall. (Values given are the mean for 1990 and 1991 in tonnes; Source: unpublished data from the Scottish Office Agriculture and Fisheries Department)

Haddock	4016
Cod	1066
Whiting	298
Saithe	284
Megrim	192
Anglerfish	170
Ling	110

Other species of which 10–100 t were caught: Catfish; squid; skate; plaice; mackerel; spurdog; lemon sole; witch; halibut (*Hippoglossus hippoglossus*); tusk (*Brosme brosme*); pollack

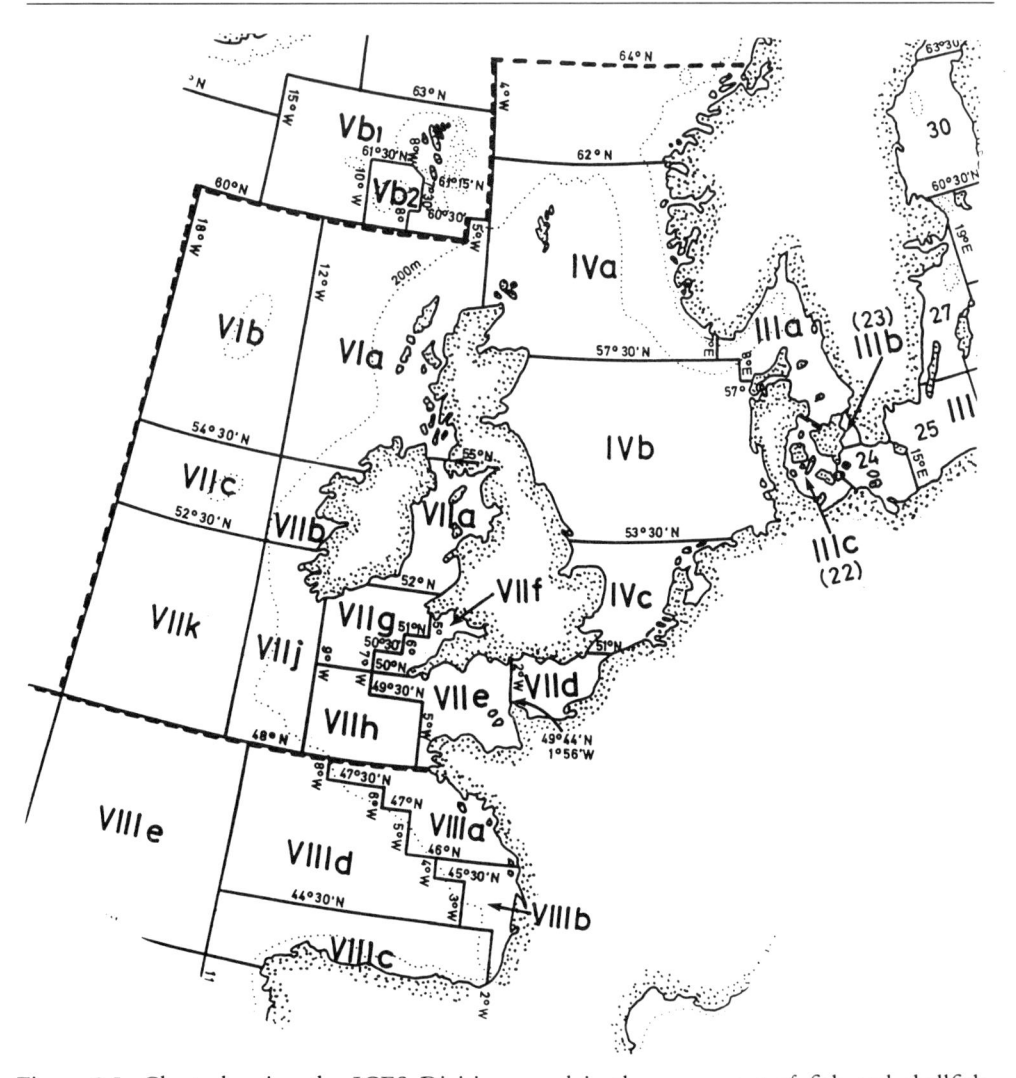

Figure 9.5. Chart showing the ICES Divisions used in the assessment of fish and shellfish stocks.

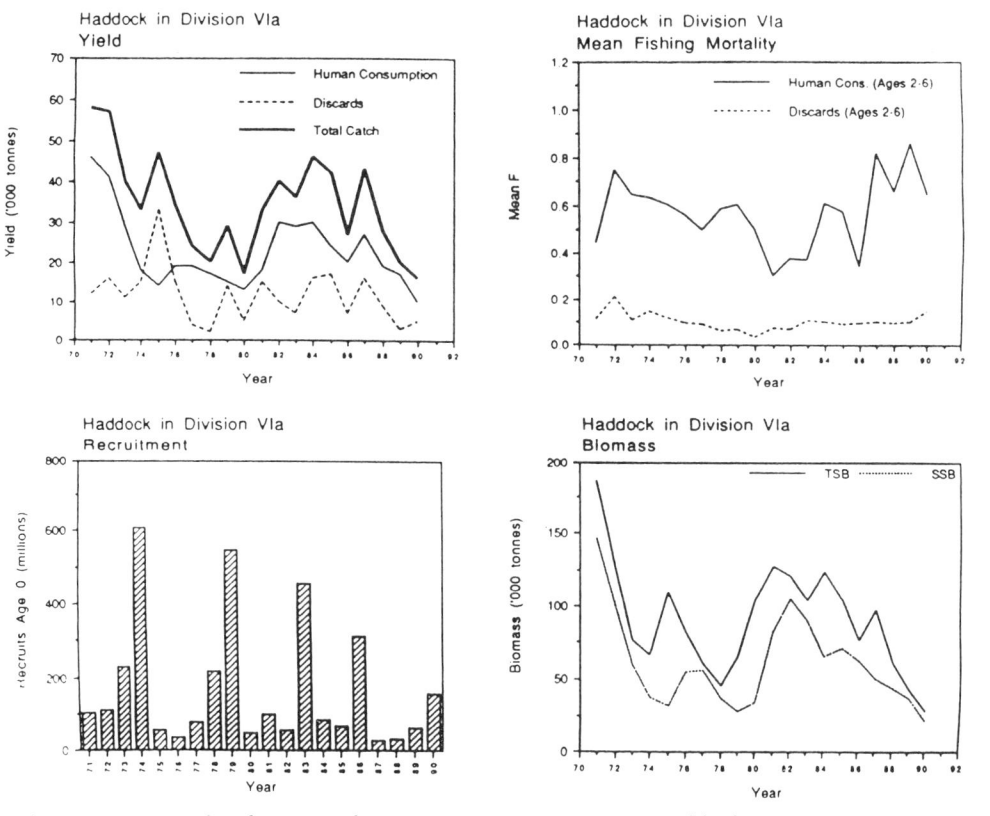

Figure 9.6. Example of outputs from an ICES assessment – Haddock in ICES Division VIa (see Figure 9.5) The figures show: a) The annual catch broken down into human consumption landings and discards; b) The estimated instantaneous fishing mortality rate F (arithmetic average for the age groups 2–6 years old); (an F of 0.6 roughly equates to removals by fishing of 41% of the stock alive at the beginning of the year); c) The recruitment of 0-group haddock by year (estimated number of haddock in their first year of life at 1 July in millions); d) The estimated total (TSB) and spawning stock biomass (SSB) at spawning time.

that they are probably also fully exploited (i.e. any further increase in fishing on them is not expected to result in any long-term increase in yield).

With the exception of sprat, the stocks of pelagic fish exploited in Scottish waters are in general in an acceptable state. In the western mackerel stock, which migrates between spawning grounds to the west of Ireland and feeding grounds in the North Sea and Norwegian Sea, recent recruitment has been at a fairly high level and the stock appears to be fairly stable. The stocks of herring in the North Sea and to the west of Scotland have increased since the fisheries were closed in the late 1970s and early 1980s.

Industrial fisheries in the area of the Scottish islands are currently at a low level. The Shetland sand eel fishery began in 1974, reached a peak of around 52 000 t in 1982 and subsequently decreased. Following a series of poor year-classes, the fishery was closed in 1991. There is evidence that the year-class spawned in 1991 was much more abundant than those spawned in the previous few years (Anon, 1993). The fishery for sand eels to the west of Scotland takes place in the North Minch and around North Rona and the Flannan Islands. The fishery started in 1980, rose to a peak of 24 000 t in 1986 and 1988 and landings have diminished since the closure of the two fishmeal factories on the Outer Hebrides. Landings from this fishery are now made into Shetland.

Table 9.5   Results of 1992 ICES assessments of fin fish stocks which are exploited at least partly within the 'island' area shown in Figure 9.1. ICES areas are shown in Figure 9.5
Source: Anon (1993)

Species	Stock Unit	ICES areas	Fishing mortality rate	Size of spawning stock	Comments and ICES advice
Cod	North Sea	IV	High	Lowest recorded	Fishing effort should be reduced
Haddock	North Sea	IV	Record high level	Recovering from a very low level	Fishing effort should be reduced
Whiting	North Sea	IV	High	Below long-term average	Fishing effort should be reduced
Saithe	North Sea	IV and IIIa	High	Very low	Fishing mortality should be reduced
Plaice	North Sea	IV	Moderate	At long-term average	No increase in long-term yield from any increase in fishing mortality
Cod	West of Scotland	VIa	High	Lowest recorded	Fishing effort should be reduced
Haddock	West of Scotland	VIa	High	Low	Fishing effort should be reduced
Haddock	Rockall	VIb	High	Well below average	Variable stock: fishing mortality should be reduced

Table 9.5   (cont'd)

Species	Stock Unit	ICES areas	Fishing mortality rate	Size of spawning stock	Comments and ICES advice
Whiting	West of Scotland	VIa	High	Below long-term average	Fishing effort should be reduced
Saithe	West of Scotland	VIa and b	Fairly high	Lowest recorded	Fishing mortality should be reduced
Megrim	West of Scotland	VIa and b	Fairly high	Not estimated	Fishing mortality should not be increased
Anglerfish	West of Scotland	VIa and b	Fairly high	Not estimated	Fishing mortality should not be increased
Hake	Northern stock	IIIa, IV, VI, VII, VIIIa,b	Moderate	Low and decreasing	Capable of sustaining present level of fishing, but protection of juvenile hake needed
Mackerel	Western stock	VI, VII, VIIIa,b, Vb, IIa, and IVa from July to December	Moderate	Stable at long-term average level	Migrates into North Sea in second half of year; present level of fishing acceptable
Herring	Northern and central North Sea	IVa,b	Moderate	Fairly stable at moderately high level	The stock is not currently overfished
Herring	West of Scotland	VIa (north of 56 N)	Uncertain	Probably above recent average	Probably not currently overfished
Herring	Clyde	VIa (Firth of Clyde)	Low	At a low level	Fishery should be kept at lowest possible level to enhance recovery

Table 9.5   (cont'd)

Species	Stock Unit	ICES areas	Fishing mortality rate	Size of spawning stock	Comments and ICES advice
Sandeel	Shetland	IVa (Shetland area)	Fishery closed	Stock low but expected to recover as a result of good 1991 year-class	Fishery should remain closed until firm evidence of recovery
Sandeel	West of Scotland	VIa	Very low	At recent average level	Stock 'virtually unexploited'; no advice given

Less is known about the state of most stocks of shellfish. The only species whose stocks are assessed by ICES is *Nephrops norvegicus* (Anon, 1993). While the sizes of the stocks of this species have not been estimated, there is information on the intensity of exploitation (Table 9.6). While the stocks do not appear to be in any danger, most of them may already be subject to 'growth overfishing' – the long-term yield could be increased by reducing the amount of fishing on them. No quantitative assessments have been carried out on other stocks of shellfish by ICES, but national assessments have been made. The results are given in Table 9.6.

Table 9.6 Available information about shellfish stocks with Scottish landings of more than 100 t in the 'island' area shown in Figure 9.1
Source: *Nephrops* stocks (Anon., 1993); other species (unpublished information from SOAFD Marine Laboratory)

Species and stock	Landings at Scottish ports in 1991	Comments
Nephrops norvegicus (a) Noup (NW of Orkney)	200 t	Landings fluctuate due to fluctuating effort and catch-per-unit-effort
(b) North Minch	2780 t	Fishing at about optimum level
(c) South Minch	4210 t	Over-exploited; would benefit from reduction in effort

Table 9.6   (cont'd)
Source: *Nephrops* stocks (Anon., 1993); other species (unpublished information from SOAFD Marine Laboratory)

Species and stock	Landings at Scottish ports in 1991	Comments
(d) Firth of Clyde	3030 t	Probably over-exploited; abundance relatively low. A precautionary TAC is set for b, c and d combined
Lobster	543 t	Over-exploited (Hebrides and Orkney)
Edible crab	4998 t	Over-exploited at Shetland, moderately exploited in Hebrides. No detailed information
Green crab	346 t	No detailed information
Velvet crab	1723 t	No detailed information
Scallop	2672 t	West coast stock at rather low level following poor recruitment. Some reason for concern
Queen scallop	190 t	Two small fisheries: Shetland and Firth of Clyde
Periwinkle	1717 t	Local hand gathering

References

Anon., 1992a. *Scottish Sea Fisheries Statistical Tables 1990*. The Scottish Office Agriculture and Fisheries Department, Edinburgh, pp. 62.

Anon., 1992b. *Scottish Sea Fisheries Statistical Tables 1991*. The Scottish Office Agriculture and Fisheries Department, Edinburgh, pp. 57.

Anon., 1993. *Reports of the ICES Advisory Committee on Fishery Management, 1992*. ICES Cooperative Research Report 193, Pt 1, pp. 389.

Bailey, R. S., Hislop, J. R. G. and Mason, J. 1979. The fish and shellfish resources in seas adjacent to the Outer Hebrides. *Proceedings of the Royal Society of Edinburgh*, **77B**, 479–94.

Bailey, R. S., McKay, D. W., Morrison, J. A. and Walsh, M. 1986. The biology and management of herring and other pelagic fish stocks in the Firth of Clyde. *Proceedings of the Royal Society of Edinburgh*, **90B**, 407–22.

Gordon, J. D. M. 1981. The fish populations of the west of Scotland shelf. Part II. *Oceanography and Marine Biology Annual Review*, **19**, 405–41.

Gordon, J. D. M. and De Silva, S. S. 1980. The fish populations of the west of Scotland shelf. Part I. *Oceanography and Marine Biology Annual Review*, **18**, 317–66.

Hislop, J. R. G. 1986. The demersal fishery in the Clyde Sea area. *Proceedings of the Royal Society of Edinburgh*, **90B**, 423–37.

Lucas, C. E. 1987. The story of fisheries research in Scotland. In R. S. Bailey and B. B. Parrish (Eds), *Developments in Fisheries Research in Scotland*. Fishing News Books Ltd, Farnham, 11–18.

Mason, J., Newton, A. W., McKay, D. W. and Kinnear, J. A. M. 1985. Fisheries in the Orkney area. *Proceedings of the Royal Society of Edinburgh*, **87B**, 65–81.

Poxton, M. G. 1992. Towards a strategy for the conservation of marine fish in Scotland. *Proceedings of the Royal Society of Edinburgh*, **100B**, 141–67.

10 Marine Mammals in Scottish Waters: Research Requirements for Their Effective Conservation and Management

P. M. Thompson

Summary

1. The waters around the Scottish islands support a rich assemblage of marine mammals.

2. Two species of seal occur in very large numbers, with 40% of the world population of grey seals. Twelve species of cetacean are regularly observed.

3. As far back as Neolithic times there is evidence of islanders using whale products.

4. Active whaling was carried out particularly in the Northern Isles, but these various activities ceased completely in the early years of the twentieth century.

5. Whales are increasingly becoming a tourist attraction and there are a growing number of commercial enterprises exploiting this element of our marine heritage.

6. Basic biological information is still required for even the most common and well studied species. Much more research is required to ensure the continued recovery and conservation of many species of marine mammal.

The wholeness of [the grey seal's] life story remains unknown to me and I can see years of work ahead. What are the paths of their migrations to and from the isolated breeding grounds? How wide does the stock of each island range? Do the seals of each breeding-ground form closed cities.. and if so, are there the occasional wandering adventurers moving between cities as are found in the nations of men? When do the great seals first breed, and to what age do they live?

Frank Fraser Darling, *A Naturalist on Rona*, 1939

10.1   Introduction

The waters surrounding the islands of Scotland contain a rich assemblage of marine mammals (Thompson, 1992). Approximately 40% of the world population of grey seals (*Halichoerus grypus*) occur in the area, with all key breeding sites being found on islands. A minimum of 20 000 common seals (*Phoca vitulina*) also occur around the Scottish coast, similarly with the main concentrations found around islands. We know little about the extent or size of cetacean populations in Scottish waters, but 12 different species have been observed regularly in recent years (Evans, 1980). Sperm whales (*Physeter macrocephalus*) and fin whales (*Balaenoptera physalus*) are usually confined to offshore areas as they migrate between their northern feeding grounds and southern breeding areas. In contrast, some groups of bottlenose dolphins (*Tursiops truncatus*) and harbour porpoises (*Phocoena phocoena*) may remain in coastal waters for most of their life. For most species, however, groups probably range widely in offshore waters and move inshore only occasionally, perhaps on a seasonal basis. These include the minke whale (*Balaenoptera acutorostrata*) and killer whale (*Orcinus orca*) as well as the smaller dolphins, such as Risso's dolphin (*Grampus griseus*) and white-sided dolphin (*Lagenorhynchus acutus*).

The presence of marine mammals in these waters has provided an important resource for our island and coastal communities. This paper describes the changing ways in which this resource has been utilized and illustrates how human activities may also affect the resource indirectly. It then outlines the information required for an assessment of the current state of the resource and for its effective management. The main body of the paper then presents an overview of current research on marine mammals and identifies future research requirements.

10.2   Historic Utilization

Fragments of seal bones from neolithic middens suggest that man made use of seal products in Scotland from earliest times. In the Northern Isles, seals were caught at local haul-out sites and longer expeditions were made from Orkney and the Outer Hebrides in the nineteenth century to collect grey seal pups and adults from offshore breeding beaches (Fenton, 1978; Bone, 1990). The distances travelled to obtain seals suggest that the grey seal was comparatively rare at this time and reports indicate that the regular hunt for both adults and pups at sites such as Haskeir led to a serious reduction in numbers (Bone, 1990). The Grey Seals Protection Act (1914) eventually reduced this killing and breeding groups increased rapidly during the present century when many islands were deserted by their human inhabitants. Hunters turned their attention to common seal pups and heavy hunting for skins in Shetland during the 1960s led to concern about local population levels (Tickell, 1970) and the introduction of the 1970 Conservation of Seals Act. Grey and common seals can still be hunted under licence but the value of skins has dropped and hunting for skins has ceased.

Whale remains in middens at Skara Brae in Orkney suggest that whales have also been utilized since the neolithic period (Berry, 1985). More recent hunting for whales by Scottish coastal communities falls into four main types, all of which are represented well in the Northern Isles. The first was the traditional drive for pilot whales, carried out at least as far back as the sixteenth century and recorded as recently as 1903. The technique was similar to that employed in the Faroese grind although, unlike the Faroese, the Orcadians and Shetlanders did not eat the meat. Instead, they sold the blubber and left the carcass to rot on the beach (Fenton, 1978). The second phase of whaling was conducted outside Scottish waters but, nevertheless, closely involved communities from coastal towns. This Arctic whaling peaked in the latter part of the eighteenth century, when many boats stopped in Orkney and Shetland to pick up crew on their way to Greenland and the Davis Straight. With each boat requiring up to 25 men, and as many as 253 boats stopping in Shetland in a single year, there were obvious impacts on the local culture and economy. This phase of whaling lasted many years, but by the late 1800s stocks of right (*Eubaleana glacialis*) and humpback (*Megaptera novaengliae*) whales had been severely over-exploited and few boats continued working in the Arctic. By this time, the explosive harpoon had been invented and the Norwegians had established shore-based whaling for the faster baleen whales. Strange as it may seem today, anti-whaling demonstrations by Norwegian fishermen led to a ban on whaling in northern Norwegian waters in 1904, forcing Norwegian whaling companies to establish alternative shore stations. Four stations were built in Shetland and one on Harris. Each having one to three catcher boats and hunting blue (*Balaenoptera musculus*), fin, sei (*B. borealis*), and a few humpback, sperm and northern bottlenose (*Hyperoodon ampullatus*) whales. Between 1904 and 1929, 6823 of these large whales were landed at Shetland stations and a further 2759 whales brought ashore on Harris included 94 right whales (Brown, 1976). By the time that these Scottish stations closed, whaling in the Antarctic was well established and many men from the Northern and Western Isles were employed in the industry until whaling from British ports became uneconomic and ceased in 1963.

10.3 Current Utilization

Rising public interest in marine mammals has now resulted in the opportunity to exploit our wildlife resource in less direct ways. Commercial whale watching first started on the southern Californian coast in the 1950s and has since developed into a major tourist industry in several countries. In Scotland there have been natural history tours to observe seals for many years, but it was only in 1989 that Sea Life Cruises of Mull offered the first whale watching trips. Although several species may be encountered, this company base their cruises on the regular occurrence of minke whales in the waters around the Hebrides. More recently, boat trips have been run to observe the resident bottlenose dolphins in the Moray Firth, while the regular occurrence of dolphins close to shore offers potential for land-based observation. Whale and dolphin watching therefore provides a new and growing opportunity to base commercial enterprises on our marine heritage. Opportunities for the public to observe seals and whales at close quarters also play a major role in current initiatives to improve public understanding of marine environments in general.

10.4 Current Direct and Indirect Effects

Directed kills of cetaceans in Scottish waters have now ceased and large scale culls of seals were abandoned in the late 1970s. Nevertheless, some shooting of seals still occurs around fish farms and fishing operations to prevent damage to stock or catches.

In addition, marine mammals may be caught incidentally by fishermen. There is only limited information on the nature and extent of this by-catch, but it appears that grey seals, common seals and harbour porpoises are the species most likely to be caught in Scottish waters (Northridge, 1988).

Boating activity may also cause disturbance to some species, either due to direct interference with feeding and social activity, through engine noise interfering with cetacean echolocation or by direct injury through collisions. Noise disturbance may also result from seismic or military activity.

A wide variety of contaminants are now present in marine waters and there has been concern that these may affect the health of marine mammals. Currently there is more interest in the effects of organochlorine compounds such as DDT and PCBs. These compounds are lipophilic and can be found at high concentrations in marine mammals, even when environmental levels are quite low (Morris *et al.*, 1989). Other contaminants such as oil and domestic sewage may also affect marine mammals but the significance of these remains uncertain.

Human activities may therefore affect the quality of marine mammal habitats through pollution. In addition, intensive fishing or activities such as gravel extraction may result in changes in food availability or habitat structure. While this range of potential threats to marine mammals is well known, there is a lack of information with which to assess the relative importance of these threats or to compare their impact with natural mortality levels. Consequently, it is currently impossible to assess whether or not any additional mortality caused by these activities is sustainable.

10.5 The Need for More Information

Recognizing that this lack of information constrains our ability to protect stocks of marine mammals, the recent Agreement on the Conservation of Small Cetaceans of the Baltic and North Seas (ASCOBANS) has outlined a range of studies which signatory governments should support. This agreement is an annex to the UN Bonn Convention on the Conservation of Migratory Species and applies to all toothed cetaceans except sperm whales. The agreement includes proposals for (a) studies of status and seasonal movements of populations and stocks (b) identification of areas of special importance to their survival and (c)

(Above) A single point mooring (SPM) in Scapa Fow, Orkney; part of the Flotta Oil Handling Terminal.

(Right) The Oil Handling Terminal at Sullom Voe, Shetland.

(Below) Stornoway Harbour, a cruising yacht alongside a local creel fishing boat.

(Above) Canna harbour, a safe anchorage for local fishing boats, visiting yachts and dive party boats, with the Rum (NNR) Tertiary Volcanic Complex shrouded in cloud.

(Right) A close encounter between a kayak and a bottlenose dolphin.

the identification of present and potential threats to the different species. In particular it suggests that studies under (a) should include improvement of existing methods to establish trends in abundance, stock identity and population dynamics, while those in (b) should focus on locating areas of importance for breeding and feeding. A wide range of studies are required under (c) and include research on feeding ecology and sensory biology, with special regard to the effects of pollution, disturbance and interactions with fisheries.

Section 10.6 reviews recent and current research which is relevant to the conservation and management of marine mammals in Scottish waters. Although ASCOBANS applies only to toothed cetaceans, similar data requirements exist for the effective management of other marine mammals. This paper therefore focuses on the research requirements identified in the ASCOBANS, concentrating on ecological studies in Scottish waters and highlighting those which have been carried out on populations on or around our islands. In addition, information is presented on studies of more general problems which may provide information on management problems affecting Scottish populations.

10.6 State of Knowledge and Current Studies

10.6.1 *Cetacean populations*

For much of this century, information on the occurrence of cetaceans in UK waters has been available only from whaling records (Brown, 1976) or from reports of stranded animals collected by the Natural History Museum since 1913 (Fraser, 1974). However, trends in these stranding records cannot be used as a measure of population status and geographical variations in reporting quality and passive transport of corpses mean that these data provide only crude information on distribution.

Since the 1960s, additional information on cetacean distribution has become available through networks of voluntary observers (Evans, 1980; Evans *et al.*, 1986; McBrearty *et al.*, 1986). Over 1000 observers from around the UK now contribute to the Mammal Society Cetacean Group's sighting scheme, the co-ordination of which has recently been taken over by the newly formed Sea Watch Foundation. Such schemes provide important information on the occurrence of cetaceans around Scotland but, because of their limited coverage, can only follow changes in relative abundance in localized areas. Shore-based sighting schemes are therefore of most use where small cetaceans form resident or semi-resident groups in inshore areas. In the Moray Firth, a coordinated shore-based survey provided a minimum estimate of 62 for the size of the local population of bottlenose dolphins (Hammond and Thompson, 1991) while regular watches at key sites give an indication of seasonal movements in the area. However, variations in the probability of sighting an animal make these techniques unsuitable for monitoring population trends. Current studies therefore aim to estimate population size using capture-recapture analyses on photographs of naturally marked individuals (Hammond, 1990).

For most species of cetaceans the assessment of population size and trends requires dedicated systematic surveys using planes and/or boats (Hiby and Hammond, 1989; Heide-Jørgensen *et al.*, 1992). The only large-scale systematic survey which provided some coverage of Scottish waters has been the international North Atlantic Sightings Survey (NASS) in 1987 and 1989. Although designed primarily for large whales (Øien, 1990), the data have been used to estimate abundance of harbour porpoise (Bjørge and Øien, 1990) and pilot whales in some areas including parts of the northern North Sea.

A significant improvement in our current understanding of cetacean distribution and abundance should result from an international survey to take place in the North Sea, Kattegat, Skaggerak and Channel in the summer of 1994. The survey is aimed primarily at assessing porpoise distribution and abundance, but data from all cetaceans will be collected and analysed. The UK's Sea Mammal Research Unit (SMRU) is leading the project in collaboration with institutes from several other European countries. Major funding for the project has recently been granted from the EC through the LIFE programme.

Although systematic surveys such as NASS and the 1994 North Sea survey are essential if we are to estimate cetacean abundance, it is important to note the limits of the information which they can provide. First, they only determine distribution at one time of year, usually in summer when survey conditions are optimal. Second, surveys for abundance provide no information on population identity. There is a high degree of linkage between different geographical areas in the marine environment. This makes it extremely difficult to assess what constitutes a population, particularly where one is dealing with a highly mobile species. It is therefore essential that studies addressing population identity are carried out in parallel with any large-scale survey. In the past, studies have generally been based on morphometric differences between populations (Berry, 1969; Kinze, 1990) but recent advances in molecular genetics have permitted more detailed studies to be carried out on a range of species (Hoelzel and Dover, 1989). Third, these are usually one-off surveys and therefore provide no information on trends in abundance. Furthermore, the coeficient of variation of at least 0.2 mean that a long-time series would be required to identify trends.

Studies of cetacean life history have generally been based on the analysis of carcasses. Harbour porpoises, for example, are frequently found dead around the Scottish coast and may also be caught incidentally in fishing gear. The relatively large number of carcasses obtained over the period 1985–92 have permitted the SMRU to investigate population parameters such as growth and reproductive rates (Martin *et al.*, 1990). Mass strandings of pilot whales also provide large samples for similar studies on this species (Martin *et al.*, 1987) and a major international programme was based on samples collected during the Faroese grind (Donovan, Lockyer and Martin, in press).

For most small cetaceans, however, carcasses are found only occasionally and it may be many years before meaningful analyses can be performed. An alternative approach to the study of cetacean population parameters is through longitudinal studies of recognizable individuals. Elsewhere, these photo-identification studies have estimated population abundance, mortality rates, age of first breeding and calving intervals for a variety of species including killer whales (Olesuik *et al.*, 1990), humpback whales (Clapham and Mayo, 1987) and bottlenose dolphins (Wells and Scott, 1990). In Scotland, such studies are underway on bottlenose dolphins in the Moray Firth (Wilson *et al.*, 1992), while potential exists for work on species such as the Risso's dolphins which occur regularly around the Western Isles. However, cetaceans are long-lived species, often calving only every two or three years. Such studies will therefore need to be continued for many years before data can be used to estimate population parameters.

10.6.2   *Seal populations*

Since 1970, the Natural Environment Research Council (NERC) have had a statutory responsibility to provide government with information on the status of seal populations in UK waters. Information on seals is therefore more detailed than that available for cetaceans, particularly for grey seals which can be surveyed annually using aerial photography over terrestrial breeding colonies (Ward *et al.*, 1988). These data indicate that Scottish grey seals have increased in number at an average of 4–5% per annum (Natural Environment Research Council, 1985), although there has been variation in growth rates among sites (Hiby *et al.*, 1993).

Unlike grey seals, common seals do not remain ashore throughout the breeding season and surveys at haul-out sites provide only minimum estimates of population size. Telemetric data on haul-out patterns have permitted estimates to be made of population size in Orkney (Thompson and Harwood, 1990) but, for most areas, surveys provide only an index of population size. Surveys for common seals have also been made less regularly than those for grey seals and there is little quantitative information on population trends. Nevertheless, other North Sea populations are known to have increased in size in the decade before the 1988 phocine distemper virus outbreak (Heide-Jørgenesen and Härkönen, 1988) and it seems likely that UK populations were also stable or increasing. Following developments in the technique used for surveying common seals, a complete survey of the Scottish coast began in 1988 and was completed in 1993 (Harwood *et al.*, 1991). Sites on Mull, Lismore and in the Moray Firth have been monitored each year since 1988 and repeat surveys will be made in other areas every five years or so (C. Duck, SMRU, personal communication, 1992). Information on trends in common seal abundance should therefore become available over the next 5–10 years.

Although there are good estimates of the number of seals present at different breeding and haul-out sites, information on the extent of genetic interchange between sites is limited. Tagging schemes for both grey and common seals have shown that pups can move long distances soon after weaning (Boyd and Campbell, 1971; Bonner and Witthames, 1974) but there are few records of where marked pups subsequently breed. Similarly, little is known of the extent of adult movements between breeding sites. Recent work by SMRU has highlighted the potential for using photo-identification techniques on the more distinctly marked female grey seals to study movements and population parameters (Hiby and Lovell, 1990). Recent advances in molecular techniques can also be used to determine interchange between sites, particularly as DNA can be obtained relatively easily from seals by blood sampling. A collaboration between SMRU and the Institute of Zoology is assessing the extent of genetic interchange between different grey seal breeding sites (M. Walton and H. Stanley, personal communication, 1992). Similar studies are being undertaken on North Sea common seal populations, where the possibility that the regional differences in mortality seen during the 1988 epizootic have a genetic basis is being investigated by a group from Cambridge University (S. Goodman and J. Pemberton, personal communication, 1992).

Studies of grey seal population structure and reproduction have been carried out on material resulting from culls during the 1960s and 1970s (Hewer, 1964; Harwood and Prime, 1978) but comparative data for common seals from UK populations are not available. The grey seal's terrestrial breeding habits have also provided good opportunities for detailed marking and observational studies and much work has been carried out on island National Nature Reserves such as North Rona and the Isle of May. Many of these studies have been directed towards an understanding of the dynamics of the population, for example by studying dispersal and survival (Boyd and Campbell, 1971), while others have explored more theoretical questions on reproductive energetics and mating patterns (for example, Fedak and Anderson, 1982; Anderson and Fedak, 1987).

10.6.3 *Identification of key areas*

Ecological studies of cetaceans are being carried out on three species in Scottish waters. Bottlenose dolphins in the Moray Firth have been studied by Aberdeen University and SMRU since 1989 and Oxford University has also carried out work in the area since 1990. Oxford University has also been studying harbour porpoises in Shetland since 1989, carrying out observations throughout the islands but concentrating its behavioural work at three key sites: Sumburgh Head, Quendale Bay and Mousa Sound (Evans and Gilbert, 1991). Whale watching trips organized by Sea Life Cruises involve studies of the minke whales around Mull and, in 1992, International Fund for Animal Welfare scientists have been working with the company to expand this research programme (V. Papastavrou, J. Gordon and R. Fairburn, personal communication, 1992). These studies vary in nature and detail but all aim to assess variations in the behaviour and distribution of animals in relation to factors such as undersea topography, diurnal, tidal and annual rhythms.

Studies such as these are essential to understand how animals utilize a local area, but larger scale survey work is needed to put the importance of these particular groups in perspective. One of the most important functions of the 1994 international cetacean sightings survey is that it will identify where the main concentrations of both porpoises and other species occur in summer. More detailed ecological studies of the type outlined above can then be focused on these areas. Using the results of sightings surveys to relate cetacean distribution to oceanographic or bathymetric features may provide additional information on why animals are utilizing different areas. Work of this kind has been carried out elsewhere in the North Atlantic and has shown that the distribution of some of the more oceanic cetaceans is related to ocean fronts and the continental shelf break (Hain *et al.*, 1985; Brown and Winn, 1989).

The identification of seal breeding sites is obviously more straight-forward and key sites along the Scottish coast have been identified and afforded protection through SSSI or NNR status. The last five years have also seen significant advances in our understanding of seal feeding distribution. VHF and acoustic telemetry have been used to show that common seals generally remain in the same areas throughout the year, feeding within 50 km of their haul-out sites (Thompson and Miller, 1990; Thompson *et al.*, 1992). Whereas recent acoustic and satellite tracking studies indicate that grey seal behaviour is more variable, with some individuals travelling extensively around the UK coast during the non-breeding season (Thompson *et al.*, 1991; McConnell *et al.*, 1992; SMRU, unpublished data).

10.6.4   *Present and potential threats*

Of all the threats to marine mammals, organochlorine pollution has received most attention in recent years. Studies of contaminant levels in Scottish grey seals, common seals and harbour porpoises have been carried out since the 1960s, primarily by the Scottish Office Agriculture and Fisheries Department (SOAFD) Marine Laboratory in Aberdeen (Holden, 1978; National Environment Research Council, 1983; Hall *et al.*, 1992). The combination of small sample sizes, high analytical costs and species-, age- and sex-related variations in contaminant levels make detailed comparison between areas difficult. Nevertheless, it appears that organochlorine contamination in Scottish animals is generally low compared with levels found in the southern North Sea. Relatively high levels were, however, found in common seals from south-west Scotland during the 1988 phocine distemper epizootic and the significance of locally high levels of contamination in this and other areas deserves further study.

More important is the lack of data on the biological effects of observed levels of organochlorine contamination. For obvious practical reasons, most research on this question has related to seals. Experimental studies in the Netherlands have shown that common seals suffered reduced reproductive success when fed a high PCB diet (Reijnders, 1986) but there is no information on the threshold levels at which such effects occur. It seems likely that marine mammals also suffer the immunosuppressive effects of organochlorines seen in other mammals (Safe, 1984) and it has been suggested that this may have exacerbated the effects of PDV infection in more polluted parts of the North Sea during 1988. Further experimental work in the Netherlands is now assessing the effect of organochlorine compounds on common seal immune status (P. J. H. Reijnders, Netherlands Institute of Forestry and Nature Research, personal communication, 1992). In addition, field studies have been carried out on grey seals on the Isle of May to relate the organochlorine burden of grey seal females to the development and functioning of their pup's immune system (P. Pomeroy and A. Hall, SMRU, personal communication, 1992).

More general information on the causes of death of marine mammals beached or stranded around the English and Welsh coast is being collected through a Department of Environment funded project at the Institute of Zoology. The project was started in 1990 and was extended in 1992 to cover the coast of Scotland, where strandings are reported to the Scottish Agriculture College Veterinary Investigation Centre. Where possible, post-mortems are carried out on fresh specimens to establish cause of death and to collect biological samples for studies being carried out throughout Europe. The scheme therefore provides baseline information on the number of animals coming ashore around Scotland and will increase the chance of identifying disease outbreaks.

Examination of beached cetaceans for net marks will also provide some information on the number of animals being discarded after being caught incidentally in fishing gear. Voluntary schemes have been started by the Ministry of Agriculture, Food and Fisheries (MAFF) and SOAFD to encourage fishermen to report by-caught animals and land them for scientific study. However, voluntary schemes of this nature have failed in other countries and there is a need for more systematic studies to be carried out to assess the extent and nature of the by-catch problem. One potential method for reducing this problem is to make nets more visible to cetaceans. Work on this subject is being carried out by a team from Loughborough and Cambridge Universities who have carried out experiments in the Moray Firth to observe the behaviour of bottlenose dolphins around a net fitted with acoustic reflectors (Klinowska *et al.*, 1992).

Significant increases in our understanding of marine mammal feeding ecology are required before the less direct interactions between fisheries and marine mammals can be assessed. Almost nothing is known of the diet of cetaceans in UK waters. Direct observations of foraging animals tend to be biased towards prey which are taken at the surface (Barros and Odell, 1990), and beached animals generally have empty stomachs unless they have died traumatically. Traumatic deaths are often associated with fishing activity, so even this information on diet may be biased towards commercially fished species. Information on seal diet is more readily available, although all the techniques available for dietary studies have potential biases (Pierce and Boyle, 1991). Nevertheless, analysis of faecal samples from both grey and common seals around the Scottish coast indicate that seals take a wide variety of species and that their diet may vary according to location (Rae, 1973; Hammond and Prime, 1990), season (Pierce *et al.*, 1991) and between years (Thompson *et al.*, 1992). Thus seals appear to be opportunistic predators, generally taking prey which are locally or seasonally available, The consequences of such changes in diet and the potential impacts of either natural or anthropogenic driven changes in food availability are unknown.

Since 1987, Aberdeen University has been carrying out research for the Scottish Office Agriculture and Fisheries Department on the feeding and population ecology of common seals in the Moray Firth. Marked between-year differences in diet have been observed and longer term work aims to relate such dietary changes to measures of body condition, individual growth rates and reproductive parameters. These studies should therefore provide an indication of the likely impact of changes in food availability on the dynamics of common seal populations.

Disturbance is widely recognized as a potential problem for marine mammals, but is extremely difficult to study without the researchers themselves causing at least some disturbance to the animals. Regular disturbance at seal breeding sites can cause disruption of the mother–pup bond, or reduce suckling times, but relatively little is known of the consequences of disturbance to cetaceans. There are several aspects to this problem. Underwater noises may interfere with cetacean social or feeding behaviour, while harassment by boats could cause animals to move elsewhere or may result in direct injury by collision. Oxford University, Marconi Underwater Systems Ltd and Dyfed Wildlife Trust recently assessed the effect of different engine noises on the behaviour of bottlenose dolphins in Cardigan Bay. These studies indicated that Jet skis could only be detected from a range of about 80 m while speedboats were heard when approximately 400 m away. Thus Jet skis would not cause widespread noise disturbance, but their high speed, erratic course and short detection distance could increase the potential for collisions (Evans, 1992). Elsewhere in the world, whale watching trips are believed to have caused changes in the distribution and movement patterns of whales, but it is not known if this has any long-term impact on the individual whales.

10.7 Future Research Requirements

Our understanding of Scottish marine mammal populations has increased considerably in recent years. Nevertheless, there remain large gaps in the data required to conserve these species.

10.7.1 Population status

Of particular concern is the lack of information on the status of any of our cetaceans. Current studies of the Moray Firth's bottlenose dolphins will provide baseline data which can subsequently be used to assess population status. However, small-scale studies such as this cannot be used to determine the status of more wide-ranging species. The 1994 international cetacean sightings survey is a first step towards establishing the status of some of these species but is only a single survey intended to provide a baseline. Its results must therefore be used, with those from related genetic analyses of population identity, to identify suitable areas for continued monitoring. This will be neither easy nor cheap, but if governments are serious about their commitment to monitoring the status of cetacean populations then they must realize that these aims require long-term and systematic monitoring programmes.

10.7.2   Factors affecting population trends

Information on population status is currently available for Scottish grey seals and existing programmes will subsequently provide data for some common seal populations. Nonetheless, the long time-series of grey seal population estimates illustrates a further research need. We know that the UK population is increasing and that the rate of increase varies between colonies. What we do not yet understand are the factors which affect the growth of grey seal colonies. On the Monach Isles, for example, why have some islands seen an increase in pup production from 1300 to 5000 over the last 10 years while others have remained stable (Hiby *et al.*, 1993)? To answer such questions we need more detailed research on population dynamics to be carried out alongside monitoring programmes. Without such work we will only be able to document rises or falls in population size. Instead, we must ensure that we possess the necessary understanding of the causes behind such trends in order to assess whether management action can or should be taken, In particular, we must determine how populations respond to natural environmental fluctuations so that we can assess the relative importance of the anthropogenic threats which face marine mammals.

10.7.3   Habitat requirements

As a signatory to the recent EC Habitats and Species Directive, the UK has an obligation to have special regard to the conservation of marine habitats important to the life and reproduction of cetaceans, grey and common seals. Another research priority should therefore be to determine the habitat requirements of these species. Initially, we should attempt to assess what factors affect the distribution of the few species or populations where we have reasonable data on marine distribution. If, for example, it can be shown that the distribution of foraging seals in the Moray Firth or porpoises in Shetland can be related to particular bathymetric, oceanographic or sediment features, this may provide an indication of important habitats elsewhere around Scotland. If species distributions overlap then data on the more easily studied seals and birds may also help highlight key cetacean habitats.

10.7.4 Present and potential threats

We also need more information on the threats which these species face. As described earlier, we require more systematic recording of by-catches in order to understand the nature and extent of this interaction with the fisheries. Current schemes to record stranded marine mammals should also be continued on a long-term basis to help determine this and other causes of mortality. These studies must be supported by, for example, histological and contaminant analyses, while further methods need to be developed to assess the biological effects of pollutants. This work should include a continuation of current studies of contaminants such as PCBs and DDT, primarily to monitor the improvements in water quality which should result from agreements at the 1990 North Sea Ministerial Conference. However, attention should also be paid to other contaminants which may also affect these species, for example polybrominated biphenyls, hydrocarbons, radionuclides and novel pathogens.

Further studies of particular threats are clearly important, but we must be careful not to become preoccupied with studies of the health of dead marine mammals. Accurate reporting of by-catches might tell us that 100 porpoises die in nets each year, but this statistic is meaningless unless we know more about the population from which these animals were taken. If it was a population of 1000 porpoises then there is a clear problem, if there were 100 000 then this bycatch would be insignificant. It is therefore essential that we extend the basic research on the status, dynamics and ecological requirements of key Scottish marine mammal populations as outlined above. Given that the life-span of most of Scotland's marine mammals is in excess of 20 years such studies must be long-term in nature. In contrast, most of the work described in this paper is carried out on short-term funding, often relying upon charitable support. The recent Agreement on the Conservation of Small Cetaceans of the Baltic and North Seas should provide a forum for identifying research and monitoring priorities in this area. We must hope that this will result in the necessary support for the long-term research programmes required to achieve the aims of this Agreement.

Acknowledgements

I would like to thank everyone who has provided information on their current research and to thank Phil Hammond and an anonymous referee for comments on an earlier draft of this manuscript.

References

Anderson, S. S. and Fedak, M. A. (1987). Grey seal energetics: females invest more in male offspring. *Journal of Zoology*, **211**, 667–79.

Barros, N. B. and Odell, D. K. (1990). Food habits of bottlenose dolphins in the southeastern United States. In S. Leatherwood and R. R. Reeves (Eds), The Bottlenose Dolphin, Academic Press, San Diego, 309–28.

Berry, R. J. (1969). Non-metric skull variations in two Scottish colonies of the Grey seal. *Journal of Zoology*, **157**, 11–18.

Berry, R. J. (1985). *The Natural History of Orkney*. William Collins Sons & Co. Ltd., Glasgow.

Bjørge, A. and Øien, N. (1990). Distribution and abundance of harbour porpoise, *Phocoena phocoena*. In Norwegian waters. Paper SC/42/SM3 submitted to the IWC Scientific Committee meeting, June 1990.

Bone, M. (1990). The Slaughter of Selchis: Notes on seal hunting in the Outer Hebrides. *Hebridean Naturalist*, **10**, 7–16.

Bonner, W. N. and Witthames, S. R. (1974). Dispersal of common seals (*Phoca vitulina*), tagged in the Wash, East Anglia. *Journal of Zoology*, **174**, 528–31.

Boyd, J. M. and Campbell, R. N. (1971). The Grey seal (*Halichoerus grypus*) at North Rona. *Journal of Zoology*, **164**, 469–512.

Brown, C. W. and Winn, H. E. (1989). Relationship between the Distribution pattern of right whales (*Eubalaena glacialis*), and satellite-derived sea surface thermal structure in the great south channel. *Continental Shelf Research*, **9**, 247–60.

Brown, S. G. (1976). Modern whaling in Britain and the NE Atlantic. *Mammal Review*, **6**, 25–36.

Clapham, P. J. and Mayo, C. A. (1987). Reproduction and recruitment of individually identified humpback whales, *Megaptera novaeangliae*, observed in Massachusetts Bay, 1979–1985. *Canadian Journal of Zoology*, **65**, 2853–63.

Darling, F. F. (1939). *A Naturalist on Rona*. Oxford University Press, Oxford.

Donovan, G., Lockyer, C. H. and Martin, A. D. (in press). Biology of northern hemisphere pilot whales. *Report of the International Whaling Commission Special Issue 14*. I.W.C., Cambridge.

Evans, P. G. H. (1980). Cetaceans in British waters. *Mammal Review*, **10**, 1–52.

Evans, P. G. H. and Gilbert, L. (1991). The distributional ecology of harbour porpoises in the Shetland Isles, North Scotland. In P. G. H. Evans (Ed.), Proceedings of the 5th Conference of the European Cetacean Society, Sandefjord, Norway, pp 131., Cambridge.

Evans, P. G. H., Harding, S., Tyler, G. and Hall, S. (1986). *Analysis of cetacean sightings in the British Isles, 1958–1985*. Unpublished Report to the NCC, Cetacean Group of the UK Mammal Society.

Evans, P. (Ed.) (1992). UK Sightings Scheme. In *The Marine Forum for Environmental Issues*, KKS Printing, London, 28.

Fedak, M. A. and Anderson, S. S. (1982). The energetics of lactation: accurate measurements from a large wild mammal, the grey seal (*Halichoerus grypus*). *Journal of Zoology*, **198**, 473–9.

Fenton, A. (1978). *The Northern Isles: Orkney and Shetland*. John Donald Publishers Ltd., Edinburgh.

Fraser, F. C. (1974). *Report on Cetacea stranded on the British Coasts from 1948–1966*. No. 14, British Museum (Natural History), London.

Hain, J. H. W., Hyman, M. A. M., Kenney, R. D. and Winn, H. E. (1985). The role of cetaceans in the shelf edge region of the western North Atlantic. *Marine Fisheries Review*, **47**, 13–17.

Hall, A. J., Law, R. J., Wells, D. E., Harwood, J., Ross, H. M., Kennedy, S., Allchin, C. R., Campbell, C. A. and Pomeroy, P. P. (1992). Organochlorine levels in common seals (*Phoca vitulina*) which were victims and survivors of the 1988 phocine distemper epizootic. *Science of the Total Environment*, **115**, 145–62.

Hammond, P. S. (1990). Capturing whales on film – estimating cetacean population parameters from individual recognition data. *Mammal Review*, **20**, 17–22.

Hammond, P. S. and Prime, J. H. (1990). The diet of British grey seals (*Halichoerus grypus*), in W. D. Bowen (Ed.), Population biology of sealworm (*Pseudoterranova decipiens*) in relation to its intermediate and seal hosts. *Canadian Bulletin of Fisheries and Aquatic Sciences*, **222**, 243–54.

Hammond. P. S. and Thompson, P. M. (1991). Minimum estimate of the number of bottlenose dolphins (*Tursiops truncatus*) in the Moray Firth. *Biological Conservation,* **56,** 79–88.

Harwood, J., Hiby, L., Thompson, D. and Ward, A. (1991). *Seal stocks in Great Britain.* Surveys conducted between 1986 and 1989. NERC Newsjournal.

Harwood, J. and Prime, J. H. (1978). Some factors affecting the size of British grey seal populations. *Journal of Applied Ecology,* **15,** 401–11.

Heide-Jørgensen, M.-P., Mosbech, A., Teilmann, J., Benke, H. and Schultz, W. (1992). Harbour porpoise (*Phocoena phocoena*) densities obtained from aerial surveys north of Fyn and in the bay of Kiel. *Ophelia,* **35,** 133–46.

Heide-Jørgensen, M.-P. and Härkönen, T. (1988). Rebuilding seal stocks in the Kattegat-Skaggerak. *Marine Mammal Science,* **4,** 231–46.

Hewer, H. R. (1964). The Determination of age, sexual maturity, longevity and a life-table in the Grey seal (*Halichoerus grypus*). *Proceedings of the Zoological Society of London,* **142,** 593–624.

Hiby, A. R. and Lovell, P. (1990). Computer-aided matching of natural markings: a prototype system for grey seals. *Reports of the International Whaling Commission,* 57–61.

Hiby, A. R. and Hammond, P. S. (1989). Survey techniques for estimating abundance of cetaceans. *Reports of the International Whaling Commission,* 47–80.

Hiby, A. R., Duck, C. and Thompson, D. (1993). Seal stocks in Great Britain. *NERC News,* **24,** 30–1.

Hoelzel, A. R. and Dover, G. A. (1989). Molecular techniques for examining genetic variation and stock identity in cetacean species. *Report of the IWC* (Special Issue 11), 81–120.

Holden, A. V. (1978). Pollutants and seals – a review. *Mammal Review,* **8,** 53–66.

Kinze, C. C. (1990). Non-metric analyses of harbour porpoises (*Phocoena phocoena*) from the North and Baltic Seas: implications for stock identity. Paper SC/42/SM35 submitted to the IWC Scientific Committee meeting, June 1990.

Klinowska, M., Goodson, D. and Bloom, P. (1992). Progress in the development of efficient warning devices to prevent the entrapment of cetaceans (dolphins, porpoises and whales) in fishing nets. *ICES Marine Mammals Committee, N:17, 1–21.*

Martin, A. R., Reynolds, P. and Richardson, M. G. (1987). Aspects of the biology of pilot whales (*Globicephala melaena*) in recent mass strandings on the British coast. *Journal of Zoology,* **211,** 11–23.

Martin, A. D., Lockyer, C. H., Northridge, S., Hammond, P. S. and Law, R. J. (1990). Aspects of the population biology of the harbour porpoise, *Phocoena phocoena,* in British waters: a preliminary analysis of recent bycaught and stranded animals. Paper SC/42/SM53, Submitted to IWC, June 1990.

McBrearty, D. A., Message, M. A. and King, G. A. (1986). Observations on small cetaceans in the north-east Atlantic Ocean and the Mediterranean Sea: 1978–1982. In M. M. Bryden and R. Harrison (Eds), Research on Dolphins, Clarendon Press, Oxford, 225–49.

McConnell, B. J., Chambers, C., Nicholas, K. S. and Fedak, M. A. (1992). Satellite tracking of grey seals (*Halichoerus grypus*). *Journal of Zoology,* **226,** 271–82.

Morris, R. J., Law, R. J., Allchin, C. R., Kelly, C. A. and Fileman, C. F. (1989). Metals and organochlorines in dolphins and porpoises of Cardigan Bay, west Wales. *Marine Pollution Bulletin,* **20,** 512–23.

Natural Environment Research Council. (1983). *Contaminants in Marine Top Predators.* Report to DoE. Publication Series C, No. 23. NERC, Swindon.

Natural Environment Research Council. (1985). Seal stocks in Great Britain: surveys conducted in 1983 and 1984. *NERC News Journal,* **3,** 12–13.

Northridge, S. (1988). *Marine Mammals and Fisheries: A Study of Conflicts with Fishing Gear in British Waters.* A report commissioned by Wildlife Link's Seals Group. 140pp.

Øien, N. (1990). Abundance of northeastern Atlantic stock of minke whales based on shipboard surveys conducted in July 1989. Paper SC/42/NHMil8 submitted to the IWC Scientific Committee, June 1990.

Olesiuk, P. K., Bigg, M. A. and Ellis, G. M. (1990). Life history and population dynamics of resident killer whales (*Orcinus orca*) in the coastal waters of British Columbia and Washington State. In P. S. Hammond, S. A. Mizroch and G. P. Donovan (Eds), *Individual Recognition of Cetacea*, IWC, Cambridge, 209–44.

Pierce, G. J. and Boyle, P. R. (1991). A review of methods for diet analysis in piscivorous marine mammals. *Oceanography and Marine Biology Annual Review*, **29**, 409–86.

Pierce, G. J., Thompson, P. M., Miller, A., Diack, J. S. W., Miller, D. and Boyle, P. R. (1991). Seasonal variation in the diet of common seals (*Phoca vitulina*) in the Moray Firth area of Scotland. *Journal of Zoology*, **223**, 641–52.

Rae, B. B. (1973). Further observations on the food of seals. *Journal of Zoology, London*, **169**, 287–97.

Reijnders, P. J. H. (1986). Reproductive failure in common seals feeding on fish from polluted coastal waters. *Nature*, **324**, 456–7.

Safe, S. (1984). Polychlorinated biphenyls (PCBs) and polybrominated biphenyls (PBBs): biochemistry, toxicology, and mechanism of action. *CRC Critical Reviews in Toxicology*, **13**, 319–95.

Thompson, D, Hammond, P. S., Nicholas, K. S. and Fedak, M. A. (1991). Movements, diving and foraging behaviour of grey seals, *Halichoerus grypus*. *Journal of Zoology*, **224**, 223–32.

Thompson, P. M. and Harwood, J. (1990). Methods for estimating the population size of common seals (*Phoca vitulina*). *Journal of Applied Ecology*, **27**, 924–38.

Thompson, P. M., Wood, D. G., Tollit, D. J. and Miller, D. (1992). Seasonal and between-year differences in harbour seal *Phoca vitulina* foraging activity. *ICES Marine Mammals Committee CM 1992*, N15, 11pp.

Thompson, P. M. (1992). The conservation of marine mammals in Scottish waters. *Proceedings of the Royal Society of Edinburgh*, **100B**, 123–40.

Thompson, P. M. and Miller, D. (1990). Summer foraging activity and movements of radio-tagged common seals (*Phoca vitulina* L.) in the Moray Firth, Scotland. *Journal of Applied Ecology*, **27**, 492–501.

Tickell, W. L. N. (1970). The exploitation and status of the common seal (*Phoca vitulina*) in Shetland. *Biological Conservation*, **2**, 179–84.

Ward, A. J., Thompson, D. and Hiby, A. R. (1988). Census techniques for grey seal populations. In S. Harris (Ed.), *Mammal Population Studies*, Symposia of the Zoological Society of London. Oxford University Press, Oxford, 181–191.

Wells, R. S. and Scott, M. D. (1990). Estimating bottlenose dolphin population parameters from individual identification and capture-recapture techniques. In P. S. Hammond, S. A. Mizroch and G. P. Donovan (Eds.), *Individual Recognition of Cetacea*, IWC, Cambridge, 407–15.

Wilson, B., Thompson, P. M. and Hammond, P. (In Press). *The Ecology of the Bottlenose Dolphins (Tursiops truncatus) in the Moray Firth*. Proceedings of the Sixth Conference of the European Cetacean Society, San Remo, Italy.

PART THREE
SUSTAINABLE USE OF OUR MARINE HERITAGE

PART THREE
SUSTAINABLE USE OF OUR MARINE HERITAGE

The links between people and the islands of Scotland are many and varied, developing since the mists of time. For some it has been a love affair with the wide open spaces and the inexplicable draw of the sea. For most it has been a way of life, a need to survive. There is, for example, the old saying that Orcadians are farmers and part-time fishermen, while the Shetlanders are fishermen and part-time farmers.

The sea is renowned for its rich wealth of natural resources and people have not been slow in developing ways of harvesting this wealth. The evidence of this dependence can be traced back as far as the neolithic inhabitants of Skara Brae on Orkney, some 5000 years ago. In the middens of this settlement there have been found large numbers of limpet and whelk shells which were no doubt collected from the surrounding shores where they are still plentiful. In addition, there were various whale bones which would have been gathered opportunistically when one of these great creatures managed to strand itself among the islands. The whales are no longer there in the numbers they once were but sadly they occasionally, and quite unaccountably continue to strand themselves on the shores of these islands. It is perhaps a sign of changing attitudes that when there is a danger of such strandings occurring, such as the incident of the five sperm whales in Scapa Flow early in 1993, we now try to help them return to the open sea rather than drive them on to the shore to be killed and used.

The island way of life has until very recently meant that there must be an almost total self dependence and a community spirit. Jim Hunter reflects on the changes to the island way of life. The lifestyle on many of the islands was a crofting one reaping a harvest not only from the land but also the sea. The potting and in-shore fishing either with baited long line or drift net provided a sufficient catch to supplement the diet without endangering the existence of the populations of fish. Progress has resulted in greater fish catching power and the commercial pressures of the modern world. The local fisheries which for generations have provided a sustainable livelihood for the islanders have now been opened up to others who do not have the same empathy with their environment. It is important that we learn from past experiences and are not afraid to grasp the nettle when it is required.

Whereas to many people the islands are home and a place to make a living, they are to an increasing number of others a place to relax and pursue sports and other pastimes. Brian Wilson examines the increasing use of the islands and their surrounding waters by those either seeking solitude and an escape from the day-to-day rat race of mainland Britain or those participating in more energetic recreational pursuits.

Jim Munford and David Donnan examine the rich harvest of living resources which are obtained from the sea. Fishing and the collection of seaweed have been carried out by islanders for centuries, and more recently the clean, unpolluted waters around the Scottish islands have attracted large numbers of fish farms.

In some cases an increased awareness of a need to 'be green' has meant that attention is being directed to other traditional resources. Seaweed has been gathered by generations both as a fertilizer for the land and also in a small way as a raw material in the chemical industry. Much of this was collected as drift weed or 'tangle' which was cast up at the top of the shore. Indeed, it is still possible to see bundles of this being dried along the shore in Orkney and the Western Isles. New uses are being developed and the increase in the demand for alginates is putting increased pressure on this resource. Instead of hand collecting stranded weed, machinery is now being developed to take large quantities by ripping it off the seabed. The potential damage of this type of activity to the sublittoral communities of animals and plants, as well as to the nursery grounds of commercially fished species, is considerable. It is in circumstances of this sort, where there is the potential for a sustainable harvest, that great care must be taken in the early planning to ensure that long term damage is not inadvertently done.

With all living resources there is theoretically at least a sustainable level at which they can be harvested. With non-living resources it is not so much a question of whether it is sustainable but whether it is an acceptable loss in terms not only of the raw material but also of the quality of life.

Raw materials are constantly required 'in the name of progress' and the islands of Scotland and the waters surrounding them have these in a rich abundance. Alan McKirdy focuses on oil exploration which has so changed the way of life in Shetland and Orkney over the past 20 years or so and examines the implications of the quest for aggregates. The islands are there because of their resistance over the ages to the forces of the sea and this is to a large degree the result of large deposits of rock. Rock is an essential component of nearly all the major construction projects undertaken. It is needed for concrete, roads, coastal defences and other uses. Advances in technology and current economic conditions make it practical to develop coastal super quarries and some of the Scottish islands are prime targets for such developments. Such projects present a range of dilemmas. Will the development bring prosperity to local people, and if so is it worth the associated decline in quality of the environment? Do we understand all of the implications of such a development and the scale of the impact? The range of issues involved is often much more diverse than at first appears. In all these cases very careful thought has to be given to the proposal before any final decisions are taken.

An ariel view of Loch Maddy on North Uist.

The tombolo connecting St Ninian's Isle to the mainland of Shetland.

(Above) Small pocket beaches of white sand and off shore skerries at Valtos, (Western Lewis).

(Right) The columnar structure of the tertiary basalt lava cliffs on Canna, with a small sea cave and a flock of auks on the sea.

It is not always activities or developments on the islands themselves which have an impact. The discovery of oil in the North Sea and more recently off the western shelf has had a large and long-lasting impact on both Orkney and Shetland. The islands have in many ways benefited from the development and the money that it has brought in, but again there is a price to pay. The way of life and the tranquillity of these islands has been inextricably altered and there is the ever present threat of an accident which could affect the environment on which so many islanders depend. It is perhaps ironic but nonetheless prophetic that the recent major oil spill in Shetland, when the *MV Braer* went aground spilling 84 000 tonnes of crude oil, had nothing to do with the local oil industry. This simply demonstrates the size of the threat which the marine environment is continually under and the international nature of the problem. The event of a major incident, such as that of the *MV Braer*, receives the attention of the international media, but the ongoing chronic pollution which is affecting the marine environment largely goes unnoticed.

Of all the resources which are to be prized and jealously protected in the seas around the islands of Scotland, it is the quality of the waters which must come first. Martin Hall rather prophetically reviews the threats from various sources of marine pollution to the coastline of Shetland. Inevitably, even without the benefit of hindsight, he highlights oil pollution as a major threat. Almost everything which goes on in the sea is dependent on clean water. The fish which are hunted by the fishermen could not survive in polluted waters. The great diversity of animals and plants for which the seas around the islands are so important are intolerant of pollutants. The increasing numbers of visitors who come to the islands throughout the year do so to enjoy the clean environment and the wildlife.

The sea is a wonderful living resource which we should not be afraid to use and enjoy. As such it is something which it is worthwhile protecting and conserving. There are so many different interested parties who have a wish to exploit the sea, and the potential for conflict is considerable. The following chapters serve to highlight the main types of issues which have to be taken into account and in so doing draw on specific examples. It is not an easy task to achieve sustainable development but in the case of the marine environment we have the examples of past practices by many of the island communities from which we can learn and hopefully go forward into the future.

11 From West Highland Survey to Scottish Natural Heritage: The Beginnings of a Sustainable Development Strategy for the Highlands, the Islands and Their Surrounding Seas

J. Hunter

Summary

1. The traditional way of life of island communities is being lost, in large part due to human greed and modern technology.

2. The rural economy is based on agriculture, forestry, fisheries, mineral extraction and country sports all of which contribute to the draw-down of Scotland's natural capital. The capacity of the natural heritage to sustain a wide range of uses is questioned.

3. There must be a commitment to maintaining Scotland's resource base. The environmental objectives and the economic needs of the islands would be best served by bringing the management of these resources as close as possible to the local communities.

11.1 A Fisherman's Perspective

Marvig is one of the many crofting settlements which developed, in the course of the nineteenth century, around those tidal creeks and inlets which are so characteristic of the part of Lewis known as Pairc. Once the little bay below the township was filled with the fishing boats on which most local families depended for their livelihood. Today the bay is empty, and when, a year or so ago, I called on Duncan MacLennan, a Marvig man whose own connection with the fishing lasted for nearly 50 years, I was left in no doubt as to what, in the opinion of one of the last of its practitioners, had resulted in the total collapse of the industry with which Marvig, like the rest of Pairc, had so long been so closely involved. 'Human greed and modern technology between them killed the fishing,' Duncan MacLennan told me, (Hunter, 1992).

Duncan's favoured fishing technique was drift-netting. It is now recognized to have been a first-rate means of conserving the herring stocks on which the Hebridean fishing industry primarily depended because of the way a drift net takes only the more mature fish. Drift-netting was long scorned by Duncan MacLennan's mainland competitors.

'First they abandoned the drift net for the ring net,' Duncan explained. 'That brought them bigger catches. Then the ring net was given up for trawling. That brought bigger catches still. Then came purse seine nets. They enclose an area of sea as big as Hampden Park and bring in herring by the ton.'

Duncan MacLennan was forced to sell his boat when herring fishing was finally banned for several years in a belated and desperate attempt to protect endangered stocks which traditionalists like himself had warned were increasingly imperilled but which they had been told repeatedly were capable of being fished intensively forever. The fact that Duncan was right, while much of the fishing industry was wrong, is not much consolation. Attempts to get the few surviving drift net boats exempted from the herring fishing ban were unsuccessful. As generally happens when a natural resource begins finally to give out, those whose exploitation of it was sustainable went down with those whose exploitation of it most certainly was not.

Duncan showed me photographs of his successive fishing vessels and talked about what has been happening to the Minch on which he spent most of his working life. Seabirds of all kinds are scarcer than they were, in Duncan MacLennan's opinion. So are whales. So also, of course, are the fish on which so many species – to say nothing of Pairc's human population – once depended.

There are nine villages in this south-eastern part of Lewis. Just before the First World War, when the Hebridean fishing industry was at its height, their total population was some 2240. Now, in all of Pairc, there are fewer than 450 people. Where previously there were five schools there is now only one. Where once there were more than 500 pupils there are now about two dozen. Here, as elsewhere in Lewis, economic life stagnates. Yet all around are some of the most potentially productive oceans in the world.

'The rural economy has traditionally been founded upon agriculture, forestry, fisheries, mineral extraction and country sports,' Scottish Natural Heritage stated earlier this year. But many of these activities, our July policy document continued, 'have been contributing to a draw-down of Scotland's natural capital. Significant elements of our natural heritage have deteriorated . . . This degradation calls into question the capacity of the natural heritage to sustain the range of uses to which it is subjected.' (Scottish Natural Heritage, 1992)

There is no part of Scotland to which these comments are more readily applicable than the Highlands and Islands. They apply, as already indicated, to the experience both of Duncan MacLennan and the wider community to which he belongs. They apply to much else besides; to our natural resource base in its entirety; to the land as well as the sea.

What remains to be seen is the extent to which Scottish Natural Heritage will be successful in gaining acceptance, both from politicians and from the population generally, for an approach which, when previously urged on government, was steadfastly ignored.

11.2 West Highland Survey

'The Highlands,' Frank Fraser Darling concluded nearly half a century ago, 'are a devastated countryside and that is the plain, primary reason why there are now so few people and why there is a constant economic problem'. This might be an 'unpalatable fact', Fraser Darling observed. But it was one of critical importance all the same. No Highlands and Islands policy which failed to take account of it could 'hope to achieve rehabilitation' (Darling, 1955).

Underlying all such comments, as expressed repeatedly in the course of the publicly funded West Highland Survey which he supervised in the later 1940s, was Frank Fraser Darling's intense interest in the extent to which the productive capacity of the Highlands and Islands had been reduced as a result of the way in which the region's natural resources had not been so much managed as abused. It is his uniquely comprehensive approach to such issues that makes Fraser Darling such a pivotal figure in the modern history of the North of Scotland. The nature of his ecological insights, unfortunately, has been somewhat obscured, in our own times, by influential segments of the environmentalist movement becoming more concerned with particular aspects of the North of Scotland ecosystem than with the well-being of that ecosystem as a whole.

Take, for example, the issue of landscape and its preservation – a topic to which an enormous amount of lobbying energy has been devoted. It is surely more than a little ironic that so much environmentalist effort has gone into safeguarding a countryside which, for all that its outward appearance is undeniably attractive to many people, has been shaped in part by the very processes which Frank Fraser Darling so abhorred; processes now considered by Scottish Natural Heritage to have depleted those natural capital reserves which so urgently require to be replenished.

The stark and treeless hillsides which are generally thought to contribute enormously to the scenic value of the Highlands and Islands are – from the ecological standpoint adopted by Frank Fraser Darling and taken up, it would appear, by Scottish Natural Heritage – the end product of this 'draw-down of natural capital' which Scottish Natural Heritage has pledged itself to reverse.

The Highlands and Islands, Fraser Darling concluded nearly half a century ago, 'are unable to withstand deforestation and maintain productiveness and fertility. Their history has been one of steadily accelerating deforestation until the great mass of the forest was gone, and thereafter of forms of land usage which prevented regeneration of tree growth and reduced the land to the crude values and expressions of its geological composition' (Darling, 1955).

The resulting barrens might appeal to the urban seeker after wilderness, Frank Fraser Darling conceded. 'But if the jaded townsman attains to an ecological knowledge and appreciation,' Fraser Darling continued, 'he will not necessarily wish his wilderness to be the desolation caused through devastation of land by his own species . . . Man-made devastation is no environment for psychological health in a people as a whole' (Darling, 1955).

There is room, of course, for debate as to the precise extent to which the loss of tree cover in the Highlands and Islands in the course of the last two or three millenia is to be attributed to human action. But those of us with an interest in the region's natural environment can have no quarrel with Fraser Darling's stress on the need for remedial measures.

What the Highlands and Islands required above all, in Frank Fraser Darling's opinion, was a measure of 'rehabilitation'. And such rehabilitation, he insisted, must spring from a profoundly ecological understanding of what had gone so seriously awry. 'The art and science of wild-life conservation,' Fraser Darling wrote, 'is that which brings stability or regular rhythm into a disturbed habitat . . . and renders it productive of material and spiritual values.' (Darling, 1955).

This, though the phrase had not been coined in Frank Fraser Darling's day, is reminiscent of attempts to give a ready meaning to a concept we think central to the SNH approach; the concept of sustainable development.

11.3 The Scottish Natural Heritage Approach

Any policy of sustainable development in our part of the world, SNH insists in its *Agenda for Investment in Scotland's Natural Heritage*, must commence with the replacement of some proportion of what it is that has been lost. (Scottish Natural Heritage, 1992) It is by way of implementing this philosophy, it can be argued, that Scottish Natural Heritage, here in the Highlands and Islands, has given a high priority to initiatives such as the native birchwoods scheme which was launched in the course of last summer and which we are funding jointly with Highland Regional Council and Highlands and Islands Enterprise.

Here are the beginnings of that 'rehabilitation' for which Frank Fraser Darling called so long ago. It is as fully in accord with Fraser Darling's thinking as it is with our own *Agenda for Investment in Scotland's Natural Heritage* that our woodland project will be organized in such a way as to strengthen and diversify both the crofting and hill farming structures to which Fraser Darling devoted so much attention.

Our contention that the human population of the Highlands and Islands have a great deal to gain from the restoration and regeneration of the region's much-depleted natural resources was his contention also. It was a contention quite explicitly set aside by the decision-makers of Frank Fraser Darling's time. Our task, in the 1990s, is to make it stick. And to make it stick in the context of the marine environment every bit as much as in the possibly more familiar setting of policy for land use.

11.4 Highlands and Islands Fisheries

Our seas in the North of Scotland are as rich as our land is generally poor. The Highlands and Islands, which account for only a tiny fraction of UK agricultural output, are responsible for almost half the UK's total fish landings. These landings (some 220 000 tonnes with a first-hand value of £102 million in 1991) make the Highlands and Islands one of the most important fish-producing areas in the European Community. (These and subsequent statistics are drawn from Highlands and Islands Enterprise, 1992)

It is a further measure of the abundant nature of our marine resources, as compared with their terrestrial equivalents, that fishermen, unlike farmers, receive no operating subsidies. Public investment in our fisheries has been confined very largely to the provision of assistance in connection with equipment and infrastructure – boats, harbours, processing facilities and the like. There is not, and has never been, any maritime counterpart to the enormously expensive support mechanisms required to keep our agricultural economy in being.

Just as the global fishing industry is widely thought to have passed the total annual catch (some 100 million tonnes) which the world's seas can reasonably be expected to sustain, so fisheries in Highlands and Islands waters are exhibiting more and more indications of the strains which inevitably arise when any natural resource is exploited so vigorously as to endanger its capacity for regular renewal. What began to be observed of Highlands and Islands forests in the eighteenth century and of Highlands and Islands hill grazings in the nineteenth century is starting to be true of Highlands and Islands fisheries in the twentieth century: the year on year expansion of production is ceasing to be possible.

Annual fish landings in the Highlands and Islands increased steadily until the latter part of the 1980s. Now continuous growth threatens to give way to equally continuous contraction. The result, aggravated by the fact that similar difficulties are arising in other EC waters, could well be renewed dislocation of the type which, in an earlier period, deprived Duncan MacLennan's Pairc of its stake in the Minch fishery. Then Hebridean drifters were displaced by boats from other parts of Scotland. Now competition emanates from further afield.

The Highlands and Islands fishing industry consists of some 3250 fishermen manning some 1250 vessels. Only 104 of these vessels are engaged regularly in the demersal fishery; only 15 fish for pelagic species. The overwhelming bulk of the Highlands and Islands fleet, about half of which consists of boats of less than 10-m registered length, concentrates mostly on shellfish. Add to these statistics the fact that some 50% of Highlands and Islands fishing boats are more than 16 years old and there begins to emerge a picture of an intrinsically vulnerable industry; an industry which consists largely of small and elderly vessels operated by one-, two- or three-man crews; an industry which, because of its general inability to operate far from base, is basically dependent on the fish and shellfish stocks in its home waters.

Today these stocks are under growing pressure. That pressure began to mount with the enforced retreat of British fishing fleets from Iceland and Faroe in the 1960s and 1970s. It is a pressure which our EC membership has intensified considerably. And increasingly imminent reforms to the European Community's Common Fisheries Policy threaten to make matters even worse.

The European Community treats marine fish stocks as a common property resource and increasingly exercises sovereignty over them – to the extent that the EC acts as a single coastal state in international fisheries negotiations.

This means, in principle, that the seas surrounding the Highlands and Islands can be fished by fishermen from every corner of the European Community.

Important exceptions to this general rule are to be found in those Highlands and Islands waters which are the subject of derogations obtained by successive British governments from the EC. Derogations now apply to the Firth of Clyde, the Sea of the Hebrides, the Minch and the the so-called Orkney-Shetland Box. These areas are reserved largely for UK-registered vessels and, while this does not protect Highlands and Islands fishing interests from the considerable catching power wielded by vessels from the Scottish east coast, for example, it does safeguard much of our coastal waters from the still greater catching power exercised, in particular, by the French and Spanish fleets.

These arrangements are currently at risk. Vessels from other EC member states can register in the UK in order to gain access to UK waters and UK catch quotas. The recent formation of the European Economic Area, linking major fishing nations like Norway and Iceland to the EC, poses questions as to how their interests are to be accommodated in the Common Fisheries Policy. This policy is, in any case, about to be reviewed in such a way as to endanger the continued existence of the various derogations on which so much of our fishing fleet depends.

If these derogations were to be lost completely, which is perfectly possible because of the long-standing EC commitment to the equal-access principles enshrined both in the Treaty of Rome and the more recent measures establishing a single market right across the European Community, then there is a considerable likelihood of European mainland fleets obtaining a wholly dominant position with regard to Highlands and Islands fisheries.

This would be to permit history to repeat itself with a vengeance; for it is arguable that both the economic and ecological problems of the Highlands and Islands have their origins in the tendency, over a long period, for the region's natural resources to have been exploited primarily for the benefit of essentially external interests.

11.5   A Pattern of Exploitation

During the eighteenth and nineteenth centuries, the relationship between the Highlands and Islands economy and the economy of the rest of the UK was largely neo-colonial in character. The economic function of the Highlands and Islands, in other words, was similar to that of those colonies which countries like Britain were then acquiring overseas. Just as the typical tropical colony, for example, supplied the rubber, cocoa and other commodities required by UK industry, so the Highlands and Islands also served as a source of certain raw materials. Among the more important of these Highlands and Islands materials were timber, wool and kelp – the latter being a crude industrial alkali manufactured from seaweed.

Since no industrial sector of any consequence developed in the Highlands and Islands, the region was deprived of the value added to its products in the course of manufacturing, and because the ownership of key natural resources was vested in individuals (most notably the region's landlords) whose commitment to reinvestment in the local economy was generally minimal, even the considerable wealth resulting from sales of raw materials delivered next to nothing in the way of long-term local benefit.

Thus the substantial estate revenues generated by the kelp industry, far from being channelled into productive projects, were, in the words of one contemporary observer of the early nineteenth century Highlands and Islands, 'bartered for the merest baubles' – being spent almost entirely on the 'residences, dress, furniture and equipages' which were the standard objects of the land-owning fraternity's conspicuous consumption (Somers, 1848).

From a Highlands and Islands viewpoint, then, the commercial exploitation of natural resources was conducted, for much of the eighteenth and nineteenth century at any rate, in such a way as to secure no very positive return. It was also conducted in such a manner as to have almost wholly negative social consequences. These included, of course, the various calamities known as the Highland Clearances; the removal of many thousands of families from inland straths and glens being a necessary prelude to the introduction of the intensive sheep farming techniques which were established in order to allow North of Scotland landlords to meet the massive southern demand for wool; the subsequent settlement of many of these families on diminutive coastal crofts being the equally essential means of providing the cheap labour which the region's landowners required to have on hand if they were to satisfy the burgeoning market for kelp.

While the strictly human implications of these developments have been comprehensively studied, their ecological impacts have received rather less attention – though Frank Fraser Darling, for one, was in no doubt as to the very large extent to which the environmental devastation he discerned in the Highlands and Islands could be attributed to inherently short-sighted resource exploitation of the type I have just described.

The quest for profit was such as to result in the removal of much of what remained of the natural woodland cover of the Highlands and Islands. It was also such as to ensure that hill grazings were subjected to uses more intensive by far than those associated with the transhumance regimes practiced traditionally by those families who had been evicted to make way for sheep. Thus it came about that, well before the nineteenth century's close, sheep farming interests were themselves increasingly lamenting the extent to which the land's carrying capacity was in steep decline.

The pattern of resource exploitation established in the North of Scotland in the eighteenth century, then, was essentially extractive in an ecological as well as in an economic sense. It resulted in the Highlands and Islands losing a significant proportion of their natural capital – in the shape, for instance, of their forests and their grazings – while simultaneously failing to retain any significant share of the financial capital accruing from the commercial development of these assets.

Putting the ecological dimension to one side for the moment, it is clear that, from a purely economic perspective, something of this historic pattern survives into the present. Modern forestry certainly provides the Highlands and Islands with a measure of employment. However, the ownership of forestry ensures that its capital-generating potential is exercised mainly for the benefit of interests extraneous to the North of Scotland. The same is generally true of fish farming. It is true, too, of the offshore oil industry and of still more recent forms of resource utilization such as those associated with large-scale coastal quarrying of the type already going on in Morvern and likely to occur in Lingerabay and other places.

The two resource-based industries which do not conform to this general model are, of course, agriculture and fisheries; one, as is well known, being founded firmly on family-farming and crofting; the other, as is perhaps less generally appreciated, being very similar in its management structure.

11.6 Towards a Sustainable Fishery

The overwhelming majority of the 1250 boats which constitute the Highlands and Islands fishing fleet belong to their skippers, crews and the families of both. Company-owned vessels are practically unknown. The typical Highlands and Islands fishing skipper, as a result, is no mere employee; he both generates and invests capital on a not inconsiderable scale. Like the family farmer, the fisherman is a valuable source of entrepreneurial talent and leadership in comparatively remote rural communities where such skills and abilities would otherwise be in very short supply.

It is this structure which would be so severely jeopardized in the event of the various Common Fishery Policy (CFP) derogations which the United Kingdom currently enjoys being lost in the course of the Policy's looming renegotiation. Were Spanish, French and other interests to prevail in the course of that renegotiation, something which is by no means unlikely in view of the European

Community's growing adherence to the equal-access principle, then Highlands and Islands fishermen will be exposed to competition of a type they have not encountered before; competition emanating from those technologically-sophisticated, heavily-commercialized, largely company-owned foreign fleets which are presently excluded from much of our inshore waters.

There has been talk of altering the EC structural fund arrangements to help the more directly affected localities in the Highlands and Islands cope with the consequences of such a development – the European Commission taking the view that such funds would assist our more traditional fishing communities to adjust to their loss of fishing income by diversifying their economies. As has been pointed out to the European Commission by Highlands and Islands Enterprise among others, however, the availability of EC structural funds would, of itself, accomplish very little in fishing communities of the Highlands and Islands type – for the simple reason that the economies of these communities are not susceptible to meaningful diversification.

Highlands and Islands Enterprise has consequently suggested to the Commission that the Common Fishery Policy's restructuring might include the concept of Temporarily Dependent and Permanently Dependent Zones; Temporarily Dependent Zones being places where local economies could, over a period of years, be made less reliant on fishing; Permanently Dependent Zones being areas where there is no realistic economic alternative to fishing of the traditional type. if such a policy were to be adopted, in the HIE's opinion, then most of the fishing communities in the Highlands and Islands – certainly most such communities in the Northern Isles, on the West Coast and in the Hebrides – would merit designation as Permanently Dependent Zones for CFP purposes.

Zonation of this type is presently being advocated for social and economic reasons. It should also be advocated for environmental reasons.

Suppose, for example, there were to be a Permanently Dependent Zone (PDZ) covering the Minch and the Sea of the Hebrides. Its primary purpose would be to protect our fishing communities from external competition which would otherwise overwhelm them. A closely related purpose might be the conservation of fish stocks and the protection of the overall marine environment within the general confines of the PDZ. And both the socio-economic and environmental interest could arguably be served by the same means – an insistence on the West Coast and Hebridean fishery being prosecuted by the more traditional and less destructive methods still employed by the bulk of the West Coast and Hebridean fleet.

A Permanently Dependent Zone, in other words, could readily constitute the maritime equivalent of an Environmentally Sensitive Area (ESA). For just as ESAs are intended to promote low-intensity farming, so a PDZ might be designed in such a way as to promote low-intensity fishing. And just as the ESA approach is especially fruitful in a crofting context, so the PDZ approach might be equally beneficial in the context of those Highlands and Islands fishing communities which, like their crofting counterparts, still operate in such a way as to impose minimal pressure on natural resources.

Nor would it necessarily be sufficient, from this viewpoint, to exclude Continental fishing interests from our inshore waters. Controls might also have to be exercised over those UK fishermen who, for all that they have so-called historic rights to west coast fisheries, have contributed substantially to the depletion of our marine resources. It was not Spaniards and Frenchmen, after all, that Duncan MacLennan had in mind when he told me that 'human greed' had destroyed the old-style herring fishing in the Minch.

This is not to imply that Highlands and Islands fishermen, or Highlands and Islands crofters, for that matter, are themselves entirely guiltless of environmentally disruptive practices. It is to suggest, however, that the natural resource which is controlled by those local communities which depend directly upon that resource is more likely to be managed sustainably than the resource which is freely available for external exploitation.

Scottish Natural Heritage is committed to maintaining Scotland's common resource base. We are most likely to accomplish this if we can ensure that the people closest to the natural resources we wish to conserve and enhance have a vested interest in such conservation and enhancement. That is why both our environmental objectives and the economic needs of the Highlands and Islands will be best served, in my opinion, by bringing resource-management – and, if necessary, resource-ownership – as close as possible to those Highlands and Islands communities which have already suffered so enormously as a result of their long-standing inability to exert any meaningful control over our region's natural assets.

A period of at least a century would be needed, or so Frank Fraser Darling thought, to repair our natural fabric and to get the Highlands and Islands even into something approximating to a state of environmental health. Skillful management would also be required. He was in no doubt as to what its sources ought to be. 'There are three bodies in Scotland,' Fraser Darling commented towards the end of the 1940s, 'that should be able to work in close cooperation and to rid their minds of narrowly pragmatic notions. The Department of Agriculture has great power and owns half a million acres; the Forestry Commission also has power, plantations and land; the Nature Conservancy has little land as yet but may be expected to develop ideas and techniques in conservation and the ecology of land use. We wait for the lead to be given.' (Darling, 1955).

Frank Fraser Darling was to wait in vain. It is profoundly to be hoped that, this time round, we can do rather better.

References

Fraser Darling, F. 1955. *West Highland Survey: An Essay in Human Ecology*. Oxford University Press, Oxford.

Highlands and Islands Enterprise. 1992. *A Sea Fisheries Strategy for the Highlands and Islands*. Inverness.

Hunter, J. 1992. *Scottish Highlanders: A People and their Place*. Mainstream, Edinburgh.

Scottish Natural Heritage. 1992. *Agenda for Investment in Scotland's Natural Heritage*. Edinburgh.

Somers, R. 1977. *Letters from the Highlands on the Famine of 1846*. first published 1848, reprinted Melvens, Edinburgh.

12 RECREATION AND ACCESS

B. Wilson

Summary

1. There is an ever increasing range of outdoor recreational pursuits with scope for further expansion. A major challenge is posed in ensuring the compatibility of these with both the wildlife and local economy of the Scottish islands.

2. Successful outdoor tourism and recreation are based on very high quality environment, scenically beautiful, pollution free and rich in wildlife. There is a very large element of the wilderness factor to be taken into account.

3. The remoteness and limited accessibility of many of the Scottish islands protects them from over exploitation.

4. Recreation needs to be managed to ensure that damage does not result from over exploitation or insensitive developments.

5. Greater understanding through education and communication will help protect the natural resource. Appreciation of the problem leads to concern and on to involvement and a feeling of at least a degree of responsibility.

12.1 Introduction

Under the heading 'Recreational Demand Bound to Increase', the Highlands and Islands Development Board (HIDB) Magazine *North 7* claimed in 1972 that 'Industrial Development has only just touched the fringes of the Highlands, and specific Islands – they remain an undeniable focus and centre for an increasing range of outdoor activities'. It went on to say that, 'The challenge is to ensure that Recreational Developments are compatible with the interests of conservation, wildlife, study of wildlife and the local economy – some of which are themselves forms of recreation for large groups of people'.

Twenty years later, in 1992, it seems that those claims are still valid. The subject of this paper is the still-increasing range and demand of recreational pursuits, and the challenge posed in ensuring their compatibility with the wildlife and local economic interests of the Scottish islands.

Not only are the Scottish islands an important asset to the recreation industry in the stunning range of recreational opportunities they present; the recreation industry is itself of immense economic importance to Scotland.

I will suggest that the recreational potential of the Scottish islands has perhaps not yet been fully utilized, and provides scope for further expansion.

Also, whereas traditional 'environmental' stances have tended to see recreational activities as potentially damaging to the natural environment, I will argue that such damage is minimal in the context of some of the major current threats to our seas and coastlines – and that a more cooperative approach between 'environmentalists' and 'recreationists' could lead to improved 'codes of conduct' and a 'common cause' lobby for environmental protection.

'Recreation' – like 'Conservation' – is an anomalous and woolly term, meaning many things to many people. Among its several definitions one would expect to find elements of sport, tourism, leisure, adventure, heritage, exploration and other such terms. To many islanders, recreation is still 'something done here by people from elsewhere'; some of whom wish to blast wild or managed creatures out of land or water; others enjoy getting sodden, cold and sore in boats!

One certainty is that the diversity and range of recreational pursuits available today has increased beyond anything *North 7* could have dreamed of in 1972. Among the various pursuits covered by the more generic uses of the term 'Recreation' in this paper are – yachting, boating, kayaking, surfing, windsurfing, powerboat and waterskiing, walking, climbing, cycling and all-terrain biking, sub-aqua, fishing, angling, golfing, sand-yachting, parascending, birdwatching, whale-watching and archaeology – to name a few. In addition to the list of conventional pursuits (both aquatic and terrestrial), a considerable degree of ingenuity and eccentricity can also be found among the forms of recreation being pursued throughout the Scottish islands today.

This range and diversity is inevitably something quite baffling to those unfamiliar with the pursuits in question, many of which, at times, seem shrouded in their own mysterious rules, rewards and purposes. But no matter how trivial these various pursuits may seem to non-practitioners, it is plain that their followers – in many cases – take them very seriously indeed, and are willing to pay for the privilege.

Tourism is now recognized as one of Scotland's biggest industries. Recreation is probably the major *de facto* land use in many parts of Scotland, and is probably very near the top of the list of the '10 major uses of our island coasts', bringing considerable revenue into the Scottish economy.

A Scottish Tourist Board (STB) 1989 Visitor Survey into expenditure generated by recreation showed the following:

Recreation	*Expenditure (in millions of £)*
Hiking	272
Watersports	210
Golf	131
Mountaineering	55
Salmon	53
Shooting	20
Skiing	11

The revenue generated by watersports can be seen from the above results to be considerable. And while the survey was not restricted to island, or even, coastal, areas the recreational assets of the Scottish Islands will have contributed greatly towards the figure quoted. This is hardly surprising when one pauses to consider the scale and quality of the resource.

Scotland not only has 7866 islands, but claims >60% of the total UK coastline. The quality of the Scottish coast for recreation is such that Shetland has hosted the European Sea Angling Championships; Thurso has hosted the World Surfing Championships; Tiree hosts an annual 'Wave Classic' international windsurfing event; the combination of clear water, marine life and wrecks draws divers from all over the world (see Section 12.5); the west coast cruising grounds are among Europe's finest for yachtsmen and canoeists. What the island golf courses lack in manicure, they make up for in sheer beauty of location. On the whole, given the vast range of sites, shores, aspects, heritage and even climates of our three major island groups, perhaps the full recreational – and therefore economic – potential of the Scottish isles is still largely underutilized.

In many remote areas recreation may present an opportunity to develop what could be a valuable – and sustainable – local resource, within a context where other alternatives are scarce, and perhaps potentially far more damaging.

Mathieson and Wall (1982) described recreation as 'The temporary movement of people to destinations outside their normal places of work and residence, the activities undertaken in these destinations, and the facilities created for their needs'.

This description recognized facilities as an integral factor in the notion of recreation, a factor which is also vitally important in the economic relationship between recreational pursuits and the local economy. In many cases all it takes is provision of basic, low cost accommodation, wet-weather facilities, signposting and information, and improved local access points for the local area to be able to benefit from existing recreational visitors, and perhaps even to attract more. In some situations this approach has changed a problem to an opportunity, whilst also maintaining scale, local character, and minimum impact.

The Inner Hebridean island of Tiree is a case in point. For many years Tiree had been an international Mecca for windsurfers. Because of a lack of local facilities, accommodation and provisions, the windsurfers arrived every year – in the cold and wet season – in camper-vans filled with provisions bought on the mainland, and parked in areas without even litter or sewage facilities. This led to a certain amount of local antagonism, which was featured on a TV documentary about the island. Today, the people of Tiree are well aware of the windsurfing 'asset'. Organizations like the Hebridean Trust have recognized the need to provide accommodation and facilities, which in turn create a certain amount of seasonal wealth and employment on the island. In addition, local people have now gained skills and qualifications in the sport themselves, and are well placed both to control, and to benefit from its developing popularity.

On Shetland the Islands Council has set up the Shetland Amenity Trust in order to increase and develop local facilities for recreation, heritage and environmental protection throughout the Shetland Isles: and a similar initiative is now under way on the southern isles of the Outer Hebridean chain.

Even without suggesting outrageous developments such as bowling greens on the machair, or bungee jumping from the Skye bridge – it often seems that almost any proposal for increased exploitation of the recreational potential of the Scottish countryside is likely to meet with antagonism and opposition from the protective environmental lobby. The 'traditional' Environmentalist approach has been to panic: to assume that increased, recreational use of wild land – especially if someone is making a living from it – is not only self-limiting, but also damaging to the environment, and a threat to the well-being of other species. This sort of 'them and us' attitude leads familiarly to the entrenched positions which have characterized many of the recreation/conservation debates of the last decade – most notably the debate over development of ski facilities. Conservationists, worried about losing valuable habitat and approaching situations from a pessimistic viewpoint, often seem unwilling to grant any concessions, and perceive the recreation as a major threat to all that they hold dear. Recreationists feel equally pessimistic, as the conservation lobby seems to win every planning dispute. This leads to increased self-interest and defensiveness, and far away from the direction of cooperation.

These are entrenched stereotypes which lead to little progress on either side. I would like to go on to examine the more pragmatic stance of working with and harnessing change, of recognizing the rights and values of other interest groups, and of finding common ground.

12.2 Resources

Tourism based on outdoor recreation is crucially dependent on a very high quality environmental resource; scenically beautiful, pollution free and rich in wildlife.

Unlike some resource categories, the recreational resource is largely 'in the eye of the beholder'. However, most recreationists' analysis would probably include some element of 'wilderness' as important (unspoiled countryside, and access to it). Despite the fact that it is almost impossible to define the notion in detail, many would consider it as Scotland's greatest asset.

Access too can be considered as a recreational resource, and in the context of the Scottish islands access has both an enabling and a limiting role to play in the recreation equation. Limited access, or accessibility, is without doubt the major factor in minimizing recreational impact on the islands at present. Factors like remoteness and physical inaccessibility; distance (and time) from major population centres; limited ferry timetables and destinations; cost of access by boat; weather; dangerous conditions for small boats; shortage of harbours; limited accommodation; and midges – all contribute to protecting the Scottish isles from recreational overuse.

Many of these factors are being steadily eroded by better maps, guidebooks and information; better road, rail and ferry links; Ro-Ro ferries; causeways and inter-island bridges; increased use of yachts and power boats; better clothing and equipment technology; lengthening recreational season; midge repellents and nets. However, for the moment the buffer of remoteness and limited accessibility still largely protects the islands – substantially reducing the honey-pot pressures that affect more accessible sites of similar quality. Apart from some busy areas of Skye, most island mountain areas show far less physical erosion than comparable areas on the mainland. And island beaches are far less affected by sand-dune trampling damage than those on the mainland.

The impact of recreational use on the countryside is usually classified under (a) physical wear and tear, and (b) disturbance to wildlife. Under (a), with reference to the Scottish Isles, might be listed path erosion by walkers and bikers; sand-dune erosion due to badly sited caravan sites, inappropriate or increased usage; machair erosion by wheeled vehicles, caravans and increased trampling; damage to cliff vegetation by climbers; litter, sanitation and fire damage from camping. Under (b) might be landings on remote nesting sites by yachtsmen and other small boat users; disturbance, for example, to nesting birds by beach users; disturbance, causing increased predation on eggs and young due to adult birds being scared off nests; dogs and horseriding in sensitive areas; noise – from power boats and jet skis; general increased people-presence; collecting, bait-digging and hunting, including sub-aqua.

Certainly these things do happen; there are legitimate causes for concern about loss of habitat, disturbance, and environmental deterioration; and these concerns are shared by many people.

However, within the areas of the Scottish islands there are very few cases where recreation *alone* is having a serious adverse impact. Furthermore, apart from a few well-known problem habitats and localized impacts, it seems possible that much of the information regarding disturbance is inaccurate, lacking in thorough research, or merely anecdotal.

Some sports do have a severe local impact on a specific site which can then become the kind of key issue which leads to a widespread image of controversy and conflict out of all proportion to the actual effects. On the other hand, there will be cases where recreational pressures, on badly planned and provisioned sites, may eventually increase above a manageable level, requiring careful and decisive management in the near future. Such changes will need to be monitored closely and continuously.

Complacency regarding the potential effects of uncontrolled recreational growth must be guarded against. However, we must be very careful to retain a sense of perspective regarding the damage and disturbance associated with recreation, especially when compared with that from other sources. In many cases, the types and scales of problems and impacts from recreation are limited compared with other sources of damage, disturbance and pollution threatening the same areas.

Apart from the occasional 'slick' of sun-tan oil, recreation is more often associated with localized physical and geographical damage than with pollution, contamination, enrichment or large-scale engineering or development works. Thus, with the possible exception of illegal collection and disturbance of rare and protected species recreational damage is far less prominent and disturbing in the context of the Scottish islands than for example: pollution from sewage outfalls, dredge spoil, dumping or bilge tank flushing; over-fishing, and industrial species catches, and by-catch levels; sea-floor dredging and suction techniques; MOD bombing and shelling practices; general loss of coastal habitat; superquarries; increased plastic litter of marine origin; oil spillages; nuclear waste discharges; submarines and tankers; coastal industry and engineering.

12.3 Common Concerns

I believe that concern over these latter issues should be at the forefront of our thinking about the Scottish marine environment – and it is important to recognize that conservationists by no means have a monopoly on that concern. Although the recreation and tourism sector has never been vocal enough in demonstrating its interests in a high-quality, clean, safe environment – and while those interests may be largely self-centred – they are nonetheless valid and heartfelt.

In many situations outdoor recreationists are ideally placed not only to enjoy and appreciate the richness of the marine environment, but also to observe and monitor changes, damage and threats to that environment, and to 'sound the alarm' – thus performing an important 'watchdog' function in areas where otherwise such damage might easily slip by unnoticed. Recreational divers, for instance, were among the first to alert conservationists to the damage done to the sea floor by dredging; they also play an important role in organizations such as the Marine Conservation Society (MCS). Surfers and windsurfers have recently formed a vocal lobby regarding inshore pollution and water standards – 'Surfers Against Sewage' (SAS). Recreational interests have put considerable pressure on the development of fish farming on the basis of access and navigational rights, water purity and wild fish stocks, and the scenic impact on inshore waters. On the simplest level, litter and dangerous contaminants on remote beaches are more likely to be noticed and reported by families actually using those beaches in a recreational sense, than by scientists who might just chance to pass by.

In short, though the concern might be self-centred, or related to a narrow, sectional interest, it is often directed at the same target, and may serve to strengthen considerably the environmental lobby. I would like therefore to focus on the common ground between conservationists and recreationists, and on blurring the polarity between these groups, as a basis for reducing the environmental impact of recreational pursuits.

The MCS Report on Coastal Zone Management (CZM), entitled 'A Future for the Coast' (Gubbay, 1990), lists a number of concerns about the marine and coastal environment held in common between recreational and conservation interests. Their survey showed these concerns to be: trawling/overfishing; fish farming practices; military use of coastal areas; pollution levels in inshore waters; water quality; litter on beaches; the role of Crown Estate Commissioners; and the lack of integrated planning processes for coastal areas. Not only is there a considerable overlap between conservationists and recreationists in terms of common environmental concerns; there are also important affinities between the two camps which tend to blur the imagined dichotomy. Far from being mutually exclusive, the two groups are actually highly compatible. Natural history or field study, for example, could be considered as a 'recreational' activity; Bird watching is almost a 'sport' for many people; and sports like climbing, canoeing or diving can be an important route to increased environmental awareness. Some birdwatchers will walk further in a year than many ramblers; whereas some ramblers will see more birds – and perhaps disturb fewer. Instead of stressing the antagonisms, we should concentrate on building the way forward out of the cooperation, affinities and common ground.

The Scottish Conservation Projects Trust (SCP) specializes in achieving practical conservation projects by involving volunteer workers. Many of these projects take place on the Scottish islands each year, involving people in a recreational capacity giving their time and energy towards environmental improvement. Similarly, the annual 'Da Voar Redd Up' on Shetland, and other beach cleaning projects such as the 'Great Mull Atlantic Cleanup' (SCP) of 1989, involve a recreational approach to practical conservation. Even solutions to recreational problems such as footpath erosion and sand-dune damage, have been approached with considerable success through recreational involvement.

The educational value of experience must be recognized. It is estimated that people retain approximately 10% of what they hear; 30% of what they read; 50% of what they see; but a full 90% of what they do. This is important, for people may well learn most about the natural environment of the Scottish isles by personal experience, and through relating environmental problems to their own interests. Appreciation of the problems will lead to concern, and perhaps eventually involvement or at least a degree of responsibility.

Realistically, if relations between conservation and recreation are to avoid needless and unproductive stand-offs, there will need to be a major improvement in communication and understanding – and much closer joint involvement in management and planning.

Greater understanding requires a willingness on both sides, and a re-examination of common assumptions. For example, it is easy for environmentalists to assume that everyone surely has a basic awareness of marine processes. However, closer examination shows that this is simply not so. In fact a general lack of awareness concerning many important and fundamental processes of the marine environment pervades society, from the general public to planners, managers and developers. Sometimes this involves an ignorance of opportunities, dangers and threats to the coastal zone; or an ignorance of certain damaging practices relating to sensitive breeding sites and seasons. At other times it may simply mean a lack of awareness of how best to use the coastal zone and marine environment sustainably.

So, although some individuals using the marine environment will have some environmental awareness, a large portion of users may well be entirely unaware of their potential impact. While these are not such a serious threat to the environment as the minority who deliberately pursue damaging practices in full awareness of their impact, we must acknowledge the management challenge posed by a large sector of users who are basically well-intentioned, but simply lack information. Conservation has yet to become fully part of the culture of many recreational pursuits. There is an opportunity here for the environmental sector to provide an educational input into these pursuits via instructor schemes, manuals, codes of conduct and equipment suppliers, (see Section 12.5).

Just as the recreational sector occasionally lacks basic ecological awareness, so conservationists sometimes lack a basic knowledge of the sports they are dealing with. Sensitive management will need to recognize the distinct variations and subcultures within different sports, as well as the different aims, motivations and impacts of their participants. For example, canoeists may be island-hoppers, coastal tourers, solo or group paddlers, surfers or racers. Divers may be trophy-hunters, wreck spotters, photographers, salvagers or sport-fishermen. If conservationists are to communicate more effectively with recreationists, they will also have to appreciate the strengths, weaknesses and concerns of the organizations and individuals concerned. This too is part of the sharing of information, and has at least been started in the MCS report and survey mentioned above.

Among areas of concern within recreation are the absence of a unified lobby for recreation, and the lack of legislative backing making general provision for recreational interests; lack of availability of environmental information; maintaining access; difficulties in conveying information and advice to non-affiliated practitioners; difficulties in influencing private landowners; lack of information on impacts and levels of different recreational activity; conflicts of interest with other recreational claims. Both from recreational, and conservation management points of view therefore, there is a need to know more about the following: numbers participating in different recreational pursuits; extent of participation; seasonality of use; impact (noise, litter, collecting etc.); economic value to the local area; real/imagined/potential problems; environmental opportunities (e.g. for education/monitoring). In short, a structured survey, providing a projected assessment of the long- and short-term impacts of many recreational pursuits is required.

12.4   Management

At present levels most recreational conflicts should be soluble – or even pre-empted – by sound management, planning and education. Even as recreational demands among the islands become more specific, and environmental constraints become imperative, some forms of zone management, resource management, or visitor management may prove effective controls.

These methods, however, imply constraints on recreational access to various extents. Yet the very idea of constraints and restrictions may be contrary to the ethos of sports such as rambling, sailing or kayak touring which at present enjoy virtually unlimited access, and are largely unaware of their impact on the environment. Acceptance of such constraints (for example for seasons or at locations) will have to be largely voluntary, and therefore depend on effective communication, presentation of convincing evidence of their necessity (of the actual impact of the recreational pursuit), and on avoiding a polarized 'them and us' approach.

Management constraints on recreational access among the Scottish islands – and how these are to be applied – will be among the major challenges facing Scottish Natural Heritage in the next few years. Policing and physical restraint are generally impractical, requiring large resources, and often causing more damage/disturbance than the recreational presence itself. Besides, it is to be recognized that most disturbance and damage are unintentional – and that most effective improvement and damage-limitation will be achieved from within the sports themselves by means of committee responsibility, in-house magazines, codes of practice, voluntary agreements and close seasons, internal research, internal disciplinary procedures, advance planning, and byelaws.

If we wish to retain sanctuaries and safeguards for our wildlife, scenery free from visual pollution and areas where we may still seek the peace and freedom so important to the human spirit, with the minimum of regulations, restrictions and policing, the representative bodies for both recreation and conservation will have to work together diligently and thoroughly to achieve a substantially improved level of harmony and understanding, preferably before the potential conflicts become actual.

12.5   Sub-aqua – A Case Study

Sub-Aqua 'diving' is one of a number of specialist recreational pursuits which enables – even depends upon – access to an area of the natural environment which was previously relatively undisturbed, and which is potentially very vulnerable to increased human presence. It is a non-competitive sport, offering 'something for everyone' at various levels of involvement, from adventurous wreck explorers to those who would rather wallow in secluded coves and admire the rich variety of marine life in Scotland's coastal waters.

The waters around Scotland's islands offer some of the richest, most beautiful and challenging dives in all Europe. The remains of Spanish galleons and a myriad of other wrecks adorn the seabed, while the mixture of relatively cold and warm, clean waters supports an exciting and unique range of wildlife.

As the popularity of recreational diving increases, more and more pressure is being placed on popular dive destinations. Advanced divers, fully experienced in the weather and tidal conditions of the Scottish seas, and with access to fast and capable boats and vastly improved equipment, are now regularly diving on the remotest stacks, skerries and sanctuaries around our island coasts. While this must be an exciting and challenging opportunity for the divers themselves, it does mean that areas previously unvisited by human beings are now experiencing considerable pressure. The increased human pressure in itself is bound to cause a certain amount of disturbance, but the real damage associated with this form of recreational access is from the irresponsible collection of, and interference with, wildlife – for example, lobsters and crabs.

Lobsters are under pressure throughout Scotland's coast and islands due to commercial creel fishing, an important island industry. Since almost all accessible sites are regularly, and quite intensively fished by creel boats, the relatively innaccessible pinnacles, rock-stacks and remote skerries are among the last safe havens for these crustaceans, and other wildlife. Divers now have access to all the stacks and skerries between Glasgow and St. Kilda, with St. Kilda itself being a very popular dive destination. Not only is St. Kilda under diving pressure, but sites used as bad-weather alternatives, or en-route stop-overs – such as Loch Maddy, Canna and Canna reef – are also beginning to suffer diver-fatigue.

Of course some divers have a great conservation awareness, and approach their sport from a viewpoint of wildlife appreciation and minimum impact. However, there are others, in reasonably large numbers, whose uncontrolled collecting/hunting, and careless descent and buoyancy techniques are resulting in very real damage and disturbance to the underwater environment. Some divers are simply unaware of conservation problems and precautions; others are boldly flaunting or ignoring the codes of conduct. The problems in managing or controlling this sort of exploitation and damage are common to many other problems of recreation and access in that:

1. Restrictions and 'No Access' policies are fairly futile because (a) they tend to further advertise the asset; (b) they are logistically difficult, and often damaging to enforce in remote and sensitive areas; and (c) they simply challenge the defiance of maverick participants.

2. A certain proportion of any specific recreationist category will be unaffiliated to that sport's controlling or advisory body – and therefore unaligned with, or merely unaware of the codes of conduct and responsibility promoted by that body.

Aware of the actual and potential impact of divers on the environment – not only in Scotland, but throughout the world – the Professional Association of Diving Instructors (PADI) has launched Project AWARE (Aquatic World Awareness, Responsibility and Education). This scheme is an excellent example of the regulating body of a recreational pursuit taking a concerted and systematic approach to in-house training in environmental responsibility, as part of the participant's regular training.

PADI has 1800 centres worldwide; with 79 centres in the UK. At present only one of these is located in Scotland (The Puffin Dive Centre at Oban). However, with 400 000 people each year being introduced to the marine environment through PADI, the importance and content of the Project AWARE scheme are to be commended.

Project AWARE involves divers in education programmes, aquatic conservation activities and beach clean-ups. It has a corporate commitment to preserving the world's underwater resources, and is now running specialist underwater naturalist courses. At the Puffin Dive Centre near Oban, an initiative to develop an Underwater Nature Trail – with associated waterproof leaflets – recently won the Glenfiddich Living Scotland Award in conjunction with SCP's Operation Brightwater campaign. (For more information contact the Professional Association of Diving Instructors, c/o Puffin Dive Centre, Laggan, Glenshalloch, Oban PA34 4QJ.)

This trail, along with the whole Project AWARE approach, will encourage divers to observe and photograph wildlife, rather than to hunt and collect, and will galvanize a code of environmental conduct for Diving. With proper direction, education and information, the growing number of recreational divers could become an effective and influential group of environmental advocates. The problem of maverick, unaffiliated participants remains, as it will in other pursuits, but – with the essential help and input of conservation and environmental groups and experts, equipment manufacturers and the media – many more recreational groups will be able to develop codes of environmental awareness and protection to the standard and quality of their present technical guide books and safety codes.

References

Gubbay, S. 1990. *A Future for the Coast? – Proposals for a UK Coastal Zone Management Plan*. Marine Conservation Society.

Mathieson, A. and Wall, G. 1982. *Tourism: Economic, Physical and Social Impacts*. Longman, London.

13 THE SUSTAINABLE USE OF THE RENEWABLE MARINE RESOURCES OF THE SCOTTISH ISLANDS

J. G. Munford and D. W. Donnan

Summary

1. The islands of Scotland have a marine tradition based on their use of the natural resources of the sea although their full commercial exploitation is a fairly recent phenomenon. Today, use of these resources requires holistic management to ensure sustainability and to integrate the use of the coastal seas with the neighbouring land.

2. Conservation is a legitimate component of this stewardship; indeed it is fundamental to its success. The importance of stochastic events in coastal waters in deciding species distribution suggests that conservation should be inclined towards habitat protection and maximizing potential for recovery.

3. Until our understanding is adequate to the task, a precautionary approach should be adopted. An important component of such an approach is the monitoring of both human activities and their impact on the environment.

4. The aim of stewardship of the island inheritance should be development that meets the needs of the present without compromising the ability of future generations to meet their own needs. In the context of islands this may best be achieved through local strategies under localized management.

13.1 Conservation and Sustainability

The concept of conservation is capable of many interpretations (Munford, 1991) ranging from site-related management to broadly based environmental management with the objective of sustainable development (Table 13.1). Arguments for conservation can arise either through moral conviction or a pragmatic view of ecosystem management for long-term human gain without endangering those natural checks and balances that ensure our own survival.

Table 13.1. Definitions of conservation

Restoration	A return to some past ideal state
Preservation	Maintenance of present state
Moral imperative	Obligation of human stewardship
Scientific imperative	Ecological necessity
Balanced sustainable development	Integration of conservation with economic and social evolution through management

In marine conservation it is usual to separate the conservation of commercially exploited species, which is the duty of the fisheries departments, from the broader conservation objective that encompasses all species whether they are directly exploited or not. The concept of area selection and designation is fundamental to terrestrial conservation, as defined by the Wildlife and Countryside Act 1981, but its use in marine conservation needs critical examination.

Areas selected for conservation protection on land are both easily identifiable and can usually be managed as a unit. In the sea this is not normally possible except over relatively large areas. Certainly the form of protection evidenced on land is hardly practical at sea except in limited special sites. Baxter and Munford (1992) have suggested that an holistic view of the coastal environment is required to promote long-term conservation, and *inter alia* sustainable development. They recognized that in coastal waters it is not possible to divorce land use from this overall strategy. The Scottish islands and the indented western mainland coastline illustrate a close relationship between land and sea.

The objective of marine conservation management should be habitat protection rather than species conservation *per se*. Management should maximize the potential for marine species to reproduce successfully and maintain their populations within the sea as a whole, rather than directly intervene in the conservation of specific species, or assemblages of species, at particular locations. This reflects both our inability to alter or modify to any great extent the underlying hydrodynamic and ecological forces at work, but also the marine ecosystem has a remarkable capacity to recover from localized over-exploitation. There will always be some special areas that require a stringent management regime. These might be areas of such a character as to be particularly vulnerable or fragile, or which display particular qualities that warrant their use for research or education, or perhaps more importantly refugia from which re-population of exploited areas can occur. Such local measures should be seen as an addition to the general thrust of protection of the innate diversity through sustainable use.

An holistic view to management incorporates the exploitation of the renewable and non-renewable elements within our marine natural heritage and the need to conserve them. The concept that binds them is sustainability.

A recent publication *Caring for the Earth* (IUCN/UNEP/WWF, 1991) published as a successor to the *World Conservation Strategy* (IUCN/UNEP/WWF, 1980) has offered a definition of a sustainable activity as one that can, for all practical purposes, continue forever.

In the coastal marine environment, stochastic events have an important role in determining the suite of species present at a location at any particular time (see Chapter 4). The effects of autumnal and winter storms can have greater impact than normal human exploitation (for example Dare, 1973). It seems unreasonable, therefore, to curtail exploitation or development of the coastal marine environment to preserve a particular suite of species that may well change through natural forces within the space of a few years. However, it is a reasonable objective to maximize the potential for recovery by ensuring that any change in the environment is reversible and does not result in any gross modification of the ecosystem. Thus the World Commission on Environment and Development (WCED) (1987) defined sustainable development as meeting the needs of the present without compromising the ability of future generations to meet their own needs, or improvement of the quality of human life while living within the carrying capacity of the supporting ecosystem. The concept of sustainable use is of value when applied to living resources as it limits their exploitation to rates within their capacity for renewal. Thus, in simple terms, for a fishery to be sustainable recruitment and mortality must balance. Management's principal task is to maximise fishing mortality compared with natural mortality without endangering the potential for recruitment.

Caring for the Earth gives nine principles of a sustainable society from a worldwide perspective many of which are particularly appropriate to islands.

The concept of sustainability, used within an holistic management framework, must attempt to balance the needs of conservation with development. It indicates that the development or use of a resource should be appropriate to local environmental, as well as social needs. It also implies that aspirations for

Table 13.2.   The nine principles of a sustainable society

Respect and care for the community of life

Improve the quality of human life

Conserve the Earth's vitality and diversity

Minimize the depletion of non-renewable resources

Keep within the Earth's carrying capacity

Change personal attitudes and practices

Enable communities to care for their own environments

Provide a national framework for integrating development and conservation

Create a global alliance

---

individual gain need to be controlled for the greater benefit of society and the environment. Nowhere is this more evident than in islands.

13.2   Utilization of Natural Resources

13.2.1   *Fishing*

While fishing is an important subsistence activity, its commercial importance to the economy of the Scottish islands is a relatively recent phenomenon. It is in Shetland that economic dependence is most evident (Goodlad, 1992). Whereas 12% of the Western Isles workforce is dependent on fishing and fish farming compared with 1.4% for Scotland as a whole, 29% of the Shetland workforce relies on this sector for employment (Table 13.3).

Table 13.3. The dependence of the Shetland workforce on fishing and fishfarming (after Goodlad, 1992)

	Numbers employed	*Percentage of total Shetland workforce of 10 400*	*Sector as a percentage of total*
Fishing (direct)	485	16	
Fishing (ancillary)	330	11	27
Processing (direct)	578	19	
Processing (ancillary)	780	26	45
Fish farming (direct)	386	13	
Fish farming (ancillary)	452	15	28
Total	3011		

The earliest Scottish islanders left behind them middens of sea-shells. Although, in terms of food value, it takes up to 140 limpets to equate to a pound of meat (Grimble, 1985), sustainable exploitation of the natural shellfish was not a problem as the population was small and mobile. The continued dependence on the natural productivity of the sea is shown by the artefacts found at Skara Brae on Orkney. The inhabitants of the settlement at Jarlshof on Shetland dating from 1000 BC fished for cod, collected shellfish and hunted seals. Dr Johnson (1924) described Donald MacLean of Coll in the following words, 'He is as complete an islander as the mind can figure. He is a farmer, a sailor, a hunter, a fisher'.

Fishing was an integral part of the crofting economy but could not be developed by the islanders for their full benefit because of lack of investment. The first *Statistical Account of Scotland* (Anon., 1799) records that John MacLeod of Harris recommended the 'judicious selection of proper stations on the sea coast for the prosecuting of the fisheries, and manufactures established for constant employ of fishermen's families.' Also that the local families should be 'free to prosecute the fisheries for their own immediate benefit, and made to feel the advantage of working for themselves.' This suggestion was offered to draw people away from the commercial gathering of kelp that was later to prove so ruinous (see below). The Minister for Stornoway noted in the *New Statistical Account* (Anon, 1845) that the island lacked suitable boats for deep sea fishing, but codling, saithe and sole were caught in inshore waters. Later, Leverhulme promoted fisheries, which he saw as the sole solution to the islands problems. He wanted to find a solution to the cycle of scarcity and glut by introducing canning as an addition to the traditional kippering, salting and pickling. Before the end of 1918 he had set up the Mac Line Drifters and Trawlers Company, but the boats were to be his property not the islanders'. With his death in 1925 these projects stopped. Geddes (1955) associates the era of Leverhulme with a surge in island vitality, a lively debate and questioning of values, but the developments brought little lasting good.

Barra and South Uist in common with the rest of the Outer Hebrides saw tentative development of fisheries following the collapse in the kelp market, but suffered greatly during the clearances of the 1850s. The staple diet of the islanders in the 1890s appears to have been salt herring and salt ling. The Sea Fisheries Regulation (Scotland) Act 1895 protected the livelihood of the outer Hebridean fishermen but was not used, as it might have been, to close the Minch to foreign boats. The Sea League founded by Sir Compton MacKenzie (MacKenzie *et al*, 1936) sought to alter this situation by saving the Minch from foreign, including English, trawlers. However, by the time the Minch was closed in 1964, the traditional long lining and ring netting fisheries of the islands had been destroyed by exhaustion of the fish stocks. The crofter-fisherman (Nicolson, 1990) of the islands using traditional boats could not compete with the full-time east coast fishermen, but embodied the natural link between land and coastal sea that is fundamental to current thinking on marine conservation.

The islanders of Shetland and Orkney maintained a continual close association with fishing and the sea despite various attempts to deprive them of this income by their overlords. In the eighteenth century the islanders had to pay their land rent in fish and were not permitted to sell their catch elsewhere. By the end of the seventeenth century, the fish that had once been easily caught by line in inshore waters were no longer available. The landlords provided and owned the bigger boats required for the new haaf fishing (hav = ocean in Scandinavian). The coming of the Highlands and Islands Development Board in 1967, together with the development of the North Sea oil fields, marks a change in this history of exploitation of the human population if not the sea fish.

The history of island fishing is of subsistence with development restricted by limited investment. The restraining factors were economic and technical, not any concept of sustainability.

Development of fishing in the Highlands and Islands of Scotland has recently been the subject of a paper produced by Highlands and Islands Enterprise (HIE) (Anon., 1992a). The paper acknowledges the importance of fishing for many remote communities and sees the sustainable exploitation of valuable fish stocks as essential to their future prosperity. The paper advocates a management strategy that will safeguard the resource for future generations as well as taking account of present needs. Within the HIE area it is estimated that 2.6% of the total workforce are directly employed in this sector of the economy without taking account of those employed by the processing and ancillary industries. The fishing fleet consists of some 1250 vessels of which half are under 30 feet registered length. Shellfish harvesting is the major activity with over 90% of the boats engaged in this sector. Only the Northern Isles have a significant demersal fishery. Public investment in the fishing industry of the Scottish islands will probably concentrate on the development of fisheries infrastructure. The long-term return on this investment is dependent on a sustainable management strategy for the stocks. It is therefore pertinent to review the success of management thus far.

Holden (1991), reviewing the operation of the Common Fisheries Policy (CFP) of the European Community, finds that it is generally unsatisfactory and unenforceable. The structural component of the policy has been implemented independently of the conservation policy that has resulted in increased pressure on the stocks at a time when they can least sustain it. There have been some notable achievements such as the regulation of beam trawling. The fleet is largely Dutch and Dutch scientists have taken a significant lead in evaluating the effect of this gear on the bottom fauna as a whole, not just the target species (NIOZ/RIVO/RWS/DNZ, 1990). They demonstrated that fishing with a beam trawl changed the structure of the benthic community. Holden believed that the CFP had not been operated with the objective of rationally managing the renewable fish stocks of the Community. At best, he concludes, the policy has prevented the situation in 1983, when the policy was adopted, from deteriorating further. He advocates sustainability achieved through licensing of vessels and the limitation of fleet size. While stressing that it is not possible to divorce economic objectives from biological considerations, he pays scant regard to the secondary effects of fishing on non-target species. It is difficult to see how such a policy can be integrated with the type of sector development advocated by the HIE for developing island economies, except if this development is limited to the shellfish sector and that this sector remains only loosely controlled by the CFP.

Greenpeace (Anon., 1992b) in reviewing European fisheries drew particular attention to the secondary effects of fishing. They argue that the CFP should have as a guiding principle the minimizing of environmental damage. However, it might be more practical to determine an acceptable level of impact, taking into account the aspirations of the fishing community and the society in which they live.

Of all means of fishing, perhaps creeling for shellfish best typifies the sustainable use of the sea around islands. A recent survey of commercially exploitable shellfish around Scotland (McKay, 1992) examined the availability of mollusca along the west coast, Orkney and the Moray Firth. Most of the species are not currently exploited in this country, but, given the wider appreciation of shellfish on the continent, this is not likely to remain the case. The environmental impact of the chosen fishing method, suction dredging, was also reported on by both McKay (1992) and Hall *et al.* (1990). Their work indicated that any discussion of sustainability must address the effect of a fishery on non-target species. Evidence from Italy, where suction dredging for bivalves has a longer history, shows (Valli *et al.*, 1981) that fishing not only removes the target species, but also changes (coarsens) the substrate allowing other species to become more common. This is of significance if any broad conservation strategy is to be based on habitat protection as advocated by Baxter and Munford (1992).

Any use of mobile fishing gear, such as trawls, carries with it the risk of general environmental damage. It is not suction dredging alone that carries this threat, although this method above others has been regulated through the Inshore Fishing (Scotland) Act 1984. Atkinson (1989) when investigating the effect of trawling on the benthic megafauna of Loch Sween found little impact on those species inhabiting burrows, although the sea pen *Virgularia mirabilis* (O. F. Muller) occurred at lower density in areas subject to trawling pressure although this species can retract into the sediment. The sea pen *Funiculina quadrangularis* (Pallas), which cannot retract, appears to suffer damage after trawlers have operated in the locale (personal observation). A review of beam trawling, otter trawling and scallop dredging found that the latter was the most damaging to the substrate and *Modiolus* beds in Strangford Lough (Anon., 1990). This confirmed an earlier report by Fowler (1989) that such dredges, when towed by powerful fishing vessels, were capable of moving boulders the size of small cars.

A strategy that meets the aspirations of the fishing community dependent on mobile gear while safeguarding the livelihood of static gear fishermen and conservation is needed. It may be that the development of static gear fisheries by island communities can provide the basis of a sustainable economically viable inshore fishery.

13.2.2 Aquaculture

The guiding principles of aquaculture development are all too often to maximize yield and economic benefit (Pillay, 1977) without reference to the environment. Munford and Baxter (1991) in reviewing conservation and aquaculture stressed that progress could be made based on the long-term interest of both in protecting the environment.

Fin-fish farming has developed into a major component of the islands' economy with the majority of seabed leases for salmon farms. Salmon farming is a major employer in the islands and it is a significant factor in halting the decline of many island communities (Table 13.4).

Table 13.4. Number of people employed in fin-fish farms in Shetland, Orkney and the Western Isles in 1991 (SOAFD, 1992)

	Full-time	Part-time	Total
Shetland	202	102	304
Orkney	38	22	60
Western Isles	187	43	230

The exponential growth of salmon farming is now slowing giving a gross annual salmon production in Scotland of 40 593 tonnes in 1991 up from 32 350 in 1990 with an estimated production in 1992 of 37 698 tonnes (Scottish Office Agriculture and Fisheries Department, 1992a). Of the total 1991 production of salmon, 43% can be ascribed to the Western Isles, Orkney and Shetland combined. The Inner Hebrides' and Argyll islands' production cannot be readily isolated from the published statistics, but it would be reasonable to assume at least half the total salmon production of Scotland is island based.

Shetland is now responsible for 26% of the total Scottish production of farmed salmon. The revenues, legal powers and confidence gained from the earlier development of the offshore oil industry permitted the Shetland Islands Council to formulate principles for site allocation that were to become a model for good management. These have been modified in the light of experience to permit the industry to move into deeper waters and reduce environmental impact now that the technology required is available (Anon., 1991a). In other parts of Scotland the Crown Estate Commissioners followed the strategy outlined in their guidance notes on the siting of fish farms (Anon., 1989), but in both cases the emphasis has been placed on encouraging development.

Husbandry techniques have gradually changed to combat the effects of the bacterial disease furunculosis and the ectoparasitic salmon louse. It is becoming increasingly common to introduce fallowing of sites, and sometimes whole lochs, at the end of the production cycle. Stocking densities are also being reduced. In 1991, figures for Scotland (Scottish Office Department of Agriculture and Fisheries, 1992a and b) indicate that of those sites that were allowed to fallow the majority did so for between 8 and 26 weeks. Very few sites are left fallow for a year or more.

This increased tendency to fallow requires an operator to possess at least two sites. With the large number of leases that are already held, there are very few areas suitable for salmon farming left for additional sites and conflict for space with alternative users of the marine environment will increase.

Munford and Baxter (1991) have recently reviewed the various environmental impacts of fin-fish farming, which are summarized in Table 13.5.

Table 13.5. The impacts of fish farming on the environment

Changes in plankton
Removal of suspended sediment
Deoxygenation of the water column
Eutrophication of the water column
Organic pollution of the bottom
Physical modification of the seabed
Creation of artificial habitats
Invertebrate pests
Introduction of non-native species
Release of farmed species
Genetic selection
Chemical treatments
Vertebrate predators
Shore facilities

To this list must now be added the use of wild species for fish farming. Salmon farmers seeking a 'green' alternative to use of dichlorvos for lice control have used wrasse as cleaner fish. There is, however, an environmental cost as to date the wrasse are all wild caught. The impact of this fishery is unknown and catch data are not available. If this 'green' option is to be truly environmentally benign then hatchery methods need to be developed.

It is important to stress that, for the most part, the impacts associated with fish farming are apparently reversible. Indeed the most dramatic effects can be reduced by careful site selection. Increased water depth and current both reduce the worst effects of faecal and waste food deposition on the seabed and eutrophication. Predators such as seals can be controlled by non-destructive means, although these are not 100% successful (Howell and Munford, 1991) and site selection remains a useful adjunct.

The distribution of shellfish leases is largely similar to that of the fin-fish industry except in contrast that there are very few shellfish leases in Shetland. Compared with the fin-fish industry, there are relatively few people employed in shellfish farming. The importance of this industry is nevertheless high in the island crofting communities.

Shellfish farming has often been considered more environmentally benign than fin-fish farming. A recent report produced for the conservation agencies by the Institute of Offshore Engineering (Anon., 1991b) has tended to support this view, while highlighting the environmental impacts that almost of necessity arise from any intensive cultivation practice.

There are six species of shellfish cultured in the islands. Most leases in Scotland (35.8%) are held for the Pacific oyster, *Crassostrea gigas* (Thunberg) with a steady increase in production from 507 000 in 1986 to 2 300 000 in 1991. There has been a recent revival of interest in the cultivation of the native or flat oyster, *Ostrea edulis* (Linnaeus), (5.8% of leases) and production is smaller but on the increase.

There are few mussel, *Mytilus edulis* (Linnaeus), farms in either Orkney or Shetland but in the Western Isles and the islands off the mainland they are much more common. It is a similar position for the scallops, *Pecten maximus* (Linnaeus) and queen scallops, *Aequipecten opercularis* (Linnaeus). The production of scallops in culture is expected to increase steadily over the next few years as both large and small businesses reach the end of the production cycle. In addition, there have been improvements in the collection of scallop spat which have meant a higher ratio of the more valuable scallops to queens. Finally, there have been experimental trials conducted involving the Manila clam, *Tapes* (*Ruditapes*) *philippinarum* (Adams and Reeve).

The range of species available to the shellfish industry should permit the choice of the best biological and economical option to ensure success. A simple comparison of mussel and oyster culture best typifies the choices faced by the island-based prospective shellfish farmer. Mussels are the least expensive in terms of set-up and running costs. Generally the seed mussels are freely available from natural spat fall. The species is robust and needs minimal care. Indeed in the outer islands the principal predator of mussels, the eider, is often absent (Galbraith, 1992). It would appear at first sight that this species would be ideal when compared with the non-native Pacific oyster which has no natural spatfall and, therefore, cultivation is dependent on hatcheries that might be as far away as Guernsey. The set-up and running costs are also higher. It is only at the post-harvest stage that the limitations imposed by an island become evident. The home market is limited and transport costs are high. Faced with this economic reality, the development of a sustainable island industry seems linked to the high unit price oyster (MacLeod, personal communication, 1992). Whatever the final solution, it should be noted that the island share of the Scottish shellfish industry is falling (Scottish Office Agriculture and Fisheries Department, 1992b).

13.2.3 Seaweed harvesting

Several species of marine seaweeds growing around the coast of the Scottish islands have been exploited or have the potential for exploitation. The most important of these are the knotted wrack *Ascophyllum nodosum* (L.) Le Jolis, and kelp, mainly *Laminaria hyperborea* (Gunnerus) Foslie. The coralline red algae known as maerl, which is exploited elsewhere, is also found around the islands.

In the eighteenth century and into the nineteenth, Orkney and the Western Isles were the main centres for the kelp industry in Scotland. The industry was originally for the production of potash and soda used in the soap and glass industries. On Orkney this kelp industry dominated the economy from 1780 to 1830 and employed up to 3000 people (Thompson, 1983). The huge profits went to the landlords who under Scots law owned the foreshore and its contents. This money often passed straight to the mainland and was not used for island development, which contrasts unfavourably with the development of a broadly based island economy by the Campbells of Islay. Indeed, the gathering of kelp for export was often at the expense of basic tillage of the land, which resulted in its neglect (Grimble, 1985). Discovery of a foreign substitute, Spanish barilla, destroyed the lucrative trade. The collapse of the kelp market and its revenues may well have assisted in the wholesale introduction of sheep whose consequences are well enough known. People driven to less fertile areas must have found the natural harvest from the sea to be vital.

After the 1840s the declining industry was maintained on a smaller scale by the discovery of iodine in seaweed ash. However, a cheaper source of iodine was found in the Chilean nitrate deposits. The Scottish kelp industry was virtually ended (Johnston, 1985) following the termination of the price agreement between Chile and Britain in 1935.

In 1883, the English chemist E. C. Stanford discovered that alginate could be extracted from brown seaweeds including *Ascophyllum* and *Laminaria* (De Roeck-Holtzhauer, 1991). The uses of alginate are reviewed in Guiry and Blunden (1991). It is for this industry, run by Kelco, that a residual seaweed industry using drift plants remains in the islands. The collection of stipes is a major crofting activity with a tonne of dried stipes fetching around £150. It is thought to involve around 30 people on the Western Isles and Tiree and up to 150 on Orkney (Briand, 1991).

Ascophyllum nodosum continues to be harvested by hand in Scotland. Along the sheltered eastern coasts of the Western Isles this activity provides employment for about 60–70 people (Briand, 1991). Most of this harvest is sent to a processing plant in Girvan, again for the production of alginate by Kelco.

Laminaria is currently only collected as drift with negligible environmental impact. Harvesting of living kelp forests would be entirely different in terms of its effects on the ecosystem. In the 1950s, the then Institute of Seaweed Research in Scotland investigated the distribution and extent of *Laminaria* around Scotland (e.g. Walker, 1954) and ways of exploiting this resource. More recently, Johnston (1985) has drawn attention to the potential for harvesting around the coast of Orkney.

In Norway, since about 1965, a dredging technique has been employed for kelp harvesting. The dredge is towed through the kelp forest and plucks the plants off the rock. Up to a tonne, wet weight, can be taken in a single dredge. A recent Norwegian study of the recovery of exploited *Laminaria* forests found that recolonization of harvested areas did occur. However, after 4 to 5 years the height of the plants was only two thirds that of comparable unharvested areas. Biomass of the harvested areas was also reduced to 17–18 kg/m² compared with 27–41 kg/m² in unharvested (Sivertsen, 1991). *Laminaria hyperborea* is notable for its rich epifaunal and epiphytic communities and the diversity of these is reduced in harvested areas up to four years after harvesting (Svedsen, 1972).

To ensure a sustainable harvest, and to avoid lasting damage to the *Laminaria* forest, one of the most critical factors will be the period allowed between harvesting. The above would suggest that adequate regrowth would occur in 4 to 5 years, but a longer period would be required for full recovery of the associated epiphytic and epifaunal communities. Sivertsen (1991) recommended a 6 to 7 year harvesting cycle based on his growth and recruitment data.

The role of the kelp forests in the inshore ecosystem is not well understood, but there is evidence that particulate and dissolved organic matter originating from the kelp is highly important. There is also a strong link between the kelps and a wide range of organisms beyond the obvious kelp/grazer food chain (Duggins *et al.*, 1989). Over-exploitation and subsequent reduction of productivity could, therefore, have quite far reaching knock-on effects as kelp forests also act as a nursery ground for some commercially important fish (e.g. whiting) and scallops. It is also thought that in the Western Isles, the large kelp forest helps to absorb a lot of the energy of the waves arriving from the West. This is particularly important off the Atlantic coast of the Uists, where the gently sloping nature of an offshore platform with its attendant kelp forest, reduces the impact of the breakers on the sandy beaches. This in turn protects the machair, a coastal grassland of high conservation value.

Sustainable exploitation of *Ascophyllum* can be achieved providing the plant is harvested by cutting so that vegetative regeneration of the remaining plant can occur. It has been found that, when an area is cleared of *Ascophyllum* completely, *Fucus vesiculosus* and *F. spiralis* rapidly invade and it may take from 3 to 8 years for mature populations of *Ascophyllum* to re-establish (Seip, 1980). The key to successful management of the resource will again be the period between harvests. Currently, a 2-3 year rotation is used in Scotland (Briand, 1991), but further research is required to ensure sustainability.

Maerl, marketed primarily as a soil conditioner, is dredged off the coasts of Cornwall and Brittany in France. It consists of a mixture of small, red coralline algae (2–10 mm in diameter) the most common species of which are *Phymatolithon calcareum* (Phallas) Adey et McKibbin and *Lithothamnion coralloides* P. Crouan et H. Crouan. Live maerl is generally found in areas exposed to currents usually between 10–18 m depth in the UK, but over time dead maerl can be transported by currents to create banks that may be metres deep. It is found around many of the islands, but its precise distribution and extent are not well known. Although there is no current exploitation in Scotland, there have been proposals to dredge for maerl here on a trial basis. Exploitation of live maerl could never be considered sustainable. The slow growth rate of the plant, only 1 mm per year, means that regrowth could not make up the deficit caused by exploitation. Exploitation of maerl deposits of a sub-fossil nature can be considered similar to other capital dredging. Living maerl beds with their associated rich and unique community of plants and animals are of high conservation value and exploitation should be discouraged.

13.3 The Future for Island Development

It is evident that a management strategy for the sustainable use of the renewable resources of the islands of Scotland must integrate the aspirations of the people with the needs of the environment. In formulating such a strategy it would be wise to review present management, and previously discounted options, to determine if the modern Scottish islands can usefully profit from the lessons of the past. For example, the development of an island inshore fishery could well be assisted by a local approach to control and regulation. Presently this is not possible as regulation is largely through prime legislation, the Inshore Fishing (Scotland) Act, which aims to take a national overview of all fisheries. This is not true in England and Wales where a more local focus for inshore fisheries has been adopted through the use of Sea Fisheries Committees. When the legislative framework for this option was being drafted it was presumably not thought to be a useful strategy for the Scottish fishing industry based as it then was on a distant water fleet using trawl gear and a coastal fishery employing static gear. This situation has now changed. Fewer distant water grounds are available to the Scottish fleet and the pressure on the inshore grounds is increasing. It might be argued that such local control of fisheries is no longer an option. Britain's membership of the European Community and the Common Fisheries Policy seems to indicate that inshore fisheries will soon become accessible to the whole EC fleet, although the important Shetland Box recently commented on by Goodlad (1992) and the Northern Isles Fishermen's Associations and Councils (Anon., 1992c) suggests that local communities can receive preferential treatment. The concept of subsidiarity might offer a mechanism whereby the regulation of inshore fisheries could remain in the control of the nation state. In the case of the Scottish islands with a long tradition of inshore fisheries, albeit principally at a low level of exploitation, it seems sensible to reappraise the local control option. However, the environmental base, on which fishing and fish farming so closely depend, must also be protected. The sea's bounty was available to all who had the ability to harvest it. This can no longer be the case. Management now requires to integrate the needs of old and traditional industries alike with the special requirements of conservation.

Without addressing the political framework within which this management might be developed, it is pertinent to review the tools that are available. Modern resource management implies a modelling approach whereby accurate predictions can be made of the consequences of management options. This further requires that the complexities and inter-relationships of the system to be regulated are understood. While scientific data may be available in some cases, they are usually not synthesized in such a way as to make their use in coastal management simple.

The concepts needed to manage the relationship between people and coastal seas are not well understood, particularly the need to manage the coastal zone ecosystem as a whole. Without a clear understanding of the environmental consequences of a particular development, it seems sensible to proceed with caution. In terms of the sustainability definition proposed by the WCED, we should conserve the capacity within the natural world to sustain itself thereby maintaining the options for future generations.

The publication *Caring for the Earth* offers a list of actions that would encourage sustainable management of the coastal resource (Table 13.6).

Table 13.6.   Action to ensure the sustainable use of the marine resource

---

Develop a national policy on the coastal zone and ocean.

Establish a mechanism to coordinate the planning and allocation of uses of the coastal zone.

Allocate marine resource users rights more equitably among small-scale, large-scale and sport fisheries, and give more weight to the interests of local communities and organizations.

Use an ecosystem approach for management of marine resources.

Conduct information campaigns to raise the profile of coastal and marine issues; and include a strong marine component in environmental education in all countries.

Promote marine protected areas.

Conserve key and threatened marine species and gene pools.

Place high priority on preventing marine pollution from land-based sources.

Adopt procedures for effective prevention of pollution from ships and offshore installations, and for rapid response to emergencies such as oil spills.

Ratify or accede to the United Nations Convention on the Law of the Sea (UNCLOS) and other international legal instruments and develop an effective regime for sustainable use of open-ocean resources.

Expand and strengthen international cooperation, both regionally and among funding agencies and intergovernmental organizations.

Promote inter-disciplinary research and exchange of information on marine ecosystems.

Not all these are directly applicable at the level of the coastal resources of the Scottish islands. However, there is an interesting note of similarity between these proposals and the Government's response to the report on coastal zone protection and planning produced by the House of Commons' Select Committee on the Environment (Department of the Environment, 1992) which suggested that one mechanism for implementing local strategies appropriate for local needs is to use a local forum to achieve consensus.

It is true that the sea, and the natural riches that it contains and sustains, shows a remarkable ability to recover from over exploitation, but the expectation shown by Nicolson (1990) that the fishing industry should recover and strengthen as it has done in the past can no longer be relied upon. Only through an integrated holistic management of the coastal sea can recovery be expected. Such management, or better stewardship, integrating development with conservation offers the prospect of a sustainable future for the islands of Scotland and their marine inheritance.

References

Anon., 1799. *The Statistical Account of Scotland*, 21 vols, 1791–9, HMSO, Edinburgh.

Anon., 1845. *New Statistical Account of Scotland*, HMSO, Edinburgh and London.

Anon., 1989. *Marine Fish Farming in Scotland: Development Strategy and Area Guidelines.* Crown Estate Commissioners, Edinburgh.

Anon., 1990. *The Impact of Commercial Trawling on the Benthos of Strangford Lough.* Department of Economic Development Report TI/3160/90.

Anon,, 1991a. *Simplified Guidelines to Council Fish Farming Policy, August 1991.* Shetland Islands Council, Lerwick.

Anon., 1991b. *A Review of the Nature Conservation Implications of Molluscan Shellfish Farming.* Institute of Offshore Engineering, Edinburgh, IOE 90/1073.

Anon., 1992a. *A Sea Fisheries Strategy for the Highlands and Islands 1992–1996.* Highlands and Islands Enterprise, Inverness.

Anon., 1992b. *Net Losses, Gross Destruction: European Fisheries in Crisis.* Greenpeace, London.

Anon., 1992c. *The 1992 Review of the Common Fisheries Policy: Proposals to improve the Shetland Box Licensing Scheme.* Shetland Fishermen's Association, Orkney Fisheries Association, Shetland Islands Council, Orkney Islands Council.

Atkinson, R. J. A. 1989. *Baseline Survey of the Burrowing Megafauna of Loch Sween PMNR and an Investigation of the Effects of Trawling on the Benthic Megafauna.* Nature Conservancy Council CSD Report No 909.

Baxter, J. M. and Munford, J. G. 1992. Towards a marine nature conservation strategy. *Proceedings of the Royal Society of Edinburgh*, **100B**, 185–94.

Briand, X. 1991. Seaweed harvesting in Europe. In Guiry, M. D. and Blunden, G. (Eds), *Seaweed Resources in Europe*, John Wiley and Sons, Chichester, 259–308.

Dare, P. J. 1973. *The Stocks of Young Mussels in Morecambe Bay, Lancashire.* Shellfish Information Leaflet, Ministry of Agriculture Fisheries and Food.

Department of the Environment, 1992. *Coastal Zone Protection and Planning*, Cm 2011, HMSO London, 1–28.

De Roeck-Holtzhauer, Y. 1991. Uses of seaweeds in cosmetics. In Guiry, M. D. and Blunden, G. (Eds), *Seaweed Resources in Europe*, John Wiley and Sons, Chichester, 83–94.

Duggins, D. O., Simenstad, C. A. and Estes, J. A. 1989. Magnification of secondary production by kelp detritus in coastal marine ecosystems. *Science*, **245**, 170–73.

Fowler, S. L. 1989. *Nature Conservation Implications of Damage to the Seabed by Commercial Fishing Operations.* Nature Conservancy Council Contract Report No. 79.

Galbraith, C. 1992. *Mussel Farms: Their Management alongside Eider Ducks.* Scottish Natural Heritage, Edinburgh.

Geddes, A. 1955. *The Isle of Lewis and Harris.* Edinburgh University Press, Edinburgh.

Goodlad, J. 1992. The role of fisheries in Shetland economy. *Shetland Fishing News*, July, 10–11.

Grimble, I. 1985. *Scottish Islands.* British Broadcasting Company.

Guiry, M. D. and Blunden, G. 1991. *Seaweed Resources in Europe.* John Wiley and Sons, Chichester.

Hall, S. J., Basford, D. J., Robertson, M. R. 1990. The impact of hydraulic dredging for razor clams *Ensis* sp. on an infaunal community. *Netherlands Journal of Sea Research*, **27**(1), 119–25.

Holden, M. 1991. *The Future of Common Fisheries Policy*. World Wide Fund for Nature, London.

Howell, D. L. and Munford, J. G. 1991. Conservation and aquaculture, aquaculture and the environment 1991. In De Pauw, N. and Joyce, J. (Eds), *European Aquaculture Society Special Publication No 16*, Gent, Belgium, 339–64.

IUCN (The World Conservation Union), UNEP (United Nations Environment Programme) UNEP, (World Wide Fund for Nature) WWF. 1980. *World Conservation Strategy*, Gland, Switzerland.

IUCN (The World Conservation Union), UNEP (United Nations Environment Programme) UNEP, (World Wide Fund for Nature) WWF. 1991. *Caring for the Earth, A Strategy for Sustainable Living*, Gland, Switzerland.

Johnson, S. 1924. Journey to the Western Islands of Scotland. In Chapman, R. W. (Ed.), *Johnson's Journey to the Western Isles of Scotland and Boswell's Journal of a Tour to the Hebrides*. Oxford University Press, London.

Johnston, C. S. 1985. The seaweed potential of Orkney waters. *Proceedings of the Royal Society of Edinburgh*, **87B**, 1–14.

McKay, D. W. 1992. *Report on a Survey around Scotland of Potentially Exploitable Burrowing Bivalve Molluscs*. Fisheries Research Services Report No. 1/92, Scottish Office Agriculture and Fisheries Department, Aberdeen.

MacKenzie, C., Campbell, J. L., and C. Borgstrom. 1936. *The Book of Barra*. George Routledge and Sons, London.

Munford, J. G. 1991. Conservation – What's in a word. *Fish*, **23**, 50–1.

Munford, J. G. and Baxter, J. M. 1991. Conservation and aquaculture. Aquaculture and the environment 1991, in De Pauw, N. and Joyce, J. (Eds), *European Aquaculture Society Special Publication No 16*. Gent, Belgium. 279–98.

Netherlands Institute for Sea Research (NIOZ), Netherlands Institute for Fisheries Investigations (RIVO), North Sea Directorate (RWS/DNZ). 1990. *Effects of Beamtrawl Fishery on the Bottom Fauna in the North Sea*, BEON Rapport 8.

Nicolson, J. 1990. The sea, in Hetherington, A. (Ed.), Highlands and Islands: a generation of progress. Aberdeen University Press. Aberdeen.

Pillay, T. V. R. 1977. *Planning of Aquaculture – An Introductory Guide*. FAO, Fishing News Books, London.

Scottish Office Department of Agriculture and Fisheries, 1992a. *Results of Annual Survey of Fish Farms in Scotland*.

Scottish Office Department of Agriculture and Fisheries, 1992b. *Results of Annual Survey of Shellfish Farms in Scotland*.

Seip, K. L. 1980. A computational model for growth and harvesting of the marine alga *Ascophyllum nodosum*. *Ecological Modelling*, **8**, 189–99.

Sivertsen, K. 1991. Cleared areas and regrowth of kelp following harvesting operations at Smola, County of More Og Romsdal. *Fisken Og Havet*, **1**, 1–45.

Svedsen, P. 1972. Noen observasjoner over taretraling oggjenvekst av stortare, *Laminaria hyperborea*. *Fiskets Gang*, **58**, 448–60.

Thompson, W. P. L. 1983. *Kelp Making in Orkney*. The Orkney Press, Kirkwall.

Valli, G., Nodari, P. and G. Zecchini-Pinesich, G. 1981. Osservazioni statistiche sulla pesca di *Chamelea gallina* (L.) e di altri mollusca bivalvia e gastropoda nel Golfo di Trieste. Nova Thalassia, **5**, 75–96.

Walker, F. T. 1954. Distribution of Laminariaceae around Scotland. *Extrait du Journal du Conseil International Pour l'Exploration de la Mer*, **20**(2), 160–66.

World Commission on Environment and Development. 1987. *Our Common Future*. Oxford University Press. Oxford.

14 DEVELOPMENT OF OUR PHYSICAL RESOURCES – SUSTAINABILITY IN PRACTICE?

A. McKirdy

Summary

1. Developing our physical resources in a sustainable way is one of the biggest challenges of our age. Consumption of hydrocarbons and aggregates has risen inexorably throughout this century, with no sign of decline.

2. Levels of aggregate production are set to increase rapidly in Scotland if the proposed development of the new breed of superquarries become reality.

3. Development of oil and gas reserves in the North Sea also continues apace with many new fields due on stream before the end of the century.

4. The purpose of this paper is to review exploitation of our physical resources, particularly rock, sand and hydrocarbons, from the coastal and marine environment of the Scottish islands against a background of sustainable development.

14.1 Introduction

It is self-evident that physical resources such as rock and hydrocarbons are non-renewable on a human timescale and, therefore, their exploitation is inherently unsustainable. Jacobs (1991), in his book on the *Green Economy*, argues that 'since they (non-renewable resources) do not regenerate, all output reduces their stock. If sustainability means constant stock levels, it would require us to stop using fossil fuels and minerals altogether. Of course, this would be no help to future generations, since, if they were bound by the same sustainability principle, they could not use them either'.

So our goal must be that of sustainable development where the needs of the present are met without compromising the ability of future generations to meet their own needs. (World Commission on The Environment and Development, 1987).

As society's unquenchable requirement for aggregate and hydrocarbons grows, so the far-flung islands of Scotland are included within the widening 'area of search' for these commodities. Exploitation of our physical resources is nothing new, but the scale of the North Sea operation and the proposed superquarries, if they are approved, are many orders of magnitude greater than anything that has gone before.

Development of our physical resources are considered under the following headings:

1. Aggregate from superquarries

2. Marine-dredged sand and gravel

3. Maerl dredging

4. Marine dredged chromite and olivine

5. Extraction of beach sand and gravel

6. Islay wave power project

7. North Sea oil and gas exploration and production

14.1.1 Aggregate from superquarries

Aggregate is now an internationally traded commodity. Crushed rock is no longer supplied entirely from within the country promoting larger construction projects and current practice within the minerals industry reflects this change. Glensanda, currently Scotland's only superquarry, already exports a proportion of its annual output of two million tonnes to the US and Germany. This trend is set to continue if currently planned extraction operations are granted permission.

Scotland is potentially a rich source of crushed rock aggregate. Much of the country, including many of the islands, is underlain by crystalline rocks, either of igneous or metamorphic origin, which are ideally suited for use in the construction industry. However, these reserves have been little exploited to date as, traditionally, aggregate has been quarried within 50 miles or so of its eventual end-use. As the *modus operandi* of the industry has changed, so the area of search has been extended to include the entire coastline of Scotland.

The minerals industry is largely untouched by the concept of sustainable development. The oft-repeated truism that 'minerals can only be worked where they are found' is given as the main justification for inappropriately-sited mineral working. However, as the motive for winning and working minerals is entirely profit-related, the industry as a whole has, to date, been opportunistic rather than strategic in its exploitation of the mineral resource. Applications arise where a suitable deposit exists, the land is available, a gap in the market has been identified and a private company thinks they have a better than even chance of getting permission from the mineral planning authority. Planning procedures exist to make the process more strategic and in keeping with local, regional and national requirements.

Sustainability has not been a primary consideration in the determination of quarrying applications to date. The concept is somewhat alien to this traditional industry and many would say that quarrymen have managed quite satisfactorily without it since Man first hewed stone. However, the issue of sustainable use of a finite resource is now on the agenda as it is tackled by the National Planning Policy Guidelines on 'Land for Mineral Working' recently issued in draft by the Scottish Office.

They acknowledge the difficulty of assessing whether the exploitation of a non-renewable resource constitutes a sustainable activity and also poses the key question whether the man-made asset created through the use of the mineral will be of greater value to society than the natural asset that is lost. The draft Guidelines make specific reference to the development of coastal superquarries, which are considered to offer a number of attractions. However, these economic benefits should, accordingly to the draft Guidelines, be reconciled with:

- environmental designations of national importance (such as Sites of Special Scientific Interest (SSSI) and National Scenic Area (NSA));
- the unique scenic quality of much of the west coast of Scotland and the islands;
- its remoteness and designation as a preferred coastal conservation zone;
- the importance of tourism to the national and local economy;
- the legitimate interests of the local community.

Such guidance is helpful in defining the meaning of an acceptable development in practice, although these definitions leave room for some debate when applied to individual cases.

The general presumption in favour of mineral extraction is nevertheless preserved, providing that acceptable environmental standards can be achieved and maintained. However, given the outstanding quality of the natural resource, especially the Inner and Outer Hebridean Islands, it is perhaps doubtful whether there are many locations where the benefits of large scale mineral extraction could outweigh the environmental losses.

The draft Guidelines also stress the benefits of using mineral and construction wastes as an alternative to primary aggregates and this process of effectively recycling construction material may obviate the need for some pristine deposits of rock, sand and gravel to be exploited.

There is certainly scope for the amount of secondary or recycled material used in the construction of roads, buildings and other civil engineering projects to increase in future years. Material is supplied by the minerals industry in response to the precise specification for each contract, so if standards change, then material largely discarded at present as waste, such as oil shale, colliery spoil and pulverized fuel ash (PFA), could be used to a much greater degree than at present. This area is the subject of current research. Clearly this practice will limit the degree to which pristine reserves will be required, so the increased use of recycled material will contribute towards the wise use of our natural reserves of rock, sand and gravel.

The concept of developing very large coastal quarries, with an average annual output many times that of conventional extraction sites, was first put forward in the 'Verney Report' commissioned by the Department of the Environment and published in 1976. It described coastal superquarries as one of a number of potential solutions to the problem of aggregate supply. When the Scottish Development Department published its own national planning guidelines a year later, it confirmed this view. '. . . on planning grounds a coastal exporting superquarry could, in principle, be acceptable if a scheme can be put forward which minimizes damage to the environment'. A Scottish Office report published in 1980 on 'The potential for a large coastal quarry in Scotland' demonstrated that the superquarry concept was technically feasible and went on to identify five specific locations: South Harris, Loch Ewe, Loch Linnhe (where Glensanda is now developed), Kentallen and Walls (Shetland). These were ranked in order of their desirability from an environmental viewpoint and also the suitability of the rock to be exploited.

A more recent contribution to the debate is a report commissioned by the Department of the Environment entitled *Coastal Superquarries to supply South-east England Aggregate Requirements*', which was published in 1992. The terms of reference for this study included the identification of suitable locations and broad environmental impacts of superquarry development, but little consideration was given to the concept of sustainable development.

The authors of the report chose to narrow the scope of the study by ruling out 'sandstone and gneiss because of the difficulty of identifying suitable deposits from a desk study alone'. Also omitted are the Moine Schists, which underlie much of Lochaber, for example, and outcrop extensively on the coast. Such omissions impair the value of this study as there is no technical reason why these rock types could not be exploited in the same way as the lithologies included in the study, which are as follows: limestone, granite, diorite, gabbro, ultrabasics, anorthosite, andesite and basalt.

A number of specific locations were considered during the preparation of the report and it concludes that 'possible locations . . . include many with severe and varied environmental constraints. Some areas are likely to be excluded because of the significance of specific SSSI impacts and many suitable locations for coastal superquarries, on technical grounds would conflict with touristic, heritage or ecological consideration'.

14.1.1.1 Case study – proposed superquarry at Rodel, South Harris
As an illustration of potential impacts of a superquarry development on the coastal and marine environment, the application by Redland Aggregates Limited to develop the anorthosite resource of South Harris is examined in some detail.

The application area lies east of Roineabhal and covers a total of 459 hectares. It is proposed that the initial output will be around 1 million tonnes per year, achieving a final figure of 10 million tonnes per year if there is sufficient demand for the product. The application area is split by the Finsbay to Rodel road, so it is proposed that separate mineral extraction operations should take place to the east and west of the road. The main face would gradually advance westwards up the mountainside towards Roineabhal but the existing ridgeline and skyline would not be breached. At its highest point, this main western face is planned to be some 370 m high, but with a stepped appearance reflecting the benched method of working.

As the quarry develops, so the main quarry face would move westward. The quarry floor would be deepened to make the development of a sealoch a viable restoration option. Restoration blasting has been proposed to reduce the visual impact of the main quarry face, creating scree slopes to blend in with the natural topography (Figures 14.1 and 14.2)

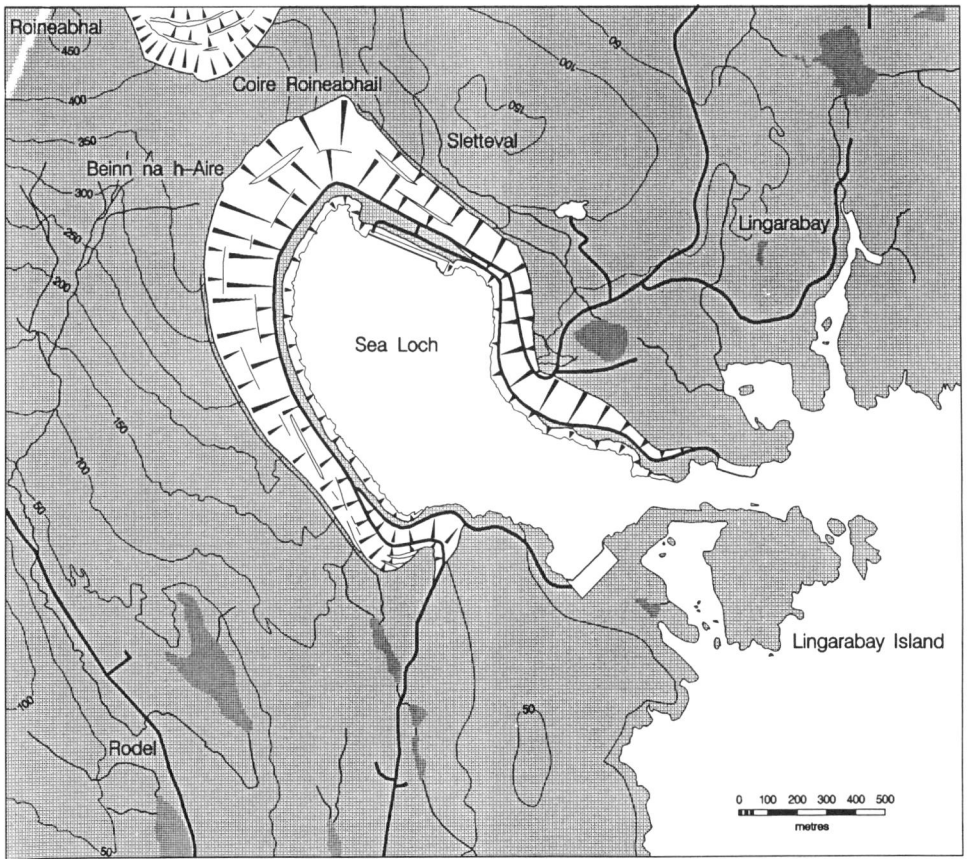

Figure 14.1. 'Indicative ultimate landform' - how the superquarry at Rodel might be restored (after Redlands Aggregate Limited, 1991).

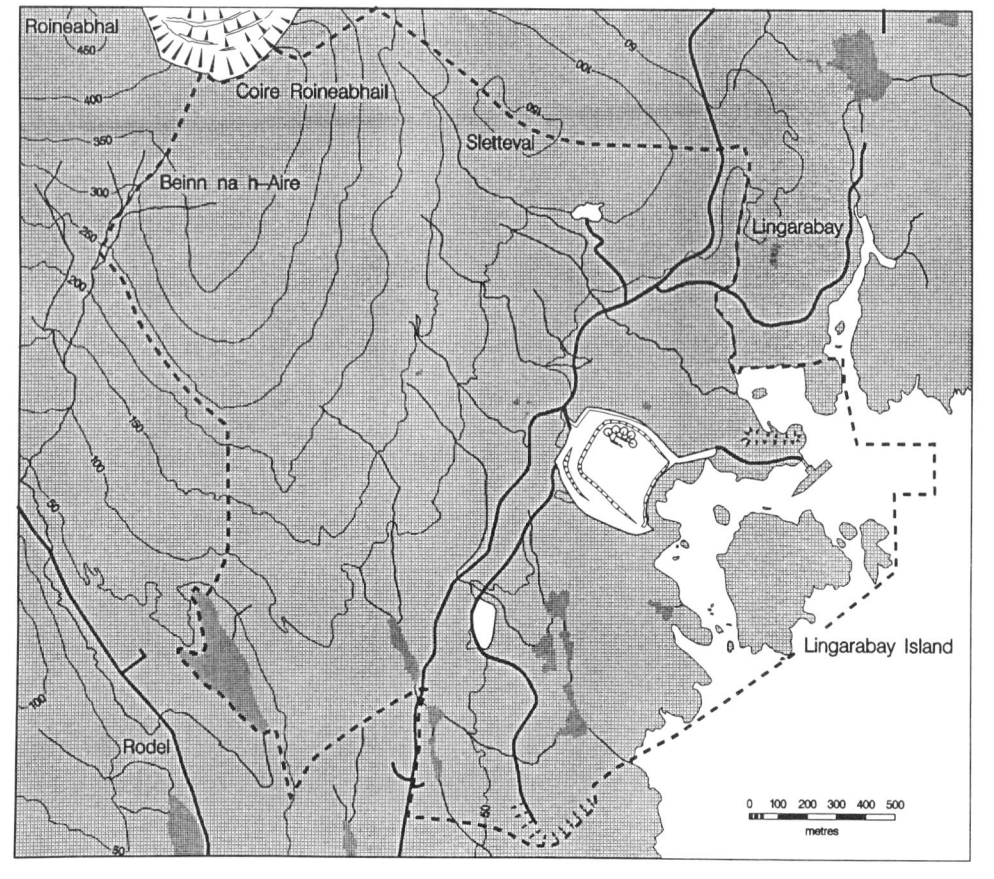

Figure 14.2. Initial quarry development at Rodel (after Redlands Aggregate Limited, 1991)

14.1.1.2 Impact of the 'Rodel superquarry' on the natural environment

Despite efforts to ameliorate the effects of quarrying by restoration works, the biggest impact by far would be on the scenery of South Harris. A quarry on this scale would considerably affect Roineabhal, which is itself part of a National Scenic Area. Other impacts would include silt run off from the quarry operations and the possibility of water contamination or foreign species being introduced through ballast water dumped by the rock carrying tankers.

Tankers arriving from many destinations abroad would have to discharge their ballast water before taking on board their cargo of crushed rock. In some parts of the world, ballast water has introduced non-native species which have adversely affected local fisheries.

Silt entering the coastal waters adjacent to the quarry site would cause changes to the local marine environment, with the likelihood that shellfish grounds would be affected. The increased marine traffic with the attendant pollution and general disturbance would also take its toll on the natural environment.

Some of these environmental effects can be observed at Glensanda, the UK's only working coastal superquarry. Further work is underway to assess the effect of this superquarry on the environment, so that in evaluating future applications for mineral extraction on this scale, current experience will inform our opinion.

The anorthosite body which is earmarked for exploitation extends over many square kilometres, so, environmental consideration notwithstanding, removal of part of the resource to satisfy a considerable proportion of the nation's aggregate requirements is arguably a wise use of a finite resource. However, if the output of crushed rock from this quarry is simply to be added to the world supply, then the argument for quarrying at this particular site is more difficult to justify.

14.1.2   *Marine sand and gravel dredging*

Marine-dredged sand and gravel has not made a contribution to the supply of aggregate in Scotland to date, but there is no doubt that resources do exist which could be exploited. Although planning permission under the Town and Country Planning Act is not required unless the proposed extraction site falls within the area of an administrative Region, controls are in place to regulate the dredging industry. In fact, the way in which new applications are handled has recently been streamlined and this 'Government View' procedure makes provision for early informal discussions with a wide range of statutory consultees, including SNH.

However, marine sands and gravel deposits which are commercially exploited may only be replenished over a prolonged period so there is a clear need for the resource to be developed in a responsible way. The marine environment is particularly sensitive to change and conflicts with nature conservation interests have arisen in English waters, where aggregate extraction is commonplace. The main areas of conflict identified by Eno (1991) are as follows.

1. **Destruction of habitat and fauna.** Aggregate dredging can cause destruction of habitat and benthic invertebrate populations and have adverse effects on fish spawning grounds. Disturbance to marine mammals and birds, through both the removal of existing substrate and the smothering of organisms by material rejected over board by the dredger may also occur.

2. **Suspension of fine sediment.** Dredging causes suspension of sediment in the water column which may affect phytoplankton growth, clog fish gills and affect filter feeding organisms. Also, on settling, the sediment can alter the nature of the substrate by blanketing shellfish beds and altering sediment characteristics of spawning grounds.

3. **Remobilization of toxic substrates.** Fine sediments act as a sink for many toxic compounds introduced into the marine environment. Remobilization of these substances from the sediment into the water column can occur at dredging sites and where dredged material is dumped.

4. **Recovery potential.** Dredging of sand from sand banks has little long-lasting affect on the biology of the seabed, whereas dredging through fine sediment deposit to get to the gravel underneath causes longer term effects which may persist for 10 years.

5. **Effects on the coastline.** Dredging has been known to accelerate foreshore erosion. Dredging may affect the adjacent coastline by interrupting the offshore/onshore sediment transfer, causing beach drawdown or creating a more aggressive near-shore wave climate. The net effect of any of these changes may be to create a need for coastal protection or sea defence works to be constructed.

14.1.3 Maerl dredging

Maerl is a calcareous algae of the family *Corallinacea* which has been dredged from British waters. It is used in a crushed form as a soil conditioner on acidic soils and can also be used as a food additive.

Where the maerl is dead, exploitation in moderation is not necessarily at odds with good conservation practice, but exploitation of live maerl, which usually supports very rich infaunal communities is to be discouraged. This practice is not widespread, although recently a prospecting licence was issued to search the seabed off Barra, South Uist.

14.1.4 Offshore chromite and olivine resources

Marine deposits of chromite and olivine have recently been located some 3 km south-east of Rum. The upper layers of sand contain some 70,000 tonnes of the mineral chrome spinel, averaging 32% Cr_2O_3 at a grade of nearly 1%, together with 1.5–2 million tonnes of olivine, averaging 47% MgO at 25% grade. Accompanying deposits of ilmenite and vanadiferous magnetite, and traces of platinum group elements, have also been detected. The sand size and freshness of the minerals are favourable for extraction (Beveridge *et al.*, 1991). The potential conflicts with marine nature conservation are similar to those associated with aggregate dredging. However, despite the apparent commercial attractiveness of this mineral deposit, no attempts have been made to exploit it at anything other than reconnaissance scale.

14.1.5 Extraction of beach sand and gravel

Quarrying beach sand and gravel at some locations on the Scottish islands probably extends back several centuries. Material is removed from beach environments for use in construction or to sweeten agricultural land. For the majority of the Hebridean islands, significant glacial deposits which form the main source of sand and gravel for the building trade in other parts of the country, are absent. This shortfall in supply, especially on Lewis, mainland Orkney and Islay, is largely made up by extraction from the intertidal and immediately adjacent areas of the coastal zone. This situation is complicated by the crofters involved in this practice, who regard beach sand and cobble extraction as a traditional right. Where sediment supply is sufficient to replenish the material which is removed, the beach system remains in balance. However, the natural process of longshore drift and transfer of material onshore may not match the rate of extraction and the beach level may drop as a consequence. Other manifestations of this imbalance are sand blow-outs and accelerated marine erosion.

In the 1970s, around Broad Bay near Stornoway the situation deteriorated to such an extent that a Coast Protection Order was issued, which required any person taking material from below high water mark to do so under permit (Ritchie and Mather, 1970).

As well as their widespread use as source material for the construction industry, Hebridean beaches are also a significant source of lime-rich shell sand deposits, which have been used to reduce the pH of acidic agricultural soils. Ritchie and Mather (1970) report that 'during the period from 1960–69, no less than 11,838 acres of land were improved in Lewis together with a further 3,031 acres in the outer islands of Inverness-shire. Application rates were approximately 8 tonnes of shell sand per acre. Since one tonne of shell sand approximates to one cubic yard in volume, the volume of sand extracted in Lewis alone *could* amount to as much as 90,000 cubic yards.

As most of the extraction is concentrated on a very small number of beaches, it becomes very clear that the effects of shell sand extraction on the 'sand-budget' of the beaches and dunes can be very considerable'.

Sustainability in the context of exploiting the beach, sand and gravel resource, can be simply defined. A balance must be struck between the material which is being removed and the rate at which it is being naturally replenished by waves, currents and tides. If an equilibrium can be achieved, then the net effect of sand and gravel extraction on the coastline will be neutral. Where the quantity of material removed by man exceeds the rate of natural replenishment, the coastline may retreat or exhibit other signs of instability, such as beach level lowering. Where uncontrolled extraction is taking place and warning signals exist that the natural system is being exploited to a degree which is unsustainable, the coastal environment will continue to degrade. Under extreme conditions, such weakening of the coastline's natural defences against the sea may lead to flooding or dramatically increased rates of coastal erosion.

Extraction continues at a number of locations including Eoropie and Barvas machairs on Lewis, Laggan Bay on Islay and Burray Links on Orkney where it is still regarded as a right to remove beach sand and cobbles for local use. However, it is in the interests of all concerned that this resource is wisely used and is not exploited beyond its capability to self-sustain.

14.1.6 *The Islay wave power project*

In terms of sustainable development of our physical resources, use of a renewable resource such as wave power is readily justified. Many large-scale wave prototypes were constructed and tested in the 1970s, but none have been commercially developed. The most promising wave energy technology, at present, is small in scale and shore-based. It makes use of natural coastal gullies, both to concentrate the energy in the waves and also to minimize environmental disturbance. Water oscillating back and forth in the gully can then be used to force air through a turbine which is coupled to a generator which produces electricity.

A prototype of this design was constructed on the west coast of Islay, funded by the Department of Energy. The device spans a natural rock gully in relatively shallow water and resembles an upturned box with a submerged open bottom. Both the conceptual design of this device and its method of construction are novel. It is now providing valuable information on the commercial prospects for on-shore wave power technology and will also be a marine test bed for its continuing development.

The electricity produced by this device is already being fed into the distribution grid on the island. Commercial devices based on this concept could be used to provide electrical power for isolated communities or to support local grid supplies.

14.1.7 North Sea oil and gas exploration and production

The development of North Sea oil and gas reserves has been on an opportunistic basis and exploration companies have exploited to the full hydrocarbon finds which they have made. As the recoverable reserves are clearly finite, a point will be reached with each oil or gas field where they cease to be economically viable. Although enhanced recovery techniques can be used to extend the life of individual fields, some are already reaching the point of exhaustion. Development of the North Sea resource is without any accepted concept of sustainable development and exploitation of the oil and gas resources has taken place in a way which is entirely driven by market forces. It is arguable that given the hostility of the environment in which these operations are being undertaken and the complex nature of the technology involved, the oil companies have no alternative but to extract the resource in its entirety. Thoughts of leaving some oil or gas under the seabed in the hope that future generations will revisit the field and complete the extraction process are impractical and would make most of the more marginal fields uneconomic. Sustainability in practice may also take the form of proving economic prospects but leaving them in place for future generations to bring ashore.

Again, this is an impractical proposition as exploration costs incurred in locating and proving the resource have to be recovered. We are, therefore, left with the inescapable conclusion that each individual act of resource exploitation is of itself inherently unsustainable and that sustainability in practice is to ensure that a sufficient reserve has been identified worldwide that will satisfy requirements for future generations.

The possibility of oil and gas resources under the North Sea has been known about since the 1930s (Turnbull, 1991). However, it was not until the mid-1960s that exploration and production of hydrocarbons from the North Sea began on a major scale. Oil from the Argyll Field was first to be landed in June 1975 and, at that stage, 10 major hydrocarbon prospects were under development (Hallet *et al.*, 1985). Since that time, prodigious efforts have been made by the exploration companies in developing and producing the fruits of the North Sea.

14.1.7.1   Exploration for oil and gas in the North Sea

The large-scale geological structures which might hold commercially viable reserves of hydrocarbon are obscured by first the sea and then a cover of non-productive younger strata. Investigative methods have been developed to penetrate these obstacles and to determine the nature of the rocks hidden from view. Detailed information about deeply buried rock layers and structures, such as folds and faults, has been obtained by seismic survey and, as a result, the main structural elements of the UK continental shelf are known (Figure 14.3).

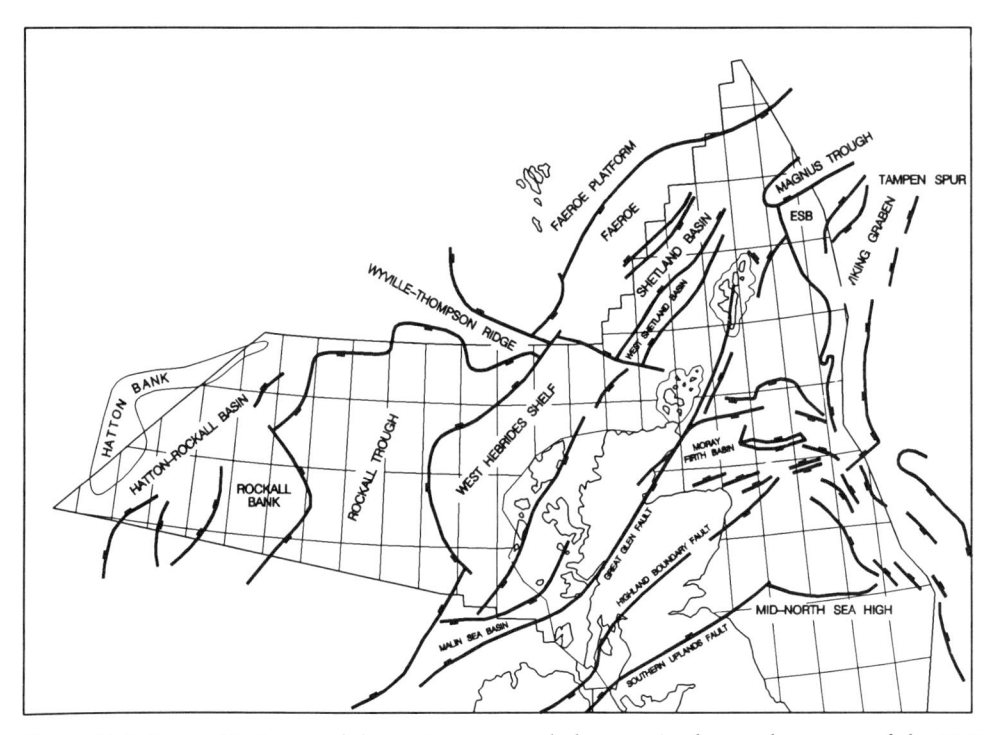

Figure 14.3. Generalised map of the major structural elements in the northern part of the U.K. continental shelf (after Beveridge, Brown, Gallacher and Merrit. In Craig 1991)

The most striking feature is the development of the Viking Graben, a major 'valley', now filled with sediments, which run the length of the northern sector of the North Sea. The distribution of productive oil and gas fields shown in Figure 14.4 clearly shows the relationship between this valley system and the major hydrocarbon reserves.

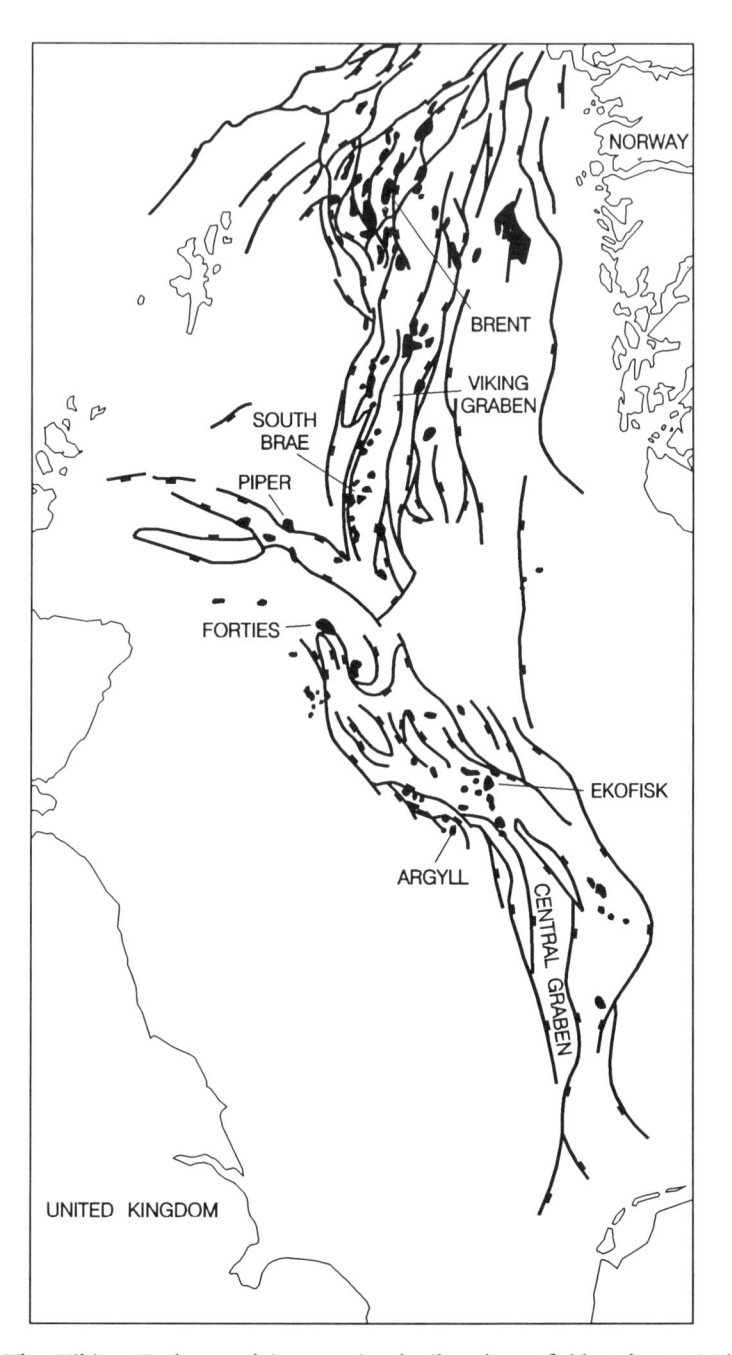

Figure 14.4. The Viking Graben and its associated oil and gas fields (after British Museum (Natural History) and Geological Museum, 1989)

The impact of oil exploration and development on the island communities of Shetland and Orkney in particular has been considerable.

Europe's largest oil and liquefied gas terminal is sited at Sullom Voe on Mainland Shetland and the oil marine base for much of the service activity in the North Sea is concentrated in Lerwick. Pipelines carrying crude oil come ashore at Sullom Voe and Flotta; the latter being the only significant onshore oil-related development in Orkney. The impact on these remote communities is already well documented (Blackadder and Baster, 1991) ; the most significant being increased employment prospects and a drift away from the more traditional pursuits such as fishing and agriculture.

Environmental impacts have also been monitored with equal vigour. Until the grounding of the *MV Braer* in January 1993, there have been no large-scale releases of oil from a tanker wreck or pipeline leak, but regulated releases and minor spills have had a cumulative effect on the marine and coastal environment. Hydrocarbon levels in waters and associated sediments where oil related activities are focused, have given rise to some concern (McIntyre and Turnbull, 1991). Particular concern about the environmental impacts of the oil industry has been demonstrated at Sullom Voe, where the Shetland Oil Terminal Environmental Advisory Group (SOTEAG) has been established. Together with its predecessor, the Sullom Voe Environmental Advisory Group, a clear picture of the existing environment, including a comprehensive description of the habitats potentially at risk was compiled. This work is the baseline study against which the ongoing environmental monitoring programme is now compared.

Levels of chemical contaminants in different parts of the environment, as well as an assessment of the effects of these chemicals, is an integral part of the environmental monitoring programme. Great care is taken to distinguish the effects of chemical contaminations from natural changes in populations of plant or animal and their supporting habitats.

14.1.7.2   On shore oil exploration

Exploration has also taken place in the inshore coastal waters of the Minch and off Barra (classed as onshore for the purposes of licensing) and on Skye and Mull. Although no wells have been drilled in these areas to date, seismic survey work has been completed. The geology of these 'onshore' areas is similar to that of the productive North Sea basins, so recoverable reserves may be identified in future.

14.1.7.3   Oil production: The future

Oil production peaked in the mid-1980s, (Figure 14.5) but there are sufficient resources for this industry to be viable well into the next century. Further exploration will undoubtedly continue, with smaller, more marginal fields being brought on stream. If oil prices climb, 'enhanced recovery' techniques

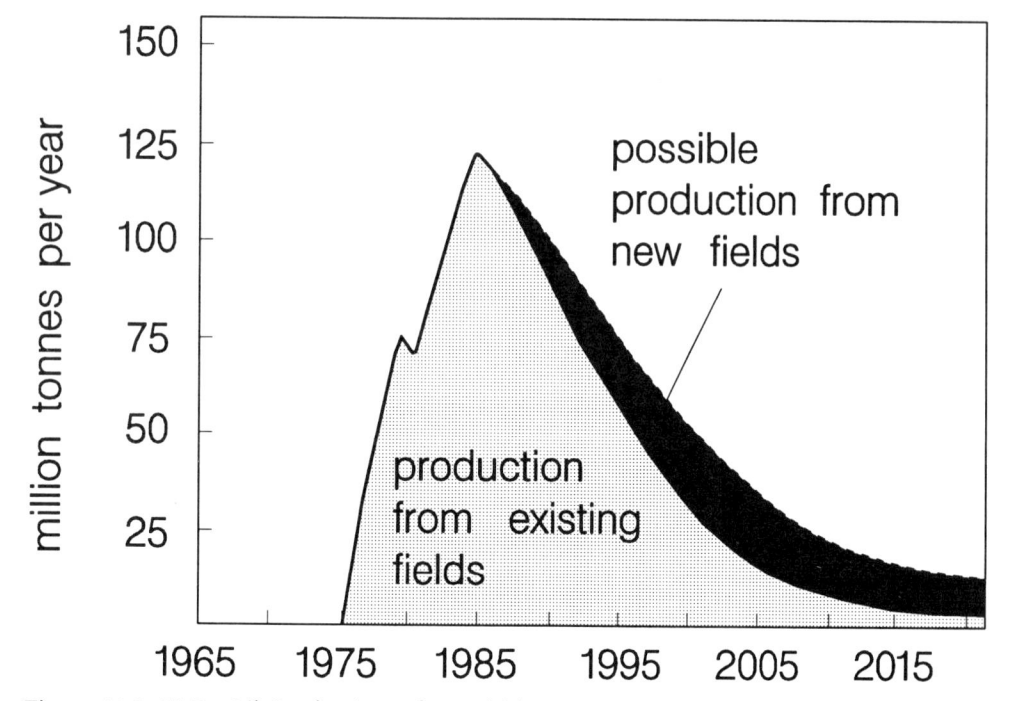

Figure 14.5. U.K. Oil Production (after British Museum (Natural History) and Geological Museum, 1989)

may be employed to increase flow ratio and yields, helping to squeeze more out of the existing fields.

However, it is likely that all the extractable oil and gas will ultimately be removed from the extant fields, both onshore and offshore, and they will be abandoned. 'Abandonment' procedures are being developed to minimize the impact of this process on the environment. Steel platforms may be cut off to permit safer navigation; concrete platforms relocated and sunk in the ocean deeps and pipelines flushed and left on the seabed.

14.3 Conclusions

This brief review of the ways in which our physical resources have been exploited leads to the inescapable conclusion that the concept of sustainable development has not conditioned activities to date.

The process of resource exploitation is largely driven by the rate at which materials are required and the price which a particular commodity will fetch in the market place. This 'market forces' philosophy is best exemplified by the way in which the North Sea oil and gas resources have been exploited, where peak levels of production in the mid-1980s coincided with high commodity prices and concerted worldwide economic growth. This situation is in stark contrast to the long-term prospects for the North Sea, where all the recoverable hydrocarbons will have been removed by the early part of the next century. Similar observations can also be made on the proposals to develop superquarries along the west coast of Scotland in that no attempt has been made to apply the principle of sustainable development and that each new application or proposal is opportunistic rather than strategic.

Magnus Magnusson, in his address to the Natural Environment Research Council in November 1992, argued that market forces will always tend towards over-consumption and the exploitation of the reserves which are cheap to work will be targeted, irrespective of the impact on the environment. These impacts on the natural heritage, as well as those on the local communities in the shadow of such developments, are frequently not reflected in the cost of the material produced. Consequently the market is not likely to encourage any form of sustainable development of resources as the environmental costs are not 'internalized' or put in simpler terms, the environmental and human costs are ignored. This situation will continue until robust and unambiguous guidelines for mineral extraction are established so that the needs of society and not just the economic imperatives of industry can be met in the most environmentally acceptable way.

For the concept of sustainable development to take root and guide our national policy on the exploitation and use of non-renewable resource, there must be a re-evaluation of current practice.

Strategic planning must replace opportunism and positive encouragement should be given to national regulatory authorities and local councils to think and act in the best interests of our shared environment.

The need for these raw materials is unlikely to diminish in future years, so the demand that society will make on the countryside and the marine environment will increase. People need houses, roads and fuel for their cars, but society also demands that our heritage of wildlife sites and landscapes are preserved. It is surely not beyond us to make adequate provision for both.

References

Arup Economics and Planning, 1992. *Coastal Superquarries to supply South-east England Aggregate Requirements*. Research Report for the DoE.

Beveridge, R., Brown, S., Gallacher, M. and Merritt, J. 1991. Economic Geology. In Craig, G. Y. (Ed.), *Geology of Scotland*, Alden Press, Oxford, 545–86.

Blackadder, G. A. and Baster, J. 1991. Oil and remote communities – Shetland and Orkney. In Cairns, W. J. (Ed.), *North Sea Oil and the Environment*. Elsevier Applied Science, London and New York. 165–91.

British Museum (Natural History) and the Geological Museum. 1989. *Britian's Offshore Oil and Gas*. British Museum (Natural History), London.

Eno, N. C. (Ed.) 1991. *Marine Conservation Handbook*. Nature Conservancy Council, Peterborough.

Hallett, D. Durrant, G. P. and Farrow, G. E. 1985. Oil exploration and production in Scotland. *Scottish Journal of Geology*, **21** (4), 547–70.

Jacobs, M. 1991. *The Green Economy: Environment, Sustainable Development and the Politics of the Future*. Pluto Press, London.

Magnusson, M. 1992. Sense and Sustainability, Homage to Frank Fraser Darling. *Natural Environment Research Council Annual Lecture* (unpublished).

McIntyre, A. D. and Turnbull, R. G. H. 1991. Environment. In Cairns, W. J. (Ed.), *North Sea Oil and the Environment*, Elsevier Applied Science, London and New York. 27–56.

Redlands Aggregate Limited, 1991. *Rodel, Isle of Harris, A Planning Application.*

Ritchie, W. and Mather, A. 1970. *The Beaches of Lewis and Harris.* Unpublished report to the Countryside Commission for Scotland.

Scottish Development Department Report, 1977. *Aggregate Working.* National Planning Guidelines.

Scottish Development Department Report, 1980. *Potential for a Large Coastal Quarry in Scotland.* Preliminary Research Report.

Scottish Office, 1992. *Land for Mineral Workings' National Planning Policy Guidelines,* (in draft).

Turnbull, R. G. H. 1991. Resources, environment and development – a summary. In Cairns, W. J. (Ed.), *North Sea Oil and the Environment.* Elsevier Applied Science, London and New York 7–12.

Verney Report, 1976. *Aggregates: The Way Ahead.* Report to the Advisory Committees on Aggregates, HMSO.

World Commission on the Environment and Development, 1987. *Our Common Future,* Oxford University Press, Oxford.

15 THE PROBLEMS OF POLLUTION AND LITTER IN THE SEAS AROUND THE SCOTTISH ISLES: THE SHETLAND PERSPECTIVE

M. R. Hall

Summary

1. Marine pollution is a major, multi-faceted problem in the seas around the Scottish islands.

2. Litter in the sea and along the shore is derived from many different sources. It, more often than not causes no more than visual offence but in some cases more dangerous materials may be washed up. With suitable motivation local islanders can be mobilized to help clean-up this problem.

3. Salmon farming results in a variety of substances being introduced and subsequently accumulating in the environment. The Shetland model of requiring fish farmers to carry out inexpensive benthic monitoring is described.

4. The North Sea oil industry has had a major impact on the Shetland Islands with the development of the Sullom Voe oil terminal. The different precautions and regulations imposed on the various operations and the coordination of the environmental monitoring through the Shetland Oil Terminal Environmental Advisory Group are discussed.

5. The vulnerability of all the Scottish islands to outside influences as demonstrated by the Braer oil spill is highlighted in a postscript to this paper.

15.1 Introduction

Living on an island group does not, as you might believe, make people insular. On the contrary, people tend to see things from a distance with an overview perspective. Shetland Islanders are, therefore, acutely aware of their marine heritage and the litter and pollution problems affecting the marine environment from the Sea of Japan to nearer home in the Wadensee, where pollution appears to be seriously affecting traditional fish breeding grounds.

Shetland is located at the northern end of the North Sea on its border with the Atlantic Ocean and is some 589 miles north of London and 220 miles west of Bergen in Norway at a latitude of 60° North, level with the tip of Greenland. It is made up of over 100 islands, 14 of which are inhabited, covering an area of 567 square miles with a total length of coastline in excess of 900 miles. The population of Shetland is approximately 23,000, the main population centre being Lerwick on Mainland, the name of the largest island.

There are three National Nature Reserves in Shetland and 70 Sites of Special Scientific Interest. Shetland is of considerable importance, at national and international levels for several species of animals and birds, providing as it does a habitat for a large proportion of the British population of whimbrel (*Numenius phaeopus*) (95%), great skua (*Stercorarius skua*) (76%), red-throated diver (*Gavia stellata*) (75%), red-necked phalarope (*Phalaropus lobatus*) (70%) and arctic skua (*Stercorarius parasiticus*) (61%) and of course Shetland otters (*Lutra lutra*) which are greatly dependent on the marine environment.

It is thus readily apparent from both the economic and ecological points of view that maintaining the cleanliness of the environment, particularly the sea, is vital to Shetland.

Its proximity to major oil fields has also made Shetland an ideal location for the oil industry and we now have Europe's largest crude oil terminal situated at Sullom Voe. Shetland also collects what appears to be a high proportion of sea-borne litter from both the North Sea and the Atlantic Ocean. In addition, its long coastline and relatively clean environment have made it an attractive location for fish farming.

This paper is limited to the three high profile areas of concern to the people of Shetland, namely those of sea-borne litter, fish farming and, of course, oil exploration and production.

15.2 Legislative Background

The legislation relevant to Shetland's litter and pollution problems is abundant and complex, stemming from the UK, the European Community and other international sources. To discuss it in detail would require a separate paper. I will, however, outline briefly the legislation in force at the present time to give a flavour of the problem.

15.2.1 UK legislation

The mainstay of the UK's legislation for controlling pollution is the Control of Pollution Act 1974 which allows us to control effluent discharges to the marine environment. It is primarily enforced by the River Purification Authorities.

The other main Act dealing with marine pollution is the Food and Environmental Protection Act 1990, which replaced the 1974 Dumping at

Sea Act. This Act is enforced by a combination of local government, central government and River Purification Authority officers. It brings into effect decisions taken at the 1972 Oslo Convention dealing with prevention of marine pollution caused by dumping at sea from ships and aircraft and also decisions taken at the 1972 London Convention on the prevention of marine pollution by dumping of wastes and other matters.

Shetland also has its own legislation, the Zetland County Council Act, which was enacted in 1974 as a result of fears regarding the development of the oil industry. This legislation allows control of development in coastal waters and has been put to effective use in Shetland.

Other Acts of note are the Litter Acts, the Water Acts, the Prevention of Oil Pollution Acts, the Public Health Acts and the Civic Government (Scotland) Act.

The enforcement of the UK legislation is thus carried out by diverse groups of people, including local government officers, River Purification Authorities, central government officers and other agents who have become very effective and built up a wide range of expertise. The system has, on the whole, worked well and has had a good deal of local accountability and control.

In order to rationalize the situation and avoid confusion and duplication of effort the Government decided to build on this earlier system by the introduction of integrated pollution control as embodied in the Environmental Protection Act 1990. However, before integrated pollution control was implemented the Government announced proposals for the formation of Environmental Protection Agencies in England and Wales and in Scotland the Scottish Environmental Protection Agency (SEPA). This may well be the single most important step taken this century in the protection of our environment. The implications of such an Agency are immense. This paper will not discuss the implications except to say that we must all strive in the forthcoming months to ensure that, when the Scottish Environmental Protection Agency is established, it is in a form which still has local accountability and control and is properly funded.

15.2.2 European Community law

New EC Directives on environmental issues, which have to be incorporated into UK legislation are a frequent occurrence. These have a direct effect if the provisions are clear, concise, unconditional, unqualified and leave no discretion to member states. Problems, however, do occur where this is not the case as different member states put their own interpretation on the Directives.

15.2.3 Other international law

Other international controls stem mainly from the 1973 International Convention for the Prevention of Pollution from Ships, as modified by the International Protocol of 1978 (Marpol 73/78) and are implemented in this country by Department of Transport Merchant Shipping Notices.

The most significant of these is M 162 – Prevention of Pollution of the Sea by Garbage from Ships and Offshore Installations, garbage is defined as 'ship's operational waste'. This makes it illegal to deposit garbage in the North Sea. The creation of such a 'garbage free' area and others of its kind throughout the world is, on the face of it, a great step forward. However, in most cases the garbage is still disposed of at sea beyond these areas and, given the right wind and tide conditions, it still ends up on the same beaches.

Controls of this nature are also difficult to enforce. For example, a Shetland Islands Council Pollution Control flight witnessed a cargo boat, *en route* from Amsterdam to Norway, within a North Sea special area, but beyond UK coastal waters in international waters 18 miles west of Shetland, cleaning out her holds which were full of coal dust in preparation for her next cargo. The coal dust was simply being washed into the North Sea. The UK Government's initial reaction was that no contravention of the Marpol Protocol had been committed as this was not 'garbage', that is, ship's operational waste. Shetland Islands Council disagreed in the strongest possible terms and the Government agreed to contact the ship's flag state concerning the incident.

It is obvious from the above example that the enforcement of international law is complex and fraught with loopholes and scope for interpretation. Also given the absence of any recognized International Court, it is not clear by whom and in what manner these laws are to be enforced. These issues must be addressed with urgency.

Section 15.3 deals in detail with the three subjects noted earlier, ranging from the chronic problem of seaborne litter to fish farming's chronic and acute problems to the disastrous scenario of a one-off major oil spill.

15.3   Seaborne Litter

Seaborne litter is a chronic pollution problem in its most visible form and for this reason it is emotive and attracts a great deal of public attention. There is little evidence of any acute litter problems causing major environmental disasters and, on the whole, litter has very little effect on the environment. However, a single incident can be dramatic and dangerous to both humans and marine life, for example disposal of old flares or hypodermic needles.

The problem of littering our seas and shores can be overcome without the need for scientific solutions or sophisticated technical equipment. It is simply a case of getting people to discharge their waste to a reception facility which they know will be removed to an approved disposal site. However, the experience of experts working in this field suggests that it would be easier to resolve the issue if it were a complex, acute scientific problem, rather than a more low-key chronic one.

In the short term this problem is not going to go away and in Shetland, with its 900 miles of coastline, the local authority does not have the resources to deal with seaborne litter which, of course, dries out and becomes windborne litter affecting all of Shetland. As a result, using income from the oil industry,

Shetland established the Shetland Amenity Trust, charged with improving the amenity of Shetland. While it plants trees, builds walls and renovates old buildings, a major part of its work is the collection and disposal/recycling of waste, including sea- or windborne litter.

One of the major initiatives taken by the Shetland Amenity Trust was the formation of Shetland Anti-Litter Enterprise which, in its four years of operation, has done a great deal to highlight the problems of litter by campaigns, educational projects and promotional activities. Through these activities people's attitudes to 'chucking their bruck over da banks' or off the fishing boat have greatly changed.

However, without doubt, its greatest visible achievement is 'Da Voar Redd Up', which is Shetland's annual Spring clean involving over 2,000 people annually (10% of the population). Through this the Shetland population personally cleans up approximately 50 beaches and some 250 miles of verges over a period of three days, filling in excess of 7,000 black bin bags. This event has gained a number of prestigious prizes including a Queen Mother's Award.

It is indeed fortunate that local authorities in the rural areas of Scotland, where our scenic beauty is greatest, can rely on volunteers to clean up these areas, as resources from the Government are not forthcoming. There is not much hope, in these days of government cut-backs, of more resources being allocated and for this reason our attention should be focused on educating the offenders and securing international enforcement and control, administered at local, national and international levels.

15.4   Fish Farming

Fish farming has grown rapidly in the last five years in Shetland with the total annual value of fish farmed since 1990 exceeding the value of the traditional fish catching industry. The result has been a 'rash' of fish farms breaking out in almost every suitable Voe in Shetland.

The siting of these fish farms is easily controlled through the powers of the Zetland County Council Act 1974, which is a very useful piece of legislation. However, this did not allay the people of Shetland's fears with regard to the possibility of chronic or acute pollution effects from the industry. These fears were proven to be well founded. In 1987, at a time when the fish-farming industry was still growing, a salmon farmer disposed of a large quantity of TBT anti-fouling paint by pouring it into the sea, causing the sterilization of a small geo and significant effects to the marine community within half a mile on each side of the geo. The offending person was prosecuted under the Control of Pollution Act 1974 and the Food and Environmental Protection Act 1985.

This incident, together with the public outcry concerning the general use of TBT, prompted the fish-farming industry in Shetland to impose a voluntary ban on the use of this anti-fouling paint prior to legislation being enacted. Shetland Islands Council's Control of Pollution Act Consents require applicants to keep a Register of any chemical or medical treatments and to notify the Environmental Services Department 24 hours before any such treatment is given. In addition, the fish farming industry itself employs a veterinary surgeon who oversees the administration of drugs to the salmon as well as issuing general guidance on the treatment of fish.

If the Control of Pollution Act Consent is adhered to and the guidelines are followed then the risk of another acute incident is minimized.

The other main concern is the chronic effect of pollution from fish farms, in particular from waste food and fish excrement.

Monitoring pollution from fish farms could be done by chemical sampling and analysis of the sea or analysis of the biological effects of the farm on the environment. We set the criteria that monitoring should be repeatable, use standardized techniques and reports, and should eliminate as many variables as possible. We felt that it should be operable by non-specialist staff so that various people would be able to undertake the work. It should also be able to give us comparisons with previous results and, if possible, allow comparison from farm to farm. Since the Environmental Services Department does not employ chemists or marine biologists it was essential that any results were both meaningful and easy to interpret. It was also necessary to be able to attribute any effects found to a particular farm and not to another source.

Chemical monitoring for routine purposes was dismissed because of interpretation difficulties and the number of variables involved, for example, from which side of the cage was the sample taken; at what depth; the weather conditions at the time of sampling; the tide conditions; the time of day and the time from the last feed input. In addition there were no experts or set standards to use as a baseline for interpretation. Fish farms could also have 'blamed' agricultural run off or a neighbouring fish farm for some of the pollution.

A technique involving seabed monitoring, developed by Sarah Fowler, was adapted to our needs. This technique involved the classification of the seabed type from fine mud through six stages to gravel, a series of standardized photographs and a report along a transect line. It used *Begiatoa sp* for assessing the conditions, as this organism only grows at the interface between aerobic and anaerobic conditions and is therefore very useful as a marker. At a series of meetings between Shetland Islands Council, the Nature Conservancy Council and representatives of the fish farming industry, a seabed monitoring methodology was finally agreed.

Shetland Islands Council now includes this approach as part of a fish farmer's 'Consent to Discharge'. The farmer in carrying out the necessary monitoring work in-house employs a contractor, with the Environmental Services Department carrying out an audit of 10% of the fish farms in Shetland, chosen at random on an annual basis.

A report by the Nature Conservation Bureau Limited concluded that the methodology required by the Shetland Islands Council Department of

Environmental Services (as Islands River Purification Authority) for self monitoring by marine fish farmers under the Control of Pollution Act 1974 Discharge Consents is inexpensive, repeatable and readily interpreted by the Authority. Results examined to date have been generally of high standard, with very few reports turned down because of poor quality. Where serious pollution effects are noted, the Authority may then take any steps considered appropriate (by requiring more detailed monitoring to determine whether the pollution levels are unacceptable or by limiting stocking densities).

Examination of the results obtained from previous Nature Conservancy Council fish farm surveys has indicated that visual surveys provide similar levels of information on pollution gradients to the appraisal of macrofauna in small core samples taken along transects. Other authors have suggested that benthic monitoring to detect pollution gradients need not be carried out to such a detailed level as has generally been the practice in the past.

15.4   Oil Pollution Prevention/Control Procedures

When exploration for oil and gas began in 1970 the people of Shetland were concerned that large numbers of companies would try to develop separate facilities and that there would be a proliferation of facilities along Shetland's coast. In order to prevent this, and to be in a position to exert some control over the situation, the then local authority, Zetland County Council (now Shetland Islands Council), obtained their own legislation through Parliament in the form of the Zetland County Council Act 1974. This gave Shetland Islands Council wide ranging powers, the most important of which in relation to oil development are:

- to exercise jurisdiction as harbour authority in various areas throughout Shetland, including Sullom Voe where Europe's largest crude oil terminal is situated;

- to construct, maintain and operate works in coastal areas;

- to grant licences for other bodies to construct works in the coastal areas;

- to provide the vessels necessary to carry out these functions, including tugs;

- to remove obstructions in harbour areas, including wrecks;

- to appropriate land in a harbour area;

- to issue general and special directions to shipping;

- to make bylaws.

These powers enabled Shetland Islands Council to enter into an agreement with the oil industry on the construction and use of Sullom Voe Terminal – The Ports and Harbours Agreement. The most important aspect of the agreement, in environmental terms, is that the oil industry is responsible for cleaning up pollution either within or originating from Sullom Voe, to the satisfaction of Shetland Islands Council. To this end the industry provides the necessary equipment and staff.

With the advent of oil there was great concern about the effects of the oil industry on the environment of Shetland and as a result an Environmental Monitoring Group was set up called Sullom Voe Environmental Advisory Group. This later gave way to a new group called the Shetland Oil Terminal Environmental Advisory Group (SOTEAG) under the chairmanship of Professor George Dunnet, then head of the Zoology Department of Aberdeen University. The Group is representative of all the interests involved – fishing, crofting, Shetland Bird Club, Scottish Natural Heritage, the oil industry, Shetland Islands Council and others. Base data were established and a continuous monitoring programme undertaken. The group was instrumental in recommending where effluent outfall pipes should be located to provide the greatest dilution effect and where they would be least harmful to marine life.

Recommendations were also made as to the acceptable limit of oil content in the water. Plans showing environmentally sensitive areas and areas of prolific wildlife activity, were produced with guidelines for the use of dispersant chemicals for combating oil pollution.

It would be unfair to suggest that SOTEAG was solely responsible for the production of all the environmental protection strategies which were adopted. However, it was and still is the only Group in existence in which all the interests in Shetland are represented and it is in this aspect that its strength as a responsible and unbiased Environmental Advisory Group lies.

To discharge its functions properly, Shetland Islands Council created a Ports and Harbours Department, now called the Marine Operations Department, during the latter part of 1975. This Department was given the responsibility of managing the day-to-day affairs of the port of Sullom Voe. It also advises Shetland Islands Council on marine matters and where appropriate, in conjunction with the Environmental Services Department, on environmental matters throughout the whole of Shetland. It was envisaged during those earlier years that there would be a requirement for a long-term commitment to prevent oil pollution. An Oil Pollution Control Section within the framework of the Marine Operations Department was therefore formed and plans devised to prevent oil spillages and manage any clean-up operation when it occurred.

Shetland Islands Council Anti-Oil Pollution Plan was born. This Plan now forms part of the Department of Transport's East Coast of Scotland Marine Survey District Plan and incorporates procedures for cleaning up oil pollution which has not originated in Sullom Voe. It is applicable to the whole coastline of Shetland out to the limits of territorial waters.

The Sullom Voe Oil Spill Advisory Committee, (SVOSAC), was formed to advise Shetland Islands Council and the oil industry on the best means of implementing efficient oil spill clean up procedures within Sullom Voe. SVOSAC was responsible for the production of the Sullom Voe Harbour

Oil Spill Plan which is a detailed document setting out the various actions to be taken in the event of oil pollution. In the plan oil spills are categorized in terms of the size of the spill and there are explicit details on actions to be taken under each category heading. The plan also incorporates lists of anti-pollution equipment available, details of environmentally sensitive areas, lists of the responsibilities of the various parties to the plan and lists of telephone contacts.

The membership of SVOSAC consists of representatives of Shetland Islands Council, the Terminal operator (BP), the Department of Trade and other parties responsible for the transshipment of oil within the Harbour Area. The Terminal Manager and Shetland Islands Council's Director of Marine Operations alternate as Chairman of the Committee. The Committee can also call upon outside expertise. SVOSAC has a close liaison with SOTEAG and the latter Committee is always consulted before any new oil pollution clean-up method is brought into effect, for example the removal of oil polluted beach material or the use of dispersant chemicals in a particular area.

15.4.1 Port operations

Port Control and Pilotage are situated in the Port Administration Building at Sellaness, thus providing visual surveillance of the manoeuvring area on the jetties. In addition, there is comprehensive radar coverage of the whole pilotage area including a feature which sets up theoretical boundaries within the shipping channels with an audible alarm sounding if a ship approaches them. Vessels can be equipped or labelled, with a readout of their course, speed and distance being provided. Control of shipping movements, however, commences much earlier, with approaching ships having to contact the port and complete a check list 24 hours prior to arrival.

On arrival the ship waits at one of the two pilot stations which are 11 and 8 miles from the Port Administration Building respectively. Pilots board by fast launch or, in severe weather, by helicopter. Tugs meet each vessel soon after the pilot boards and will escort the ship both in and out of the harbour. The tugs are operated by Shetland Towage which is a joint venture between Shetland Islands Council and two leading British tug companies. The Port Authority specifies that all ships which exceed 200 m must be attended by four tugs during any berthing operations. The number to be used for smaller ships is also laid down. There is no scope for the unscrupulous ship-owner to compromise safety by saving money on towage charges.

Port Control is staffed continuously by a pilot. In addition, whenever there is a vessel alongside the jetties, another pilot is on standby in the Port Administration Building in case it is necessary for a ship to be moved in a hurry. Since Shetland lies in the track of most of the transatlantic depressions and can be subjected to exceptionally high winds at any time of year, Port Control is also equipped with various items of meteorological equipment, including remote weather stations at two locations. In addition, the Council has a contract with the UK's Meteorological Service whereby forecasters are on site to provide the Port Controller with up-to-date information.

It is unusual in the UK for Port Control to be staffed by pilots, and this might be considered excessive. However, the philosophy is that the pilot on board the ship must have complete confidence in the information that is provided from ashore and that the best way of ensuring this is for it to be provided by a colleague who fully understands the problems.

15.4.2 Offshore oil pollution prevention procedures

All the systems and operational procedures designed into the Port of Sullom Voe performed as expected and caused cautious optimism and a degree of satisfaction to everyone who had been involved in the design stages. It was, therefore, a profound shock to all concerned when, late in the evening of 30 December 1978, a large tanker became involved in an accident during a docking manoeuvre, which resulted in the spillage of about 1200 tonnes of heavy fuel oil from one of the vessel's bunker tanks which had been ruptured on impact with the jetty structure. A spillage of fuel oil had never been seriously contemplated – the Port had never been designed to handle fuel oil – and the equipment available for dealing with the clean-up had been procured on the premise that any large-scale spillage would be light North Sea crude oil.

This incident received wide publicity, much of it unwarranted. It was strongly suspected at the time that some tankers approaching or leaving Sullom Voe, aware of the publicity given, would be tempted to discharge their own oil-polluted ballast into the sea in the knowledge that the pollution would be considered to have originated from the other vessel. Whether such practices were resorted to is difficult to assess but, shortly after the incident, reports of oil pollution from various parts of the Shetland coastline were received, investigated and confirmed. Analysis of the oil showed that the pollution was consistent with an origin in a vessel's 'dirty' ballast tanks.

Swift action had to be taken to counteract this new threat to the environment, but as the pollution had emanated from vessels navigating normally well to seawards of the territorial limits, then beyond three miles of the coast, there was no legal action which Shetland Islands Council could take against such offenders. It would have been possible to prosecute British flag vessels in the UK courts under the provisions of the Oil Pollution Act 1971, assuming sufficient evidence could be procured. However, there were at the time few methods by which evidence could be procured to initiate legal proceedings. Analysis of beached oil and its comparison with the contents of a suspected vessel's cargo tanks is not usually in itself sufficient to take legal action.

The problem was overcome by securing an Agreement with the oil industry, which states that every vessel proceeding to Sullom Voe will retain on board at least 35% of the vessel's summer deadweight in the form of ballast, fuel oil, fresh water and stores and that where it has been found necessary to load additional ballast this too shall be retained on board for discharge to the shore reception facilities at Sullom Voe. The Agreement also contains penalty provisions which give the oil industry the right to refuse to load offending vessels, provided there is sufficient proof to warrant such action.

The aircraft currently in use is a Bolkow 105 helicopter, a 5 man twin-engined aircraft which is also used to transfer marine pilots to and from tankers, and as an aerial platform to direct oil spill clean-up operations. The Port Engineer also uses the helicopter to maintain remote lights and navigation marks. To monitor the situation the Harbour Authority has chartered a light aircraft and conducts reconnaissance flights on a daily basis. It is fitted with radar and marine-band vhf radio. The trained observer is equipped with cameras and a camcorder. Support is also given to the Council's anti-pollution activities from a variety of different sources including the RAF, the Department of Trade, HM Coastguard, civil airlines, lighthouse keepers, fishing craft and other sources. Through the publicity given by the media the local population also rapidly respond to any oil pollution sighting.

15.4.3   Pollution prevention

Due to the limitations of modern pollution clean-up equipment in the sea conditions experienced in Shetland, it is considered that prevention is much better than cure. The provision of well-trained and experienced personnel, efficient and well-maintained equipment and clear and unambiguous rules and regulations are all seen as part of the preventative process. However, other measures are also in place, the most important of which is probably the establishment of an 'area of avoidance' around Shetland.

By the middle of 1979 several reports had been received of large tankers passing dangerously close to the islands and skerries off Shetland. This raised the possibility of an accident similar to that involving the '*Amoco Cadiz*, which broke down close to shore and was unable to manoeuvre to a position of safety. It was, therefore, decided to establish a '10-mile area of avoidance' around Shetland, based on response time, as the only tugs regularly present are those at Sullom Voe operated by Shetland Towage Limited. Research showed that this would allow prompt and effective action to be taken in the event of a total machinery failure.

Unfortunately, the Government of the day would not support this scheme on the grounds that traffic levels were too low and the scheme was never submitted to the International Maritime Organization (IMO). However, support from the Terminal participants was forthcoming and it was written into the charter parties of all ships using Sullom Voe that they should comply with the scheme. Masters are required to provide the Port Authority with details of their intended courses and positions both inwards and outward from a distance of 200 miles of the port. On receipt of this information it is checked by Port Control and the ship is advised of any noncompliance. In addition, the Authority's hired-in helicopter is useful to check that vessels are, in fact, complying with the scheme.

While the scheme is generally successful there have been occasional reports that some tankers were not complying. Research indicated that the vessels involved were not bound to or from Sullom Voe but were merely 'passing' and, therefore, would not necessarily be aware of the scheme. Efforts were resumed to gain Government support for promoting the scheme at IMO in order that details would appear on the charts of the area. In November 1991 IMO finally ratified the 'area of avoidance'. It is somewhat ironic that the scheme was rejected in 1979 when traffic levels were higher than in 1992 when it was accepted. Perhaps this is an indication of a change in the public perspective of environmental protection which has occurred in the intervening years.

15.5 Postscript – The *MV Braer*

Since this Paper was written the *MV Braer* ran aground on Shetland on the morning of 5 January 1993. I believe this accident could have been avoided if comprehensive Vehicle Traffic Systems were in place similar to those developed for Sullom Voe traffic. If our Scottish islands are to be protected the whole question of shipping standards, qualification of crews, crew manning levels and the implementation of shipping management and vehicle traffic systems has to be reviewed and improved upon.

15.6 Conclusions

We are slowly winning the war against pollution but there are still a great number of individual battles to be won and in preparing for these battles the following points must be given consideration:

1. Prevention is better than cure. We must continue to educate polluters and persuade them to minimize pollution at every opportunity, whether by stopping the small boat owner from dumping garbage or getting a multinational company to improve its treatment and disposal facilities.

2. There must be effective policing of the marine environment with effective enforcement and control integrated at local, national and international levels with courts which are recognized internationally and empowered to hand out internationally agreed penalties no matter when and where the incident occurs.

3. Accidents will happen and where it is known that a potential pollution risk exists, all necessary measures must be put in place ready to be implemented quickly and effectively.

In conclusion it is suggested that the experience of the Shetland Islands Council has been that it is possible through innovative methods to go a long way to protect the environment effectively, provided that the objectives are clear to all concerned and that effective steps are taken to achieve those objectives.

EPILOGUE:
THE MARINE HERITAGE OF
THE ISLANDS OF SCOTLAND

J. M. Baxter and M. B. Usher

16.1 The Background

The islands of Scotland and the seas surrounding them support a great wealth of natural resources, both living and non-living. People have exploited many of these resources for centuries, and until relatively recently this harvesting has been notable for the manner in which it has been done and the respect shown for the balance of nature; in a very real sense the harvesting seems to have been done on a sustainable basis.

In more recent times the various natural and anthropogenic pressures on both the natural resources of the islands and the surrounding seas have increased. The level of exploitation of various fish stocks has taken on far greater proportions, with an increasingly international dimension. When the local control and the associated empathy with the environment is lost, the risk of excessive, non-sustainable exploitation increases. Many of the living resources appear to have a fragile existence which can easily be disrupted; recruitment on an annual basis cannot always be guaranteed. The non-living resources, by their very nature, are finite and their exploitation can have far reaching and very long-lasting effects on both the island culture and the environment. The overriding factor is the naturally highly dynamic character both of the various environmental parameters and the different natural resources. Changes occur as a result of forces which we do not yet fully comprehend and thus there is always the danger that any interference on our part to halt, reverse or control an 'undesirable' trend may simply exacerbate the problem or create another problem elsewhere.

The marine environment of Scotland is receiving increased attention from developers, fishermen, conservationists and those enjoying recreational activities. In the face of this increased activity there is a growing recognition that the natural resources around our coast are worth protecting and managing properly. The debate on how best to achieve protection while still permitting and even encouraging development was opened at a conference organized by the Nature Conservancy Council for Scotland (Baxter and McIntyre, 1993) and further developed by Professor George Dunnet in the 1992 Newth Lecture (Dunnet, 1993). The various authors in this volume have addressed a range of topics which together highlight many of the reasons why the islands of

Scotland and their surrounding seas are so prized. The wildlife of the islands and the livelihoods of the islanders themselves depend on the cleanliness of the waters around the island's coasts. Unpolluted waters are essential to help to sustain and improve the islanders traditional way of life, to provide a market for a pure and valued marine harvest and to promote tourism and recreation in the islands. Clean water is thus the most valuable resource of all, but pollution is a problem which recognizes no boundaries and in many instances its origin is outside the control of the local population.

16.2   A Shetland Islands Example

The grounding of the *MV Braer* on 5 January 1993, at Garths Ness on the southern tip of Shetland, demonstrates the vulnerability of the Scottish islands to outside events. The tanker was using the Fair Isle Channel, a piece of sea some 39 km wide, on passage from Norway to Canada, carrying 84 000 tonnes of 'Gulfaks' crude oil taken from the Norwegian sector of the North Sea. The vessel was Liberian registered, American owned, with an international crew and a Greek master. Early on the morning of 5 January 1993 it had nothing to do with Shetland, although on a number of previous occasions she had called at Sullom Voe to uplift cargo. Events developed rapidly as the *MV Braer* drifted helpless, eventually striking the rocky south coast of the Shetland Mainland soon after 1100 hours on that wintery morning.

Shetland Islands Council had recognized the possibility of a major oil spill occurring around its coast because of the oil handling terminal at Sullom Voe. As a result the Council had taken all reasonable precautions to prevent an incident happening and to deal with an emergency in the unfortunate event of one happening. What took place and where it happened could not have been predicted, a fact which is true for the whole coast of Scotland, neither could the sequence of events which followed. The full impact of the incident is unlikely to be revealed within the next year or two, but the immediate effect on the island's wildlife, and the implications for the islanders and their way of life, cannot be minimized.

A survey of the shores around the south-west coast of Shetland, carried out three months after the incident, revealed that in the immediate vicinity of the wreck many of the common shore species were absent from habitats in which they would normally be present. Most obvious was the lack of limpets (*Patella vulgata*) and littorinid snails from the rocky coasts around Garths Ness. Moving further away from the wreck site the level of mortalities in these species was greatly reduced. A survey of the sublittoral flora and fauna showed even less signs of impact although during the period of the incident when the very severe storms were at their worst, considerable numbers of some species including the razor shell (*Ensis* sp.) and various fish such as ling (*Molva molva*) and wrasse (*Labrus* sp.) were washed up dead (Scottish Natural Heritage, 1993a and b). These surveys formed only a small part of a comprehensive and coordinated programme of work which aimed to monitor, among other things, the dispersal of the oil, the concentrations of oil in the water and sediments, the effect on the fisheries and aquaculture industries and the impact on the deeper water benthos (Scottish Office Agriculture and Fisheries Department, 1993). The programme of work was coordinated by the Ecological Steering Group for the Oil Spill in Shetland (Scottish Office Environment Department, 1993).

The ramifications of an incident of this scale spread throughout the island community. The flesh of stocks of farmed salmon became tainted, resulting in the fish having to be destroyed; inshore fishing was affected with a temporary Fishery Exclusion Zone being declared. Wildlife suffered with 1542 seabirds reported killed and another 235 recovered oiled but alive; seals and otters were probably affected and important archaeological sites were lightly oiled. The reputation of Shetland depends on its image of having a clean and pure environment. There were genuine fears that the revenues from both tourism and the natural products harvested from the seas around Shetland would be put at risk.

Monitoring the impact of the oil spill on the natural environment will have to continue for some time, not only to ensure that a full picture of the effects on the Shetland environment and the local communities can be gained but also to enable us to learn lessons from the event. A comprehensive range of studies are planned or underway (Scottish Office Environment Department, 1993); a number of these is listed in Table 1.

Incidents of the scale of the *MV Braer* are newsworthy and consequently receive considerable attention in the national and international press. The potential for another '*Braer*' cannot be ignored, and the Scottish islands are all vulnerable as they are adjacent to the main shipping lanes, namely the Fair Isle Channel and the Pentland Firth in the north and the Minch in the west. Most oil pollution incidents, however, pass almost unnoticed by the general public. In a period of 6 months between January and June of 1993 there were 24 reported incidents or potential incidents of oil pollution in Scottish waters (Figure 1), of which 13 were in the inshore waters around the islands of Scotland, from Rockall, Benbecula and Skye in the west to Orkney and Shetland in the north and Inchcolm in the east. The scale of most of these incidents is unknown; most are the result of tankers washing out ballast tanks while in transit or small accidents associated with oil exploration and production activities. Many other even smaller incidents in harbours, marinas and out at sea regularly occur but go unrecorded. Individually these small events are probably of only very minor impact, but their cumulative effects, together with all the other potentially damaging activities which take place in the marine environment, are of greater concern.

16.3 Integrated Management

The range of activities which take place in the marine environment is great, from fishing and seaweed harvesting to jet skiing and SCUBA diving. It is all too easy to focus on one particular activity and link this to a single issue. For example,

Table 1   A selection of the studies proposed or under way to monitor the long-term impact and recovery of the Shetland environment (adapted from Scottish Office Environment Department, 1993)

Studies on the movement and fate of the oil
   Numerical models of surface and sub-surface water around the south-west coast of Shetland and further afield
   Investigation of how droplets of oil were carried as spray onto the land
   Biodegradation of oil by micro-organisms in seabed sediments
   Wave refraction models to measure mixing and energy processes at the time of the spill
   Deployment of seabed instrument west of Shetland to measure processes of resuspension under actual storm conditions
   Investigations of interaction between oil droplets and sediments
   Effect of mixing energy and dispersants used during the oil spill on the droplet size of the spill
   The study of the changes in the oil levels contained in seabed sediments especially in relatively deep water basins

Studies of the effects on terrestrial ecosystems and species
   Survey of the effects of oil spill on otters
   Level of hydrocarbons in otter carcasses
   Short and long-term effects of oil spray on coastal soils, including dunes and cliff slopes
   Pre-breeding tystie population survey and monitoring of cliff-nesting seabirds
   Winter monitoring of seabird and seaduck populations
   Sub-lethal effects on seabirds
   Monitoring of Arctic terns and Arctic skuas
   Seabirds monitoring on NNRs (Noss and Hermaness)
   Seabird diets and breeding success, Foula, Yell Sound and Hermaness
   Seabird ringing programme, counts, breeding success and diets
   Counts of seabirds at sea
   Seabird monitoring (particularly puffins and storm petrels)
   Photointerpretation of airborne contamination of land
   Vegetation survey of the Quendale Bay SSSI sand dunes

Studies of the effects on marine ecosystems and species
   Study of the effects of oil on sandeel stocks
   Pathological studies of stranded cetaceans to identify involvement of oil from the spill
   A survey and count of common seals in south-west Shetland as an index of population change
   Population dynamics of selected coastal sites to determine rate and amount of recovery
   Effects of the oil spill on intertidal ecology and monitoring of recovery
   Survey and monitoring of subtidal habitats
   Chemical/macrobenthic monitoring in Sullom Voe and Yell Sound
   Temporal and spatial monitoring of the benthic meiofauna and macrofauna
   Sampling and analysis of water and plankton around the south Shetland Peninsula
   Organoleptic and chemical analysis of farmed salmon for quality assurance procedures
   Rocky shore monitoring in Sullom Voe and Yell Sound including special studies of dogwhelks
   Quantitative rocky shore surveys at five rocky shore sites and two sandy shores in south Mainland Shetland
   Succession on rocky shores around south Shetland Peninsula
   Independent market sampling programme on fish quality outside the exclusion zone

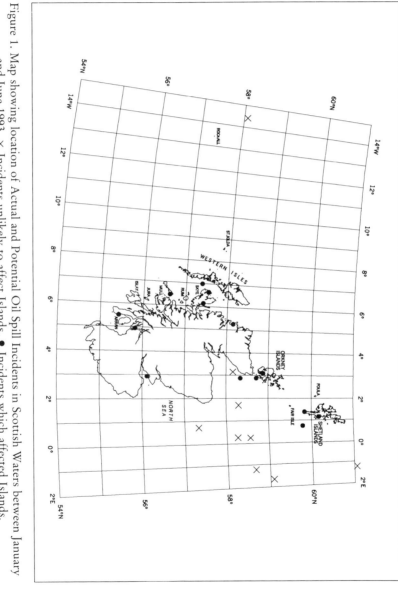

Figure 1. Map showing location of Actual and Potential Oil Spill Incidents in Scottish Waters between January and June 1993. × Incidents unlikely to affect Islands. ● Incidents which affected Islands.

the decline in certain seabird numbers and their breeding success in Shetland was linked to the decline in sand eel numbers which was in turn attributed to increased fishing effort. While it is more than likely that the increased fishing effort had a part to play in the situation, it is unlikely that a simple relationship of this type provides the full explanation. Seabird numbers themselves had been increasing for a period of years, thus creating additional pressure on their prey species, and changes in water currents around Shetland are also thought to have had some influence on the distribution of the prey, sand eels (Wright and Bailey, 1993). The fluctuations in numbers of many species in the marine environment are the result of natural, stochastic events, which are impossible to predict. Thus in assigning any 'cause and effect' relationship it is important to take as integrated and holistic a view of the situation as possible.

Coastal Zone Management is a concept which is receiving increased attention and debate in a wide variety of fora. Scottish Natural Heritage, through its Marine and Coastal Issues Task Force, is examining the efficacy of this type of approach in providing protection for the wider marine environment. The House of Commons Environment Select Committee on Coastal Zone Protection and Planning, which reported in 1992, highlighted the need for an integrated approach and this is acknowledged in the Government's Response (Department of the Environment, 1992). There has been, for many years, a perceived division between what goes on in the sea and what takes place on, or is derived from, the land. This division is a misconception which is only slowly being broken down. Many activities which have been carried out on land in the past have assumed that the sea is a bottomless receptacle able to absorb as much waste as people produce. Similarly, with many living resources, such as fish and shellfish stocks, when levels of exploitation were less than they are currently and the fishing effort was locally based, there was an impression that an adequate continued availability of the resource was assured. Increasingly powerful boats and sophisticated machinery have opened up what was always essentially a global common to far greater exploitation by vessels from a much wider geographical area. The number and diversity of activities on land and at sea which influence the islands are very great and subject to many different controls at local, national and international level. Prosecuting one activity often brings people into conflict with others wishing to carry out another activity and it is the accommodation of these various aspirations, while ensuring the well-being of the natural environment, which is the challenge which must be met. Fundamental to ensuring sustainable use of the resources in general is the establishment of far greater understanding of the complexity of the system and the limits of its capacity to adapt to changes.

In order to achieve any sort of effective protection for the marine environment it is essential that there is local involvement in, and ownership of, any initiative. It is not possible, nor necessarily desirable, to turn the clock back to a time when all activities were carried out at a low, relatively inefficient level. The appreciation by the islanders of their heritage is, however, invaluable in helping to control the level of development, but this caring long-term attitude is one which must be universally held. Integrated management of the coastal zone is an exciting vision which, if it is to be fulfilled, will require a much greater appreciation of the value of the natural resources around our coast and in the seas. The conference on which this book is based is one further small step in this process of education and inspiration. The marine environment and all that lives in it are there to be enjoyed and exploited but within a management framework which takes account of the dynamic nature of the systems, the limitations imposed by ensuring sustainable exploitation of both renewable and non-renewable resources, and most importantly the requirements of the local human communities and the populations of animals and plants. In order to achieve this aim there is a need for an increased understanding of the science, economics and sociology of the marine and coastal environment associated with the Scottish islands. Technological advance is often perceived to have destroyed or polluted so much of the marine environment; what we must do is to harness technology, to develop new techniques – that will mean that the future management of the resources is more sustainable than our attempts at the moment.

16.4 The Need for Further Knowledge

A great wealth of scientific information already exists detailing the natural resource of the islands of Scotland, not least the work carried out by the Marine Nature Conservation Review of the former Nature Conservancy Council and now of the Joint Nature Conservation Committee. Records and comments have been assembled over many years and some notable naturalists such as Frank Fraser Darling (Fraser Darling, 1970; Fraser Darling and Boyd, 1989) have given much attention to some of these remote areas. Despite all of these efforts there is still a great deal to be discovered. In the intertidal and subtidal environments, in particular, many areas remain unsurveyed.

A survey of the island of Canna in 1993 by staff of the Aquatic Environments Branch of Scottish Natural Heritage revealed a rich and varied coastline and marine environment with many species rich communities and unusual habitats. There are many more such records to be gathered which will add further to our knowledge and understanding of the value of the natural heritage of the Scottish islands.

Canna may be said to encapsulate all that is memorable and important about the Scottish islands. The crystal clear waters which surround the island lap against shores backed by towering basalt cliffs, which themselves provide hunting areas for peregrines (*Falco peregrinus*), golden eagles (*Aquila chrysaetos*) and white-tailed eagles (*Haliaetus albicilla*). The re-introduction of the white-tailed, or sea, eagle to Scotland is a success story which should inspire us all. The few people thus far who have been privileged enough to see this majestic bird soaring above the cliffs of the Scottish islands cannot fail to be in awe and wonder. The cliffs are also home during the breeding season to large numbers of seabirds which feed in the surrounding waters and include razorbills (*Alca torda*), guillemots (*Uria aalge*), puffins (*Fratercula arctica*), gannets *(Sula bussara)* and fulmars (*Fulmaris glacialis*). The coastal waters support populations of both common (*Phoca vitulina*) and grey (*Halichoerus grypus*) seals, and otters (*Lutra lutra*) can be observed feeding along the shore. In and around the Sound of Canna groups of harbour porpoise (*Phocoena phocoena*), killer whale (*Orcinus orca*) and minke whale (*Balaenoptera acutorostrata*) can be seen. Occasionally basking sharks (*Cetorhinus maximus*) are sighted, feeding off the phytoplankton which thrives in the clear oceanic waters. The coast around Canna has examples of a wide range of habitats from exposed to sheltered rocky shores interrupted by isolated sandy bays (Table 2). The subtidal habitats are also rich and varied with the kelp extending to depths of over 20 m in the clear oceanic waters. The sheltered sandy bottomed bays support eelgrass (*Zostera marina*) beds. The deeper underwater cliffs are covered by dense, colourful growths of dead man's fingers (*Alcyonium digitatum*) and plumose anemones (*Metridium senile*) together with many other species. In the deeper waters where even SCUBA divers cannot reach there are extensive sandy and muddy plains supporting large populations of scampi (*Nephrops norvegicus*) and where the trawlers have not scoured the bottom there are stands of the elegant sea pen (*Pennatula phosphorea*).

The scenery around Canna is spectacular and the sailing and diving in the area is of the highest standard. Canna is a place of peace and solitude and through the eyes of a visitor may even seem idyllic, especially on a warm summer's day. The local people on Canna exploit both the land and the sea, but even this small close-knit community cannot escape the influence of the twentieth century. Fishing boats from both the east and west coast trawl the seabed for scampi (*N. norvegicus*) and in places the shores are littered with the discarded plastic debris from all types of vessels – fish boxes, torn nets, fenders, plastic containers. In Canna harbour it is a common sight to see the seabed near the pier littered with discarded undersize fish; these would have become the future for the fishing industry. These are sad and unnecessary scars, inflicted often by people who hope to enjoy the fruits of the marine environment. The message of sustainable production has still to be learned.

16.5 Conclusion

The *MV Braer* was a timely and salutary reminder of the vulnerability of our islands to outside influences and every effort must be made to prevent such an event happening again. It is also important, however, to recognize that there are many other damaging activities going on each day which are not given the same high profile media coverage. It is right that we should be shocked and outraged by the sudden and unpredicted events of a major pollution incident but we should be equally outraged by the many other activities which threaten our marine heritage.

Table 2 Summary of the principal intertidal habitats found around the coast of Canna

Rocky shores

Shore topography	Wave exposure	Dominant assemblages
Steep and vertical rock	Very exposed	Upper shore: *Verrucaria maura*; *Porphyra umbilicalis* Mid-shore: limpets and barnacles Lower shore: *Alaria esculenta*
Steep and vertical rock	Exposed	Dominated by limpets and barnacles, with *Laminaria digitata* and/or *Alaria esculenta* in the upper sublittoral zone.
Wave-cut platforms	(a) Exposed	Dominated by limpets and barnacles with *Fucus vesiculosus f. linearis*.
	(b) Moderate	Dominated by fucoid algae
	(c) Sheltered	Dominated by fucoid algae including *Ascophyllum nodosum*
Boulder shores	(a) Exposed	Sparse fucoid cover
	(b) Sheltered	Dominated by fucoid algae with *Laminaria digitata* in upper sublittoral zone.

Sedimentary shores

Sediment type	Surface features	Infauna
Muddy coarse sand with widely scattered boulders	*Fucus serratus* clumps; Mats of filamentous algae *Chorda filum* and *Arenicola* mounds.	*Lanice conchilega* *Arenicola marina* *Echinocardium cordatum* *Dosinia exoleata*
Muddy coarse sand with stones	*Fucus serratus* clumps; Mats of filamentous algae *Chorda filum* and *Arenicola* mounds.	*Lanice conchilega* *Arenicola marina* *Echinocardium cordatum* *Venus verrucosa*
Muddy coarse sand with stones	*Fucus serratus* clumps; Mats of filamentous algae and dense *Arenicola* mounds.	*Nephtys* spp. *Arenicola marina*
Muddy sand	Areas of decaying algae.	*Cerastoderma edule* *Angulus tenuis*
Soft mud	No obvious surface features	*Scrobicularia plana* *Cerastoderma edule* *Corophium volutator*

The example of Canna serves to illustrate how much there is still to learn about our islands and how much they have to offer us. The islands of Scotland and the surrounding seas truly contain a great wealth of natural heritage and tradition. This book is an attempt to raise the profile of the island habitats and to encourage everyone to cherish them and to work for their long-term protection and their sustained yield of fish, seaweed, aggregates and energy. The essential characteristic of the islands is the unpolluted nature of the surrounding seas, and hence the quality of the life for both people and wildlife that inhabit these coasts.

References

Baxter, J. M. and McIntyre, A. D. 1992. Marine conservation in Scotland. *Proceedings of the Royal Society of Edinburgh (Section B)*, **100**, 1–204.

Department of the Environment. 1992. *Coastal Zone Protection and Planning. The Government's response to the Second Report from the House of Commons Select Committee on the Environment*, HMSO, London.

Dunnet, G. M. 1993. The Newth Lecture. Scottish Natural Heritage and the Marine Environment. *The Scottish Association for Marine Science. Newsletter 7*, April 1993.

Fraser Darling, F. 1970. *Wilderness and Plenty*. BBC Publications, London.

Fraser Darling, F. and Boyd, J. M. 1989. *The Highlands and Islands*. (Third Edition), Collins, London.

House of Commons Environment Select Committee. 1992. *Coastal Zone Protection and Planning*. (Second report), HMSO House of Commons Paper 17–1, Session 1991–92.

Scottish Natural Heritage. 1993a. *Effects of the 'Braer' Oil Spill on the Marine Biology and Sites of Earth Science Interest in the Shetland Islands*. Bulletin No.1, Scottish Natural Heritage, Edinburgh.

Scottish Natural Heritage. 1993b. *Effects of 'Braer' Oil Spill on the Marine Biology in the Shetland Islands*. Bulletin No. 2, Scottish Natural Heritage, Edinburgh.

Scottish Office Environment Department. 1993. *The Ecological Steering Group on the Oil Spill in Shetland: An Interim Report on Survey and Monitoring*. HMSO.

Scottish Office Agriculture and Fisheries Department. 1993. *Interim Report of the Marine Monitoring Programme on the Braer Oil-spill*. SOAFD.

Wright, P. J. and Bailey, M. . 1993. *Biology of Sand Eels in the Vicinity of Seabird Colonies at Shetland*. Draft Final Report.

INDEX

Printed in UK for HMSO by (10111)Dd 0287544 C10 3/94